Where to watch
France

La Ligue Française
pour la Protection des Oiseaux

Translated by Tony Williams

CHRISTOPHER HELM
A&C Black · London

a subsidiary of A & C Black (Publishers) Ltd,
35 Bedford Row, London WC1R 4JH

Maps by Julia Welstead and Mike Madders

ISBN 0-7136-8107-1

A CIP catalogue record for this book is available
from the British Library

Typeset by Florencetype Ltd, Kewstoke, Avon
Printed and bound in Great Britain by Biddles Ltd, Guildford

CONTENTS

BOURGOGNE (BURGUNDY)

BRETAGNE (BRITTANY)

CENTRE

CHAMPAGNE-ARDENNE

CORSE (CORSICA)

FRANCHE-COMTÉ

ÎLE-DE-FRANCE

NORD-PAS-DE-CALAIS

NORMANDIE

PAYS DE LA LOIRE

THE REGIONS OF FRANCE

HOW TO USE THIS GUIDE

This book is intended for use by people who enjoy watching birds on a casual basis as well those for whom 'birding' is a passion. Its aim is to encourage people to discover the wealth of France's bird life.

The sites contained in this book should all provide interesting and safe birdwatching. However, you should follow the itineraries outlined in this guide and take heed of official notices and signs at the sites themselves.

The Itineraries

The site accounts are divided into the regions of France. For the purposes of this guide, Basse-Normandie and Haute-Normandie have been combined.

There are 279 separate itineraries; they are split into two categories covering main and secondary sites.

Main itineraries: there are 120 of these covering the major birdwatching sites in France. Each site is described under the sub-headings of 'Habitat and Timing', 'Calendar', 'Access', and 'Species'. The heading for each site details the length of the itinerary (in kilometres and miles) and the relevant IGN (Institut Géographique National) map or maps.

Habitat and Timing

This provides a precise description of the site, its biogeography and ecology, its importance within the region – either natural or historical – and its main ornithological interest. It also details any restrictions on access and the best times for visiting.

Calendar

Species that may be observed according to the season are listed in this section. This gives the reader an idea of the interest and value of the itinerary at any given time of the year. Obviously, it would be difficult, if not impossible, to see all the species listed for a season during a single visit. And of course species not mentioned may often be seen.

Access

The best routes to the site from the nearest large town or towns are detailed here. A parking site (if one exists) is also indicated. The itinerary outlined in the text is shown with corresponding numbers on the accompanying map.

Species

A quick-reference section listing the main groups of birds and some specific species to be seen at the site, and often the areas in which to look for them.

Secondary itineraries: there are 159 of these, and they are treated in a more concise manner. The nearest large town to the site is mentioned, and there is an outline of the site's natural characteristics and a list of the more interesting birds occurring in each season (if no season is given they are normally visible throughout the year, with a few exceptions).

The Maps

All the main itineraries (one exception) are accompanied by a simple map (essentially locatory) based on the relevant IGN map for the area. Three different scales of map have been used; 1/25 000 (1 inch = 250m); 1/50 000 (1 inch = 500m); 1/100 000 (1 inch = 1 km). For a more detailed look at the area you should use the relevant IGN map.

Key to the Maps

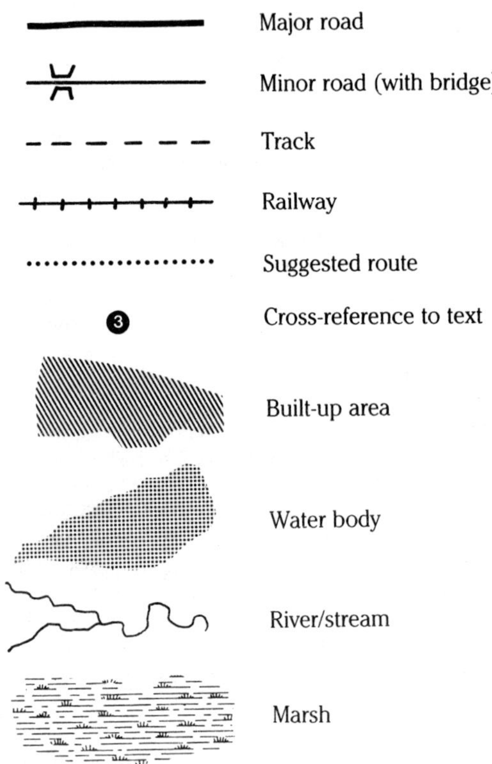

BIRDWATCHING IN FRANCE

The Seasons

Each season – even each month – has its own species of birds. If you use the same itinerary in January and July, the list of species observed will be very different. Certain species only come to France for the summer to breed, then leave for Africa to winter there; others, coming from Scandinavia or Siberia, pass the winter here. Some species only make short journeys or are sedentary, while others only pass through France on migration. So visiting the same site more than once a year – perhaps even once a week – is strongly recommended. Each month has its high point.

Spring begins as early as **February**. Greylag Geese, Lapwing and the first Golden Plover are migrating already. Buzzard and Goshawk have started displaying over the woods. Dunnock, Blackbird and Song Thrush are singing in gardens.

In **March** it is the turn of dabbling duck to move, stopping-over in large flocks, especially along the Atlantic coast. Cormorants also leave, while Black-tailed Godwit, Snipe and Ruff may stay awhile on their way north. Woodpeckers are calling and are most easily seen during this month. In the south, the maquis is full of the song of Mediterranean warblers. Elsewhere, Chiffchaffs are in full song.

In **April**, Swallows return in force, rapidly moving from the south to the north. Grebes and Coot are displaying on lakes, while waders stop-over on the coast before continuing northwards. Many migrants are returning from Africa: woods and forests are full of the song of Cuckoo, Nightingale and Golden Oriole, whereas the sunnier open countryside will be home to Hoopoe. Garganey may be surprised on inland marshes. At the end of the month, Swift invade the country and many raptors are returning, Montagu's Harrier and Short-toed Eagle among others. In the mountains, Black Grouse are displaying and Fieldfare are more active.

In early **May**, some terns are still migrating, others are now mating on sandbanks and lakes. Reed-beds are alive with the song of Reed, Sedge and Savi's Warblers, and Honey Buzzards are returning. Mudflats have numerous Knot, Sanderling, Grey Plover and Turnstone, on their way back to Siberia. This is the best time of the year for learning warblers' songs, the south coast being the best area. On lakes, noisy Black-headed Gull colonies contrast with the quieter families of duck. At the end of May, late migrants such as Marsh Warbler and Spotted Flycatcher, finally arrive. Owls, now in the middle of breeding, are less noisy. This is a good month to see some rarities, such as Broad-billed Sandpiper and Red-rumped Swallow in the south, or Collared Flycatcher nesting in Lorraine.

June is the month when most birds are nesting; the spring migration is over and at the end of the month it is possible to see the first groups of Lapwing, and the odd Green Sandpiper or Black-tailed Godwit starting the return south. In the salt-pans along the Atlantic and Mediterranean coasts, Black-winged Stilt, Avocet and Kentish Plover are active. Greater Flamingos are busy nesting at their colony in the Camargue. Bee-eaters and Black-eared Wheatears in the south, like Kittiwakes and Icterine

Warblers in the north, are all feeding young.

July sees the return of larger flocks of waders from the Arctic. In the mountains, the start of the month is a good time for looking for Ptarmigan, Snow Finch, Rock Thrush or Wallcreeper. Swallows and House Martins are still rearing young, but at the end of the month many Swift are on their way back to Africa. In effect, autumn has already arrived for the birds.

In **August**, the coast is occupied by birds that will leave later. Curiously, at this time when the weather is often very good, the forests are silent; birds are no longer singing. Most White Storks pass during this month, along with the first Black Storks. Black Kites leave us, whilst out at sea there are groups of terns flying towards the tropics.

September sees the autumn migration at full pace. At this time, herons, waders and raptors can be seen almost anywhere. Sea-watching can be more variable: shearwaters, Gannets, skuas, terns, and sometimes Sabine's Gull, are occasionally seen in large numbers, principally from pivileged sites along the Channel and Atlantic coasts. Less obvious, as they migrate at night, is the movement of insectivorous passerines which have left their breeding areas: Whinchat, Wheatear, Redstart, Spectacled Warbler and Bee-eater are noted by their absence. A good month for hunting out some rarer species, particularly waders from further north (Dotterel) or from North America (Buff-breasted and Pectoral Sandpipers among others), principally along the western seaboard.

October is another month which sees birds on the move. Cormorant, ducks and certain raptors (Sparrowhawk and Buzzard) return, as do Redwing, Fieldfare, Chaffinch, Brambling, Siskin and Redpoll. At sea, especially after a storm, there are petrels, skuas and Little Gull. Starlings invade the country, from east to west, and flocks of Rook occur on the ploughed fields. Some passerines, straying from their migration route out of Siberia, are a delight for birdwatchers; usually only well-exposed islands and coastal headlands along the Channel and Atlantic will attract birds like Yellow-browed Warbler.

Red Kites are still passing in early **November**, about the same time as the largest numbers of Crane occur. Also from the north, divers, grebes, Eiders, Common and Velvet Scoters and Red-breasted Mergansers pass along the coast. In woods and copses there is a good chance of disturbing Woodcock. Here, too, are flocks of tits which include other species – treecreepers, Nuthatches, Goldcrest or Firecrest. The extreme south of the country receives a large increase in its numbers of Robin, Blackbird, thrushes, Chiffchaff and Blackcap.

December, if there is no particularly cold spell, is calmer. The north and east of the country may receive a few more Bean Geese, and Whooper and Bewick's Swans. The duck are on their wintering grounds, as are the coastal waders. This is the time to go and see them, especially the Brent Geese along the Atlantic coast. Thrushes and finches can be seen everywhere, whilst here and there some rarer species may be seen almost anywhere: Crossbill, Grey Phalarope and Long-tailed Duck, among others. Now is the time to see some passerines from the far north, along the Channel coast; such species as Shore Lark, Twite and Snow Bunting.

January is much like the preceding month. However, if there is a spell of hard weather over western Europe, then France may see some large movements of birds, especially those normally wintering in Holland or Britain. Hundreds of Goldeneye, Smew, Goosander and Eider arrive on the coast and non-frozen inland water-bodies. Some geese, (Bean, Greylag and White-fronted) as well as swans, may arrive at the same time. Some waders – especially Oystercatcher, Curlew, Golden and Grey Plovers and Lapwing – flee the freezing conditions. You can often find a Rough-legged Buzzard or White-tailed Eagle, particularly in the north-east of the country. On the contrary, if it is mild, you can often hear, towards the end of the month, some owls calling (Eagle and Tawny) announcing the start of spring.

The Habitats

With experience, birdwatchers learn to associate any given habitat with the species that occur within it. Regular use of the proposed itineraries in this guide will allow birdwatchers to discover new sites and new species. This is why walking in the countryside looking for birds necessarily means learning more about the habitats they use. For example, by searching in a conifer wood the observer has more chance of seeing certain species – treecreepers, Goldcrest, Coal and Crested Tits, and Crossbill. Willows are host to many small insectivorous passerines. Lake reed-beds are favoured by herons, Bitterns, Water Rail, Coot and certain warblers: their uncovered edges attract species such as waders, wagtails and pipits, whereas duck and grebes are more often seen on open water.

SOME NOTES FOR BIRDWATCHERS

Before using the information in this book, please prepare sensibly for your walk in order to avoid any mishaps in the field. Here are some useful reminders:

1. Take warm clothes with you (in winter, in mountains), and perhaps a change of clothes in the car.
2. Take rubber boots, especially if visiting the coast, lakes or other wetlands (lined boots in winter). Elsewhere, comfortable walking boots are essential. Avoid town shoes and, worst of all, high-heels.
3. Binoculars are a must. A telescope is well worthwhile when looking at duck, waders and seabirds.
4. Do not forget to take an identification guide. But remember that it is there to help you, not to stop you thinking for yourself. Many excellent guides are available nowadays; *Where to Watch Birds in France* should be used in conjunction with one of these.
5. A notebook is useful. Make detailed descriptions of any birds you are unable to identify in the field so that you can research further when you return home.
6. IGN maps of the relevant areas are very useful.
7. Do not forget to take food and drink, especially if you are planning a day's outing.
8. Lastly, and most importantly, please respect the countryside and private property. Do not obstruct public or private passage-ways, tracks or entrances to fields with your car. Remember to abide by the country code; this will guarantee a trouble-free outing.

The Birdwatcher's Code of Conduct*

1. The welfare of birds must come first.
2. Habitat must be protected.
3. Keep disturbance of birds and habitat to a minimum.
4. When you find a rare bird think carefully about whom you should tell.
5. Do not harrass rare migrants.
6. Abide by bird-protection laws at all times.
7. Respect the rights of landowners.
8. Respect the rights of other people in the countryside.
9. Make your records available to the local bird recorder.†
10. Behave abroad as you would when birdwatching at home.

* A modified version of the *Birdwatcher's Code of Conduct* (RSPB *et al*)

† Observations of nationally rare species should be sent, along with a full description, to: Comité d'Homologation National, La Corderie Royale, BP 263, 17305 Rochefort Cedex, France. Addresses of local recorders can also be obtained from here.

ALSACE

1 RHINAU LAKE/KAPPEL

8 km/5 miles
Benfeld
(IGN 3817 – 1/50 000)

Habitat and Timing

The mouth of an old arm of the Rhine, the Taubergiessen became a lake in the early 1960s thanks to hydro-electric work. Although on German soil, it belongs to the parish of Rhinau. It is bordered to the west by the Rhine embankment, to the east by meadows (protected for their rich flora), and to the south by luxuriant forest (made a reserve by German legislation). Transition to the forest is gradual; a flooded woodland zone separates the two, with many standing, dead trees.

The lake is remarkable for passage and wintering water birds. The surrounding embankments offer excellent birdwatching, without frightening the birds (telescope recommended). The surrounding woodland holds six species of woodpecker. Conditions are favourable throughout the day; however the arrival of Cormorants at their roost is particularly spectacular (about 1,000 birds in January).

Calendar

Winter: Great-crested and Little Grebes; Cormorant, Grey Heron, Mute Swan, Greylag Goose; dabbling ducks (all species wintering in France), Pochard and Tufted Duck, Goldeneye, Goosander; Water Rail, Moorhen, Coot; Black-headed, Common and Herring (Mediterranean subspecies) Gulls; Kingfisher. Other less regular species include: Bean Goose, Shelduck, Red-crested Pochard, Eider.

Spring and Autumn: Osprey; Little Gull, Black Tern; some small waders (Snipe, Green and Common Sandpipers).

Breeding season: large numbers of Mute Swans (moult site); six species of woodpecker (Green, Grey-headed, Black, Great Spotted, Middle Spotted and Lesser Spotted).

Access

From Strasbourg (to the north) or Sélestat (to the south-west), take the N83 as far as Benfeld, then the D5 towards Rhinau (via Herbsheim and Boofzheim). At Rhinau, park on the side of the Rhine (French side), just after the customs post ① (passport necessary) and, on foot, catch the Kappel ferry: there are boats every 15 minutes from 6.15 am to 7.00 pm in winter, and from 6.00 am to 9.00 pm in summer (on the way out ask the time of the last boat back). Once the Rhine is crossed go southwards along the river. There are bus connections from Strasbourg (ask for times locally).

There is a good track on the eastern side of the lake which later turns westwards towards the Rhine. The first part of this track (on the embankment) ② is the best for watching water birds: numerous stops are possible. Later, on the south side of the lake ③ there are less observation points. Once at the Rhine it is possible to continue southwards for

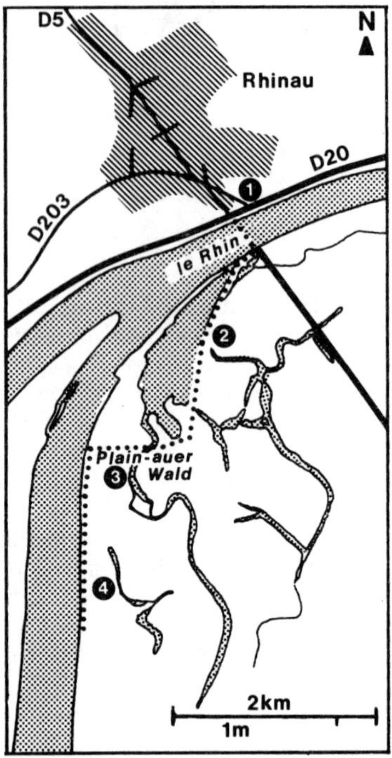

several kilometres ④; the whole of this area is important for wintering duck. Return by the same track.

Species

- Water Rail often occur along the lake shore.
- At the end of summer, Green and Common Sandpipers and Snipe often occur.
- Outside the breeding season (from October to March) there is a large Cormorant roost in the surrounding trees.
- Many Mute Swans pass the summer on the river (moult period).
- In winter large numbers of Pochard and Tufted Duck as well as Goldeneye and Goosander can be seen on the Rhine.
- Six species of woodpecker breed in the woods next to the Rhine.
- Black-headed, Common and Herring (Mediterranean subspecies) Gulls often feed along the river.

2 THE BRUCH DE L'ANDLAU

12 km/7.5 miles
Strasbourg
(IGN 3816 – 1/50 000)

Habitat and Timing

Once a vast marsh (the word 'bruch' means marshland), it is now drained. It is an area of wet hay meadows (of great botanical interest) mixed with cultivated fields, separated by woods, thickets and hedgerows. Unfortunately, many of the meadows are being replaced by maize fields. In spite of recent damage, these water-meadows are the best conserved in Alsace. It is an important breeding site for Curlew, and many birds of prey occur. Many of the passerines that occur in eastern France can also be found here. There is unrestricted access to the whole area but it is better to avoid tramping across the meadows during spring and summer.

Calendar

Winter: Hen Harrier; sedentary woodland birds (woodpeckers, tits, Nuthatch).

Breeding season: Curlew, Lapwing; many birds of prey (especially Honey Buzzard, Sparrowhawk, Goshawk, Hobby) and a large variety of passerines (notably, Icterine and Marsh Warblers, Lesser Whitethroat and Willow Tit).

Access

From Strasbourg, take the N83 towards Erstein or the N422 towards Obernai. Then take the D426 which joins Erstein and Obernai (via Schaeffersheim and Meistratzheim) crossing the bruch. Park on the west side of the Andlau ①, taking care not to impede agricultural traffic. On

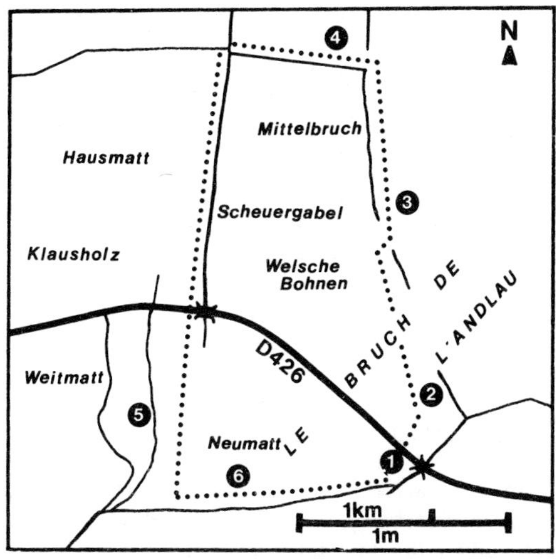

foot, follow the Andlau for a short while, then the south-western side of Danislager Wood ② and follow the wooded hedgerow. Cross the narrow part of the forest to emerge at the open meadows: where the forest joins the planted alders and poplars there is a good observation point ③. After walking 1 km (0.6 miles) northwards take the track that goes westwards, crossing the wood ④ (many woodland species). On arriving at the power lines, take the track southwards. That part of the track to the south of the tarmac road (D426) ⑤ can be interesting. Return via the side of a dense hedge ⑥.

Species

- The wooded hedgerows are good for passerines typical of eastern France: Icterine and Marsh Warblers and Lesser Whitethroat.
- In the alder and poplar woods, Marsh and Willow Tits can be seen side by side.
- On the bruch, both Curlew and Lapwing nest.
- Many birds of prey may be seen flying over this open habitat: Honey Buzzard, Sparrowhawk, Goshawk and Hobby.
- Mixed tit flocks often occur in winter, Nuthatches may mix with them.
- Great Spotted and Middle Spotted Woodpeckers are occasionally seen.
- Curlew can often be heard singing over the meadows from March to July.

3 Krafft Reservoir/Plobsheim

A large reservoir used to regulate flow on the Ill and Rhine Rivers. It is a very important area for wintering wildfowl: 10,000 to 15,000 duck depending on the winter and many other more-or-less-regular species (divers, grebes, Bewick's Swan, Red-crested Pochard, Scaup, scoters). In spring and autumn migrants include: Red-necked and Black-necked Grebes, Osprey, Little Gull and Black Tern. Leave Strasbourg on the D468 towards Plobsheim. Turn left at the traffic-lights in the village, follow signs to Rhinland. Park at Rhinland, then walk along the tracks on the reservoir side.

4 Rohrschollen Island

A wooded island bordered to the west by a canal and to the east by the Old Rhine close to Strasbourg. There are many woodland birds on the island and a large colony of Common Terns on the jetty above the hydro-electric station. In winter, there are large numbers of duck on the Alsace Canal and the Old Rhine.

From Strasbourg, leave towards Germany (Route du Rhin). Turn right at the traffic-lights just before the Vauban bridge towards 'Zone Portuaire Sud' (Route du Havre). Turn left at the second set of traffic-lights, 5 (3.1 miles) to 6 km (3.7 miles) along this road following the signs 'Usine Hydroélectrique de Strasbourg'. Once past the power-station fork right (tarmac track); stop at the large parking area.

5 Sommerley Forest

A typical Rhenish forest, unfortunately partly spoilt by forestry (logging, conifer planting etc). Rhenish forests are exceptional in Europe because of their complex structure, a large diversity of woodland plants and an abundance of creepers (ivy and clematis). There is a wide range of hole-nesting birds (Tawny Owl, Great Spotted, Lesser Spotted and Black Woodpeckers, tits, Nuthatch, Short-toed Treecreeper). The Middle Spotted Woodpecker is particularly abundant and there are many other woodland species. The site is best visited in the spring when birds are singing.

From Strasbourg take the D468 towards Plobsheim and then Krafft. Turn left (eastwards) at Krafft, immediately after the Ill outflow canal, follow the canal side and then go obliquely right as soon as possible (after about 1 km (0.6 miles)). Follow the other canal and at the second bridge go left as far as the embankment track. The numerous tracks covering the forest may be walked.

6 ÎLES DU RHIN NATIONAL NATURE RESERVE

16 km/10 miles
Altkirch
(IGN 3721 – 1/50 000)

Habitat and Timing

This is an island between the Rhine and the Grand Canal (created in 1928). The Alsace Grand Canal starts at the up-stream point with the Kembs Dam. Much of the island's 100 hectares is deciduous woodland; there are some maize fields and dry meadows. On the French side the Rhine is bordered with willows. In 1870 the river was canalised and deep digging gave rise to the appearance of two rocky bars (Barres d'Istein). These made the water course non-navigable. When the river is low, as in winter, these bars slow the flow which encourages the growth of aquatic plants and Zebra Mussels. These rocky bars are outlying spurs of the nearby Black Forest. Water birds may be seen at close quarters. The Rhine does not freeze and is the only open water in Alsace in cold winters (the light is right for the canal in the morning and the Rhine in the afternoon). Leaving the paths is forbidden. Group visiting is prohibited between 1 March and 1 July.

Calendar

Winter: Teal, Mallard, Pintail, Wigeon, Pochard, Tufted Duck, Coot, Black-headed Gull, Great Crested and Little Grebes, Goldeneye, Goosander, Mute Swan, Common Sandpiper, Snipe, Dipper, Kingfisher, White Wagtail and Water Pipit. Every year rarer birds occur: Long-tailed Duck, Eider, divers, Red-necked and Slavonian Grebes. Fieldfare and Bullfinch in the thorn trees.

Spring: Grey Heron nesting; Nightingale, Golden Oriole; Black Kite; six species of woodpecker.

Autumn: migrant waders; Osprey; Swift, three hirundines; warblers, Firecrest; Song Thrush; tit flocks throughout the day.

Access

From Mulhouse, take the A35 motorway towards Bâle, leave at the Saint-Louis exit on the D468 as far as Kembs. Pass the town and cross the sluices to the car park ① (you must park here). From the car park go

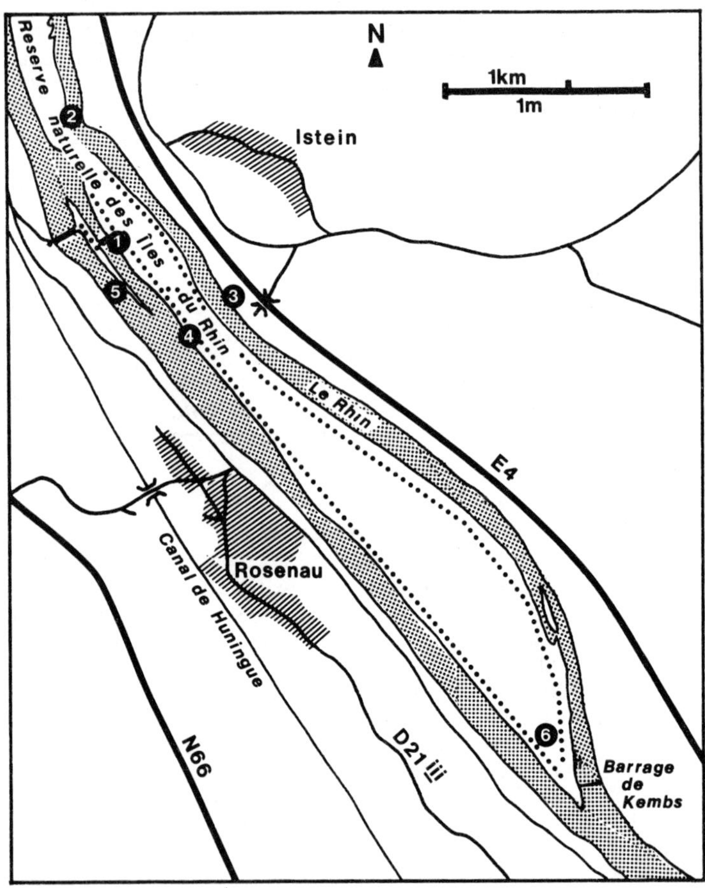

down to the causeway ②, a good observation point. Follow the Rhine up-river using the old towpath. Stop at the Barres d'Istein ③. Then, take either the traverse track ④ for the short circuit (4 km/1.5 miles), joining the canal side, then observing from the jetty ⑤ and return to the car park; or, continue along the towpath for the full circuit (12 km/7.5 miles) staying with the Rhine and its birds. Go to the point of the island ⑥. Return either using the same route or use the tarmac road along the canal side (no cars allowed) to get back to the car park.

Tufted Duck

Species

- In winter, the Mute Swan is common, there are also many ducks at the wide part of the canal, particularly Pochard and Tufted Duck. Not only are there many Mallard along the old towpath in winter, but also diving duck, Goldeneye and Goosander. Wigeon, Pintail and Gadwall gather near the jetty.
- Common Sandpiper are occasionally seen in winter. Some waders use the Rhine on their autumn migration.
- Hundreds of Cormorant and Black-headed Gulls roost on the peninsula each winter.
- The Dipper occurs on the river banks.
- Flocks of Fieldfare and Bullfinch occur in the forest during winter.
- In spring six species of woodpecker (Black, Grey-headed, Green, Great Spotted, Middle Spotted and Lesser Spotted) can be heard in the forest.
- The Kembs Dam is a good place for viewing duck.
- Grey Herons can be seen almost anywhere.

7 Michelbach Dam

At the foot of the Vosges Hills, the lake at the Michelbach Dam is in the parish of the same name. This recently-made lake may well become very good, the number of birds is increasing. There are no pleasure boats, surf-boards or fishing. The Haut-Rhin County Council and Mulhouse City Council will ensure that the lake remains free of all pleasure activities, leaving it undisturbed for the birds. There is a good walk: from the car park (with information board) take the embankment; a track round the lake passes through an orchard and a wood. This track is good at any time, except when the lake is frozen. There are many duck, and heron, grebes, Marsh, Montagu's and Hen Harriers, and Osprey. There are passerines in the forest and orchards, and waders in spring and autumn.

8 Sigolsheim Hills

To the north-north-west of Colmar lie the dry and sunny Sigolsheim Hills with their diversified landscape of Downy Oak woods, meadows with orchids, scrub and vineyards. There is a rich bird community, of particular interest are: Hoopoe, Woodlark, Stonechat and Lesser Whitethroat. From Sigolsheim go towards the military cemetery and park in the car park. From here walk along the ridge towards the oak wood on the top of the hill to the west.

9 Rixheim/Habsheim Hills

A hilly area with many orchards, hedges and scrub; this beautiful landscape with traditional farming holds a rich diversity of bird species. Some of the most interesting species are: Little Owl, Green Woodpecker, Wryneck, Stonechat, and Woodchat and Red-backed Shrikes. There is no recommended route; numerous possibilities exist by using the farm tracks within Rixheim, Habsheim, Eschentzwiller and Zimmersheim parishes.

AQUITAINE

10 BRUGES MARSHES NATIONAL NATURE RESERVE

2.5 km/1.55 miles
Bordeaux
(IGN 1536 west – 1/25 000)

Habitat and Timing

The last wetland area on the outskirts of Bordeaux (7 km/4.3 miles from the city centre). There are large water-meadows bordered by natural hedges; to the north grow ash and alder on damp ground. There are many culverts and ditches with permanent water. The meadows are managed using rare breeds of cattle. It is a stop-over site for migrants, with many breeding species as well. There is restricted access except for the public footpath. Information can be obtained at the entrance; ask the wardens for the latest updates.

Calendar

Winter: Cormorant, Grey Heron; Mallard, Teal, Pochard, Tufted Duck; Red Kite, Buzzard; Snipe and Jack Snipe.

Spring: White Stork; Grey Heron; Black Kite, Little Owl; Kingfisher; Reed, Great Reed, Sedge and Cetti's Warblers.

Autumn: Black and White Storks, Crane; Lapwing; Woodpigeon and Stock Dove; numerous passerines.

Access

From the entrance to the north of Bordeaux (Pont d'Aquitaine), continue to the end of the motorway on the N210 (northern ring road) towards Mérignac Airport. Cross the Lac de Bordeaux and leave the road after the Bruges industrial estate in the direction of Blanquefort (exit 6,

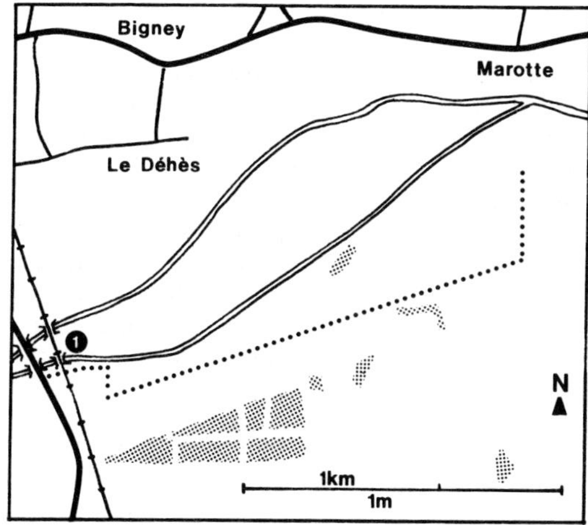

Campillau). 500 m (0.3 miles) from here at Les Quatre-Ponts, turn right (before the first bridge). Stop before or just after crossing the railway ①, continue on foot to the reserve entrance. Follow the marked footpath, use the hides next to the most productive areas. Most species occurring on the reserve can be seen from the central footpath.

Species

- Good observation point in spring or summer for Black Kite, Buzzard, Honey Buzzard, Short-toed Eagle and Kestrel.
- In spring the reed-beds are full of the songs of Reed, Great Reed and Sedge Warblers.
- Little Owls can often be seen, even during the day.
- In winter, both Snipe and Jack Snipe occur in the meadows.
- There is a Grey Heron colony (with associated Black Kites).
- In spring, Red-backed Shrikes nest in the hedgerows.
- In the marshes, not only White Stork, but often also Purple and Night Herons can be seen feeding.
- During the autumn migration various species of waders can be seen; in winter Lapwing and Golden Plover occur on the meadows.
- In winter, four species of thrush (Mistle, Song, Fieldfare and Redwing) occur on the reserve.

11 Grave Headland/Le Verdon

Grave Headland, in Verdon-sur-Mer parish, is the southern prominence at the mouth of the Gironde River. For some years, ornithologists from the LPO (La Ligue Française pour la Protection des Oiseaux) have been studying spring migration here looking particularly at fluctuations in the numbers of Turtle Dove (declining in Europe). Between March and May many other migratory species can be seen: White Stork; Honey Buzzard, Black Kite, Hobby; Collared Dove, Hoopoe, Swift (tens of thousands); larks, hirundines (the three common species and occasionally Red-rumped Swallow); Tree, Meadow and Tawny Pipits; Blue-headed Wagtail; Golden Oriole; Chaffinch, Greenfinch, Goldfinch, Linnet, Serin and many insectivorous passerines.

12 Nord-Médoc Marshes/Vensac, Saint-Vivien-de-Médoc and Soulac-sur-Mer

Nord-Médoc Marshes, between the Atlantic and the Gironde estuary, is a vast area of water-meadows, some bordered by tamarisk hedges. The marshes are particularly interesting in spring for the following species: Marsh, Hen and Montagu's Harriers; Short-toed Eagle, and Hobby, which nest nearby and come to the marshes to feed. Many passerines are seen on migration and large numbers of inland waders often stop-over: Lapwing, Golden Plover, Ruff and Redshank (especially in the spring). Watch from the N215 between Vensac and Le Verdon-sur-Mer, stopping every so often at the lay-bys. Be careful, during the hunting season (August–February) people carrying binoculars or telescopes are not particularly appreciated in the area!

13 TEICH BIRD RESERVE

3 km/1.85 miles
Audenge
(IGN 1437 west – 1/25 000)

Habitat and Timing

This area was formerly salt-marshes. Embankments were constructed in the eighteenth century to utilise the area for fish-farming. Seventy per cent of the area is covered in shallow, brackish water; levels are controlled by sluices. Some of the ponds are specially managed for birds. There is a wooded (alder and willow) border on the inland boundary. This is one of the most important wintering sites for duck and waders within the Bassin d'Arcachon, an exceptional site for nesting herons, and a major staging-post for many migrant species. You have to pay to enter. It is open every day from 1 March to 1 October, otherwise at weekends and on bank-holidays.

Calendar

Winter: Gadwall and Pintail, Teal, Pochard, Coot; Dunlin, Grey Plover, Avocet, Spoonbill; Penduline and Bearded Tits often overwinter.

Spring: Grey Heron, Night Heron and Little Egret nest; as do Shelduck and many passerines, in particular the Bluethroat. Waders occur.

Access

From Bordeaux, take the A63 motorway (towards Bayonne), and leave at exit 22 (Arcachon) on the dual carriageway turning onto the road to Teich, from here the way is signposted as far as the car park ①. Follow

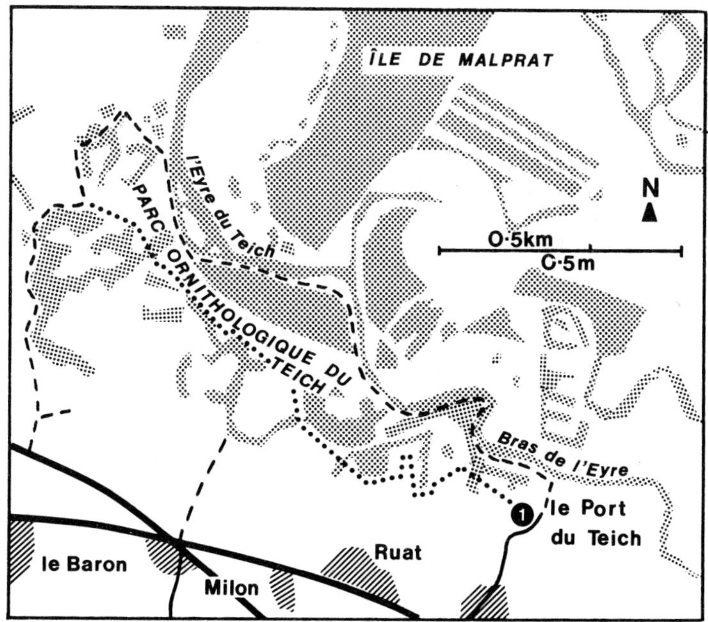

the marked footpath as far as the Bassin d'Arcachon. There are 11 hides along the path, which allow close views of the birds. Try to be at the far end of the path at high tide (tide tables are displayed at the entrance).

Species

- In winter, there are some Shoveler among the large Pintail flocks. Garganey occur in spring.
- Water Rail and Coot are present year-round.
- Nesting Grey Herons and Litle Egrets can be seen here between March and September.
- Groups of Wood, Green and Common Sandpipers occur in late summer.
- There is a Cormorant roost every winter.
- At the end of summer, flocks of Black-headed Gulls occur on the ponds.

- During the spring both Bluethroat and Reed Warbler can be seen close to the hides.
- During the migration period large numbers of Blue-headed Wagtails may occur.
- The Marsh Harrier is most often seen during the winter.
- Shelduck nest not far from the Pointe de l'Eyre.
- In winter, as in the migration period, large numbers of waders concentrate here at high tide.
- A nesting place at high tide in winter not only for Mute Swans, Shelduck, Mallard, Pintail and Wigeon, but also Great Crested, Black-necked and Red-necked Grebes.

14 The Coastal Trail/Audenge

The Coastal Trail is built on the embankment which encircles the Domaine de Certes. The path passes between the old salt-works of the Domaine and the Bassin d'Arcachon estuary (access to the diked areas is prohibited to the public). There are many salt-ponds mixed with rectilinear fields. An area rich in birds with much movement between the foreshore and nearby fields. It is best visited in spring or summer for waders; Mute Swan, Shelduck and Bluethroat all nest. In winter, from the northern embankment (Pointe de Lanton), it is possible to see many thousands of Brent Geese on the estuary. The route and car park are signposted from Audenge village.

15 HOSSEGOR LAKE

4.5 km/2.8 miles
Saint-Vincent-de-Tyrosse
(IGN 1343 west – 1/25 000)

Habitat and Timing

A natural lake, and a protected (no-hunting) coastal reserve. It is filled by the sea and surrounded by dunes on the west, north and east sides. It is also an immense mudflat at low tide. A canal links the lake with the sea, and an embankment which juts into the sea for about 100 m (110 yards) is excellent for birdwatching. The lake is a remarkable site for waders, gulls and divers in both winter and spring. The embankment is good for watching gulls flying up the canal to the lake. Visit the lake at low tide and the embankment at high tide.

Calendar

Winter: on the lake, Dunlin, Golden Plover, godwits, Curlew, smaller waders; divers, Black-headed, Little, Mediterranean, Herring, Lesser Black-backed, Great Black-backed and Common Gulls; Cormorant. On the sea, from the embankment, Kittiwake, Eider, Great Northern and Black-throated Divers, Razorbill. Also, Gannet, shearwaters and petrels.

Spring and Autumn: numerous waders as listed above and others (including Black-winged Stilt) and duck. From the embankment, watch passing Greylag Geese, sometimes Spoonbill and Sabine's Gull, and many passing passerines. To be avoided in summer because of the presence of sailboards and bathers.

Access

From the N10 main road, take the road signposted 'Hossegor–Capbreton 5 km', park at the port (railway station 5 km (3.1 miles) away, buses from Bayonne and Dax). Start at the car park ①, a good place for looking over the lake. Go southwards as far as Les Mimosas ② following the lake side

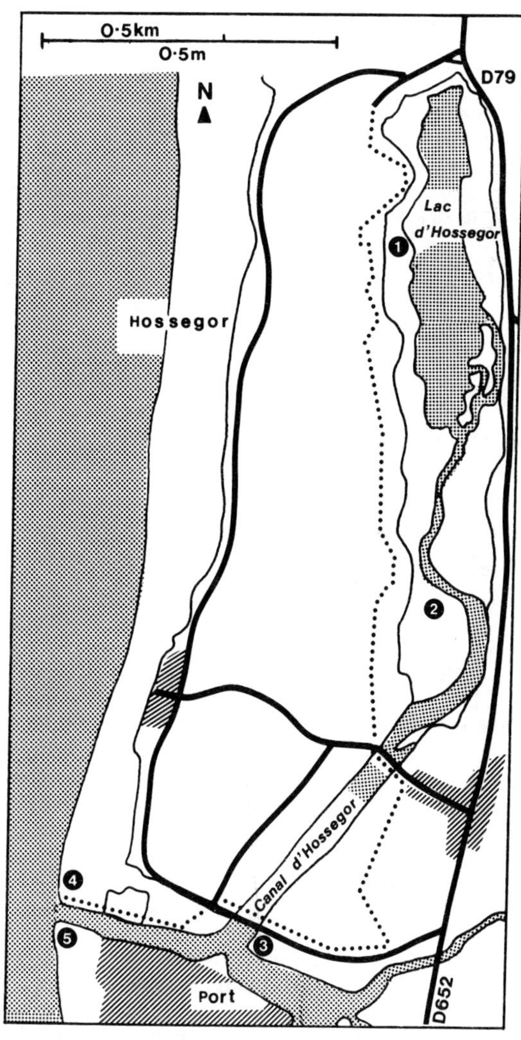

and passing by Plage Blanche. Cross the bridge on foot ③ to arrive at the northern embankment ④ for sea-watching. To get to the southern embankment ⑤, go round by car passing by the port.

Species

- Great Northern and Red-throated Divers occur on the northern part of the lake.
- There are groups of waders on the mudflats during the migration period.
- On changing tides, gulls move between the sea and the lake. There is a roost at high tide.
- Divers and Eider occur on the sea.
- There are large movements of seabirds – Gannet, shearwaters, petrels, Kittiwake and Sabine's Gull (in autumn).

16 Captieux

Large areas (recently deforested) in the Landes Forest are now used for growing maize. The vast Captieux military camp is host to hundreds of Cranes during the winter and migration periods. The cranes move between the different feeding and roosting areas, according on the one hand, to where the feeding is – maize spilt during harvesting – and on the other, to the amount of disturbance in these enormous clearings bordered with Maritime Pines. There is a hide and signposts in Lencouacq parish.

17 MAZIÈRE-VILLETON NATIONAL NATURE RESERVE

1.5 km/0.9 miles
Tonneins
(IGN 1739 east – 1/25 000)

Habitat and Timing

An old arm of the Garonne River – known as 'Gaule' or 'Gaure' – infilled at both ends, Mazière Marsh once extended for 5 km (3.1 miles), but has gradually been reduced through the years by organised drainage, particularly at the end of the nineteenth century. Work connected with 'remembrement' (re-allocation of agricultural land) in the early 1970s in Villeton parish has further spoilt this area, the last and only real witness of the changes of the river course in the 'Bassure', the local name for the whole of the low-lying flood-plain. Actually, a plan to protect and restore the habitat is being studied and work should begin soon. Access to the reserve (65 hectares) is strictly limited, and leaving the marked paths is totally prohibited.

Calendar

Autumn: Little Grebe, Mallard, Gadwall, Pintail, Shoveler, Teal, Coot; Jack Snipe and Snipe, waders; Bluethroat; Penduline and Bearded Tits; Reed Bunting. More rarely: Cormorant, Black Stork, Greylag Goose, Osprey, Crane, Aquatic Warbler.

Winter: Golden Plover, Lapwing.

Access

Leaving Tonneins (on the N113) cross the Garonne River and take the road towards Casteljaloux/Mont-de-Marsan (D120), then, about 1 km (0.6

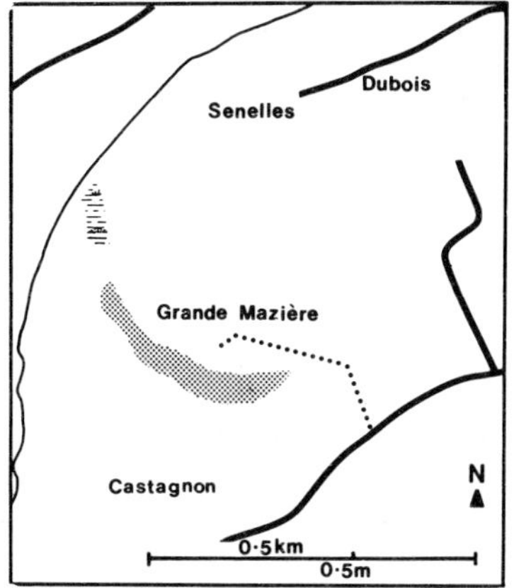

miles) after the bridge turn right onto a small public road: this leads directly to the reserve, enter only after having contacted the warden (Petite Mazière Farm).

Species

- In winter, Lapwing and Golden Plover occur in large numbers.
- The place known as Matte at Grand Mazière has many breeding species including: Blackcap, Short-toed Treecreeper and Woodchat Shrike.
- During migration, many Swallow, House Martin and Sand Martin flock over the lake hunting insects.
- Little Grebe and dabbling duck are undisturbed on the reserve (November to March).
- There are large numbers of Reed Bunting in the reed-bed in autumn, when there are also Penduline and Bearded Tits and *Acrocephalus* warblers.

18 The Confluence Area/Aiguillon

The area of confluence of the Lot and Garonne Rivers, upstream from the town of Aiguillon (access from the N113 or the motorway), is well worth a visit; according to the season many different species of bird can be seen. The Pech de Beyre, the last line of limestone hills on the right bank of the Garonne, should also be visited (many raptors, Little Ringed Plover, Bee-eater, Woodlark, Orphean Warbler). A remarkable observation point for migrants in autumn and February/March. From Aiguillon, the small valleys of the Pays des Serres on the right bank of the river, especially the Masse Valley, are worth visiting.

19 Campet Forest

Campet Forest, crossed by the N113 (Mont-de-Marsan), extends over an area of 1600 hectares, the majority of which is planted with Maritime Pines. Much recent cutting (70 per cent of the woodland) enables you to watch many interesting species (raptors, including Montagu's and Hen Harriers, passerines, including Dartford Warbler). The banks of the Avance are more suitable for such species as Woodcock. To visit this public forest, leave the N113 between Aiguillon and Port-Sainte-Marie (or at Aiguillon) towards Mont-de-Marsan; or from the motorway, leave at the Aiguillon intersection and take the road signposted Mont-de-Marsan.

20 ARTIX LAKE BIRD RESERVE

2 km/1.25 miles
Arthez-de-Béarn
(IGN 1544 west – 1/25 000)

Habitat and Timing

This is the lake of a hydro-electric dam bordered to the north and west by artificial embankments. The Pau River flows into the lake on the east and south sides forming a wooded, wet area of islands, mud-banks and channels. This area, difficult to penetrate, holds remarkable numbers of duck and waders during winter and periods of migration. Access to either the lake or the reserve is forbidden. Best watching is from the reinforced embankments, either in the morning or evening.

Calendar

Winter: many duck: Mallard, Shoveler, Pintail, Wigeon, Gadwall, Teal, Tufted Duck and Pochard; also Little Grebe, Lapwing; Black-headed Gull, Common Gull; Snipe, Grey Heron, Little Egret, Cormorant.

Spring: a breeding colony of Little Egrets and Night Herons, as well as Gadwall, Black-headed and Mediterranean Herring Gulls. Many migrants, ducks and waders. The willows hold many migrant passerines (both insectivores and seed-eaters). Osprey, Marsh Harrier and Hobby are seen.

Autumn: important numbers of herons, waders, Spoonbill; sometimes migrating White Storks and Cranes as well as many passerines and raptors.

Access

From Pau to the east, or Orthez to the west, take the N117 as far as Artix, which is about 20 km (12.5 miles) from both towns. Here take the D281 towards Mourenx. After 1.5 km (0.9 miles), just after the bridge, there is a car park on the left. The lake is visible from the road. It is only 2 km (1.2 miles) from Artix railway station (on the Paris–Lourdes line).

There are two possible routes. Either stop at the car park ① from where the lake can be watched directly, or walk to the right of the car park following the railway line on the bridge, and straight after drop to

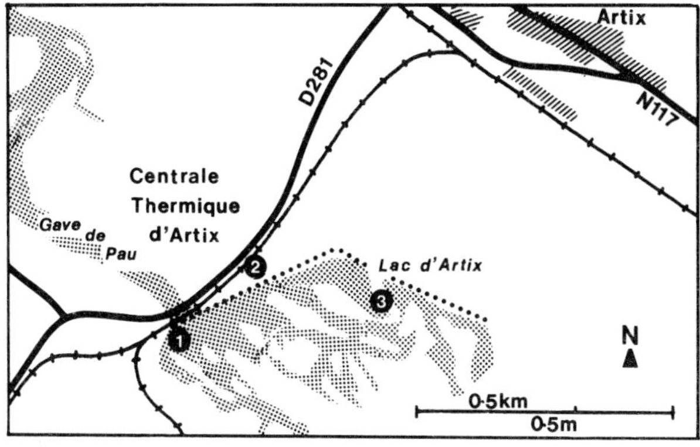

the left onto the track that follows the embankment to the most interesting site ② (the Heron and Egret colony). Then continue to follow the embankment; the path zigzags among brambles and trees. Finally, the path comes to the flooded woodland area ③ with its birds, amphibians, reptiles and mammals. Return by the same route.

Species

- There is a Night Heron and Little Egret colony.
- A good wintering site for duck.
- The mudflats are used by migrant waders.
- There is a Black-headed Gull colony.
- Osprey hunt here in April.
- In the willows, there are many passerines during periods of migration.

21 Orx Marshes

A large, 800-hectare site 15 km (9.3 miles) from Bayonne, Orx Marshes are unfortunately very much hunted over. Even so, many species of aquatic birds can be seen here; *Acrocephalus* warblers, Marsh Harrier, various herons. Walk around the peripheral embankment. A road splits the marsh in two. The flooded part is certainly the most interesting. The other part serves as a refuge for waders but is difficult to watch due to its size; only the gulls and herons are easily seen. Excellent habitat, to be visited between the autumn and spring.

22 Chingoudy Estuary/Hendaye

Chingoudy Estuary near Hendaye is a vast area of mudflats between the Bidassoa River and the Atlantic Ocean. Thanks to its somewhat inland position, it is a refuge for many waterbirds: geese, duck, waders, gulls. This reserve is best visited during migration times and in the winter (September to May) by following the D912, behind Hendaye beach.

23 Ossau Valley

About 20 km (12.5 miles) south of Pau, Ossau Valley is one of the richest and most beautiful in the Pyrénées. All the large species of raptor are commonly seen: Red Kite, Egyptian Vulture, Golden Eagle. The Lammergeier is best seen on the Benou plateau, above Bielle-Bilhères village. On the opposite slope, the cliffs at Aste-Béon have one of France's few Griffon Vulture colonies. To the north of Arudy, Bescat Plateau is of particular interest for migrant passerines. The Centre d'Écologie Montagnarde (Mountain Ecology Centre) has an exhibition, and there is information on the valley's rich natural history.

24 Orgambidexha Pass

The Col d'Orgambidexha, on the Haute-Soule, is probably the best known raptor migration watch-point in France. There is a team of experts in residence – from August to November – providing easy watching at a site once used by Woodpigeon hunters.

As early as mid-August Black Kites and Honey Buzzards can be seen crossing the Pyrenees on their way to Africa. In September – an ideal month both for the numbers and the variety of birds that pass – there are migrant Black Stork, Osprey, Honey Buzzard, Hobby, Marsh Harrier and large numbers of Swallows, especially in the second half of the month. In October it is the turn of Red Kite, Buzzard and Sparrowhawk, accompanied – from the middle of the month – by large numbers of Woodpigeons and many passerines such as Skylark, Meadow Pipit and Chaffinch. At the end of the month, and especially in early November, it is the turn of Cranes and the last of the Red Kites.

From either Oloron-Sainte-Marie or Pau go as far as Larrau then take the road towards Saint-Jean-Pied-de-Port, Bayonne and Orthez. The pass is about 10 km (6.2 miles) from Larrau. Information from: OCL, 64450 Viven. Tel: 59.04.87.50.

AUVERGNE

25 THE ALLIER VALLEY AT BRESSOLLES

10 km/6.2 miles
Moulins
(IGN 2627 west – 1/25 000)

Habitat and Timing

South of Moulins, the Allier is a wide strongly-flowing river. Meanders in the river-bed are constantly changing, and there is a lot of erosion. A mosaic of habitats – bare sandbanks, heath, willow thicket and riverside woodland in a few places – shelters a diversified avifauna year-round. It is an important migration route both in spring and autumn as well as a remarkable wintering site for duck and a nesting site for some interesting species. There is public access to the higher parts of the river-bed. A public right of way along the river banks allows for easy access along the riverside. Many accesses to the banks are private.

Calendar

Winter: Cormorant, many ducks (all the commoner species), sometimes Greylag and Bean Geese, many passerines.

Spring: Grey and Night Herons, Little Egret; Black Kite, Osprey; Stone Curlew, marsh terns, Sand Martin.

Summer: Little Ringed Plover, Hobby, Little and Common Terns, Wheatear all nest.

Autumn: Osprey, Crane, Stone Curlew, waders and many passerines.

Access

Bressolles is 5km (3.1 miles) south of Moulins on the N9. Those arriving by train can hire a bike at Moulins station. Park at Bressolles church ① for a visit to Allier Valley Bird Centre. To get to the river, continue on the N9 southwards for 400 m (440 yards). On top of the rise, turn left along a track that ends at a small car park ② on the river bank. This is a good point to look over the river and its sandbanks. Pass the barbed-wire fence and continue along the sandy bank on the edge of some private property as far as Lys Château ③. According to the condition of the river, it may be possible to descend onto the sand-bars and avoid the river inlets. Beware of the cows! Follow the château walls along the Allier, then back onto a wooded bank at Girodeaux Farm. The path overlooks a wood. Continue for 500 m (550 yards), to an entry onto Girodeaux open meadows ④ covered with willow thickets, and then onto the river sandbank. Go back by the same route or by cutting through the wood in front of the château. From Girodeaux, go back to the small car park at Bressolles either by the same path or on a small road that passes through Longvé and joins the N9. After this, you can take the N9 as far as Châtel-de-Neuvre, 13 km (8.1 miles) south of Bressolles. From the church there is a good panoramic view of the Allier Valley. The Allier River can be followed from the bridge.

Species

- Reed Bunting, Reed Warbler, Grasshopper Warbler nest in the riverside willows. Also there are large numbers of *Phylloscopus* warblers on migration.
- The Stone Curlew occurs on the sandbanks in summer, and in autumn there are sometimes large concentrations. Little Ringed Plover nest.
- Little and Common Terns fish over the river between May and August.
- Many species of wader occur on the mudflats, particularly in the autumn.
- Blue-headed Wagtail nest on the sandbanks. Sometimes, in summer, Tawny Pipit may be seen.
- There is a notable movement of Osprey both in spring and autumn, more rarely Black Stork and Crane.

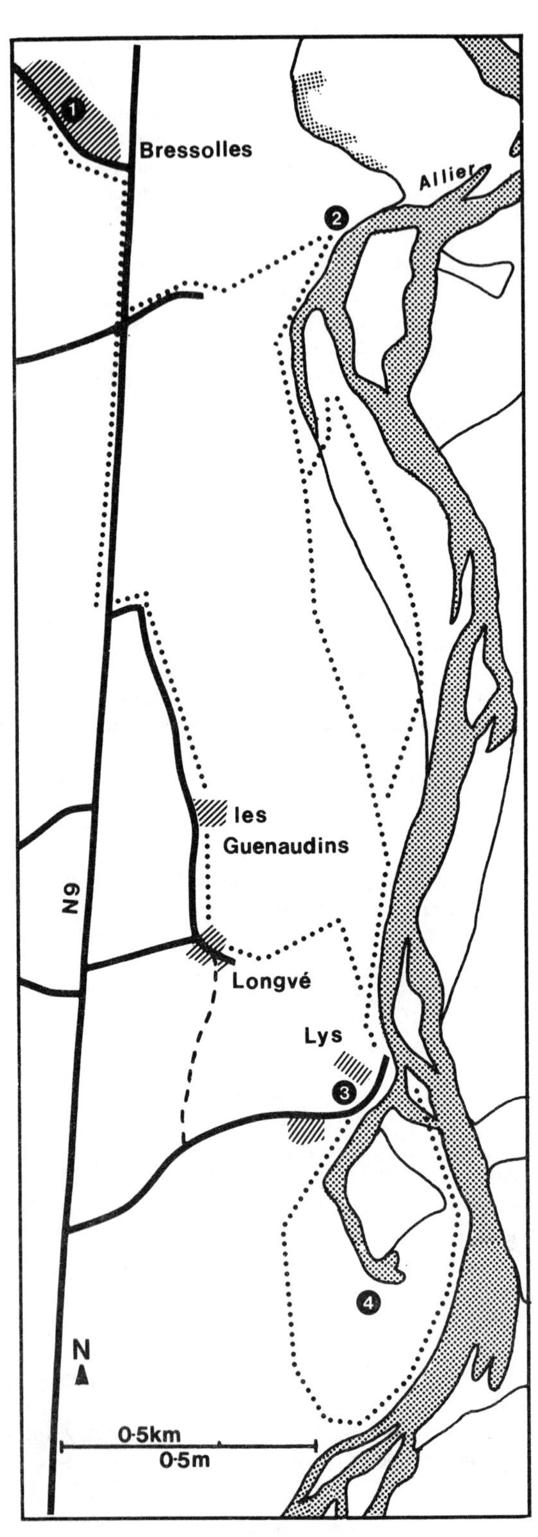

Bressolles
Allier
les
Guenaudins
N9
Longvé
Lys
N
0·5km
0·5m

- There are Sand Martin colonies on the river banks.
- Between September and March Cormorant overwinter in large numbers.
- In the spring, many passerines sing in the willow thickets: Nightingale, four *Sylvia* warblers including Lesser Whitethroat; four tits including Willow Tit.
- Mallard and Teal winter in large numbers. More rarely, sawbills, Goldeneye or divers occur on the river.

26 Tronçais Forest

Tronçais Forest is one of the best oak woodlands in Europe, with many full-grown trees and natural regeneration. The type of forestry practiced here creates a diverse habitat with many clearings and natural regrowth alongside old, mature trees (some 250 years as an ancient protected area). There are some interesting species: woodpeckers (Great, Middle and Lesser Spotted, Green, Grey-headed and Black); raptors (Booted Eagle, Short-toed Eagle, Honey Buzzard, Hen and Montagu's Harriers, Goshawk, Hobby); Nightjar and passerines such as Grasshopper, Bonelli's and Wood Warblers. Additionally, there are lakes with nesting *Acrocephalus* warblers and Black-necked Grebes. The reed-beds have roosts in late summer and winter, but the best time for the birdwatcher is between April and July. Further information is available from the C.P.I.E. (Centre Permanent D'Initiation à L'Environnement) nearby.

27 PRAT-DE-BOUC PLOMB DU CANTAL

11 km/6.8 miles
Murat
(IGN 2435 east – 1/25 000)

Habitat and Timing

Traditional summer pasture in the southern part of the volcanic Cantal range, the area around the Prat-de-Bouc (1,386 m) and the Plomb du Cantal (1,855 m) is known for its rich flora, and has a large variety of natural habitats: sloping peat-bogs, heath, stunted bushes, subalpine meadows, rocky outcrops. Because of its position on one of the Massif Central's autumn migration routes, it is (since 1982) one of seven sites in southern France studying the protection of migratory birds.

Calendar

Spring and Summer: many mountain passerines nesting: Rock Thrush, Ring Ouzel, Water Pipit, Alpine Accentor, Crossbill. Migrants include: Black Kite, Honey Buzzard, Montagu's Harrier; Dotterel (rare); swift; warblers (August); storks; Osprey, Short-toed Eagle, hirundines (September); Peregrine, Merlin, Sparrowhawk; Woodpigeon, Stock Dove; Mistle Thrush, Fieldfare, Redwing; Brambling, Chaffinch, Siskin, Greenfinch, Goldfinch (October).

Access

Prat-de-Bouc Pass is reached from Murat (N122). Park at the pass ① From August to October, there is an exhibition devoted to bird migration run by the Espaces et Recherches association at the cross-country ski school centre. Follow the track towards the ridge which starts off between two buildings. After a quarter of an hour's walk, there is a permanent observation post for autumn migrants ② (reception point). Then head towards the springs at Epie ③, now upwards towards the Plomb du Cantal, the highest point in the range ④. Go down along the

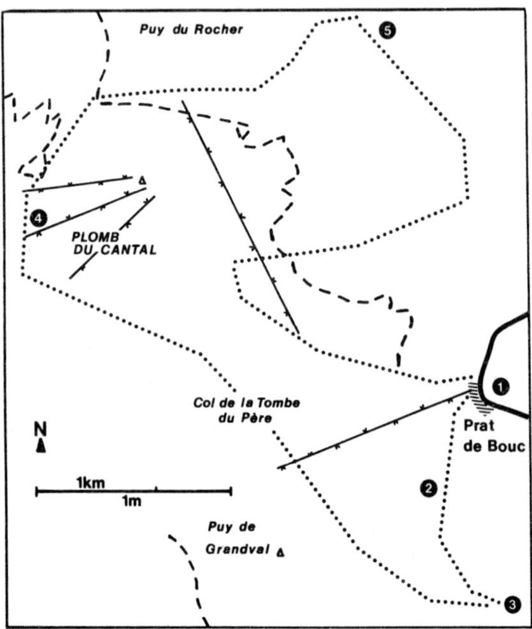

ridge towards the Cirque de Chamalières ⑤. From the Cirque return towards the pass, passing many sloping peat-bogs dispersed over the Cirque de Prat-de-Bouc (under the Plomb du Cantal), there are some typical peat-bog plants (be careful not to trample any underfoot and respect protected species). Return to Prat-de-Bouc Pass. Pay attention to the weather forecast, respect animals and fences and do not let dogs loose. The circuit, including stopping for watching, will take the whole day.

Species

- In autumn, halfway up the hillside is the perfect position for observing migrating raptors: Black and Red Kites, Honey Buzzard, Buzzard, Montagu's Harrier, Sparrowhawk, Peregrine, Merlin.
- In May and August, Ring Ouzels feed on the rocky slopes and in the bilberry scrub.
- Rock Thrush are often seen near Tombe-du-Père Pass.

- Alpine Accentors inhabit the scree, but are rare at the Plomb du Cantal.
- Water Pipits nest near the summit.
- Wheatears are omnipresent on the higher meadows and at the foot of the Plomb.
- Fieldfare and Mistle Thrush can be seen in the Cirque de Chamalières in the autumn.
- Snipe are often seen in the peat-bogs during their autumn migration.

28 LASCOLS/CUSSAC

1.5 km/0.9 miles
Chaudes-Aigues
(IGN 2536 – 1/25 000)

Habitat and Timing

Lascols 'narse' or marsh covers 100 hectares, at an altitude of 1,000 metres; it borders some habitats that are rare in the Auvergne mountains: a large water body of variable depth, open mud, grazed heath and a stream that supplies the marsh. Hunted over in the autumn, Lascols along with other wetlands in the Saint-Flour area (Nouvialou, Chassagnette, Secourieux), is of most interest during the spring. Thanks to its classification by the EEC as a zone of ornithological interest (1979), Lascols marsh benefits from special departmental protection; going into the marsh is dangerous. Watching conditions are best at sunrise and sunset.

Calendar

Spring: all of the dabbling ducks and many waders (all the shanks, Lapwing, Curlew, Golden Plover, Black-tailed Godwit). Also, Marsh Harrier, Merlin and Hobby. Five of the nesting species are at their altitudinal limit in Western Europe: Spotted Crake, Lapwing, Snipe, Curlew, Black-headed Gull.

Autumn: (mid–August to mid–September): waders; a Hen and Montagu's Harrier roost; Grey Heron; sometimes White Stork, Crane, Blue-headed Wagtail, Red-throated Pipit (rare), chats.

Access

Some 15 km (9.3 miles) from Saint-Flour (on the N9 road or the Paris–Bézieres railway line) take the road towards Chaudes-Aigues (D921). Between Bouzentes and Les Ternes turn onto the road for Cussac (D57). 700 m (765 yards) before Cussac take the fork to Lascols where there is a public car park ①. A general idea of the area can be gained from the road as long as the water level is high enough; visits are ideal for groups of no more than ten. The start of the footpath is wet. In front of the farm on the side of the narse follow the small wall, birdwatching along the way; firstly having crossed the mudflats in front of the farm to look over the widest part of the lake. Moving on a further 100 m (110 yards), stop in front of the wire cage for a general look over the various habitats ②. Then, at the far end of the narse, you can look over the

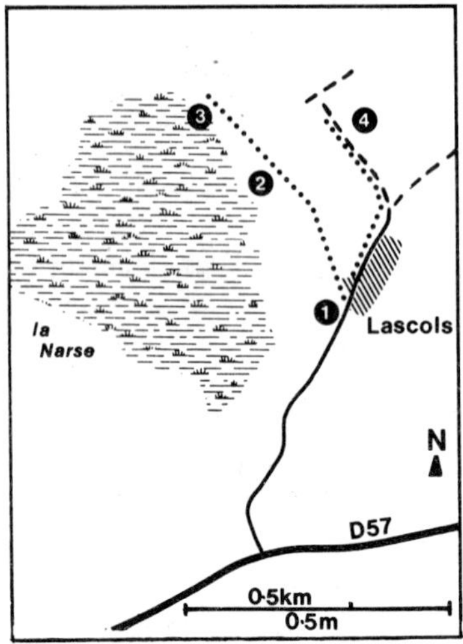

mudflats outside of the breeding season ③. Lastly, from the car park, walk through the village for an elevated view over the whole area ④. You must be quiet as many of the birds are found less than 50 m (55 yards) from the observation points, in the open. Respect the country code, please do not take dogs.

Species

- At the end of summer there is a Hen and Montagu's Harrier roost. Also an area where Black and Red Kites, Marsh Harrier (migrants) and Hobby hunt. In winter Peregrine sometimes occur.
- In the evening, it is sometimes possible to hear Water Rails and Spotted Crakes calling.
- In the spring, there is a view of the Black-headed Gull colony with the Plomb du Cantal as a backdrop. There are Whiskered and Black Terns, sometimes gulls, on migration.
- During March all the West-European dabbling ducks can be seen. Mallard, Teal and Garganey nest here.
- Throughout the spring, flocks of migrant waders can be seen, both morning and evening. In June some of the nesting birds can be seen: Lapwing, Curlew and Snipe (rare).
- White Wagtail, Whinchat and Wheatear are common breeders around the edge of the marsh.

29 Truyère Gorges

The Truyère Gorges are located along the 35 km (22 miles) between Chaliers and Paulhenc; the many wooded slopes and heaths around the hydro-electric dams are very good for birds of prey. There are many potential observation points: firstly at Longevialle (the right bank near Ruynes), an ideal spot for Osprey both in spring and autumn, also migrant pigeons and waders. Next at Cheyle viewpoint (left bank,

Fridefont) where duck can be seen in the spring, also Booted Eagle, Short-toed Eagle and both species of kite. Lastly at Turlande/Pont-de-Treboul (right bank, Pierrefort), pigeons and raptors on autumn migration; during the spring and summer, Hen and Montagu's Harriers over the heaths and Grey Heron along the river. Owls are also relatively common (Little, Tawny, Long-eared and Eagle).

30 The Dordogne Gorges

From Madic to Saint-Projet, the valley is steep-sided and wooded with many cliffs and heaths. The cliffs have been transformed into hydro-electric dams. This is a large area used by many species during the spring migration, particularly raptors. Two of the most interesting sites are at: Madic (left bank near Brot-les-Orgues) where there is a lake and marsh on the side of the Dordogne River – an excellent area for passerines (Melodious Warbler, various *Sylvia* and *Phylloscopus* warblers, Reed Warbler, Whinchat, a hirundine and Starling roost in July and August) – and the Gratte-Bruyère viewpoint (right bank), on the 'Route des Ajustants' road near Saint-Projet bridge, which is good for raptors (Black and Red Kites, Honey Buzzard, Goshawk, Booted and Short-toed Eagles). Ospreys occur on migration.

31 ROCHER DE PRADES

3.3 km/2 miles
Langeac
(IGN 2635 east – 1/25 000)

Habitat and Timing

More than 200 metres high, this basaltic outcrop dominates the Allier River, still a torrent below. Between the granitic or volcanic plateau there are many different habitats: pebble banks, riverside woods, broom heath, dry meadows and rocky outcrops, all characteristic of the Allier gorges. A haven for raptors (large diversity and good populations of some rare species) during the breeding sesason, and for rock-dwelling species.

Calendar

Winter: Raven, Great Grey Shrike, Red-legged Partridge and many Dipper. Occasionally Wallcreeper or Alpine Accentor.

Spring and Summer: many breeding raptors (Short-toed Eagle, Red and Black Kites, Honey Buzzard, Sparrowhawk, Kestrel and Hobby). On the rock itself is a colony of Crag and House Martins, with a few pairs of Alpine Swift, Raven and Rock Bunting. On the banks of the Allier, Common Sandpiper, Dipper and Grey Wagail.

Access

From Langeac, to the north-west, follow the Allier upstream on the D585. At Saint-Arcons-d'Allier take the D48. On the way out of Prades, park in

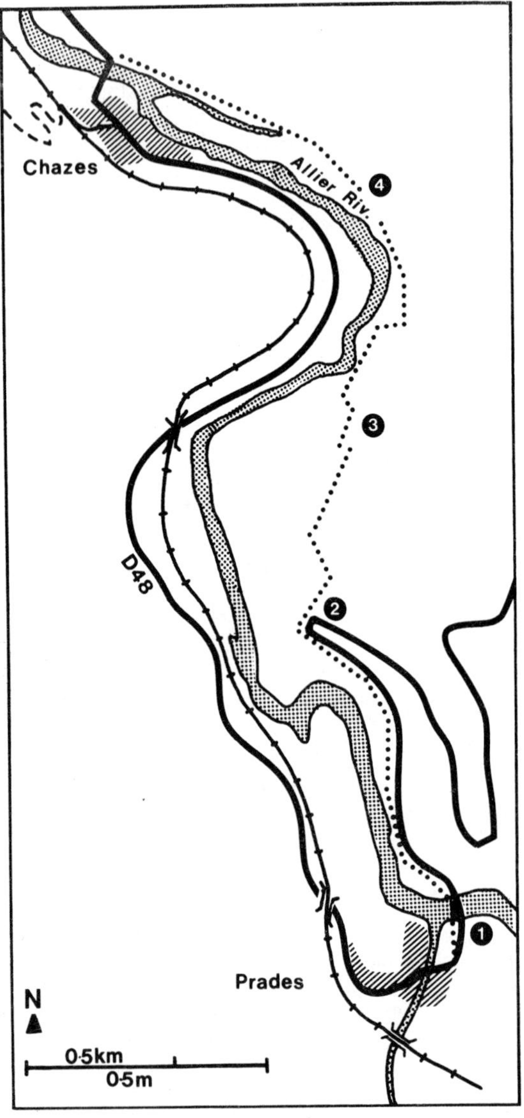

the car park at the bridge over the Allier. You can reach Saint-Privat-d'Allier on the D589 coming from Puy-en-Velay; go through the gorges on the D301 (good view of the valley) then, at Vergues, drop down to Prades on the D48. It is possible to watch birds by either going down onto the river bank or by walking around the foot of the rock ①. After looking at the rock, walk along the marked trail (follow the red-and-white stripes). Follow the road as far as the first hairpin bend ②, then take the surfaced track. After the small village of Le Pradel ③ you can look over the banks of the Allier and the heath on the other side. Continue as far as Sainte-Marie church (rocky area) ④ and rejoin the road at

Saint-Julien-des-Chazes bridge. Return by the same track or along the road. In order to understand the layout of the area and to see the birds on the plateau, it is well worthwhile climbing the mule trail from the foot to the summit of the rock.

Species

- A raptor feeding area: Short-toed Eagle, Red Kite and Hobby in the breeding season and Hen Harrier in the autumn.
- There are Raven (throughout the year), Alpine Swift, nesting Crag and House Martins.
- You can see Wallcreeper and Alpine Accentor in winter.
- There are large groups of tits.
- Dipper (throughout the year), Common Sandpiper (nesting), and sometimes Kingfisher can be seen.
- There are Rock Buntings in the breeding season.
- There are Red and Black Kites in the breeding season and Hen Harrier on migration.

32 Bas-en-Basset

On the sides of the Loire River (Bas-en-Basset parish) in the north of the department is a small depression made up of partially worked gravel-pits, scrub, arable land and an ox-bow lake (afforded special protection). In the breeding season you can find Grey and Night Herons, Lapwing, Little Ringed Plover; Sand Martin; Red-backed and Woodchat Shrikes. Raptors also hunt over the area: Short-toed Eagle, Black and Red Kites, Sparrowhawk and Hobby. During migration you can see: Mallard, Teal, Coot; Great Grey Shrike; Reed and Rock Buntings.

33 The Mezenc Massif

These volcanic hills on the Haute-Loire/Ardèche border dominate the whole area. At its foot, Les Estables (one of the highest villages in the Massif Central) is a gateway to a habitat typical of mid-altitude mountains rich in plant and animal life. In winter, Black Woodpecker, Crossbill, Coal Tit, Fieldfare and Siskin can all be seen as well as a few Snow Finch and Alpine Accentor. Ravens can be seen displaying during the first fine days of spring but it is not until the end of May that all nesting species have returned: Water Pipit; Ring Ouzel, Rock Thrush; Citril Finch and probably Woodcock. A few raptors hunt over the slopes; Short-toed Eagle, Red Kite and Hen Harrier.

34 LA SERRE/ SAINT-SATURNIN

5 km/3.1 miles
Veyre-Monton
(IGN 2532 east – 1/25 000)

Habitat and Timing

Many millions of years old, the Serre basaltic lava flow, which came from Mont Vigeral, descends as far as the village of Crest. It has been worn down by erosion and is now a volcanic ridge. It has long been used by man (grazing and crops) but of late only part is farmed and it has partially returned to its former state (grass and scrub, wooded on its sides). On its south side the Chadrat sedimentary plateau is still cultivated. This diverse countryside holds a wide variety of birds, particularly raptors and some uncommon passerines. In autumn, the heart of the Limagne (central part of the Massif Central) forms a bottle-neck. La Serre is situated at the exit of this funnel and is a good point for watching hundreds of thousands of migrant birds: raptors, storks, Cranes, pigeons and passerines. This migration has been studied since 1986. There is unlimited access to the area which is made easy thanks to the presence of many paths. The migration watch-point is manned between 1 August and 31 October.

Calendar

Spring: Short-toed Eagle, Buzzard, Honey Buzzard, Black and Red Kites, Sparrowhawk, Kestrel and Hobby all nest, as do Quail, Hoopoe, Woodlark, Red-backed Shrike, *Phylloscopus* warblers (four species) and Hawfinch.

Summer: on migration, Black Stork, Honey Buzzard, Black Kite, Montagu's Harrier. Also Tawny Pipit and Ortolan Bunting.

Autumn: Osprey, Marsh and Hen Harriers, Red Kite. Large movements of pigeons (mid-October) and passerines (especially morning and evening), sometimes Crane (early November). Also Great Spotted Woodpecker and especially Lesser Spotted Woodpecker and Great Grey Shrike.

Access

From Clermont-Ferrand take the N9 towards Issoire. At Vierge de Monton take the D213 towards Saint-Saturnin/Saint-Amand-Tallende and then the

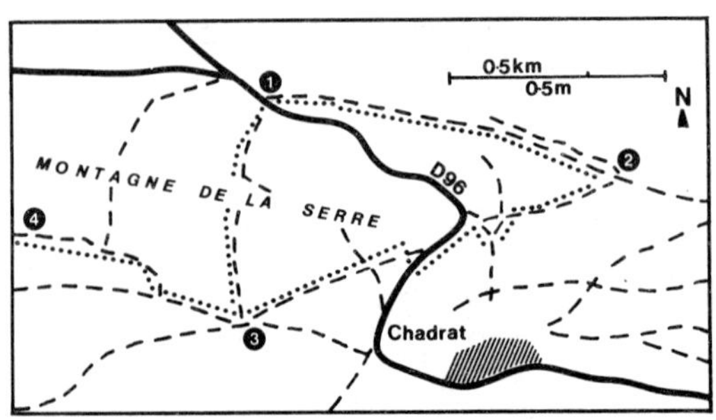

D96; cross Chadrat and continue for another 1.5 km (0.9 miles) as far as the car park on the right. You can also come up the N89 turning off at Theix and then Nadaillat (on entering the village), continue on this road for a few kilometres. There is a car park 50 m (55 yards) after the road to Chagourdat Farm. From the car park take the track; 100 m (110 yards) on is an information centre and migration study point ①. Continue along the track for 1.4 km (0.85 miles) and then turn right ② and walk as far as the road. Walk down about 50 m (55 yards) onto the track leading to the small chapel ③, then climb back up to the car park. A further walk as far as ④ is possible.

Red Kite

Species

- A migratory stop-over for Tree, Meadow and Tawny Pipits; Woodlark and White Wagtail in October. Sometimes Ortolan Bunting in September.
- An observation post during the autumn migration (1 August to 31 October) from the water-tower. You can see many species of raptor hunting.
- Parties of Hawfinch are regularly seen in autumn.
- Red-backed Shrike breed and Great Grey Shrike is seen in autumn.
- Nightjar can be heard singing on calm summer nights.
- In the surrounding woods, Coal and Crested Tits occur as well as Goldcrest and Firecrest (especially in the autumn), and you can also find Bonelli's Warbler in the breeding season.
- Again in the autumn, flocks of Mistle and Song Thrushes and Redwing often occur.
- Montagu's Harrier nest and hunt over the crops. Hen Harrier, Black and Red Kites may be seen on migration.
- Many passerine species nest in the woods, including Chiffchaff, Willow, Wood and Bonelli's Warblers.

35 The Allier Valley

The most interesting part of the Allier valley for birds lies between Pont-du-Château and Maringues. Its banks, sometimes spoilt by man's activities, have many different habitats: riverside forest of different ages, pebble banks, ox-bow lakes, fields, abandoned and working sand quarries. Many species are easily observed throughout the year. Winter visitors include: Grey Heron, Mallard, Teal and Black-headed Gull; in spring, Red Kite, Osprey, many species of duck and waders in small numbers. Grey and Night Herons, Black Kite, Hobby, Stone Curlew and Common Sandpiper all nest; Little Egret and other migrants occur in autumn.

36 Chaudefour Valley

Chaudefour Valley, in the Sancy Massif, is in Chambon-sur-Lac parish. A site protected for its plants, animals and landscape; this glacial valley is untouched by human development and may become a National Nature Reserve. Once the snow has started melting is the best time to look for Water Pipit, Treecreeper, Ring Ouzel and Coal Tit at the top of the valley. Crag Martin, Wallcreeper and Raven are all found in the more rocky parts, whilst on the higher ground you can watch Rock Thrush, Alpine Accentor, and Montagu's Harrier hunting. In the autumn the soaring raptors (Osprey, Honey Buzzrd, Marsh and Hen Harriers) mix with pigeons and passerines, all on migration.

37 The Dômes Chain

The Dômes chain of hills, one of the most beautiful volcanic complexes in Europe, lies to the west of Clermont-Ferrand. It is a vast area of peaks covered with forest and moor. A good perspective of the area can be had by visiting Vache and Lassolas peaks and the Cheire d'Aydat. There is a typical list of mountain birds: notably Tengmalm's Owl, Treecreeper, Black Woodpecker and Crossbill, as well as both 'crests in the more wooded parts. Six species of tit occur together. There is also a good list of raptors (Short-toed Eagle, Goshawk, Red Kite). Hen Harrier, Nightjar, Meadow Pipit, Whinchat and a few pairs of Great Grey Shrike nest on the heaths and in the fields. The spring (from mid-May) is the best time to visit the area, but autumn can be interesting (many Red Kites and Hen Harriers).

BOURGOGNE

38 LAVAUX DALE, GEVREY-CHAMBERTIN

7 km/4.35 miles
Gevrey-Chambertin
(IGN 3123 west – 1/25 000)

Habitat and Timing

This site consists of wooded dales typical of limestone areas. The ravine, dropping 150 m (165 yards) along its 3 km (1.85 miles), is covered with bushy wood with some cliffs. The two sides are north- and south-facing with markedly different vegetation, and there is natural scrub on the plateau above. Unrestricted access (common land) is made easier by the presence of tracks maintained by the Club Alpin Français. It is best visited in the morning or evening in spring or early summer.

Calendar

Spring: Kestrel; Woodpigeon, Turtle Dove; Black, Great Spotted and Lesser Spotted Woodpeckers; Nightjar; Dunnock; Robin, Song Thrush; Whitethroat, Chiffchaff, Garden, Wood and Bonelli's Warblers; Goldcrest.

Access

From Gevrey-Chambertin take the road towards Chamboeuf, which runs through the dale. The dale begins just after the vineyards, 100 m (110 yards) further on on the left is an ONF (Forestry Commission) car park ①. The walk follows the marked paths which cross the forest, the slopes, the bottom of the dale, cliff tops and the plateau. Follow the CAF blue track which climbs to the left through a beech wood ②; after the concrete reservoir at the first horseshoe bend, walk downhill on the unmarked track ahead. Go as far as a hollow in an adjacent small dale and turn right to arrive at the bottom of the dale ③, near a wooden hut.

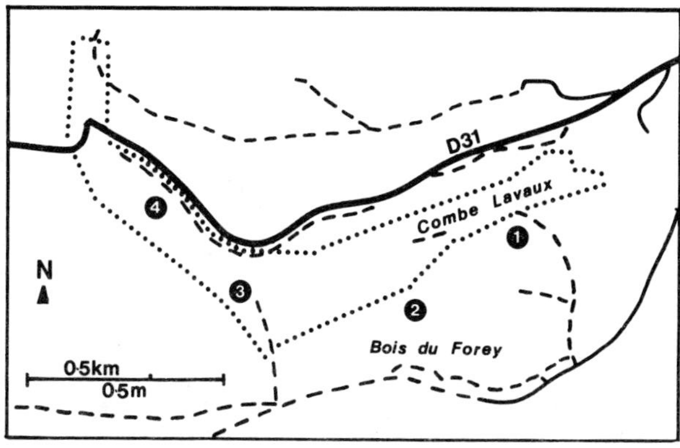

Climb up as far as a fork, then turn right to re-find the road. Cross the road into the small Saint-Martin dale opposite. Once on the plateau, turn right at the fork and follow the blue track. Follow the cliff top ④. Return to the car park via the vineyards and the D31 road.

Species

- In the beech wood, the Wood Warbler trills from a low branch.
- The Black Woodpecker's loud call and the Great Spotted Woodpecker's drumming can be heard in the wood.
- Woodpigeon and Turtle Dove are easily seen in the cool oak woods at the bottom of the dale.
- In one of the few spruces a Firecrest may be found delivering its quiet song.
- The Kestrel often passes in front of the cliff-face. The Peregrine makes occasional short appearances.
- In a clearing, Yellowhammer and Cirl Bunting may be seen and the Tree Pipit heard singing.
- On the hillsides, Dunnocks sing quietly and the Bullfinch gives its melancholy song.
- Four species of *Phylloscopus* warbler can be heard here.
- In the evening the Nightjar can be heard in the more open woodland.

39 Kir Lake/Dijon

The lake is on the left of the Paris road on the outskirts of Dijon. This artificial water body on the course of the Ouche is an interesting wintering site, to be visited between November and March. In autumn, small waders (Redshank, Dunlin) occur on the bank near the Cygne restaurant. Coot, Tufted Duck and Pochard are regular in winter. Rare birds sometimes occur; Goldeneye, Greylag Goose, Scaup, Red-crested Pochard, Eider, Common and Velvet Scoters, Shelduck, Smew, Goosander, Red-breasted Merganser. There is a Black-headed Gull roost in winter (with the occasional Herring or Common Gull). Grebes are also seen: Little Grebes and Great Crested regularly, Red-necked, Black-necked and Slavonian more rarely. Other species seen in the winter include: Dipper, Kingfisher, Moorhen, White Wagtail.

40 THE LOIRE VALLEY BETWEEN LA CHARITÉ-SUR-LOIRE AND TRACY-SUR-LOIRE

11 km/6.8 miles
La Charité-sur-Loire
(IGN 2523 – 1/50 000)

Habitat and Timing

One of the best conserved parts of the middle Loire River, locally called 'La Loire des Îles'. It is a mosaic of a large variety of habitats: gently-

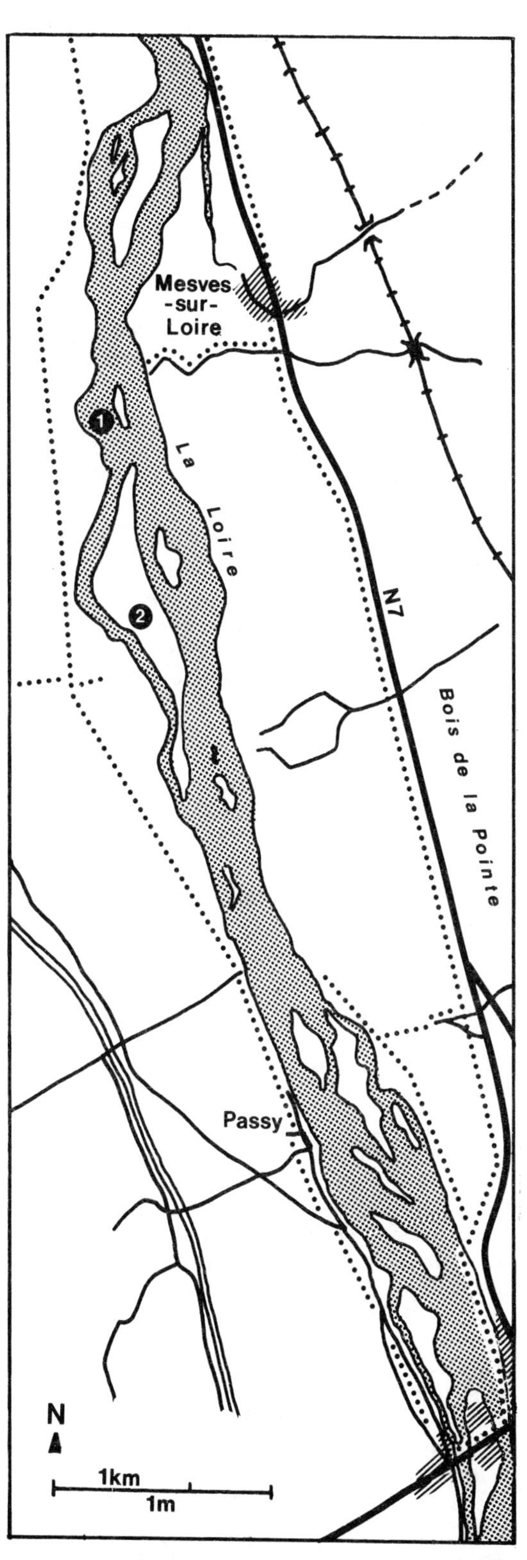
Mesves
-sur-
Loire
1
La Loire
2
N7
Bois de la Pointe
Passy
N
1km
1m

sloping banks, sometimes undermined by the current, changing mudflats, sand- and gravel-bars, dry meadows, and islets and islands with different stages of woody growth (from willow saplings and poplars to mature riverside forest). The river course is a Réserve de Chasse (strictly no hunting) along 20 km (12.5 miles). At the moment there is unlimited access, but there is a proposal to make the area a National Nature Reserve.

Calendar

Winter: Cormorant; Bean Goose, Mallard, Teal; Peregrine; Woodpigeon.

Spring and Summer: Black Kite; Stone Curlew, Little Ringed Plover; Common and Little Terns, Black and Middle Spotted Woodpeckers; Kingfisher, Sand Martin; Nightingale, warblers.

Autumn: Osprey, Common Sandpiper, Greenshank, Lapwing, calidrids and warblers.

Access

From La Charité-sur-Loire take the N7 northwards as far as Mesves-sur-Loire. At the entrance of the village turn towards the Étang Communal (public lake) ①. You can look over the Loire from various points on the track. Continue northwards as far as Pouilly-sur-Loire, then back along the D187 towards La Charité. Watch from 'La Grande Levée de Napoléon' between Les Vallées and La Cafarderie ② (closed to vehicles in parts, but it can be used again from Herry onwards). Look over the Loire from La Cafarderie.

Species

- In winter, there is a Greylag and Bean Goose roost on the sandbanks.
- Cormorants roosting to the south of Mesves-sue-Loire are easily seen in winter.
- Little Ringed Plover and Stone Curlew nest on the uncovered sandbanks in the river.
- Common and Little Terns also nest.
- Kingfishers occur along the river's banks.
- In the bushes on the side of the Loire, in May, Nightingale and Golden Oriole sing.

41 Baye and Vaux Lakes

These two lakes are on the side of a Réserve de Chasse (strictly no hunting). There is a car park at the start of an embankment which runs between the lakes; follow the signs to the Centre de Vacances de Palaiseau (Palaiseau holiday centre). It is easy to watch as long as there is not a really cold spell; ice forces the birds to move elsewhere. Birds to be seen include: Great Crested Grebe, Grey Heron (a large heronry in the private forest on the side of Vaux Lake); Red Kite; Mallard, Teal and Pochard; waders on migration and many passerines in the reed-beds (Reed Warbler, Reed Bunting); and along the lake side, Black Kites breed. You can obtain information from local birdwatchers at the warden's house (near the car park).

42 CHARETTE AND PIERRE-DE-BRESSE

10 km/6.2 miles
Pierre-de-Bresse
(IGN 3125 – 1/50 000)

Habitat and Timing

In its lower reaches, the Doubs meanders, and a mosaic of habitats is sustained by the changing river course: sand-bars, flooded willow-beds, large ox-bow lakes, and steep and crumbling banks. Outside the protection dikes there is a large cultivated plain, and to the south-west some vast water-meadows. The rich Bresse lakes (private) with lush surrounding vegetation, and the oak and Hornbeam woods are, like the village, situated on the higher land overlooking the valley. There are many water birds. Access onto the banks of the Doubs, which collapse in places, can be dangerous. The track leading to Champ Bégon is strictly private.

Calendar

Summer: herons; harriers; Corncrake, Little Ringed Plover, Curlew; Common Tern; Bee-eater, Sand Martin; Bluethroat; wetland warblers.

Spring: dabbling duck; Osprey; waders and marsh terns.

Winter: the lakes are frozen. Only the Doubs and its valley are of interest, particularly during hard weather. There are often flocks of Cormorants, Lapwings and Black-headed Gulls; more rarely, Bean Goose and northern ducks (sawbills, Goldeneye, Eider).

Access

From Chalon-sur-Saône to the west take the N73 towards Dole and Besançon. Just after Sermesse fork right towards Pierre-de-Bresse. At Charette, park below the church on the side of the Doubs at a place called Bas de Charette ①. You can also park at L'Étang Bailly. The circuit takes a day. Start, on foot, from Bas de Charette towards Lays, going as far as the small bridge. Cross and turn right immediately onto a path across the fields (vehicles prohibited). 1 km (0.6 miles) further on, cross another small bridge and continue to where four paths meet ②. Turn right towards Terrans. Cross the village by the foot of the church in the direction of Saint-Bonnet-en-Bresse. After 1 km (0.6 miles) leave the road on the right to pass Étang Bailly ③. There is a beautiful watch point from the embankment. Another kilometre (0.6 miles) further on turn right again towards Charette via the Bois de Vendues ④ and La Pommelée.

Species

- Little Ringed Plover and Stone Curlew nest on the sand-bars.
- Night Heron and Little Egret nest along the river.
- The Bee-eater rests here before reaching its breeding sites. Kingfishers can be seen.
- Corncrakes call in the meadows along the river.
- Sand Martin hunt over the water, Bluethroats occur upstream of this site.
- Blue-headed Wagtail can be seen in the meadows, Whinchats nest not far from the water.

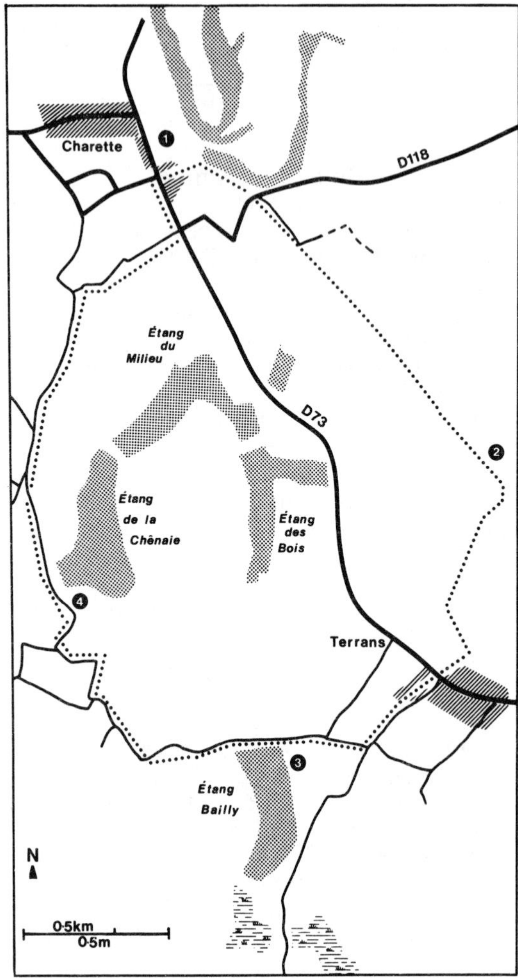

- Curlew nest in the wet meadows.
- Savi's Warblers sing around the lake, as do Reed and Great Reed Warblers.
- You can see families of Pochard (June) as well as Great Crested Grebe and Grey and Purple Herons.
- There are harriers, and Hobby hunting (rare).
- Willow Tits occur in the wood throughout the year.

43 The Saône at Marnay

For anyone passing in winter, the confluence of the Grosne and Saône Rivers, 10 km (6.2 miles) to the south-east of Chalon-sur-Saône, may well be worth a visit, particularly during very cold spells when northern water birds may occur: sawbills (three species), Eider, Goldeneye, Velvet Scoter, divers. More regularly, Tufted Duck and Pochard. In spring, Curlew and Whinchat nest, while in the summer, families of Great Crested Grebe can be seen on the river.

44 Pourlans Forest

A few kilometres north of Charette, Pourlans is a national forest managed for mature trees with a coppice understorey. Many species of raptor can be seen in spring (Goshawk, Sparrowhawk, Buzzard, Honey Buzzard, Black Kite), as well as six species of woodpecker (Green, Grey-headed, Great Spotted, Middle Spotted, Lesser Spotted, Black); also passerines of mature woodland (Firecrest, Wood Warbler, Hawfinch, Spotted Flycatcher) and birds of woodland clearings (Grasshopper Warbler, Hen Harrier, Red-backed Shrike).

45 BAS-REBOURSEAUX BIRD RESERVE VERGIGNY AND SAINT-FLORENTIN

5 km/3.1 miles
Saint-Florentin
(IGN 2719 west – 1/25 000)

Habitat and Timing

A disused gravel-pit used in the construction of the Paris–Lyon TGV railway line, Bas-Rebourseaux Bird Reserve is on the course of the Armançon River, between the railway and the Bourgogne Canal. The lake is of interest because there is a continual change of water (from the inflowing river) which produces an abundance of aquatic vegetation and fish. This constant flow also prevents the lake freezing over in winter. This, coupled with its being on a migration route, makes it a privileged site for observing many migrant and over-wintering birds. Access by vehicle is very much restricted; it is far better to visit the site on foot.

Calendar

Winter: grebes, Cormorant; Gadwall and Wigeon, Tufted Duck, Pochard, sometimes Smew or Goosander, Goldeneye; Great Grey Shrike, Water Pipit.

Spring: many dabbling duck (including Garganey), sometimes Greylag Goose (early March), Osprey; Crane; small waders and Black-tailed Godwit.

Summer: Black Kite, Kestrel; Little Ringed Plover, Common Sandpiper; Sand Martin, numerous passerines.

Autumn: Osprey; waders, terns.

All year: Grey Heron, Kingfisher.

Access

From Saint-Florentin (to the north) or Auxerre (to the south) take the N77. Between Saint-Florentin and L'Ordonnois, take the D43 towards Vergigny. On leaving Bas-Rebourseaux village take the dirt-track ① that

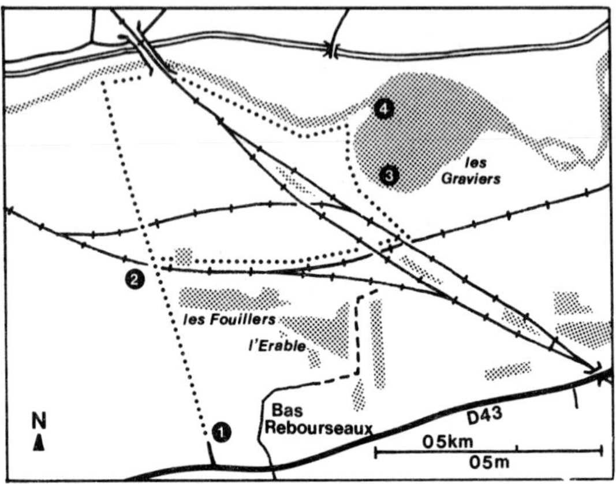

leads to the railway line. Pass the level-crossing ② and take the track to the right along the railway as far as the lake. Two observation points ③ and ④ provide views over the whole lake. Do not go round the lake to the right. Follow the river and later the overgrown hedge to arrive back at the starting place, the level-crossing.

Species

- In spring as in the autumn, Buzzard, Red and Black Kites, Sparrowhawk and Kestrel hunt over the fields.
- The Great Grey Shrike can be seen perched conspicuously, overlooking its winter territory.
- There are Lapwings on the ploughed fields.
- The lake regularly has Great Crested and Little Grebes; Black-necked Grebes sometimes join them when on migration.
- In spring and autumn the western part of the gravel-pits often has migrating waders.
- Dabbling duck, Pochard and Tufted Duck are on the lake between November and March.
- Grey Herons feed around the lake.
- Year-round, Kingfishers can always be seen.

46 Trinquelin Valley

A few kilometres south-east of Quarré-les-Tombes, after passing through the village of Trinquelin in the direction of Saint-Brisson, we find this superb valley of wet meadows surrounded by wooded slopes. From the top of Breuillot rock look over the surrounding forest for raptors (Sparrowhawk, Kites, Honey Buzzard). In the adjacent fields Hoopoe and shrikes may be encountered, and Dipper and Grey Wagtail occur on the stream.

47 Pontigny Forest

To the south of Saint-Florentin lies this varied forest (mature oak wood, conifers, clearings, lakes) with a beautiful valley and river, the Serein, along one side. There is a wide variety of species in the forest: Black, Great Spotted and Middle Spotted Woodpeckers; Wood Warbler, Willow Tit; Buzzard and Honey Buzzard. Nightjar and Tawny Owl can be heard calling in the evening; the Serein Valley has Dipper and Kingfisher.

BRETAGNE

48 SEPT-ÎLES NATIONAL NATURE RESERVE

Perros-Guirec
(IGN 074 – 1/50 000)

Habitat and Timing

This reserve is a granite archipelago 5 km (3.1 miles) off the coast at Perros-Guirec. It comprises five islands (Île aux Moines, Île Plate, Bono, Malban, Rouzic) and some smaller islets (Le Cerf and the Costans). The highest point is on Rouzic (56 m). The Sept-Îles are of most interest for their seabird colonies. The most isolated, Rouzic, has most birds: 12 species of seabird nest in spring and summer including Gannet and Puffin. Landing is strictly prohibited, except on Îles aux Moines where the lighthouse-keeper lives. This reserve, which has the largest seabird colony in France, is managed by the LPO (Ligue Française pour la Protection des Oiseaux).

Calendar

Spring: seabirds such as Storm Petrel (nocturnal), Manx Shearwater, Fulmar, Shag, Gannet, Kittiwake; Great Black-backed, Lesser Black-backed and Herring Gulls; Guillemot, Razorbill, Puffin, and Common Tern. Other nesting species: Shelduck, Oystercatcher, Rock Pipit, Wheatear, Raven.

Summer: Razorbill and Guillemot, at sea, Puffin until mid-July. The Gannets do not leave the colony before the end of September.

Winter: waders (Oystercatcher, Turnstone, Curlew, Purple Sandpiper). Grey Seals are present on the reserve throughout the year.

Access

Make your visit by boat from Trestraou beach, near Perros-Guirec; there is a car park at the top of the beach. Boats leave from Vedettes Blanches landing-stage at the extreme lefthand end of the beach for a three-hour trip around the Sept-Îles. Birds can be seen during the crossing. The boat

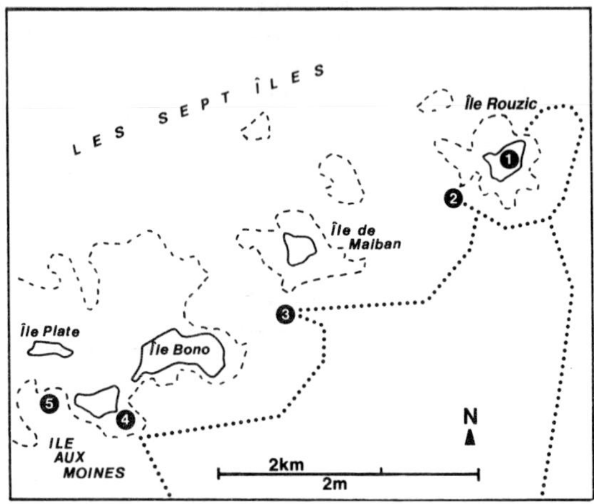

stops opposite the Gannet colony ① and in front of the Puffins at Rouzic ② and Malban ③; you can then make a one-hour visit to Île aux Moines ④, where from the foot of the ancient fort the birds on Île Plate can be watched (with either telescope or binoculars). In summer, the Île Grande Bird Station (LPO) organises the visit on Saturday mornings.

Species

- Manx Shearwaters can be seen during the boat-crossing.
- Many gulls (Great and Lesser Black-backed, Herring) and Kittiwake nest around Rouzic.
- The Gannet colony is most spectacular in the spring.
- Fulmar constantly pass in front of the boat.
- The largest number of Puffins can be seen on Rouzic.
- Many Shags nest on Malban, they can be seen on rocks drying their wings.
- Razorbill and Guillemot can be seen in the water at the foot of the island.
- The Raven often flies above Bono Island.
- Wheatear and Rock Pipit nest on Île des Moines.
- Common Terns nest on Île Plate; they can be watched from the foot of the old fort.
- Waders occur on the island, particularly in winter.
- Shelduck nest near Île aux Moins.

49 Canton Island

From Île Grande, between Trébeurden and Trégastel, go as far as the bird station from where, at low tide, you can walk to Canton Island. Waders are present year-round, especially Oystercatcher, Curlew, Turnstone, Redshank and Ringed Plover. In summer there are Whimbrel, Sandwich and Common Terns, and Shelduck. Gannet can be seen at sea. Whitethroat, Dartford Warbler, Cuckoo, Sparrowhawk and Kestrel can be seen on the heath.

50 Quellen Marsh

Some 15 km (9.3 miles) from Perros-Guirec, Quellen Marsh is on the outskirts of Trébeurden, behind Goas-Trez beach. It consists of two ponds surrounded by willows. One has Coot, Moorhen and Little Grebe nesting amongst its irises and bulrushes. The other, larger, and covered with reeds, has Reed Warblers in the spring and Teal in winter.

51 Cap Fréhel

Cap Fréhel reserve, managed by the SEPNB (Société pour l'Étude et la Protection de la Nature en Bretagne) is not far from the Sept-Îles reserve. It has nesting Shag, three species of gull, Kittiwake and a breeding colony of Razorbills and Guillemots (declining and probably now non-existent). Ravens occupy the cliffs as do Rock Dove (wild!) and Stock Dove. Black Redstart also occur, and the Melodious Warbler (rare in Brittany) nests on the surrounding heath. There are guided visits in July and August, groups are accepted from 1 April onwards.

52 Anse de Goulven (No-Hunting Reserve)

9.5 km/5.8 miles
Saint-Paul-de-Léon
(IGN 0515 – 1/50 000)

Habitat and Timing

A large, north-facing bay, the Anse de Goulven actually comprises two parts; Goulven Bay to the west and Kernic Bay to the east, separated by sand-dunes (the Keremma Dunes) which are part of a Conservatoire du Littoral (Coastal Conservancy) reserve. Primarily important for waders on migration, it is also an important area for wintering water birds.

Although there is free access, it is often better to observe from the reserve's boundaries. Dogs are strictly forbidden. Most birds are seen during periods of high tides, when they roost on the reserve (it is best to arrive two hours before high tide, and to choose a tide with a coefficient above 80).

Calendar

Winter: Mallard, Wigeon, Shoveler, Teal and Shelduck, plus Goldeneye; Dunlin, Knot, Sanderling, Purple Sandpiper, Ruff, Redshank, Greenshank, Spotted Redshank, Common Sandpiper, Ringed and Kentish Plovers, Avocet, Snipe and Jack Snipe, Golden and Grey Plovers, Curlew, Oystercatcher, Turnstone, Black-tailed and Bar-tailed Godwits, Lapwing.

Spring: migrant waders and Lapwing, Shelduck and Kentish Plover nesting.

Autumn: dabbling ducks and migrant passerines, often in spectacular numbers.

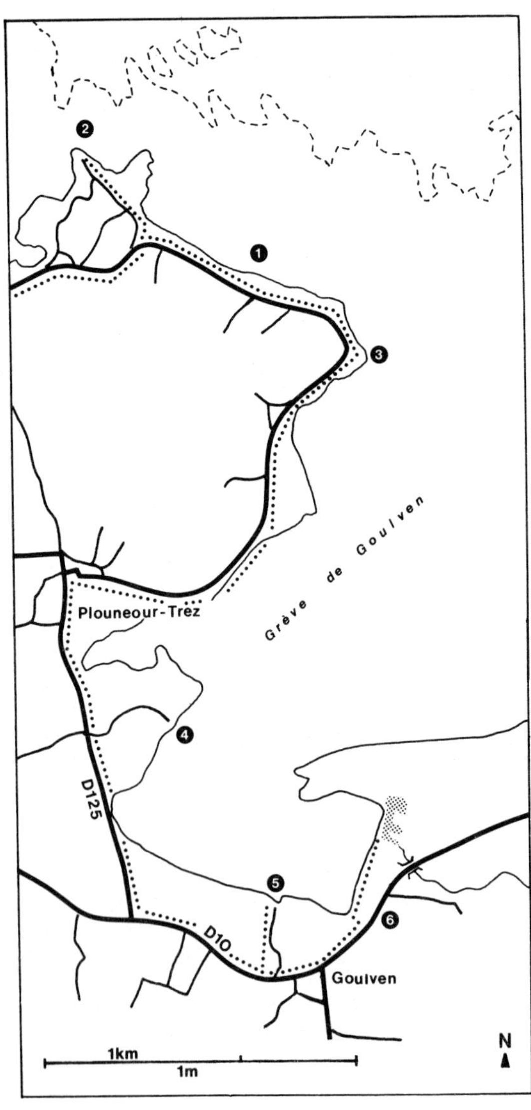

Access

From Lesneven go northwards as far as Brignogan, fork right here to Plage de Lidivic ①. Park on the car park near the football pitch (and not on the sand-dune!). Watch over the beach, especially its northern part. At the right season, or when there is a strong wind, it may be worth going to Beg-ar-Scaf Head ② to do some sea-watching. It may also be worth going to Beg-ar-Groaz Head ③. Then back in the car, and follow the coast as far as Trégueiller ④, turn left and, with caution, go as far as the sea front. Parking is possible alongside the conifer hedge on the left, be careful not to impede any farm vehicles that may want to pass. Do not go out onto the foreshore as this may frighten the birds.

Sit down on the side of the track and wait for the birds to come, the sight is rarely disappointing. Next stop is the car park at Goulven station ⑤. At high tide it is worth walking along the disused railway line. The last port of call is at Lez-ar-Mor car park (on the embankment) ⑥. Climb onto the embankment, on the left is a much used mudflat, on the right the Étang de Goulven. It is best at low tide and at a time of weak tides, to be sure the mudflats are uncovered. You can continue walking along the embankment as far as the Keremma Dunes.

Species

- In autumn there are thousands of passerines at Beg-ar-Scaf Head.
- From the head, sea-watching can be very rewarding with, in the autumn, Gannet, shearwaters, skuas, gulls and terns.
- On the beach, you can see Purple Sandpiper, Sanderling, Ringed Plover, Kentish Plover and Turnstone.
- There is a daytime duck roost on the sea (Mallard, Wigeon, Teal, Shelduck).
- Trégueiller is a high-tide roost for the bay's waders.
- From the disused railway line it is possible to see Lapwing and several species of wader on the salt-marsh.
- Wheatear and Blue-headed Wagtail occur regularly on Keremma Dunes.

53 ÎLE D'OUESSANT

16 km/10 miles
Plouarzel-Île d'Ouessant
(IGN 0316 – 1/50 000)

Habitat and Timing

The most westerly island in France, between the Atlantic and the Channel. Here there is a vast plateau dropping from east to west, ringed by a multitude of rocks and islands and a coastline of indented cliffs. There is a large bay on the west coast. Because of its exceptional interest for studying bird migration (especially passerines), it has become (1984) France's only permanent coastal bird observatory. The island also has some very impressive seabird colonies. It is France's answer to the Isles of Scilly, and it may be better!

Calendar

Winter: Gannet, Kittiwake, Razorbill, Guillemot; sometimes Glaucous Gull and Little Auk. During spells of hard weather, duck, Lapwing, Snipe, Woodcock; thrushes, Blackbird.

Spring: breeding Fulmar, Storm Petrel, Manx Shearwater, Shag; Oystercatcher, Ringed Plover; Kittiwake, Great and Lesser Black-backed and Herring Gulls, Puffin; Cuckoo, Wheatear, Dartford Warbler and Chough.

On migration: Gannet, Razorbill, skuas; Turtle Dove, Willow Warbler, shrikes, orioles and a few rarities.

Summer and Autumn: spectacular shearwater passage (Sooty, Great, Manx and Yelkouan – sometimes Little and Cory's); Fulmar, Storm Petrel; Sparrowhawk, Peregrine, Merlin; Dotterel, waders, Woodcock; Grey Phalarope, Pomarine and Arctic Skuas; Kittiwake, Sabine's Gull; terns, Razorbill, Guillemot; Wryneck, Short-toed Lark, wagtails, pipits, Wheatear, Whinchat, Redstart and Black Redstart; Redwing, Song Thrush, Fieldfare, Ring Ouzel; Icterine, Melodious, Willow, Yellow-browed and many other Warblers; Lesser Whitethroat, Firecrest, Goldcrest; Spotted, Pied and Red-breasted Flycatchers; Red-backed Shrike; Chaffinch, Brambling, Siskin, Linnet; Snow and Lapland Buntings. More rarely: Pectoral, Buff-breasted and Solitary Sandpipers, Long-billed Dowitcher, Red-eyed Vireo, from the west; Red-rumped Swallow, Greenish, Arctic, Dusky, Pallas's, and Barred Warblers, Scarlet Rosefinch, Isabelline Shrike, Little Bunting, from the east, and many other vagrants.

Access

Take the boat to Molène and Ouessant Islands from either Brest or Conquet (20 km (12.5 miles) west of Brest). It is a two-hour crossing from Brest, one hour from Conquet. The timetable varies according to the season, information can be obtained from the Service Maritime Départemental (tel: 98.80.24.68). There is a daily air service from Brest-Guipavas Airport; booking with Finist'air is essential (tel: 98.84.64.87). On the island it is better to rent a bicycle (either at the port or in Lampaul village). As to where to go on the island, just look at a map!; all of the island can be visited, but please resepct the country code. There are too many sites to give a complete list, each bit of heath

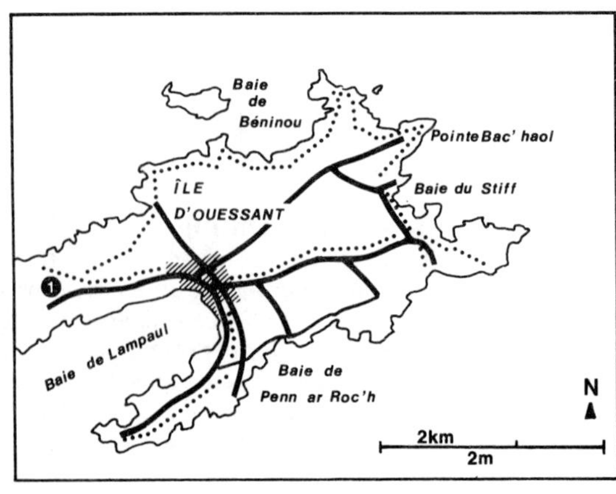

can be of interest at one time or another. However, information can be obtained from the Bird Observatory ①. The Bird Observatory can accept guests year-round. Information from Centre Ornithologique, 29242 Île d'Ouessant (tel: 98.48.82.65).

Species

- Sea-watching can be good from Creac'h Head – especially in September or October – when many seabirds may be seen: petrels, Gannet, Shearwaters, also skuas and Sabine's Gull.
- Bushes round the Bird Observatory can be good for *Phylloscopus* warblers, and 'crests in autumn.
- Wheatears are common breeders on the heath along the north coast.
- The low heath on Kadoran Head is an ideal stop-over for Dotterel.
- Fulmar and Kittiwake nest in small numbers at Bac'haol Head.
- The Vallon d'Arland is without doubt the best place in autumn for small insectivores: warblers, 'crests and flycatchers between August and the end of October.
- In spring Dartford Warbler nest in the gorse on Penn Arland Heath.
- In April you can watch Puffins on the sides of Youc'h Rock.
- There is a high-tide roost of Black-headed, Herring and Great Black-backed Gulls on Korz beach.
- Porz Doun, the extreme south-west point of the island, is the best site for waders (Oystercatcher, Ringed Plover, Redshank); Purple Sandpipers are often present amongst the other waders and Grey Phalarope may be seen after westerly gales.
- Back at Lampaul the small wood beneath the cemetery is worth watching, Red-breasted Flycatcher or Yellow-browed Warbler may be present in October.
- In October, on the stubble around Parluc'hen, Lapland or Little Buntings can be found.

54 Cap Sizun

To the west of Concarneau, in Goulien parish, this is one of the best-known sites in Brittany. Managed by the Société pour l'Étude et la Protection de la Nature en Bretagne (SEPNB), the reserve has many breeding birds that are rare elsewhere in France. Fulmar, Shag, Shelduck, Great Black-backed Gull, Kittiwake, Guillemot, Raven and Chough can all be seen. There are organised visits between 15 March and 31 August.

55 Des Cragou Reserve

In the heart of the Monts d'Arrée, in Plougonven parish, Des Cragou Reserve (SEPNB) is a vast heather heath. It is open to the public in July and August when some interesting heath-nesting birds can be seen including: Hen and Montagu's Harriers, Grasshopper and Dartford Warblers.

56 TRUNVEL NATURE RESERVE

3.5 km/2.2 miles
Trégoat
(IGN 0419 east – 1/25 000)

Habitat and Timing

At the centre of the Baie d'Audierne, this site is of international importance for nesting and migrating wetland warblers. It comprises lakes, coastal marsh, stable and moving sand-dunes in the south, reed-beds in the centre, and a large open lake inland. Gorse and Blackthorn thickets as well as elm woods surround the reserve, the access to which is strictly controlled; but higher land around its limits offers excellent bird-watching.

Calendar

Winter: many species of duck (Pochard, Tufted Duck, Teal, Gadwall, Shoveler and Wigeon); Bittern; Hen and Marsh Harriers, Merlin; Bearded Tit; Dartford Warbler.

Spring: Whimbrel, Bar-tailed Godwit and Little Gull on migration. Reed Warbler, Bearded Tit, Fan-tailed Warbler, Bittern, Purple Heron, Kentish Plover and Lapwing nesting.

Autumn: most of the European waders and American waders relatively regularly; Aquatic Warbler, Snow and Lapland Buntings.

Access

From Quimper take the road towards Plonéour-Lanvern, then Tréguennec on the D156 as far as Kermabec car park ① some 25 km (15.5 miles) from Quimper. From the car park, follow the beach to where it has been breached ②. Return on the route for about 100 m (110

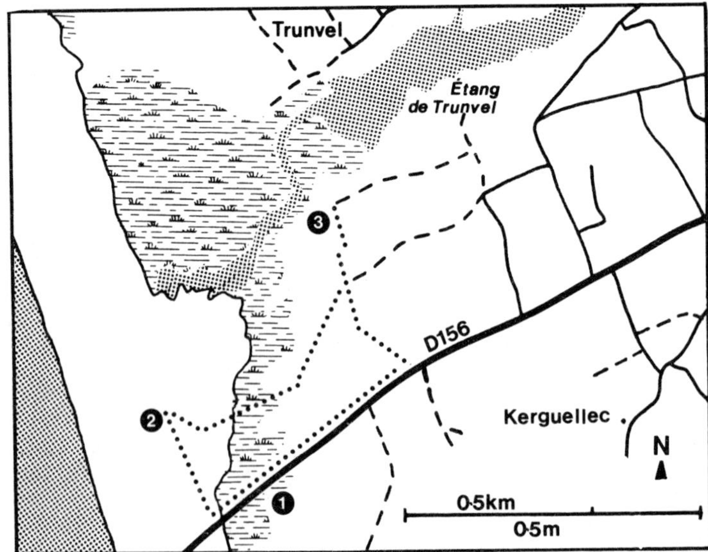

yards), then follow the reserve border north-eastwards across the dune and the marsh. This will take you to a good watch point ③. To get back to the car park take the dirt-track that leads to the D156.

Species

- In spring, godwits and Curlew occur near the breach.
- Little, Black-headed, Great, Lesser Black-backed, and Herring Gulls and terns, roost on the side of the lake at high tide.
- In spring, many wetland passerines nest in the reed-beds: Sedge and Reed Warbler, Bearded Tit, Reed Bunting.
- The Bittern is present year-round in the reed-beds, whereas the Purple Heron is present only from May to August.
- Marsh Harriers can be seen around the lake throughout the year.
- Each winter, the Étang de Trunvel holds many Tufted Duck, Pochard, Teal, Wigeon, Gadwall and Shoveler.
- Cormorant can be seen throughout the year.

57 Nérizelec Lake

Nérizelec Lake is in Plovan parish. Many waders, terns and gulls can be seen under excellent conditions on this small lagoon in August and September. In order to disturb the birds as little as possible, it is strongly recommended that you stay on the shingle-bar separating the lagoon from the sea.

58 THE WESTERN PART OF THE BAIE DU MONT-SAINT-MICHEL

13 km/8.1 miles
Mont-Saint-Michel
(IGN 1215 – 1/50 000)

Habitat and Timing

A wide salt-marsh grazed by sheep. It is possible to walk along different dikes which enclose the polders. The proposed route follows the Sentier des Douaniers (customs road), there is a right of way, and this crosses the polders on the poplar-lined dikes. The best conditions for birdwatching occur during spring tides, especially on the landward side.

Calendar

Winter: over the meadows, Hen and Marsh Harriers, Short-eared owl, Peregrine and Merlin. On the salt-marsh, many waders and dabbling duck. On the polders, Golden Plover, Lapwing, White-fronted Goose (meadows). Equally, Shelduck, sawbills, Lapland Bunting (stubble).

Autumn: important numbers of smaller waders and godwits.

Access

From Roz-sur-Couesnon take the road towards Quatre-Salines. Leave the car on the side of the road just before you reach the first dike. Walk as far as the track on the dike ①. After a few hundred metres on the dike, the track joins the Sentier de Grande Randonnée 34 (hiker's way 34) and follow this as far as the Chapelle Sainte-Anne ②. Return by the Duchesse-Anne dike.

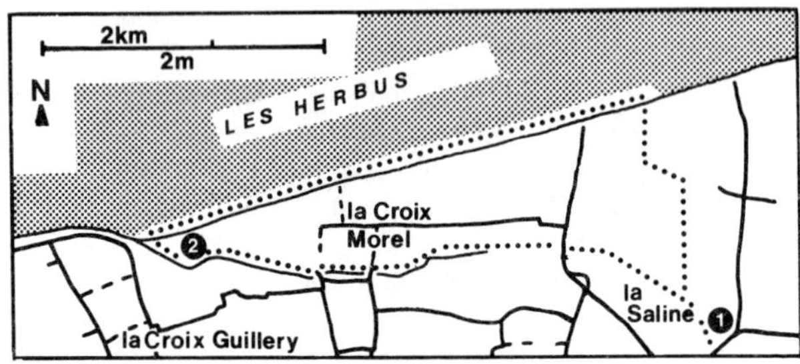

Species

- Lapland Bunting, pipits and larks feed on the polders in winter.
- In winter, Peregrine, Merlin, Short-eared owl, Marsh and Hen Harriers hunt over the meadows.
- On the meadows, Golden Plover and Lapwing can be seen in winter.
- There are large numbers of Shelduck in winter.
- Conditions are ideal for watching waders from the Chapelle Sainte-Anne during very high tides in winter.
- There are White-fronted Geese on the greener fields, but only irregularly.

Wigeon

59 GOLFE DU MORBIHAN

19 km/11.8 miles
Golfe du Morbihan
(IGN 501 tourist – 1/50 000)
Lorient-Vannes
(IGN 15 green series – 1/50 000)

Habitat and Timing

An inland sea dotted with about forty islands is linked with the sea by a narrow channel (Port-Navalo). The tidal currents are very strong at the entrance but get progressively weaker towards the interior, where they deposit sandy sediments: during an average low tide, 4,000 hectares of mudflats are uncovered, about half of which are used for farming shellfish.

An exceptional site for water birds (60,000 to 100,000 birds in winter) especially Brent Geese, duck and waders. There is a Réserve de Chasse (no-hunting zone) in its western part (Baie de Sarzeau) where ducks congregate at a traditional site (daytime roost). Conditions for observing are best three hours either side of low tide (as a reference use the time of low tide at Vannes/Penboch).

Calendar

Autumn and Winter: Brent Goose (end of October to December), dabbling duck, principally Wigeon, Mallard, Shoveler, Pintail, Teal, Shelduck (September to February), Coot; diving duck, principally Red-breasted Merganser and Goldeneye (November to March); Grey Plover, Curlew, Redshank, Dunlin, Avocet; Grey Heron, Little Egret throughout the year; Great Crested Grebe, Black-necked Grebe (August to March); Cormorant, Black-headed Gull, Common Gull (July to March).

Access

From Vannes, take the N165 towards Nantes, turn off right on the D780 towards Sarzeau/Presqu'Île de Rhuys. Most watch points can be reached by car. Start the visit at low tide, stop at Navalo ①, near the lake. Now take the road towards Saint-Armel, Centre-Bourg (town centre), follow the coast road, opposite the church, as far as the coast (about 600 m/650 yards) and the small car park ②. There are good views of birds as the water covers the mudflats (low tide plus three hours). Continue southwards. A little after Saint-Colombier, turn towards the Pointe de Trohannec ③. Now go towards Sarzeau. Some 500 m (550 yards) before reaching Sarzeau, turn right (Kerbodec) and right again at the entrance to the village: this is the road to the coast, there is a car park (at the place called Kergeorget) ④; watch during an incoming tide (low tide plus one to two and a half hours). In Sarzeau, take the road to Bénance, pass through the village of Kervoscen before arriving at Bénance. Watching is possible from the oyster port ⑤.

Species

- On the mud, Curlew and Avocet feed.
- Groups of Shelduck can be seen on the sides of emptying channels.
- Large flocks of Coot can be seen along Quistinic Island.

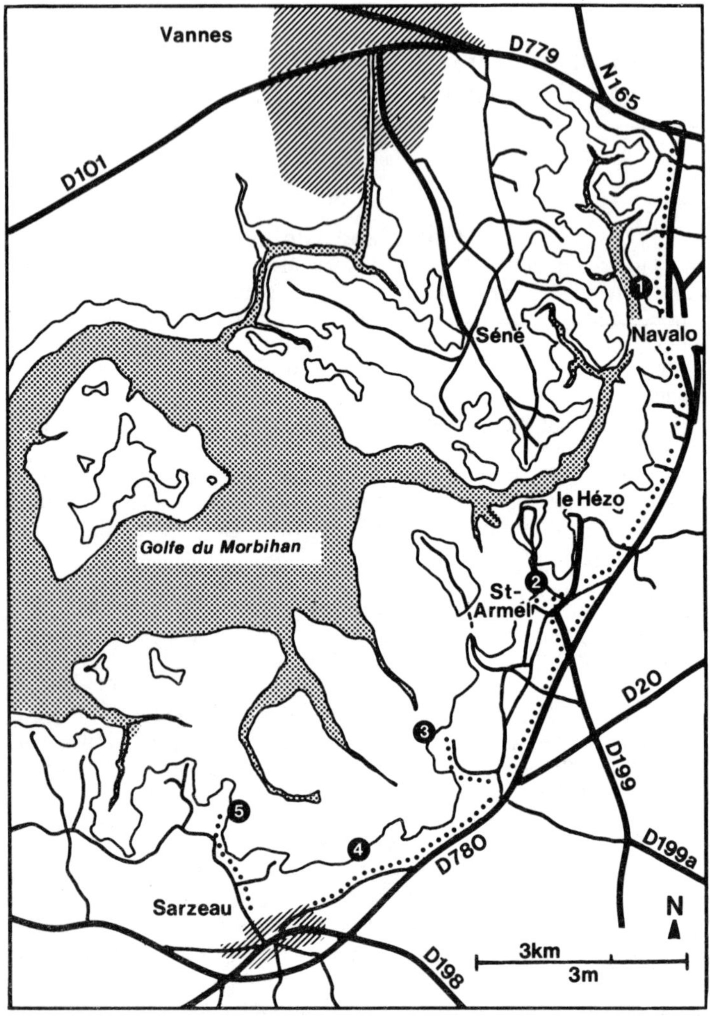

- There is a high-tide roost of Brent Geese, Shelduck and Pintail.
- In with the flocks of Brent Geese are packed flocks of Grey Plover, Knot, Dunlin, Redshank, waiting for the tide to retreat.
- Grey Heron and Little Egret are present throughout the year, whereas Spoonbill can only be seen during migration.
- On an incoming tide, Brent Geese as well as Pintail, Wigeon and Teal flock together not far from the shore close to Kergeorget Château.

60 Falguérec Reserve/Séné

Managed by the SEPNB, Falguérec reserve is just 5 km (3.1 miles) south of Vannes (route signposted). Despite its proximity to a large town, many interesting species nest here, including: Avocet, Black-winged Stilt,

Redshank, Bluethroat. At the end of summer, many waders occur here, as well as Spoonbill, gulls and terns. The reserve is open to the public between May and August.

61 Belle-Île

The SEPNB reserve, Koch-Kastell, near Saujon, is home to some of Brittany's cliff-nesting birds. There are, among others, Shag, Great Black-backed, Lesser Black-backed and Herring Gulls, and Kittiwake. That part of the island between the Pointe Saint-Marc and Pointe du Pouddon is a must, with Fulmar, Rock Dove, Raven and Chough. Marsh Harriers hunt over the nearby heath.

62 VILAINE ESTUARY

6 km/3.75 miles
La Roche-Bernard
(IGN 1022 – 1/50 000)

Habitat and Timing

There are three different components to this area: rocky coasts on the north and south banks of the estuary; a unique ochre cliff of a clay/sand mix dominates a sandy beach (the Mine-d'Or); thirdly, Bronzais coastal-bar separates a large area of inter-tidal mudflats from some old lagoon marshes. A remarkable stop-over area for ducks, waders, gulls and terns especially in autumn and winter. There is free access over the whole area which provides some excellent birdwatching opportunities, principally at high tide (rising tide at Bronzais).

Calendar

Autumn: large concentrations of gulls and terns (five species), skuas (three species); Yelkouan Shearwater, Dunlin, Ringed Plover, Curlew and Whimbrel.

Winter: many dabbling ducks (Wigeon, Pintail), and some diving ducks (Common and Velvet Scoters, Scaup). Groups of Brent Geese, Great Crested Grebe and Avocet, a few Long-tailed Duck in cold weather.

Access

From La Roche-Bernard take the D34 towards Pénestin to get to the mudflats at Bronzais ①. On reaching the village, turn right towards Tréhiguier, go about 300 m (330 yards) and park parallel to the road that skirts the estuary; a track leads to the foot of the dune. To get to Mine-d'Or ②, get back to the by-pass and go in the direction of Assérac, turn right after the petrol station towards Mine-d'Or, then take the third road on the right; 500 m (550 yards) further on turn left towards the sea. Parking is possible not far from the cliff; watch from the cliff-top. The observation point, situated between the 'Points' of Halguen and de Cofreneau, ③ is accessible by car from Haut-Pénestin: take the road towards Logui; park before you reach the beach, then on foot follow the

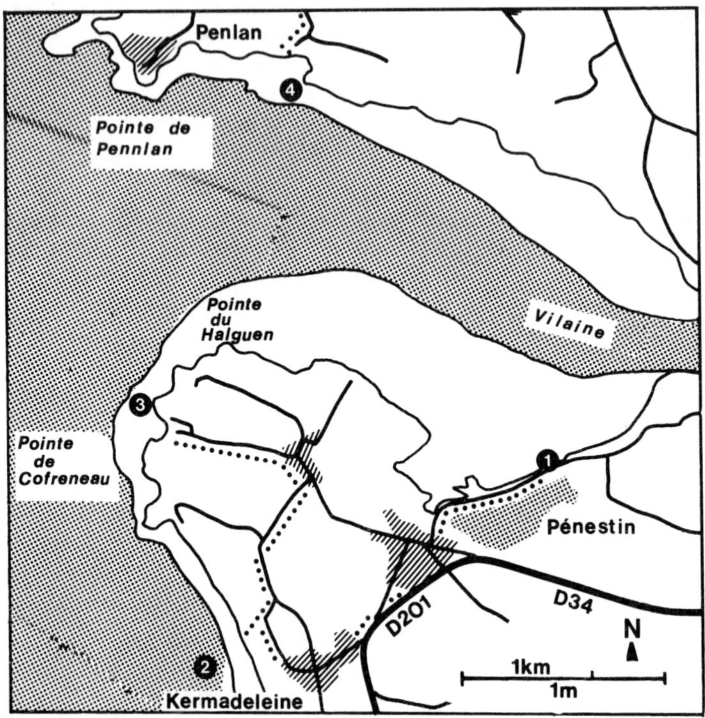

first creek northwards; this is the best place for watching.

Coming from Pénestin, cross the Arzal Dam to get to the northern shore ④. From Arzal take the road towards Billiers then the D5 towards Pointe de Penlan; 500 m (550 yards) further on turn left to Les Granges where there is a car park. Now leave eastwards on foot along the footpath on the cliff-top (good view over the estuary). The best conditions for watching are at high tide for ①, ② and ③, and at half tide for ④.

Species

- Brent Goose, Shelduck, Wigeon and Pintail can be seen on the mudflats in winter.
- In autumn and winter, there are many Curlew, Whimbrel, Godwits, Avocet, Dunlin and Ringed Plover.
- Grey Heron and Little Egret occur on the mudflats.
- Marsh Harrier can be seen over the reed-beds throughout the year.
- In winter, the commonest species is the Common Scoter, but there may also be Velvet Scoter, Scaup in varying numbers, and sometimes Long-tailed Duck.
- Great Crested Grebes are common winter visitors in front of Mine-d'Or beach; sometimes there are a few divers.
- Between August and October, both Arctic and Pomarine Skuas occur quite frequently at the mouth of the Vilaine. A few Great Skuas are seen between September and November.

- Sometimes, in mid-September, the rare Sabine's Gull stops at the mouth of the estuary.
- Yelkouan Shearwaters flock in large numbers in the evening, especially at high tide (from August to early October).
- In winter, this is the ideal spot for observing Pochard, Tufted Duck and especially Scaup, the species' principal wintering site in France.

63 Loscolo Beach/Pénestin

An interesting site in winter for watching Red-breasted Merganser, Black and Red-throated Divers, Great Crested Grebe, Razorbill and Guillemot. On the flat rocks at the point there are small numbers of Purple Sandpiper (most easily seen on an ebb tide) mixed with the Oystercatchers and Turnstones. Plage de Loscolo lies to the south of Pénestin, on the road to Asserac (turn-off at Kerfalher).

CENTRE

64 AURON LAKE

6 km/3.75 miles
Bourges
(IGN 2324 east – 1/25 000)

Habitat and Timing

A lake created to the south of Bourges in 1976, where the Auron River and its tributary the Rampenne meet. The surrounding countryside is partially urbanised, the rest conserved as a green area (fields and thickets of mature trees). There are remnants of reed-bed and marsh on the side of the Rampenne. The lake is easy to watch, and is principally of interest for the duck that occur in some numbers in winter. The island, on the western side, is protected as a reserve by a County Council order. There is unrestricted access around the whole of the lake.

The most favourable time for watching is early morning (before disturbance by water sports). There are always birds close to the island and at the southern part of the lake (at the mouth of the Auron).

Calendar

Winter: Mallard, Teal, Tufted Duck, Pochard, Coot, Black-headed Gull. Occasionally Great Northern and Red-throated Divers, Grebes, sawbills, scoters, Shoveler.

Spring and Autumn: duck, waders, terns, marsh terns, hirundines, Blue-headed Wagtail. Little Grebe, Mallard, Coot and Moorhen all nest, as do some wetland warblers and Black Kite.

Access

To get to the lake pass by the Base Nautique (water-sport centre), 3 km (1.85 miles) from the town centre, either on the road to Mazières or on the Avenue de Saint-Amand (N144). Park at the tennis court car park ①.

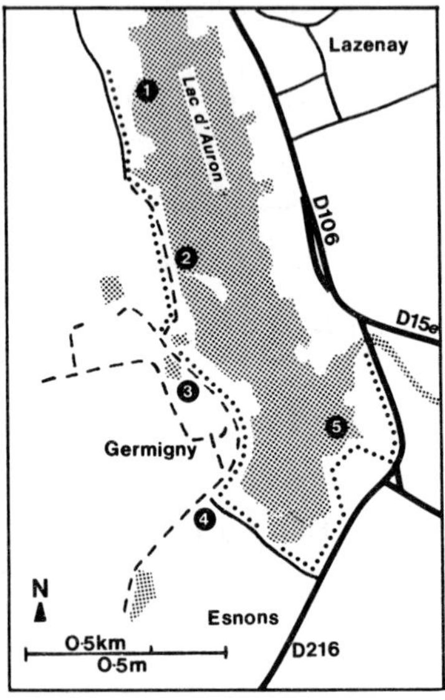

From here leave on foot and take the bank lying between the willow basin and the island reserve ②. Continue alongside the reed-bed at Germigny ③ and then walk along the banks of the Rampenne ④. A board-walk crosses the river, on the other side use the beach in order to reach Porche wooded park ⑤ and the mouth of the Auron. From here it is either back by the same route or the complete tour of the lake (6 km/3.7 miles).

Species

- Blue-headed Wagtail can be seen on the fields (on migration) or nesting behind the tennis court (May to July). Crested Larks are frequently present in winter.
- Tufted Duck and Pochard congregate above the island in winter.
- Little Grebe nest on the small private lake, but are visible from the track.
- In the reed-bed and on the wooded banks, Reed, Willow and Garden Warblers, Blackcap and Nightingale occur in the spring.
- Water and Meadow Pipits can be seen along the banks in winter.
- In spring, Cuckoo and Turtle Dove nest in Rampenne Marsh.
- The large trees are attractive to Nuthatch, Short-toed Treecreeper and Rook.
- Near Auron bridge there are some introduced Greylag Geese; when they are being fed in winter it also attracts Mute Swan, Coot, and some duck.

- Reed Warbler nest in Auron reed-bed, where Penduline Tit is sometimes seen in the spring.

65 Allogny Forest

Allogny public forest, 30 km (18.6 miles) north of Bourges (on the Orléans road D944), is situated at the limit of the Sologne and Berry Champagne country. Different species of woodpecker (including Black, Middle Spotted and Grey-headed) occur in the mature oak forest and regenerating coppices; also, Buzzard, Goshawk, Sparrowhawk and Hen Harrier. In spring, Redstart and Pied Flycatcher nest in the areas of mature woodland.

66 ÉCLUZELLES-MÉZIÈRES LAKE AND MARSH

9.5 km/5.9 miles
Dreux
(IGN 2015 east – 1/25 000)
and Nogent-le-Roi
(IGN 2115 west – 1/25 000)

Habitat and Timing

A disused sand- and gravel-pit, comprising a large lake (about 75 hectares) and two small marshy areas. The best wetland site in the department, it has many species of aquatic and Hedgerow birds throughout the year. Night Herons have nested every year since 1979, so that there is always something interesting to see between April and September. There is unrestricted access except for a few small private areas that are signposted (Chasse Interdite), and except onto the limestone hillside at Marsauceux, to the west of the lake. The area is much disturbed (sailing club, walkers, fishermen), so that it is best to visit during the week, Friday evening or early Saturday morning; avoid public holidays.

Calendar

Spring: Great Crested Grebe, Night Heron (for early April); Garganey (on migration), Shoveler; Little Ringed Plover, Common Sandpiper, Black Tern (on migration); Little Owl, Swift, Kingfisher, hirundines; wetland warblers, Nightingale, Lesser Whitethroat, Willow Warbler and Chiffchaff.

Autumn: Cormorant, Grey Heron, sometimes Greylag Goose, Teal, Gadwall, Snipe (irregular).

Winter: flocks of duck: Mallard, Wigeon, Shoveler, Pintail, Teal, Pochard, Tufted Duck; Sparrowhawk, Black-headed and some large gulls (roost), Redwing, Fieldfare, Siskin, Redpoll.

Access

From Dreux, take the D929 towards Nogent-le-Roi for 5 km (3.1 miles). At Écluzelles turn left (the bridge over the Eure), cross the village and take the first track to the left on the side of the lake, continue on foot to

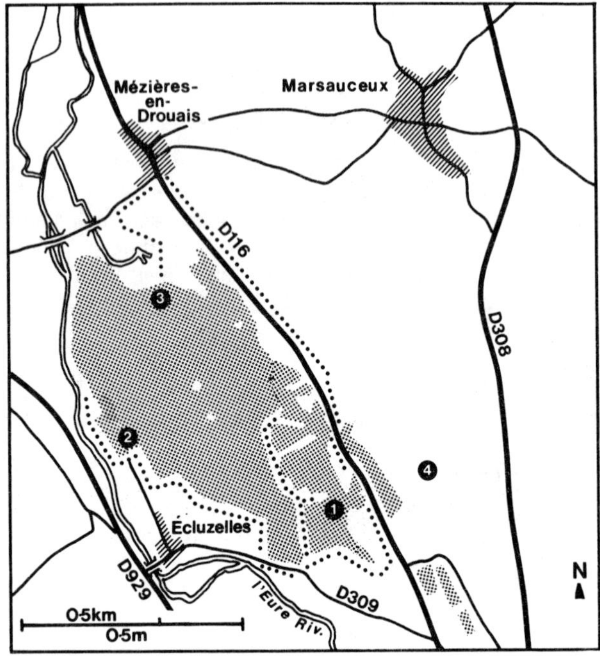

Écluzelles Marsh ①. Other observation points: on the side of the lake at the car park in front of the Aquaparc restaurant (signposted from Écluzelles) ②. Mézières Marsh: skirt round the lake on the D116 towards Mézières-en-Drouais, turn left in the village then take the track to the left after the church ③. To the west of the lake, Marsauceux hillside ④, covered in scrub, is of interest for passerines in the spring and offers a fine view of the whole valley.

Species

- There are Night Herons (early April to early October).
- Kingfishers nest here.
- There are nesting Lesser Whitethroat, Nightingale and other hedgerow passerines (singing from late April to June).
- Siskin and Redpoll winter here (November to March).
- Hirundines and Swift can be seen in the spring (April and early May).
- There are migrant terns and marsh terns.
- You can watch dabbling and diving duck (especially October to April), over-wintering and on migration.
- There are migrant Cormorants (April and October) and Grey Heron (September to April).
- Cirl Bunting and Melodious Warbler can be found on the limestone hillside.
- Look for Long-eared Owl in the spring.

Night Heron

67 Beauce Plain

To the south-east of Chartres, in a quadrilateral with its limits to the north at Auneau, to the west at Voves, to the south at Patay and to the east at the A10 motorway, a few steppe species find their last refuge in this area or are at the limit of their distribution. To improve your chances of finding such species as Little Bustard, Stone Curlew, Quail or Short-toed Lark it is best to use an IGN map to look for certain preferred habitats such as small limestone valleys (look for the contours on the map), disused quarries or military bases (view from the exterior).

Hen and Montagu's Harriers also occur here, even over fields of cereals, but they are at a low density. Most birds are migrants and the best time is therefore the spring, especially May and June. Listening for songs or calls is particularly useful in locating the steppe species. And remember that they do not sing constantly throughout the day.

68 Conie Valley

Conie Valley is well worth a visit in the spring, from Viabon (32 km/20 miles south-east of Chartres on the D10) to Marboué (on the N10 north of Châteaudun), where the valley stream rejoins the Loir River. Along these 35 km (22 miles) there are many reed-beds and small marshy areas where species otherwise rare in the region can be seen – Little Grebe, Marsh Harrier and Water Rail, for example. Some places, like Viabon, are sometimes favourable for migrating waders; Snipe, shanks and others. The banks, planted with trees and bushes, are favourable for many passerines and some woodpeckers.

69 THE LAKES OF THE BRENNE

8 km/5 miles
Saint-Gaultier
(IGN 2026 – 1/50 000)

Habitat and Timing

Many of Brenne's one thousand lakes are well known for their rich bird life.

Gabrière Lake (Bird Reserve)/Lingé: one of the biggest lakes in the Brenne. It has one of the last large reed-beds in the area (many having been removed by fish-farmers). It used to have a large area of waterlilies. Many rare species nest in the reed-beds. It is one of the best lakes in the Brenne for duck and waders in autumn (during the annual emptying), and for duck in winter. There is restricted access to the marsh and reed-beds. The road that runs along one side of the lake, and a public hide, allow views of most of the reserve's birds.

Chérine National Nature Reserve/Saint-Michel-en-Brenne: a mosaic of all the various habitats to be found in Brenne (lakes, fields, woods, heath). Rare birds nest in the reed-beds and duck on the lake; waders and marsh terns nest on three recently-constucted lakes, managed specifically for them. Herons, raptors and passerines can be watched under ideal conditions, especially during spring and summer. Large numbers of duck congregate in winter. There is restricted access, but there is a public hide.

Nearby lakes (Gabriau, Beauregard, Montmélier): some of the most beautiful and interesting lakes of the Brenne. Reed-beds, waterlilies, fields, woods and heath mix to make an harmonious landscape. The lakes can be watched from the road or public footpaths. The hides are best visited in the morning or evening.

Calendar

Spring: nesting Black-necked Grebe, Purple Heron, Bittern, Little Bittern. Gadwall, Shoveler, Pochard, Tufted Duck; Marsh Harrier, Black Kite, Short-toed Eagle, Honey Buzzard, Hobby; Whiskered and Black Terns; Savi's, Reed and Great Reed Warblers; Red-backed Shrike, Bearded Tit. Osprey, Crane, Penduline Tit, on migration.

Autumn: Shoveler, Gadwall, Mallard, Teal; Marsh Harrier, Hobby; Water Rail, Coot; Ringed and Little Ringed Plover, Dunlin, Little Stint, Spotted Redshank, Ruff, Snipe.

Winter: divers, Black-necked and Great Crested Grebes; Grey Heron, Great White Egret; Greylag and Bean Geese, thousands of duck (including sawbills – Smew the most frequent); Black-headed Gull.

Access

From Châteauroux to the east, Poitiers to the west or Tours to the north-west, go towards Mézières-en-Brenne (from Châteauroux), towards Le Blanc (from Poitiers) or towards Châtillon-sur-Indre (from Tours). The most interesting areas and the two reserves lie between the villages of Mézières-en-Brenne and Rosnay. The closest railway station is at Châteauroux (45 km/28 miles); there is a somewhat irksome 'once-a-day' bus service from here to Mézières or Rosnay. There are car parks at both

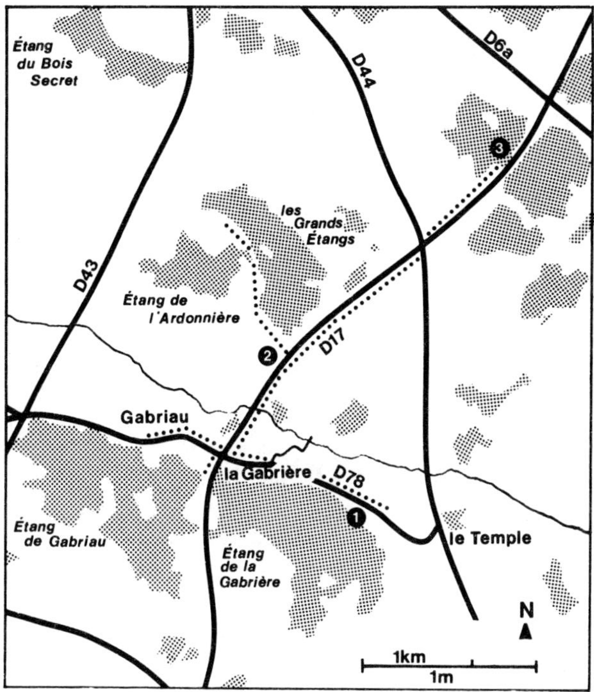

reserves; small, quiet roads elsewhere make stopping and watching easy. Watching on foot: walk along the northern sides of Gabrière and Gabriau Lakes, stopping at the reserve's public hide ①. For Beauregard, walk along the track on the southern side of the lake (entrance on the first bend on the D17), which lies between La Gabrière and Chérine, park on the left of the road ②. Still walking along the D17, which passes between Chérine and Montmélier, visit Chérine's public hide ③ about 100 m (110 yards) from the car park, opposite the disused Montmélier Farm.

Guided visits are organised at both reserves, for times and reservations: Chérine – tel: 54.38.12.24, during office hours; La Gabrière – tel. 54.37.47.47 For general information on where to go and what to see, go to the visitor centre at the Gabrière reserve (open afternoons, 2.30 pm to 7.00 pm every Saturday and Sunday, every public holiday, and all days mid–May to mid–September.

Species

- Whiskered and Black Terns hunt over the lakes from April to September.
- Many waders (Dunlin, Little Stint, Spotted Redshank, Ruff, Snipe) are easily visible on the exposed mud of the lakes in autumn.
- Marsh Harriers hunt here throughout the year, Osprey regularly occur on migration.
- In winter, Gabriau Lake like Gabrière holds many duck.
- Black-necked Grebe once nested on both Gabriau and Gabrière Lakes, they may still do so from time to time, otherwise there are good numbers in spring and early summer.

- During the summer many species of raptor can be seen (Honey Buzzard, Black Kite, Hobby). Marsh Harriers can be seen year-round.
- With luck a Bittern might be seen flying over the reeds at the back of Beauregard.
- Large numbers of hirundines hunt over the water in August and September.
- Purple Heron, Bittern and Little Bittern nest in the reed-beds at Chérine.
- It is also a good place to see Reed and Great Reed Warblers as well as the rare Savi's Warbler.
- Year-round, Montmélier Lake has many dabbling and diving duck.

70 LANCOSME FOREST VENDEUVRES

16 km/10 miles
Saint-Gaultier
(IGN 2026 – 1/50 000)

Habitat and Timing

A large forest with a wide variety of habitats: a complex mix of oaks (English and Sessile), Hornbeam, pines (Scots, Maritime and Corsican) as well as dry heather and damp moor-grass heaths. On its western edge are some high heather heaths and many lakes (Les Vigneaux, Bellebouche, Les Verdets, etc). An interesting private forest, mainly in winter and spring, for raptors and various passerines. There are, however, many public footpaths in the forest; it is best to visit in the morning or evening.

Calendar

Winter: Buzzard, Goshawk, Sparrowhawk, Hen Harrier, Red Kite, Tawny Owl, Long-eared Owl; Black and Great Spotted Woodpeckers; Marsh, Crested and Blue Tits; Goldcrest, Firecrest, Hawfinch, Bullfinch.

Spring: Black Kite, Goshawk, Honey Buzzard, Short-toed Eagle, Hobby; Nightjar, Cuckoo; woodpeckers (including Black and Middle Spotted); Whitethroat, Blackcap, Dartford, Wood and Bonelli's Warblers, Chiffchaff, Nightingale.

Summer: Tawny Pipit, Grasshopper Warbler, Great Grey and Red-backed Shrikes.

Access

From Châteauroux (to the east), take the D925 towards Châtellerault; after 20 km (12.5 miles) take the D27 towards Neuillay-les-Bois and then towards Méobecq; from here the D14 leads into the forest. Leave the car at the Rond de la Genouillerie (Genouillerie circle), or on the side of the road ①. It is possible to make a circuit of about 6 km (3.7 miles) on foot going as far as Château Robert. Take the forest track through some new plantations ②, it later crosses a mixed deciduous and conifer wood ③. The track now follows a disused lake dike (the new dike of the

Great Grey Shrike

Fosse-Noire lake is some 100m (110 yards) further back, a favourite area for rutting stags), cross the D21 and walk through the little village of La Motte, then cross the Yoson stream; the track now enters woodland dominated by deciduous trees ④. Leave the forest. The route now follows the D24 through La Caillaudière village; on the right, look across to Bellebouche Lake, to the left, Grand-Brun ⑤ with its many dead trees. Back onto the D21 which crosses the back of Grand-Brun Lake, then, at the crossroads, take the D24 back into the forest; here there is mixed woodland with new plantations ⑥. Finally, at the next crossroads, return on the D14.

Species

- On the forest edge, Red-backed Shrike and Stonechat are common.
- In early spring, Hen Harrier and Goshawk may be seen performing their display flights over the larger parcels of woodland.
- In places where the trees have been cleared, it is worth looking for Tawny Pipit, in May and June.
- Winter offers the best chance of seeing Woodcock.
- Black Woodpeckers favour oak woodland; listen for their loud calls in early spring.

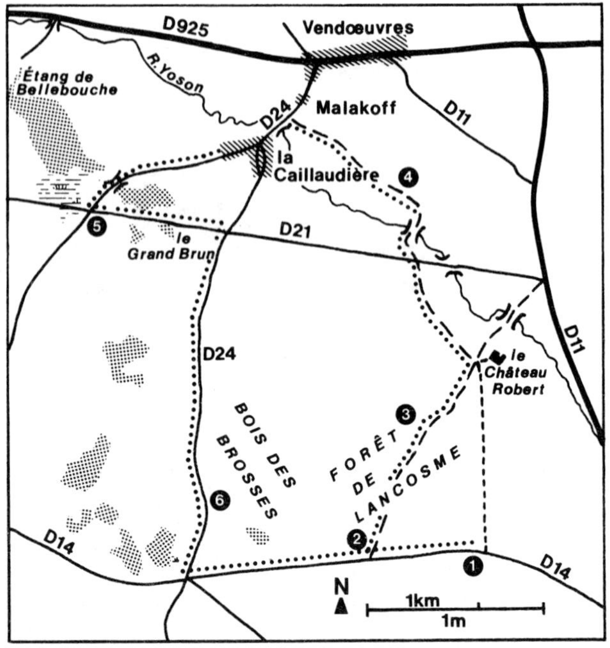

- In open habitats, Whitethroat, Blackcap, Yellowhammer and Cirl Bunting occur.
- As night falls, the calls of Tawny and Long-eared Owls can be heard.
- On Grand-Brun Lake, Great Crested Grebe, Mallard, Shoveler, Pochard and Tufted Duck occur throughout most of the year.
- Nightjars can be heard in the forest (in June) as night falls.
- In winter, the forest is livened up by groups of tits (Crested, Coal and Blue), these may contain Nuthatch, Short-toed Treecreeper, Goldcrest and Firecrest.
- In spring, Honey Buzzards glide over the forest and sometimes Short-toed Eagle occur.

71 Jean-Varenne Marsh

To the south of Issoudun, in Thizay parish, is one of the last remaining alkaline marshes of the Champagne Berrichone region. Many different species of bird can be seen here: raptors such as Hen, Marsh and Montagu's Harriers, Hobby, also Long-eared Owl, waders and ducks on migration and many passerines associated with wetlands, Cetti's, Reed, Sedge and Grasshopper Warblers among others. In spring, orchids are in bloom everywhere.

72 Creuse Valley

To the south-east of the Brenne, from Argenton-sur-Creuse, the Creuse River flows through a steep-sided wooded valley. Follow the river on the right bank as far as Eguzon. In spring as well as in winter, Dipper and Grey Wagtail can be seen near each bridge, mill or dam. In spring and summer many raptors can be seen (Buzzard, Sparrowhawk, Goshawk, Kestrel).

73 RILLÉ LAKE

8 km/5 miles
Savigné-sur-Lathan
(IGN 1722 east – 1/25 000)

Habitat and Timing

Rillé Lake, a Réserve de Chasse (strictly no hunting), was created in 1977 when a dam was built on the Lathan River in order to create a very large reservoir (5,800,000 m^3) to irrigate the horticulture and market-garden areas in the Authion Valley, above Angers. Of this 250 hectares of water, 40 hectares are used by a water-sports centre, the Complexe de Pincemaille, the area this occupies having a constant water-level. The remaining part has large fluctuations in water-level which give rise to an interesting lake side (sometimes covered sand-bars, meadows, mudflats). The lake is enclosed by a coniferous forest to the south and corn fields to the north. The whole forms a very interesting place for birds, very important for duck and waders. The most interesting times are during the autumn migration and in winter. Do not forget, that outside the Pincemaille tourist centre, the land is private without public access. But, the roads and tracks on the edge of the lake are excellent for watching.

Calendar

Spring: Cormorant, Greylag and Bean Geese, Wigeon, Pintail, Gadwall, Teal; Osprey, Marsh Harrier; Golden Plover, Lapwing, small waders, Black-tailed Godwit, Curlew, Snipe; Swift, hirundines (three species).

Autumn: Great Crested, Black-necked and Little Grebes; Grey Heron, Black Stork, Spoonbill; Mallard, Teal, diving duck; Honey Buzzard, Buzzard, Hobby, Merlin; Lapwing, small waders, Curlew, shanks; Common Tern, Whiskered Tern, *Acrocephalus* warblers; Chaffinch, Brambling.

Winter: divers, Cormorant, swans, Grey Heron; Greylag Goose, Pochard, Tufted Duck, Goldeneye; Marsh Harrier; Peregrine; Water and Meadow Pipits, White and Grey Wagtails, Siskin.

Access

Rillé Lake is 40 km (25 miles) north-west of Tours. From Tours, take the right bank of the Loire, turn at Luynes, taking the D49 as far as Rillé passing through Cléré-les-Pins and Savigné-sur-Lathan. From Rillé, continue on the D49 towards Mouliherne, after the tourist complex (hotel and camp site on the right) turn right at the small village Petit Malcombe, towards Pincemaille, park on the right before the embankment.

Suggested visiting: park at Pincemaille car park ①. Walk along the embankment, watching on the way, as far as the purification station ②

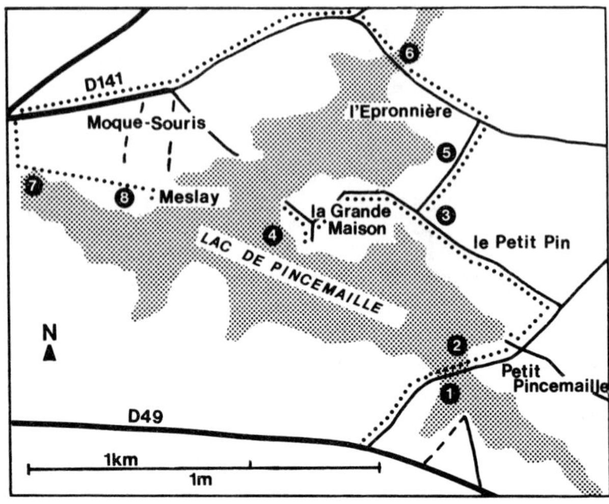

500 m (550 yards) on. Get back into the car, go towards Petit Pin, park at the Butte Noire junction ③. From here look over the surrounding fields and the Rillé 'arm'. Walk towards the Grande-Maison ④, 1 km (0.6 miles) away; cars are forbidden: the road is a private cul-de-sac. Watch to the right, over Channay 'arm'. On arriving at Grande-Maison take the old Moque-Souris road and before the fence that blocks this road, stop and look over the lake where the two arms of the lake meet. Return by the same route; after the boat-houses and houses near the apple trees, watch the Rillé arm, with the wooded shore opposite. Back in the car, go towards l'Épronnière, stopping at the reed-bed ⑤. After L'Épronnière, cross the Channay arm ⑥; park on the roadside, without blocking the traffic. Watch over the Channay arm, south and north (willows and rushes). Continue in the car turning left at Frécheau, and at Mousseaux Dam, park the car ⑦. Watch from the dam. It is possible to walk as far as Meslay (1 km/0.6 miles), watching along the way ⑧. It is worth looking at the Pierre-Saint-Urbain standing stone on the way. You can return to Rillé via Gué Morin on joining the D62 and the D49, or by the same route.

Species

- Along the embankment, during the autumn and winter, there are Water and Meadow Pipits, White and Grey Wagtails.
- In February, many Greylag Geese rest to the south of the Butte Noire.
- On the mudflats during periods of migration, there are small waders, Snipe, shanks, Curlew and Lapwing.
- Anywhere on the lake you can see Cormorants feeding. They leave to roost on the Loire.
- Grey Heron are present year-round. In September, there is a good chance of seeing Spoonbill.
- In the reed-bed on the Channay arm there are Reed Warbler, Sedge Warbler and Reed Bunting.
- The Peregrine occurs in winter, it perches on dead trees or old fence-posts in the lake.

- There is a Black-headed Gull roost in winter, a few larger gulls are sometimes mixed with them.
- From Meslay there is a decent view of the groups of dabbling duck, diving duck and Goldeneye on the lake. Grebes may also be seen here.
- Sparrowhawk, Buzzard, Honey Buzzard and Hobby may be seen in June, particularly around the southern part of the lake.

74 The Loire River (No-Hunting Reserve): from Langeais to Villandry

This part of the Loire River in the Touraine region is most interesting in the winter and during the migration period. The area can be visited between September and January by using the small roads that follow the embankments of the Loire; you will then see its gravel-bars, meadows and wooded islands. There is a Cormorant roost here, a few hundred strong, many Grey Heron, large flocks of dabbling and diving duck and a large Black-headed Gull roost, with other species present in small numbers (Lesser Black-backed, Herring, Yellow-legged, Common). During the breeding season there are Stone Curlew, Little Ringed Plover, Kingfisher, Sand Martin and Cetti's Warbler.

75 The Loire River (No-Hunting Reserve): Vouvray, Vernou, Noizay, Montlouis

Up-river from Tours, this part of the river is known for its large sand- and gravel-bars, which are more or less wooded. It is most interesting between April and June when there is a large colony of Common and Little Terns; also, Little Ringed Plover, Blue-headed Wagtail and Cetti's Warbler nest here. Black-headed Gulls sometimes breed. You can see summering Yellow-legged and Lesser Black-backed Gulls. Of all the passerine species that nest in the riverside woodland, two of the most interesting are Willow Tit and Lesser Whitethroat. The area is accessible from the marked tracks on the left bank (from the Maison de la Loire at Montlouis). The terns are specially protected.

76 SOLOGNE LAKES SAINT-VIÂTRE – MARCILLY-EN-GAULT

3 km/1.85 miles
Neung-sur-Beuvron (IGN 2221 west – 1/25 000) and La Ferté-Imbault (IGN 2222 west – 1/25 000)

Habitat and Timing

Man-made sometime in the Middle Ages, through time the lakes have become ecologically rich.

The Sologne is one of France's internationally-important wetlands. Throughout the year the lakes have a large variety of birds. In winter, hundreds of duck rest here. In spring there are many species (gulls, herons, duck and grebe). All the lakes are private, so you are advised not to leave the many roads and public footpaths. The best lakes are: des Brosses, de la Grande Corbois, de Favelle, de Marcilly and des Marguilliers.

Calendar

Spring: Great Crested and Black-necked Grebes; Grey Heron, Bittern; Shoveler, Mallard, Gadwall, Teal, Garganey, Pochard, Tufted Duck; Marsh Harrier; Water Rail; Lapwing, Black-headed Gull, Black and Whiskered Tern; Reed, Sedge, Grasshopper and Savi's Warblers.

Autumn and Winter: grebes, Cormorant, Grey Heron; Greylag Goose (November), dabbling ducks, diving duck, sawbills, Goldeneye; Buzzard, Hen Harrier, Osprey (September), Merlin; Crane (October–November); waders; Black-headed Gull, Common Gull; Brambling.

Access

From Nouan-le-Fuzelier take the D93 as far as Saint-Viâtre. To get to the Étang des Brosses ①, take the D49 on leaving Saint-Viâtre travelling towards Romorantin, take the second turning on the right (non-signposted public footpath). To get to Étang de la Grand Corbois ②, return towards Saint-Viâtre, take the first turn on the left before coming to a small triangular area. For the 'Étang de Favelle' ③, return to the square at Saint-Viâtre church, turning left just before it. Arriving at a fork, turn left on the D63 towards Neung-sur-Beuvron, going as far as Favelle. For the Étang de Marcilly ④, continue along the same road, at the crossroads turn left; the lake is 50 m (55 yards) further on. For the last lake, Étang des Marguilliers ⑤, turn round, go straight across the crossroads and the lake is 200 m (220 yards) on the left.

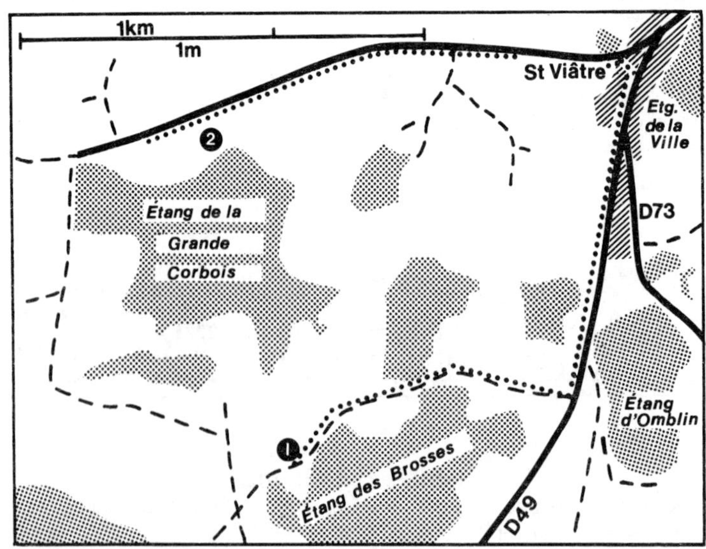

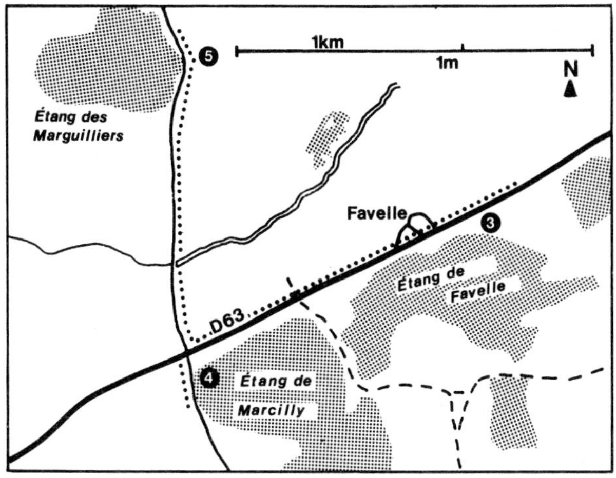

Species

- Marsh Harriers are easy to see at the Étang des Brosses, where they nest.
- Look for Reed and Sedge Warblers in the reed-beds, Savi's Warbler may be seen.
- In winter, the Étang de la Grande Corbois has good numbers of duck, Mallard, Teal, Pochard, Tufted Duck and, during hard weather, a few Goldeneye and sawbills.
- In the reed-bed at the Étang Favelle, the bizarre booming of the Bittern is sometimes heard in spring. Grey Heron nest nearby.
- Pochard, Tufted Duck and Great Crested Grebe also nnest here.
- In spring, the Étang de Marcilly is used by dabbling duck returning north from Africa: Pintail, Shoveler and Garganey.
- The Étang des Marguilliers holds the biggest Black-headed Gull colony in Sologne.
- Great Crested, Black-necked and Little Grebes nest, they are most easily seen between March and July. Pochard and Gadwall also nest.
- Black and Whiskered Terns also breed on the lake, building their nests on the waterlilies.

77 THE LOIRE RIVER: FROM JARGEAU TO ORLÉANS

18 km/11.2 miles
Orléans-la-Charité
(IGN 27 – 1/100 000)

Habitat and Timing

A part of the river which is typical of the middle Loire; most of the Loire's birds are found here. Its proximity to a large city has lead to a great deal of sand and gravel extraction; this has changed the landscape. Sand and gravel islands – strictly no access – have many nesting birds. The resulting widening of the river-bed has favoured the growth of woods and heath. Finally, dredging, sometimes over large areas (35 hectares maximum), has created habitat suitable for wintering Anatidae.

Calendar

Winter: Cormorant; Mallard, Teal, Goosander and Smew, geese sometimes; Black-headed, Herring and Common Gulls.

Spring: Little Ringed Plover, Lapwing, Stone Curlew; Sparrowhawk, Hobby; Common and Little Terns; Sand Martin.

Autumn: Osprey, shanks, small waders, Snipe.

Access

Leave Jargeau towards Orléans via the embankment. Level with Darvoy, turn right onto a track that follows the Loire ①. Above and below the first island in sight ②, look over the mudflats and the gravel-bars. The track

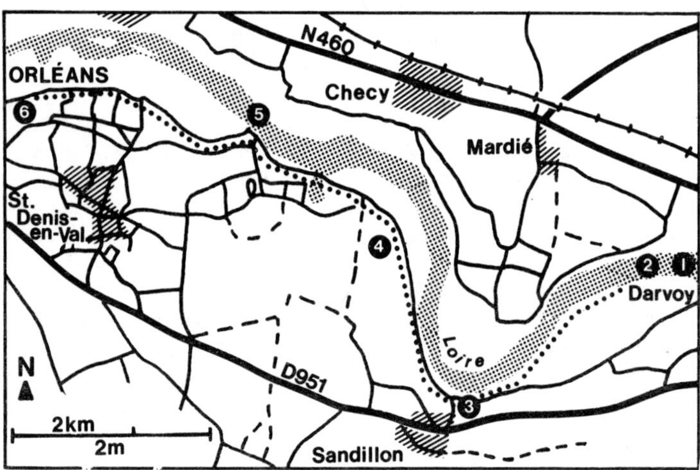

goes by a few gravel-pits before rising back onto the embankment. Stop ③, look over to Sandillon Island (special protection: no access between 1 April and 25 July) and over a broom heath. Continue along the side of the river, then on the embankment which soon leaves the river. Stop near the flooded dredge pits ④ and a few hundred metres further on at the Hawthorn-covered heath. Continue by car as far as the go-kart track ⑤: you can continue along the bank of the Loire on foot (as long as the river is not in flood). The route between here and the end goes through agricultural land with numerous gravel-pits. Finish at the railway bridge (river hunting reserve) ⑥.

Species

- In December and January there is a Black-headed Gull roost on the water.
- Sand Martins nest in the steep banks of the sand-pits.
- Many passerines nest on the banks of the Loire: Grasshopper,

Melodious and Garden Warblers, Whitethroat, Reed Bunting.
- On the vegetation-free islands, Common and Little Terns start laying in May.
- In winter, dabbling duck in good numbers occur alongside Smew, Goosander and some grebes, especially Great Crested.
- On the banks both Lapwing and Stone Curlew are threatened nesting species.
- Little Ringed Plover also nest on the islands. In autumn, waders (including Common Sandpiper, Curlew Sandpiper, Dunlin and Little Stint) occur in good numbers.
- Sparrowhawk and Hobby hunt Sand Martins over the Loire.
- In mid-winter, Cormorants assemble at their roost.

78 La Beauce around Pithiviers

Notwithstanding its uniform appearance, the area known as the Beauce (France's prairie land) has some interesting species, particularly around Pithiviers. Short-toed Lark nest on sugar-beet storage areas (from May to August) colonised by mayweed – Moncharville (Marsainvilliers), Ezerville (Engenville), Charmont-en-Beauce, Châtillon-le-Roi and Bazoches-les-Gallérandes (the sites are close to the last three villages) are known sites – but also at the Pithiviers-le-Vieil dried-out sugar-beet decantation beds (at the factory and at the flying-club); these also have Ortolan Bunting as well as waders during the two migration periods. Scops Owls inhabit those châteaux parks surrounded by stone walls. Their song is principally heard during June and July when it is warm and calm (Emerville (Audeville), Bezonville (Morville-en-Beauce) and Annorville (Guigneville)). Beware!, the Midwife Toad is common in Beauce, and to the unwary, it sounds a lot like the Scops Owl.

CHAMPAGNE-ARDENNE

79 DONCHERY BALLAST QUARRY

2.5 km/1.55 miles
Charleville
(IGN 3009 east – 1/25 000)

Habitat and Timing

A ballast quarry surrounded by wasteland recolonised by bushes; there is a lake to the west of which is a marsh (sedge and reed), alongside the D24. It is interesting thanks to the presence of two islands which serve as a refuge for migrant and nesting birds. The number of birds depends on the water-level and whether or not there are fishermen in boats. There is uncontrolled access.

Calendar

Winter: Mallard, Teal, Pochard, Tufted Duck; Coot; Black-headed Gull.

Spring: Pintail, Wigeon, Garganey; Black Tern, Little Gull.

Summer: Great Crested Grebe, Coot, Water Rail; Little Ringed Plover; Garden, Willow, Grasshopper and Marsh Warblers, Blackcap, Whitethroat, Chiffchaff; Stonechat, Blackbird, Song Thrush. Black and Red Kites fly over.

Autumn: Little Grebe, waders (Lapwing, Common Sandpiper).

Access

The quarry is between Charleville and Sedan in a triangle formed by the A203 dual carriageway, the D24 and the Meuse River.

Leave the A203 at Donchery taking the D24 towards Bosséval. Cars can be parked on the right, near the lake ①, then continue on foot along the track which follows the dual carriageway. It is possible to do a complete tour of the quarry using the fisherman's footpath. There is an observation point over the west of the quarry at ②.

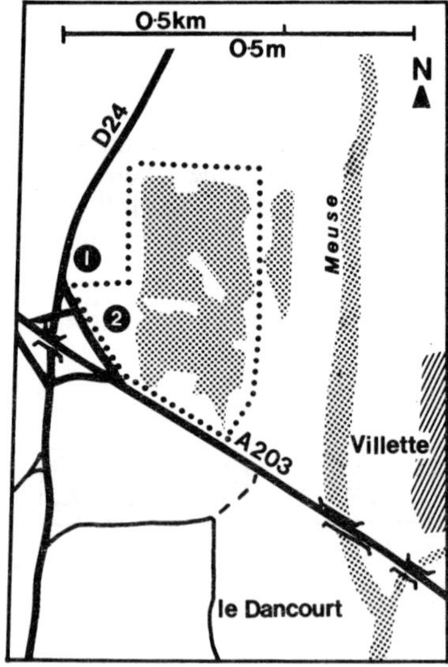

Species

- Grasshopper and Marsh Warblers nest mainly in the south-west part of the quarry.
- Great Crested Grebe nest here.
- Waders – particularly Lapwing and Common Sandpiper – frequently occur on the islands in the centre.
- Black and Red Kites are seen principally in the summer, Buzzard and Kestrel occur year-round.
- Coot and Water Rail are easily seen on the islands.

80 Aisne Valley near Attigny

Between Vouziers and Ambly this valley can be very interesting particularly for resting migrants in March. During this month, many hundreds of Pintail and Shoveler as well as some Teal use the flooded fields. Greylag Geese sometimes occur amongst them. Many thousands of Lapwing also use this site, Golden Plover mix with them. Cranes appear to be regular visitors. Meadow Pipit, White and Blue-headed Wagtails, Stonechat, Wheatear and thrushes are present. The Curlew is a rare nester.

81 Chiers Valley

Chiers Valley between Remilly-Aillicourt and Bièvres is regularly flooded in spring. Many dabbling duck feed on the flooded meadows – Teal, Garganey, Gadwall, Shoveler and Pintail – during the spring migration (mainly in March). Many Lapwing and some Snipe use the area at the same time. Use the departmental roads (those beginning with D) on the left bank of the Chiers, except near Carignan where you need to use the national road (N).

82 Bairon Lake

Some 15 km (9.3 miles) north-east of Vouziers, Bairon Lake is the largest area of water in the Ardennes. The western part is a vast reed-bed, whereas the eastern part is managed for watersports. It is best visited in winter, between November and March (dabbling and diving duck, sometimes sawbills and divers), or in the spring, April and May, when raptors gather to hunt (Red and Black Kites, Marsh Harrier, Hobby) and some rarer species put in an appearance (Purple Heron, Bittern, Black Stork). There are also some wetland passerines (*Locustella* and *Acrocephalus* warblers, Reed Bunting) and other aquatic species (Kingfisher, Grey Wagtail). Great Crested Grebe and Coot nest in large numbers.

83 FORÊT D'ORIENT LAKE

20 km/12.5 miles
Brienne-le-Château
(IGN 2917 – 1/50 000)
and Troyes
(IGN 2817 – 1/50 000)

Habitat and Timing

Forêt d'Orient Lake is man-made and of variable level; it was built in order to control the flow in the Seine. It is enclosed by the large Orient forest; most of its banks are covered with willows. The lower water-level in autumn and winter reveals large areas of wet fields and mudflats. In the north-east part of the lake there is a reserve where watersports are forbidden and there is no hunting; this results in the presence of large numbers of duck (there is restricted access). It is also an important place for Cranes, waders and duck on migration, and a wintering site for geese, White-tailed Eagle and Cormorant. Hunting is forbidden on the lake.

Calendar

Autumn: Great Crested and sometimes Slavonian and Red-necked Grebes, Grey Heron; Gadwall, Shoveler, Teal; Osprey; Crane; Lapwing, Dunlin, Little Stint, 'shanks; Black Tern, Sand Martin, Water Pipit, Wagtails.

Winter: Cormorant, Greylag and Bean Geese, Wigeon, Goldeneye, Smew, Pochard, Tufted Duck; White-tailed Eagle, Peregrine.

Spring and Summer: Bean Goose, Pintail, Gadwall, Crane. Great Crested Grebe, Goshawk, Sparrowhawk, Black, Grey-headed and Middle Spotted Woodpeckers all nest.

Access

Some 15 km (9.3 miles) to the east of the town of Troyes, on the side of the N19, the site is well signposted. A road that follows the lake's edges has many lay-bys and goes through the parishes of Lusigny, Géraudot, Mesnil-Saint-Père, making visiting easy. Get onto this road at Lusigny. About 2 km (1.2 miles) further on, park at Lusigny beach ①. Another 3 km (1.9 miles) further, to the north, it is easy to watch from the Haute Seine watersports base ②. Next, pass through Géraudot village and after about 4 km (2.5 miles) stop at the bird-hide car park ③. Walk to the hide (200 m/220 yards). Next, go by car towards Mesnil-Saint-Père. After 8 km

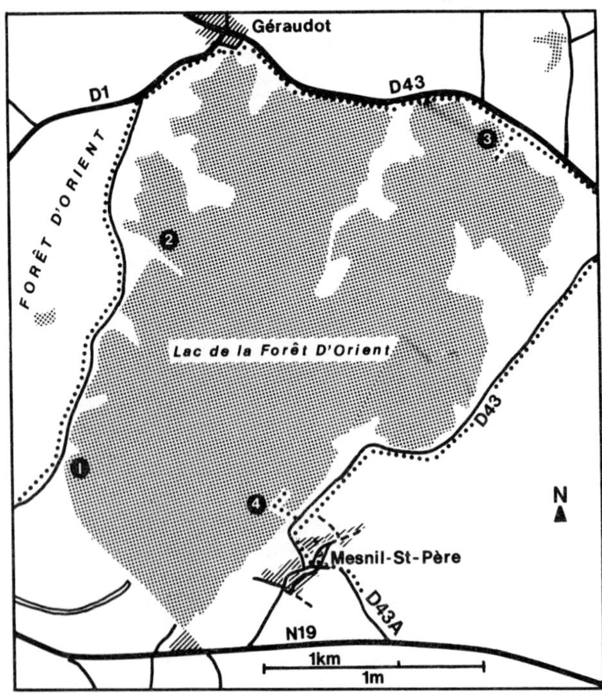

(5 miles), turn towards the marina ④: this offers a panoramic view over the site. You can start this circuit at Mesnil-Saint-Père if arriving from the direction of Bar-sur-Aube; visit the stops in reverse order. In this case, leave the N19 1.5 km (0.9 miles) after La Maison-Blanche on the D43A towards Mesnil-Saint-Père.

White-tailed Eagle

Species

- In the south during winter there is a large Black-headed Gull roost with thousands of birds; a few Common Gulls mix with them.
- From November onwards, Bean Geese winter here, as well as a few Greylag and White-fronted Geese.
- Great Crested Grebe nest. In autumn large numbers flock together here and there on the lake.
- Great Reed, Reed and Sedge Warblers and Reed Bunting nest in the reed-beds near the hide.
- In autumn, there are large numbers of duck in the reserve (Gadwall, Mallard, Teal, Pochard, Tufted Duck).
- In November and in March the lake is used by large numbers of migrant Cranes.
- Osprey (autumn) and White-tailed Eagle (winter) are sometimes seen from the hide.
- From October to December, Cormorants roost in the branches of dead trees.

- Dunlin and Little Stint stop in autumn, mixing with the large flocks of Lapwing.
- Goldeneye, Smew and Goosander are regular winter visitors. Many dabbling duck occur.
- From late November to early February, White-tailed Eagle and Peregrine can often be observed from the Mesnil-Saint-Père recreation centre.
- In September, Sand and House Martins and Swallow hunt over the lake.

84 Horre Lake

Horre Lake, 10 km (6.2 miles) west of Montier-en-Der, covering an area of 330 hectares and almost completely surrounded by forest (private), is one of France's most beautiful lakes. It is well worth a visit in spring or summer. From March to May it is used by numerous migrants (Teal, Garganey and other dabbling duck, diving duck, Osprey, Hobby, marsh terns). From June to August there are many breeding birds (grebes, herons, duck, Sparrowhawk, Black and Red Kites, harriers, Honey Buzzard), as well as many wetland passerines.

85 DER-CHANTECOQ LAKE (NO-HUNTING RESERVE)

4 km/2.5 miles
Wassy
(IGN 3016 – 1/50 000)

Habitat and Timing

This is France's largest artificial lake. There is a variable water-level according to the season; it empties progressively between July and November and starts filling from December onwards. The eastern shore is completely wooded. The western part is separated from the 'champenois' countryside (meadows, crops and woods) by a large embankment. The banks are bordered by willows of different ages, reeds and flooded scrub. A remarkable site for duck, geese and Cranes, in autumn, winter and early spring. There is restricted access onto the reserve, being totally prohibited in an area at the north-west end of the lake. However, watching is easy from the peripheral embankment. Best watching conditions occur in the afternoon and evening.

Calendar

Autumn: Teal, Shoveler, Pochard; Lapwing, Curlew, Snipe, Spotted Redshank, Dunlin. Large numbers of Cranes use the site during migration (November).

Winter: Mallard, Wigeon, sawbills, many Bean and Greylag Geese, Bewick's Swan; White-tailed Eagle, Peregrine.

Spring: spectacular numbers of Crane on passage (up to 25,000 come to roost on March evenings), Red Kite; Gadwall, Pintail; Black-headed and Common Gulls, Black Tern; passerines (notably Blue-headed Wagtail and Reed Bunting).

Cranes

Access

The route is well signposted from Vitry-le-François (to the north-west following the D13) or Saint-Dizier (15 km (9.3 miles) to the north-east on the D384). If arriving from the north, it is worth stopping on the embankment road at ① and ②, as well as at the car park at Chantecoq marina ③. There are two possibilities: either watching from next to the car on the embankment road, or on foot looking over the lake. Leave from stops ① and ②, take the embankment which follows the side of the reserve for about 1.8 km (1.2 miles). Return either by the same route or by following the D13 which crosses the forest. You are prohibited from entering the reserve.

Species

- Reed Warblers nest in the willow-beds and the small reed-beds. Stonechats also occur.
- Large numbers of Grey Heron flock together to the south-west and at the east of the lake in October and November.
- On the side of the embankments, all three wagtails may be encountered, Blue-headed (summer), White (year-round) and Grey (winter).
- Most Bean and Greylag Geese and Bewick's Swans (sometimes Whooper Swan) occupy the small islands and the point to the west, from November to March.

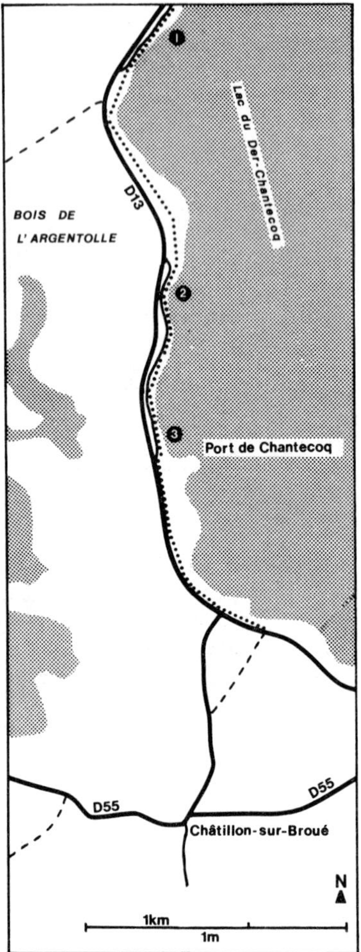

- Many waders use the western shore of the lake, particularly in the autumn, Dunlin, Spotted Redshank, Snipe, Lapwing, with smaller numbers of many other species.
- During May and April Black Tern hunt over the middle of the lake (sometimes also Whiskered and White-winged Black).
- Most Cranes come to roost on the uncovered ground between the Gros Chêne and the Ile de Chantecoq; especially in November and March.
- Not far from the Étang de Landres both Red and Black Kites hunt.
- Duck occur over most of the lake, distribution depending on the water-level. However, the area around Chantecoq marina is usually good.

86 Braux Lake, Sainte-Cohière

Some 5 km (3.1 miles) west of Sainte-Menehould, this large lake is easy to watch and is most rewarding between March and August. It has a particularly interesting list of nesting birds: various grebes, dabbling duck, Pochard, Tufted Duck; raptors (kite, Marsh Harrier); Black-headed Gull; Kingfisher, Blue-headed Wagtail; chats, warblers, shrikes. The Bittern is sometimes seen and migrants occur: herons, Hobby, Little Gull, marsh terns.

87 TROIS-FONTAINES NATIONAL FOREST

4.5 km/2.8 miles or 9 km/5.6 miles
Saint-Dizier
(IGN 3015 – 1/50 000)

Habitat and Timing

A large deciduous forest mainly comprising beech and mixed oak and Hornbeam woodland with ash, maple and alder in the many damp dells. To the north of the village is a large area that was once cultivated; it is now regenerating naturally and there are many interesting bushy areas. There is a typical collection of forest species. Many of the forestry roads are closed to cars. There is unrestricted access on foot, except to the newly-planted areas.

Calendar

All year: Sparrowhawk, Goshawk; woodpeckers (the six species, including Black, Middle Spotted and Grey-headed), tits, Nuthatch, Short-toed Treecreeper.

Spring and Summer: Honey Buzzard; Golden Oriole; Goldcrest, Firecrest, warblers.

Winter: Hawfinch, Siskin, Redpoll.

Access

From Saint-Dizier (8 km (5 miles) to the south in the Haute-Marne) take the D157 as far as the village of Trois-Fontaines-l'Abbaye. Park on the square ①. Take the small road that climbs up to the church (with an interesting view over two small lakes) ② before entering the forest. At Neuve-Grange, turn left onto a tarmac track. A part of this route crosses the old cultivated site, now scrub. For those who like a walk, there is another possibility on a longer (9 km/5.6 miles) and more forested track: take the Baudonvilliers road which passes close to the lakes. There is a pleasant little dell, the Bruxenelle, near the stream's source ③.

Species

- There is a good chance of seeing Honey Buzzard near the clearings between May and August.
- The best place to see woodpeckers is in the areas of mature woodland

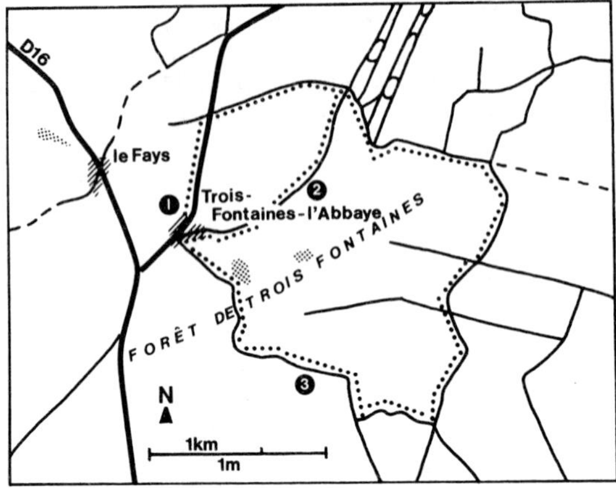

with large old trees; maximum activity in April and May and again in September.

- Wood and Willow Warblers and Chiffchaff are common where the trees are large, but far less visible after July.
- Look for Redpolls and Siskins in the wet dells in winter.
- Sparrowhawks are there throughout the year but never easy to see.
- Short-toed Treecreeper, Nuthatch, Goldcrests and Firecrests are often seen with groups of tits.

88 VILLEGUSIEN (OR VINGEANNE) RESERVOIR

4 km/2.5 miles
Langres
(IGN 3120 east – 1/25 000)

Habitat and Timing

This is a feeder reservoir for the Marne to Saône Canal (at the foot of the Langres Plateau on the Marne–Rhône–Saône migration corridor), in still unspoilt countryside (meadows, crops, woods and thickets). There is a variable water-level: the maximum being between April and June, the minimum in September and October. The foot of the dam always holds water (a length of 1.25 km/0.8 miles). There are two marshy bays, the Baie de Percey and the Baie de Vêvres; the second is crossed by the N74 (Langres to Dijon) road on a causeway and its edges are well wooded. The site is best known for the autumn migration of waders and duck and to a lesser extent for wintering duck. Numbers are never high but this is compensated for by the ease of watching at close range. There is unrestricted access but some activities (hunting, fishing, bathing, sailing) are controlled (look at the notice-boards). Part of the area is a national no-hunting reserve.

Calendar

The end of summer and autumn: Mallard, Shoveler, Teal, Pochard, Tufted Duck; Red and Black Kites, Osprey; Lapwing, plovers, small waders, Spotted Redshank, Redshank, Common Sandpiper, Black-headed Gull.

Winter: Grey Heron, Mallard, Coot.

Spring: grebes, Cormorant; many species of duck; Hobby, Red and Black Kites; *Acrocephalus* warblers, Golden Oriole, Reed Bunting. Shelduck, scoters, sawbills, terns and marsh terns on passage.

Access

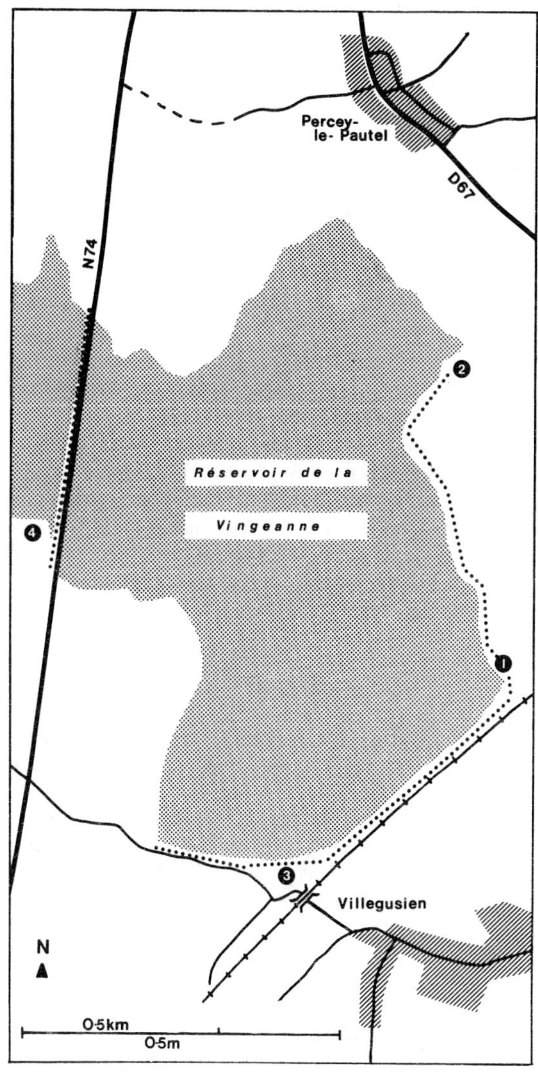

From Longeau take the D67 in the direction of Besançon. After Percey-le-Pautel turn right on the D128 towards Villegusien. Follow the lake side and park on the side of the dam ①. Skirt the lake northwards on foot/ look over the lake from the beach. On nearing the Baie de Percey ② look over the mudflats or marshy areas (depending on the water-level). Return by the same route. Caution: do not enter the no-hunting reserve (at the back of the Baie de Percey) and please do not go onto the mud, especially in the hunting season (August to February) in order not to disturb the birds. Other observation points: walk along the top of the dam ③, this offers a good view over the whole lake; or look over the Baie de Vêvres from the N74 ④, beware of the traffic. (Do not use the 'Chemin du Tour du Lac' – the peripheral path – which is not very good for watching the lake, and its use may disturb nesting birds).

Species

- The lake side is a good place for Common Sandpipers on migration.
- The site is a feeding area for marsh terns and Little Gull in April–May and August–September.
- An ideal feeding and resting area for duck in the spring, but especially in the autumn: Teal, Shoveler, Pochard, Tufted Duck, sometimes Goosander, Smew, Eider and Common and Velvet Scoters.
- When the mudflats are uncovered (August–October) this area is used by waders.
- During the migration period, the lake side is used by wagtails, and Meadow and Water Pipits.
- In spring, the lake is used by large numbers of hirundines and Swift.
- The Black-headed Gull roost is particularly impressive in February and March and between October and December.
- Kites and Osprey hunt over the lake between March and October.
- The belt of aquatic vegetation is much favoured by passerines: *Acrocephalus* warblers, Reed Bunting. Other birds to look for include: Kingfisher, Fieldfare (in the breeding season) and Lesser Spotted Woodpecker (more visible in autumn).
- Various species of grebe and Coot occur in spring and autumn. Some species use the area to feed and nest.

89 Auberive Forest

About 20 km (12.5 miles) to the south-west of Langres, this beautiful beech and oak forest on the Langrois Plateau has many woodland bird species: Sparrowhawk, Goshawk, Honey Buzzard, many woodpeckers (including Grey-headed and Black) and Wood Warbler. Hazelhen and Tengmalm's Owl can be seen with luck. The forest edge and some nearby scrub has Woodlark, Great Grey and Red-backed Shrike and other passerines. Black Storks are often seen on migration.

90 BONIFACIO AND ITS PLATEAU

6.5 km/4 miles
Bonifacio
(IGN 4256 east – 1/25 000)

Habitat and Timing

Bonifacio sits on top of a limestone cliff overlooking the sea to Sardinia opposite; it is a remarkable, historic site. The plateau, from the town to the signal-station, also on the cliff top, is covered with low maquis. In the small valleys there are some ancient gardens surrounded by high walls, used to protect the crops from the wind. Some of Corsica's Mediterranean specialities occur in the maquis.

Calendar

Spring: Cory's and Yelkouan Shearwaters, Shag; raptors; Yellow-legged Gull; Pallid and Alpine Swifts, hirundines; Tawny Pipit; Sardinian, Marmora's and Dartford Warblers; Spotless Starling; Corsican Citril Finch, Italian Sparrow, Cirl Bunting.

Winter: Gannet, Yelkouan Shearwater, Shag.

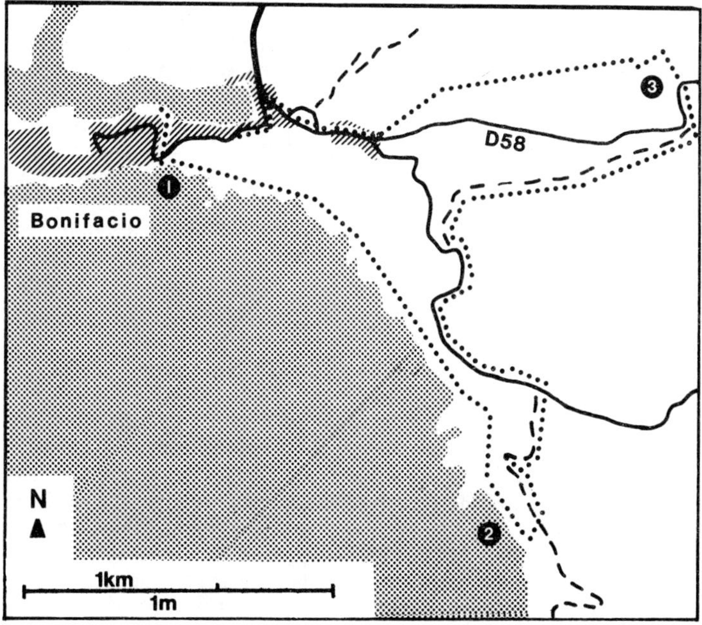

Access

In Bonifacio, climb to the Citadel from where there is a good view over the Bouches. Grain-de-Sable Island ① is at its foot; a flight of steps leads down to sea-level. A footpath starts from the foot of the citadel and follows the cliff towards the plateau. Once at the signal-station ②, there is a road suitable for cars that returns to Bonifacio, either directly or via Saint-Julien convent ③.

Species

- Spotless Starling can be seen in the town, in France they only nest in Corsica.
- In the evening you can hear Cory's Shearwaters calling over Grain-de-Sable Island, where there is a small colony.
- Sardinian, Marmora's and Dartford Warblers can be found singing in the maquis in the spring.
- Some way out to sea, Shag and Yelkouan Shearwater can often be seen passing.
- Flying close by the cliffs, both Alpine and Pallid Swifts are easy to watch.
- Look for both Corsican Citril Finch and Cirl Bunting in the maquis.
- The Italian and Corsican subspecies of the House Sparrow, the Italian Sparrow, is a common nester around the port. A close look may reveal a Spanish Sparrow.

91 The Mouth of the Liamone/ Coggia and Casaglione

This temperamental river flows into the Golfe de Sagone, 30 km (18.6 miles) to the north of Ajaccio. In summer the many habitats (reed-bed, sandbank, maquis) hold a remarkable variety of species. Water Rail, Moorhen, Kingfisher (slightly upriver), Alpine Swift, can all be found. The Osprey often occurs over the open water near the bridge. Many other species occur: Little Ringed Plover, Short-toed Lark, Red-rumped Swallow, Tawny Pipit; Great Reed, Cetti's, Reed, and Spectacled Warblers; Corn Bunting. Near the mouth of the river the following may well be seen: Turtle Dove, Red-backed and Woodchat Shrikes; Blue Rock Thrush; Sardinian and Marmora's Warblers; Cirl Bunting. Shag can be seen on the offshore islands.

92 Bavella Pass/Zonza

To the north-west of Sartène, between Levie and Solenzara, this pass reaches some spectacular scenery at the top (1,243 m). The Corsican Pine forest is home to a remarkable set of species in the breeding season: Scops Owl, Mistle Thrush, Great Spotted Woodpecker; Corsican Nuthatch, Crossbill, Treecreeper, Corsican Citril Finch, Linnet, Coal Tit. Along the Alturaghja track other species may be seen: Cuckoo, Woodlark, Water Pipit, Spotted Flycatcher. Near Aiguilles de Bavella there are: Mouflon, Golden Eagle, Lammergeier, Alpine Accentor.

93 Aitone Forest/Evisa

Going to the Niolo from Evisa via the Verghio Pass, you pass through Aitone Forest. After the chestnut woodland near Evisa there is a splendid mature conifer forest composed mainly of Corsican Pine, with some spruce and birch near the Verghio Pass. Some of the most characteristic nesting birds of this type of area can be found: Goshawk, Sparrowhawk; Woodpigeon, Great Spotted Woodpecker; Coal Tit, Corsican Nuthatch (in good numbers near Paesolu), Treecreeper, Crossbill, Siskin (irregular), Jay. Spotted Flycatchers are often present in summer.

94 BARCAGGIO/ERSA

2.5 km/1.55 miles
Luri
(IGN 4347 west – 1/25 000)

Habitat and Timing

At the northern tip of Cap Corse, this is the area where the Acqua Tignese stream forms a small delta at its mouth, with a willow-bed, a small lagoon and dunes covered in Juniper woodland. Inland there is low maquis, consisting mainly of Fumana. The complex Barcaggio maquis-dune wetland area is a good site for migrants in spring, between March and June. Other seasons are less interesting. The group, Amis du Parc, have restored an ancient oil-press which serves as a bird observatory in spring. Visitors may contact organisers of bird courses here.

Calendar

Spring: White and Black Storks, Grey and Night Herons, Little Egret, Little Bittern; Marsh Harrier, Honey Buzzard; Little and Spotted Crakes; waders, woodcock; Scops Owl, Cuckoo, Swallow, Red-rumped Swallow, House and Sand Martins; Robin, Bluethroat, Song Thrush, Redwing; Sedge, Reed, Great Reed Icterine, Willow, Wood and Garden Warblers; Chiffchaff, Whitethroat.

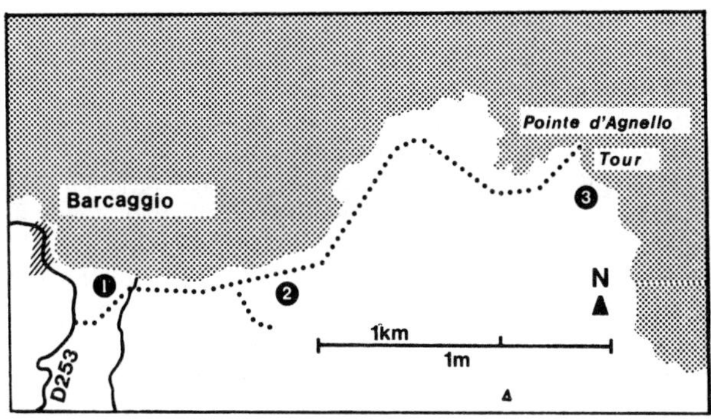

Access

From Bastia take the D80 as far as Ersa (59 km/38 miles), then the D253. Once at Barcaggio leave the car at the entrance to the village. Descend towards L'Acqua Tignese ① where the path turns right. The stream and its willow-bed is crossed by the ford. A path leads to the lagoon ② and to the dunes, as far as Agnello Tower ③.

Species

- At night the Scops Owl is often heard singing.
- In April both Swift and Alpine Swift pass in number, often accompanied by hirundines (four species, including the rare Red-rumped Swallow).
- In the willows there are often many warblers, *Phylloscopus* (three species), *Sylvia* (three species) and Icterine.
- Ringed and Little Ringed Plovers can be seen on the coast.
- In April, both Spotted and Little Crakes occur in the reed-beds.
- The lagoon holds migrant waders (especially Common and Wood Sandpipers).
- The Ring Ouzel is often to be seen near Agnello Tower in March and April.
- A little behind the hill, many Honey Buzzard and Montagu's Harrier pass on their spring migration.

95 THE SOUTHERN PART OF BIGUGLIA LAKE/ BORGO

2 km/1.25 miles
Vescovato
(IGN 4349 west – 1/25 000)

Habitat and Timing

Biguglia coastal lagoon is the largest wetland in Corsica (1,450 hectares). The proposed circuit covers the south-west part of the lake where the water has a low salt content which has encouraged a good reed-bed to develop. The interest of the lake and the coastal strip has much declined during the last twenty years due to hunting and an increase in agriculture and urban development; this has led to the disappearance of both White-tailed Eagle and White-headed Duck. Nevertheless, it is still an attractive wetland for wintering and migrant birds.

Calendar

Winter: Great Crested, Black-necked and Little Grebes; Pintail, Wigeon, Teal, Coot; Cetti's and Moustached Warblers, Chiffchaff; Penduline Tit, Reed Bunting.

Spring: Cormorant; Grey, Purple and Night Herons, Little Egret; Marsh Harrier, Red-footed Falcon, Osprey, Black and White-winged Black Terns.

Breeding season: Bee-eater, Hoopoe; Cetti's, Fan-tailed, Reed and Great Reed Warblers.

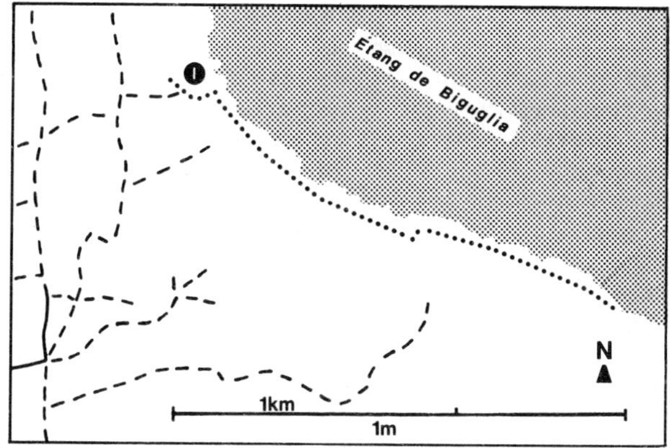

Access

From Bastia, take the N193 as far as Borgo-Revinco (15 km/9.3 miles to the south) from here turn left on the D207 for 4 km (2.5 miles). Leave the car on the side of the road where the bridge crosses the canal ①. Follow the path along the lake, between the canal and the reed-bed, for about 2 km (1.25 miles). Return by the same route.

Fan-tailed Warbler

Species

- Near the canal, listen for the 'zip' 'zip 'zip' . . . of the Fan-tailed Warbler. Stonechat, Corn and Cirl Bunting also nest.
- Purple Heron nest in the reed-bed, in small numbers.
- Reed and Great Reed Warblers sing continuously from the reed-bed from mid-April onwards. Moustached Warbler and Penduline Tit can be seen here during the winter, and Cetti's Warbler is present year-round.
- Both Marsh Harrier and Hobby nest around Biguglia and hunt over the reed-bed. In spring, Osprey and Red-footed Falcon are regularly seen (April and May).
- In winter large numbers of Pochard and Tufted Duck as well as Coot occur, also dabbling duck and Great Crested, Black-necked and Little Grebes.

96 Fango Valley/Galeria and Manso

Between Porto and Galeria, in the Filosorma region, Fango Valley is one of the most isolated in Corsica. The mouth of the Fango (property of the Conservatoire de l'Espace Littoral) is particularly well wooded with alder. Breeding species include: Sparrowhawk, Nightjar, Scops Owl, Great Spotted Woodpecker, Spotted Flycatcher, Corsican Citril Finch. Osprey regularly fish near the river's mouth. Further up the valley is Pirio Forest (an UNESCO World Heritage Site), considered one of the best mature Holm-oak woodlands. Here are such woodland species as: Goshawk, Scops Owl, Great Spotted Woodpecker, Blue and Great Tits, Blackcap and Robin.

97 VARGHELLO VALLEY/ VENACO

10 km/6.2 miles
Venaco
(IGN 4251 – 1/50 000)

Habitat and Timing

This is a large valley in the centre of Corsica between two high peaks, the Monte Cinto and the Monte d'Oro. Visiting this valley allows you to see three well-defined vegetation zones; the higher Mediterranean, the mountain, and lastly the subalpine. This diversity is responsible for a very good range of species as Mediterranean birds are seen side-by-side with mountain and forest species. In the valley bottom (490 m) there is heterogeneous maquis with Holm-oak, heath, Strawberry Tree, Juniper and Fumana. Later, the track passes through a Maritime Pine forest (on the left bank between 750m and 800 m). It crosses Varghello Valley (at the Vacchereccio bridge) and goes through part of the Solibellu Corsican Pine forest. The track eventually arrives at the Col de Tribali (1.590 m).

Calendar

Spring: Lammergeier, Golden Eagle, Peregrine, Sparrowhawk; Alpine Swift, Great Spotted Woodpecker; Water Pipit, Alpine Accentor,

Marmora's and Sardinian Warblers; Great, Coal and Long-tailed Tits; Treecreeper, Wallcreeper, Spotted Flycatcher, Crossbill, Corsican Citril Finch, Cirl Bunting.

Autumn: Dotterel are sometimes seen on the high ridges.

Access

Leave Corte on the N193 southwards. After 17 km (10.5 miles) there is a signpost indicating the valley ①. It is best to leave the car here (well parked) at the entrance to the valley and walk for a better appreciation of the changes in vegetation. Vacchereccio bridge ② is 4 km (2.5 miles) (1 hour's walk) up the valley and the Col de Tribali ③ 10 km (6.2 miles), 3½ hour's walk.

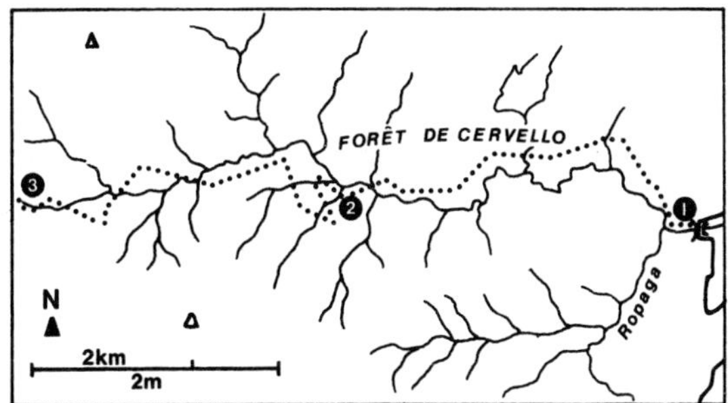

Species

- Marmora's Warbler can be heard singing in the maquis from March onwards. Both Sardinian Warbler and Cirl Bunting are also present.
- The Great Spotted Woodpecker is easily seen near Piferini.
- The pine forest is home to Corsica's famous endemic, the Corsican Nuthatch.
- Sparrowhawks hunt above the Corsican Pines.
- Watch carefully to the north, over the mountain ridges, for a chance of either Lammergeier or Golden Eagle.
- The Corsican Citril Finch can be seen near the Col de Tribali.

98 SCANDOLA NATIONAL NATURE RESERVE/ OSANI

2 km/1.25 miles on foot, the rest by boat
Corse-nord
(IGN 73 – 1/100 000)

Habitat and Timing

It is best to visit this very beautiful and ornithologically-rich reserve by boat. Scandola Peninsula is part of a collapsed volcano so that the colour and form of the rocks make this area rather special. The steep and indented coastline is used by nesting seabirds, rock-dwelling species and the symbol of conservation of the Corsican coast, the Osprey. The interior of the peninsula is covered with mixed maquis (Fumana, thickets of Strawberry Tree, heath and oak) which is home to a large range of species and an abundance of birds.

Calendar

Spring and summer: Mediterranean race of the Shag; Osprey, Kestrel, Peregrine; Yellow-legged Gull; Rock Dove, Pallid and Alpine Swifts, Crag Martin; Blue Rock Thrush; Marmora's, Sardinian, Dartford and Subalpine Warblers; Spotted Flycatcher.

Access

Take a boat, either from Porto (Vedettes Alpana – Alpana boats), or from Calvi (Vedettes Colomboline, Revellata); information on times is available in the bars around the ports. From Porto the trip lasts two or three

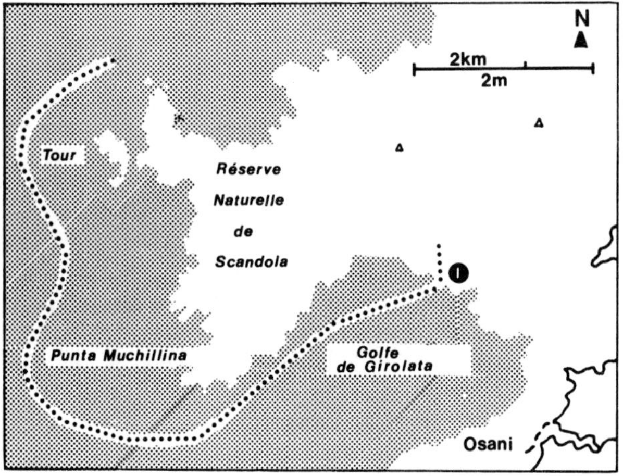

hours with the possibility of a halt at Girolata, where the surrounding maquis is interesting for the birdwatcher. From Calvi the boats leave in mid-morning, follow the coast of the reserve during the morning, stop at Girolata for lunch and return in the afternoon. In Girolata, a path leaves the village north-westwards ① and can be used for looking for passerines.

Species

- Rocks and points may have numbers of Shag.
- Along the cliffs, Pallid and Alpine Swifts stand out against the pale cliffs, Crag Martins mix with them.
- Once near Scandola, search the sky for Osprey.
- Rock Doves nest on the cliffs.
- In the spring, Marmora's, Dartford and Sardinian Warblers and Blackcap can be found.
- The Hooded Crow can be seen around Girolata village.

FRANCHE-COMTÉ

99 FRASNE NATIONAL NATURE RESERVE AND SMALL LAKE

6km/3.75 miles
Pontarlier
(IGN 3425 west – 1/25 000)

Habitat and Timing

The heart of this reserve is a very shallow lake (rarely more than one metre deep), which was created in 1960 when a marshy depression was flooded. The aquatic and marshland vegetation is well developed and many small islands have been formed. The banks are open, with only a few willows growing. Surrounded by water-meadows, it is filled from the south-west by the outflow of Frasne Lake. Frasne National Nature Reserve is to the south-east, a remarkable acid peat-bog in a diversity of evolving forms (floating, raised). There is birch and Mountain Pine woodland. The lake is a migratory stop-over for duck, gulls, terns and waders; the peat-bog is most interesting during the breeding season, and for its beautiful landscape. Access onto the reserve is controlled; marked tracks allow entry to the most interesting areas.

Calendar

Spring (April and May): many grebes and duck (Shoveler, Teal, Garganey, Pochard, Tufted Duck, Red-crested Pochard); raptors (harriers, Hobby, Red-footed Falcon, Osprey, Black and Red Kites); Black, White-winged Black and Whiskered Terns; Little Gull; most waders including Curlew, Whimbrel, Black-tailed Godwit, Lapwing, Snipe; the three commoner hirundines, Blue-headed Wagtail, Meadow Pipit, Wheatear.

Summer: Great Crested Grebe, Mute Swan, Pochard; Curlew, Lapwing; Marsh Warbler, Spotted Flycatcher; Fieldfare.

Autumn (August and September): same species as in the spring plus, Black Stork, Dunlin, Little and Temminck's Stints, Ringed and Little Ringed Plovers.

Access

From Pontarlier (19 km/11.8 miles to the north-east) take the D72 then the D471 towards Champagnole as far as Frasne (where there's a regular train service, including the TGV). From here take the D49 towards Bonnevaux: the small lake can be seen on the left of the road on leaving Frasne. Park on the side of the road near the wooden hut ① to the north-west of the lake. Watch from here or from the hillock ② to the west of the lake. On foot, follow the side of the lake from the wooden hut as far as the road (D49), follow it for 750 m (820 yards) as far as the picnic site ③ on the left of the road; the marked tracks that lead to the peat-bog leave

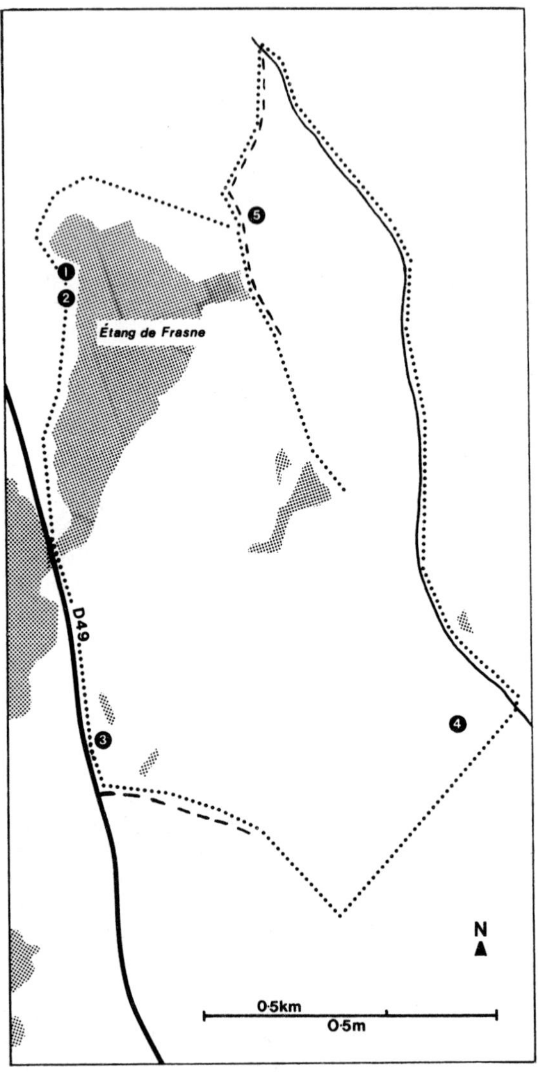

from here. Cross the forest on the tarmac track ④, turn left and walk as far as the lake's outflow ⑤. Go as far as the spruce plantation on the east side of the lake, then back to the outflow on the same track. Return to the wooded hut by the meadow.

Species

- In spring, the small islands may have waders – mainly different 'shanks.
- Great Crested Grebe, Coot and Mute Swan (two nesting pairs) can be seen year-round. Shoveler, Teal, Garganey, diving duck and Red-crested Pochard can be seen in spring.

- Although difficult to see, both Hazelhen and Capercaillie inhabit the forest.
- Crossbill occur throughout the year in the Mountain Pine forest.
- Both Nightjar and Woodcock can be heard in the woods on spring evenings.
- Marsh Warblers nest in areas where *Angelica* predominate. Spotted Flycatcher and Fieldfare nest in the spruce plantations. Redpoll breed in the birches on the side of the peat-bogs.
- Red and Black Kites, Hobby and Hen Harrier often occur in this area of meadows.
- Meadow Pipits nest on the side of the lake. Wheatear and Blue-headed Wagtail are often seen, particularly during migration.

100 Bouverans Lake

Bouverans Lake is 3.5 km (2.2 miles) to the south-east of Frasne Lake. During the breeding season the mixed beech/fir wood on the southern side of the lake has a Grey Heron colony in which also nest Raven and Black and Red kites. The wet meadow and marsh to the north-west are home to Spotted Crake, Curlew, Lapwing and Snipe. There is also a Fieldfare colony and a pair each of Hobby and Great Grey Shrike. Duck, gulls and waders are seen on migration.

101 THE MONT-D'OR MASSIF

2.5 km/1.55 miles and 5 km/3.1 miles
Mouthe
(IGN 3426 east – 1/25 000)

Habitat and Timing

One of the highest points in the region, the Mont d'Or rises to 1,463 m. On its western slopes, the beech/fir forest occurs among more open habitat (meadows, thickets and open woodland) up to 1,400 m. Here an alpine/meadow-type vegetation starts with the climate and vegetation typical of the subalpine zone. To the east, the massif is broken for more than a kilometre (0.6 miles) by a line of cliffs (200 m to 250 m in height) at the bottom of which is a large area of rocky scree. A massif remarkable for its nesting mountain and subalpine birds. There is free access at all times but the roads are not cleared of snow in winter.

Calendar

Summer: raptors (Goshawk, Sparrowhawk, Kestrel, Peregrine); Hazelhen, Capercaillie; Woodcock; Tengmalm's Owl, Black Woodpecker; Crag Martin; Water Pipit; Bonelli's and Wood Warblers; Spotted Flycatcher; Wheatear, Ring Ouzel, Fieldfare; Wallcreeper, Treecreeper, Citril Finch, Crossbill, Siskin; Nutcracker, Raven.

Autumn: a well known site for resting migrant Dotterel.

Access

From Pontarlier (to the north) take the N57 towards Vallorbe (in Switzerland) as far as Hôpitaux-Neufs. From here turn right on the D49 and then the D45 towards Mouthe. Having passed Les Longevilles-Mont-d'Or, turn left towards the Mont-d'Or and park at the summit. There are two possible walks. The first: leave the car park ①, go to the highest point on the Mont d'Or and follow the ridge northwards as far as

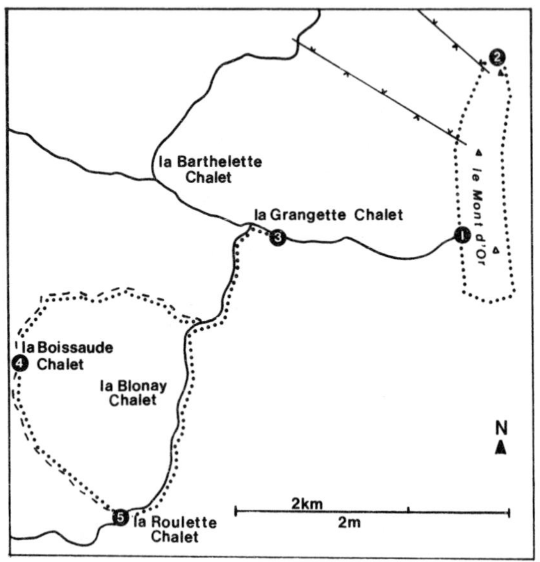

Belvédère des Chamois (the Chamois viewpoint) ②; return by the highest alpine meadows. The second walk: return down the road as far as la Grangette chalet ③ (about 1 km (0.6 mile) from the parking place), park somewhere near. Walk along the road leading to la Boissaude chalet ④ then pass near la Roulette chalet ⑤ and return to the original spot, staying on the road.

Species

- In late August and early September, with luck the Dotterel can be seen on the higher alpine meadows.
- Peregrine and Kestrel nest on the cliff-face.
- Raven also occur here (Wallcreeper too, but it's much more difficult to find – use patience, a good telescope and don't give up, even when you get a sore neck).
- Water Pipit and Skylark nest on the upper meadows.
- Wheatear are often seen perched on the small walls or piles of stones.
- Tengmalm's Owl's (a nesting bird) song, is heard from March to May.
- Crossbill, Treecreeper and Siskin nest in the forest.
- Nutcrackers also nest in the forest but are very quiet after mid-March.
- Both Hazelhen and Capercaillie nest in this part of the forest but luck is needed in order to see them, particularly for the latter.

Tengmalm's Owl

- Citril Finch, Ring Ouzel and Fieldfare nest on the forest edge and in the clearer thickets.

102 THE SERRE MASSIF

5 km/3.1 miles
Pontailler-sur-Saône
(IGN 3223 west – 1/25 000)

Habitat and Timing

The Serre Massif (altitude 400 m) is one of the rare granitic outcrops of Franche-Comté. It dominates the limestone or stony valleys of the Ognon to the north and Doubs to the south. Most of it is covered with either Sessile Oak or mixed oak/beech woodland; some plots have been planted with conifers. In a few places the forest has been cleared for sand extraction. There is also one of the few fine Sweet Chestnut woodlands to be found in Franche-Comté. The forest has an interesting list of breeding birds. There is free access at all times.

Calendar

Breeding season: raptors (Honey Buzzard, Goshawk, Black and Red Kites); Hazelhen (rare); Tawny Owl, Nightjar; Woodpigeon, Stock Dove; Black, Green, Great Spotted and Middle Spotted Woodpeckers; Tree

Pipit, Spotted Flycatcher; Wood and Melodious Warblers; all the forest tits, Golden Oriole.

Access

From Dole (to the south), take the D475 towards Gray as far as Moissey, from where the D37 on the right leads to the Fôret de la Serre. There is a disused sandpit at the entrance to the forest ①. Continue to the top and turn left on the 'Chemin de la Poste', follow this road for about 1 km (0.6 miles). Park on the right of the road ②. Go on foot as far as 'La Grotte de

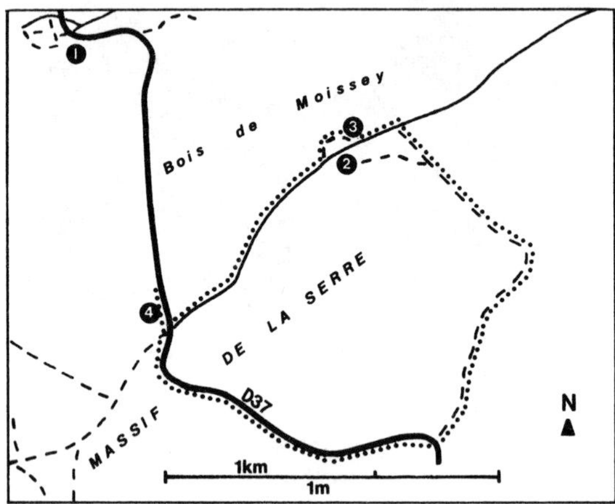

l'Ermitage' ③, then on to the source. From here take the track to the right to return to the road. Follow this for about 100 m (110 yards) to the north-east then turn right onto the straight forest track. Follow this for 700 m (765 yards) to a small dale where the track turns right. Follow it as far as the tarmac road. Take the road to the right as far as the sandpits ④. Turn around and go back to the Chemin de la Poste, then turn left and it is back to the parking place.

Species

- Little Owl nest in the wooden huts.
- Melodious Warbler and Cirl Bunting occur in the bushes on the edge of the sandpits. Golden Oriole can be seen in the surrounding trees.
- Mistle and Song Thrushes, Blackbird, Dunnock – they all occur in this part of the forest.
- Goshawk and Red Kite nest in the small valley.
- Stock Dove can be found in the beech wood.
- Great Spotted Woodpecker can be seen along the track. There are many Black Woodpecker holes and Middle Spotted Woodpeckers nest in the trees in the small valley.
- Nightjar nests on the edges of the sandpits.
- Tree Pipits occur where the forest is less dense. Grey Wagtail can be found on the side of the stream.

103 Baume-les-Messieurs Cirque

The western edge of the Jura Massif, to the north of Lons-le-Saunier, is broken by a number of steep-sided valleys called 'reculées' locally. The most interesting of these is Baume-les-Messieurs Cirque, a well-known site. This area is the vineyard of the Jura and is very mountainous. Under immense limestone cliffs, Downy Oak grows on the steep slopes and scree. The presence of Box trees shows the prevailing Mediterranean climate. There are, therefore, many southern species, including Short-toed Eagle, Alpine Swift, Crag Martin, Ortolan and Rock Buntings and Bonelli's Warbler; these occur alongside Peregrine and Raven.

104 THE LOWER DOUBS VALLEY AT PETIT-NOIR

7.5 km/4.65 miles
Pierre-de-Bresse
(IGN 3125 east – 1/25 000)

Habitat and Timing

The lower Doubs Valley, downstream of Dole, is a wide alluvial plain where crops (cereals, sugar-beet) are mixed with large meadows. Here the Doubs meanders greatly, its banks wooded. The meanders, ox-bow lakes, and sand and gravel banks form a series of habitats. A good example of these habitats can be found near Petit-Noir, especially at the meander of the Doubs where there is a vast reed-bed. In places, the right bank of the river is a sandbank two or three metres high, much loved by some riverside birds. Sand and gravel banks and riverside woodland form the dominant habitat. This is an important area for nesting species (herons, warblers) as well as those on migration (gulls, marsh terns, waders). There is unrestricted access.

Calendar

Spring (April and May): Osprey; marsh terns, Common Tern, 'shanks, Ringed Plovers.

Summer: Great Crested and Little Grebes, many Grey Herons, Purple and Night Herons, Little Egret, Little Bittern; raptors (Marsh, Hen and Montagu's Harriers, Black Kite, Hobby, Kestrel, Buzzard); Quail, Grey Partridge, Pheasant; Water Rail; Curlew, Little Ringed Plover, Stone Curlew, nesting Common Sandpiper; Little, Scops and Long-eared Owls; Cuckoo, Hoopoe, a Bee-eater colony; Turtle Dove, Lesser Spotted Woodpecker, Wryneck; Sand Martin colony, Blue-headed Wagtail; Nightingale, Bluethroat, Whitethroat, Lesser Whitethroat, Grasshopper, Savi's, Reed, Great Reed, Sedge, Icterine and Melodious Warblers; Corn and Cirl Buntings, Stonechat, Whinchat; Woodchat and Red-backed Shrikes.

Autumn (August): the same species as in spring plus large roosts of hirundines, Starlings and White Wagtails in the Vieux Doubs reed-bed.

Access

From Dole (to the north-east) take the N73 towards Chalon-sur-Saône as far as the small village of Beauchemin (about 20 km/12.15 miles). From here turn left towards Petit-Noir. On reaching the outskirts of Petit-Noir, turn immediately right and go straight on (crossing two crossroads) as far as the side of the Vieux Doubs. After turning sharp right, take the first track on the left and park on the embankment ①. For the walk, follow the embankment for about 1 km (0.6 miles) then take the farm track on the right as far as the Doubs where there is a high sandbank ②. Continue along the riverside as far as the ruins ③. Rejoin the track and go back to the embankment. Follow this as far as the south end of the ox-bow lake.

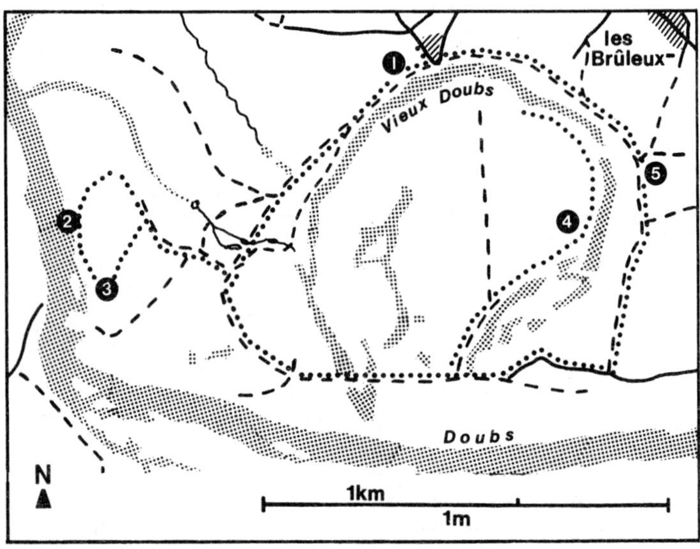

To the left and right are many ponds and bushes. The ow-bow can be watched from the track on the embankment ④, but it is a dead end, so return by the same track. Follow the river embankment as far as the south-east of the ox-bow then turn left on a track leading northwards. After crossing a small canal ⑤, follow the ox-bow as far as the starting point.

Species

- In July and August there is a hirundine and Starling roost in the reed-bed.
- Both Purple Heron and Little Bittern breed in the reed-bed, Night Heron and Little Egret do not nest but are often present in summer.
- The three harriers (Marsh, Hen and Montagu's) hunt over the water-meadows.
- Kingfisher, Sand Martin and Bee-eater all nest in the sandbanks.
- Common Sandpipers nest on the banks of the Doubs. Little Ringed Plover and Stone Curlew (difficult to find) nest on the gravel banks.
- Warblers (*Acrocephalus*, *Locustella* and *Hippolais*) as well as

Nightingale and Bluethroat nest in bushes and reeds on the side of the embankment.

- In the large trees overlooking the ox-bow lake, Lesser Spotted Woodpecker and Wryneck may be found.
- Woodchat Shrike and Golden Oriole can also be found here.
- Whinchat, Red-backed Shrike, Blue-headed Wagtail and Corn Bunting nest in the water-meadows.

105 VAIVRE-VESOUL LAKE AND FLOOD-PLAIN

4 km/2.5 miles
Port-sur-Saône
(IGN 3321 east – 1/25 000)
and Vesoul
(IGN 3421 west – 1/25 000)

Habitat and Timing

This is a 90-hectare lake built at the end of the 1970s. Urban sprawl and leisure complexes (camp site, sailing club) fringe the east, south and west sides; there is a vegetation covered island to the north of the lake. Its northern boundary is formed by the embankment of the Durgeon River with its flood-plain beyond. A footpath goes around the lake.

This is a migratory stop-over point for many aquatic species (duck, waders, gulls); the flood-plain is also interesting during the breeding season. There is unrestricted access. The northern part of the lake is protected (a reserve with no hunting or fishing). Leisure activities on the lake are prohibited during the winter months.

Calendar

Winter: dabbling duck (all the European species but especially Teal) and diving duck (Pochard, Tufted Duck, scoters, Goldeneye, sawbills); Black and Red-throated Divers, grebes (Great Crested, Red-necked, Slavonian); Shelduck, Greylag Goose, Lapwing, Curlew. There are large roosts of Water Pipit and Black-headed Gull, sometimes with Little and Common Gulls.

Spring: Black-necked Grebe, Cormorant and particularly waders, gulls and terns; all the 'shanks, Curlew, Whimbrel, Black-tailed Godwit, Lapwing, marsh terns, Common Tern, Little Gull. A stop-over site for Osprey (April), Black and Red Kites.

Summer: Garganey; Black Kite, Hobby, Montagu's Harrier; Corncrake; Curlew, Lapwing, Snipe; Blue-headed Wagtail, Sedge Warbler, Whinchat, Reed and Corn Buntings.

Autumn: Cormorant; Osprey; flocks of Lapwing and Golden Plover, Dunlin; Crane; ducks and Greylag Goose.

Access

The site is best visited in the morning (in the evening start the visit at the sailing club). From Vesoul, take the D13 towards Fresne-Saint-Mamès

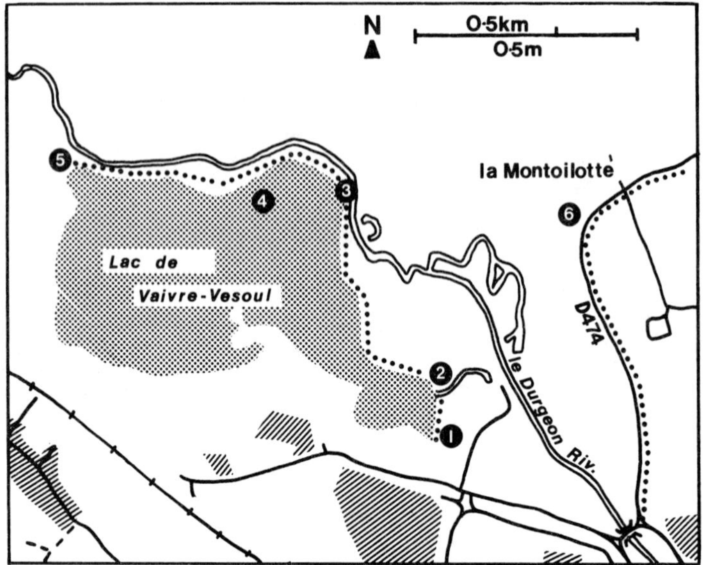

and follow the signs to the 'Lac' and the 'Camping'. Leave the car at the car park near the camp site ①. The walk: go towards the lake via the camp site, cross the wooden bridge ② and walk along the lake side on the path. Watching is possible from the embankment ③ near to the island ④. Follow the path as far as the sailing club ⑤; from here you can look over the plain to the north of the lake. Return by same route.

In order to birdwatch on the flood-plain (to the north of the lake), take the car towards Vesoul and turn left (about 800m/875 yards from the camp site) towards Pusey, passing a bridge over the Durgeon River. From here the plain can be seen on the left of the road ⑥, for a distance of about 1 km (0.6 miles). You can walk onto the plain.

Species

- A good area for nesting passerines (Sedge Warbler, Reed Bunting, Blue-headed Wagtail, Whinchat).
- Dabbling duck (Teal, Gadwall, Wigeon), diving duck (scoters, Goldeneye, sawbills), divers and grebes can be numerous in winter.
- Grey Heron, Cormorant (in winter) and duck frequently roost on the island).
- Diving duck (Pochard and Tufted Duck) feed to the north of the island.
- Waders ('shanks, Lapwing, Curlew, Snipe) rest on the plain during migration. In winter only Curlew and Lapwing occur.
- The Osprey can often be seen perched on an electricity pylon on the plain eating fish caught from the lake (in April and August).
- An area where Lapwing and Snipe nest.

106 Ognon Valley

Ognon Valley, above Marnay, is a wide flood-plain of alternating meadows and marshland. It is particularly interesting during times of migration. It is easy to see many waders (Curlew, Black-tailed Godwit, Jack Snipe, Lapwing, Golden Plover) and also Cormorant, Crane and Bean Goose. Osprey often hunt here and the three harriers nest. In the reedbeds on the side of the Ognon (or in the old ox-bow lakes of this river), Sedge, Reed, Great Reed, Savi's and Grasshopper Warblers nest, as well as Little Bittern and Water Rail.

107 The Saône Plain

Thanks to its north-east/south-west orientation, the Saône Valley is a natural corridor for many migrating species. Between Port-sur-Saône and Membrey it is particularly wide and, therefore, very attractive to migrants. Most of the area is taken up by meadows and a few crops, but there is some marshland. The Crane is seen in spring and autumn as well as Osprey, Greylag and Bean Geese and Whooper Swan. Waders are frequent: Lapwing, Golden Plover, Black-tailed Godwit and Ruff. Curlew, Montagu's and Hen Harriers and Corncrake occur during the breeding period.

108 Sundgau

Part of the Alsace Plain, consisting mainly of alluvial deposits, the Sundgau extends north-eastwards from Delle. There is undulating countryside with many forest lakes, most of the forest is made up of oak. The most interesting part lies around Faverois. In spring and autumn, terns, marsh terns, 'shanks, and small waders are all frequent; the Osprey is present between the end of March and the end of April. Black Stork occur regularly and may well nest in the neighbourhood. Among the more interesting nesting species are: Garganey and Teal, Hobby, Curlew, Little Ringed Plover and Lapwing.

ÎLE-DE-FRANCE

109 BOIS DE BOULOGNE

6.5 km/4 miles
Paris
(IGN 2314 west – 1/25 000)

Habitat and Timing

This is the last vestige of Rouvray Forest, which surrounded Paris on its northern and western sides two thousand years ago. A forest in excess of 142,000 trees, more than half of which are oak. There are three principal water bodies (Lac Supérieur, Lac Inférieur and the Mare Saint-James), created in the nineteenth century and filled by a network of streams. Most of the birds that occur are passerines. It is possible on occasion to see water birds, particularly in winter. There is unrestricted access except into the enclosures of recently-planted trees. It is best to go in the early morning in order to avoid the numerous visitors, especially in summer.

Calendar

Winter: Pochard, Tufted Duck; Black-headed Gull, northern passerines (Redwing, Fieldfare, Siskin, Redpoll, Brambling).

Spring: Willow, Wood and Garden Warblers, Chiffchaff, Blackcap, Redstart, House Martin and Spotted Flycatcher all nest. Cuckoo, Golden Oriole, Nightingale, Whitethroat, Swallow and Pied Flycatcher all occur on passage.

All year: resident species include: Tawny Owl, Green, Great Spotted

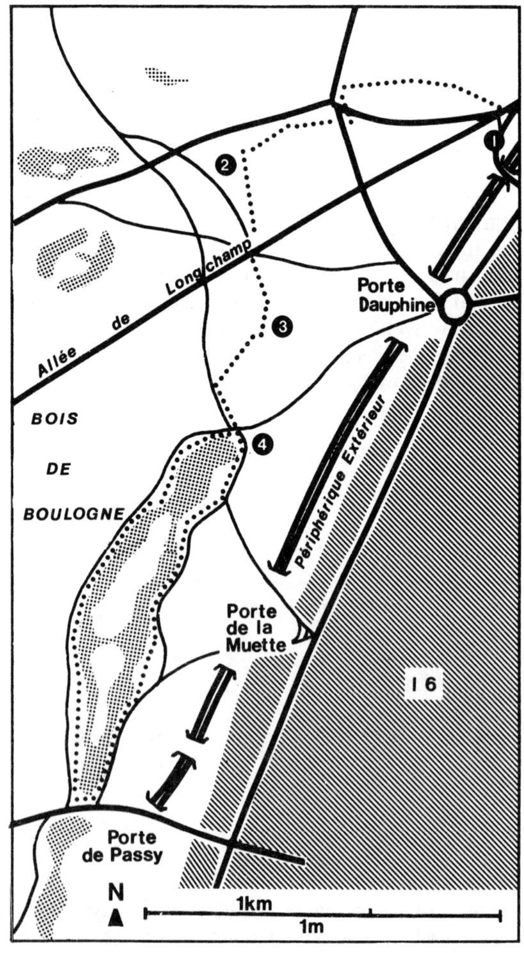

and Lesser Spotted Woodpeckers; Nuthatch, Short-toed Treecreeper, tits (seven species), Goldcrest, Bullfinch.

Access

By Paris Metro, on the N°1 line (Château de Vincennes–Pont de Neuilly); get off at Porte Maillot station (using the Côté Neuilly–avenu-Charles-de-Gaulle exit). Walk along the Rue J.-et-M.-Hackin, cross the Boulevard André-Maurois and go to the station for the Jardin d'Acclimatation narrow-gauge railway, near to where the walk begins ①. Go as far as the Carrefour des Sablons passing through a pine wood. Turn left (Route de la Porte Dauphine) then right (Allée des Marroniers). After 200 m (220 yards) turn left ② and follow the Ruisseau des Sablons (Sablons stream). Cross the Allée de Longchamp then take the sand track keeping to the right along the cycle track ③ which follows the Ruisseau d'Armenonville as far as the Route de la Muette at Neuilly. Once here, turn left to arrive at the Lac Inférieur ④; you can go right round the lake. At its southern limit you can watch over Lac Supérieur. Return by the same route.

Species

- Great Spotted Woodpecker is easily seen, especially in winter.
- Black Redstarts can be seen around buildings, Spotted Flycatchers in the larger trees.
- Around the Île des Cèdres, Garden and Willow Warblers, Chiffchaff and Blackcap can be seen in the trees between April and July.
- Nuthatch and Long-tailed Tit can be seen year-round.
- Pochard and Tufted Duck can be seen on the Lac Inférieur in winter.
- In autumn and winter, Moorhen and Coot can be seen, and more rarely Little Grebe.
- In the spring, Swifts and House Martins fly low over the water catching insects.

110 Bois de Vincennes

Bois de Vincennes is in many ways similar to the Bois de Boulogne, at least as far as birds are concerned. Above all, it is interesting for passerines; it also has water birds in winter (particularly Pochard and Tufted Duck) in greater numbers than at the other site. Like the Bois de Boulogne it is best to go early in the morning in order to avoid the general public.

111 CHANFROY PLAIN NATURE RESERVE/ TROIS-PIGNONS FOREST

4 km/2.5 miles
Fontainebleau
(IGN 2417 west – 1/25 000)

Habitat and Timing

A stony and sandy plain, dotted here and there with thorny bushes and broom. It has the appearance of steppe. There are a few permanent pools in some of the depressions. The area is most interesting for the passerines associated with this sort of habitat (rare elsewhere in the Île-de-France). In addition, such a diversity of habitats in such a small area allows for the observation of a large number of species. The best conditions for watching occur in the very early morning, when it is not too hot, and disturbance caused by walkers, who can be numerous at weekends, is at its lowest.

Calendar

Spring and autumn: migrants (Hoopoe, Cuckoo, pipits, redstarts, chats, Ring Ouzel) and raptors. Nightjar, Woodlark, Dartford Warbler and Red-backed Shrike all nest.

Access

From Fontainebleau, take the D409 at the Obélisque crossroads as far as Arbonne-la-Forêt. From here take the D64 towards Achères-la-Forêt, and about 800 m (875 yards) along this road (and immediately after the Corne-Biche Stud-farm) turn left along a forest track. There is a car park at the end of this road ①. Leave the care here (beware of break-ins!) and continue along the main track towards the plain. Many tracks cross the area passing through the better sites. Some areas are fenced-off in order to avoid the trampling of some plant species growing there. Before arriving on the plain the track crosses an interesting wooded area ②. Tracks leave to the right crossing an area of heath. The plain's ponds ③ should be looked at carefully. You can continue eastwards, on the plain,

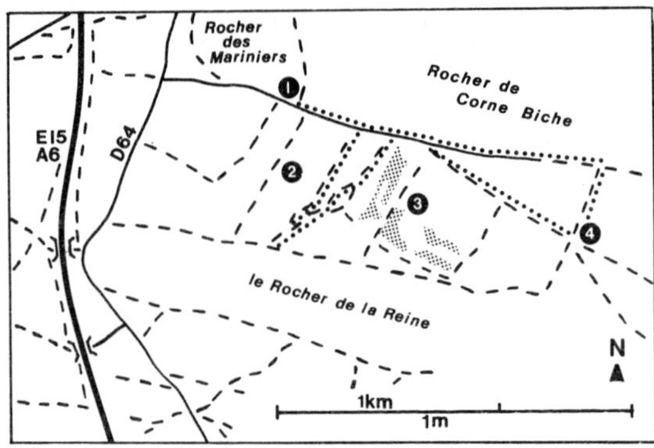

following the Allée des Fusillés forest track. After 750 m (820 yards) turn left ④, then left again 300 m (330 yards) further on, and return on this track to the car park.

Species

- In the wooded part of the plain, in spring, it is easy to find Wood, Willow and Bonelli's Warblers and Chiffchaff.
- Dartford Warbler nest in the heather.
- Woodlark nests on Chanfroy Plain; Ring Ouzel is a regular passage migrant, in April.
- The ponds have Reed Warblers in the breeding season.
- During periods of migration Stonechat, Whinchat and Wheatear can be seen perched on posts; Tawny Pipit is regularly seen on the plain in May and September.
- Buzzard, Honey Buzzard and Sparrowhawk hunt over the open parts of the plain.
- With a little luck you can see Woodcock and Nightjar.

112 Fontainebleau Forest

Fontainebleau Forest, some 60 km (37.3 miles) south-east of Paris, is a real paradise for the naturalist and particularly the birdwatcher. A spring visit to the two nature reserves La Tillaie and Le Gros-Fouteau, to the north-west of Fontainebleau, may well produce Grey-headed, Green, Black, Great, Middle and Lesser Spotted Woodpeckers, Redstart, and Pied Flycatcher (rare elsewhere in the Île-de-France) which nests here. Buzzard, Honey Buzzard, Sparrowhawk and Hobby nest in the forest. There are also all the passerines typical of the woodlands of northern France.

113 Cannes-Écluse Lakes and Surroundings

The Seine and Yonne Valleys above Montereau can be interesting for water birds throughout the year. In winter, the lakes at Cannes-Écluse have hundreds of duck (essentially diving duck). Grebes are numerous (Red-necked and Slavonian are noted almost annually), and there are often Cormorant. Rarer species may be present (divers, sawbills, Eider and scoters aren't exceptional). Further up river the many flooded sandpits are used in spring and summer by waders and gulls. The area also has a large population of breeding Common Terns.

114 SAINT-QUENTIN-EN-YVELINES NATIONAL NATURE RESERVE

1.5 km/0.9 miles
Versailles
(IGN 2214 east – 1/25 000)

Habitat and Timing

Bordered on its western side by settling-beds which intermittently contain water, the reserve is at the shallowest part of the Saint-Quentin-en-Yvelines Lake. This part, studded with areas of bulrush and reed, is remarkable for its over-wintering duck and the number of waders on uncovered mudflats in summer. Access to the reserve is strictly controlled.

Calendar

Winter: Mallard, Shoveler, Teal, Pochard, Large Black-headed Gull roost.

Spring: Great Crested Grebe, Greylag Goose, many duck; Black-headed Gull; Marsh Harrier; Black-tailed Godwit; Black Tern; Swift, hirundines; Grasshoper Warbler.

Autumn: Grey Heron, Cormorant, waders (especially 'shanks), wetland passerines.

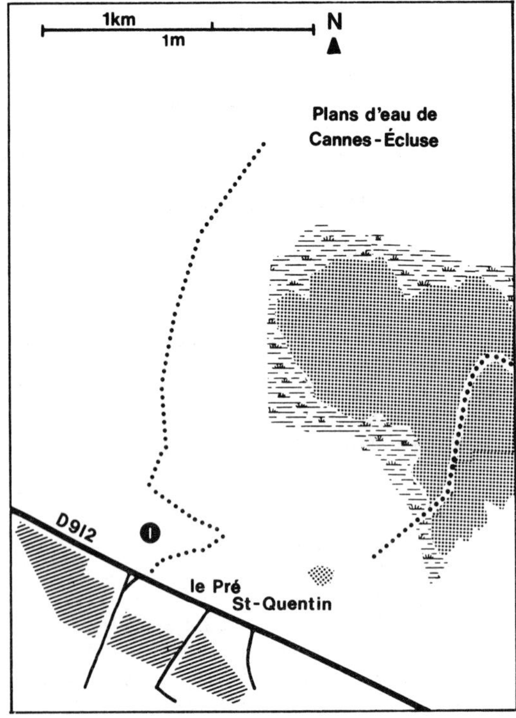

Access

From Paris, take the A13 (Autoroute de l'Ouest) as far as the Rocquencourt interchange, then go towards Dreux as far as the traffic-lights in Trappes. Turn right on the old N12 and then right again onto the car park called the 'Parc-Étang' ①. If coming by train, from Montparnasse station in Paris take trains going to Rambouillet and get off at Trappes. Cross the N10 to get to the Parc-Étang car park.

There are two ways to visit the site: – either using the free access around the periphery of the reserve, watching from points overlooking the reserve; – or a guided visit into the reserve (for small groups), except during the breeding season.

Species

- In autumn and winter, Chaffinch, Greenfinch, Goldfinch, Linnet and Bullfinch use the Blackthorn bushes.
- In spring the reed-bed resounds to the raucous cries of nesting Black-headed Gulls. There is a large roost of this species in winter.
- Mallard, Shoveler, Pochard and Tufted Duck can be seen on the lake between October and March.
- During times of migration, 'shanks and Snipe occur on the lake's mudflats and the nearby settling-beds.
- The northern part of the lake is used by roosting Grey Herons.

115 Noës Lake

At the centre of a water complex to the south-west of Paris, Noës Lake in Mesnil-Saint-Denis parish is the most important wintering site for Shoveler in the Île-de-France. It also serves as a refuge for ducks disturbed from Saint-Quentin-en-Yvelines Lake, close by. This lake is most interesting in the autumn and winter for dabbling duck (Mallard, Shoveler, Gadwall, Teal) which find relative calm even though the lake covers only a small area (about 40 hectares). For all the birds either on the water or near the edge, watch from a track that goes round the lake.

116 SAINT-HUBERT LAKES/ LE PERRAY-EN-YVELINES

9.5 km/5.8 miles (3.5 km/2.8 miles on foot, obligatory) Trappes (IGN 2215 west – 1/25 000)

Habitat and Timing

On the edge of Rambouillet National Forest, there are six lakes to the south-east of Saint-Léger-en-Yvelines Forest.

Four of these (Saint-Hubert, Pourras, Corbet and Bourgneuf), some of which are still covered with large reed-beds, are still biologically interesting and present a complex of aquatic habitats, remarkable for duck, herons and wetland passerines. There is no right-of-way to the lake edges; the embankments separating the lakes are the best places for watching.

Species

Winter: Mallard, Pochard, Lapwing, Golden Plover, Hen Harrier (open areas).

Spring: on migration, Black Tern, hirundines, Swift. Great Crested Grebe, Little Bittern, Black-headed Gull, Great Reed, Reed and Sedge Warblers nest.

Autumn: Cormorant, Grey and Purple Herons, Greylag Goose, sometimes Osprey.

Access

From Paris, take the A13 (Autoroute de l'Ouest) as far as the Rocquencourt interchange, then go towards Dreux on the N10, which you leave at the Le Perrey-en-Yvelines exit. Turn left on the N191 and go as far as the first embankment. The other embankments are visited via the D61 going towards Bréviaires. If coming by rail, catch the train at Montparnasse station in Paris going to Rambouillet, and get off at Perray-en-Yvelines station, walk to the embankment by crossing the village. The lake banks are out of bounds. From the first embankment ①, you can get to the Napoleon embankment ② by taking the track that starts behind Saint-Hubert Château. From here the first two lakes can be seen particularly well from the bridge.

Then back to the N191 and after 1.5 km (0.9 miles) turn left along the Chaussée-Neuve forestry road as far as the embankment separating the two lakes, Pourras and Corbet ③. It is possible to watch from this embankment. Then onto the plain ④, parking the car near the Ferme du

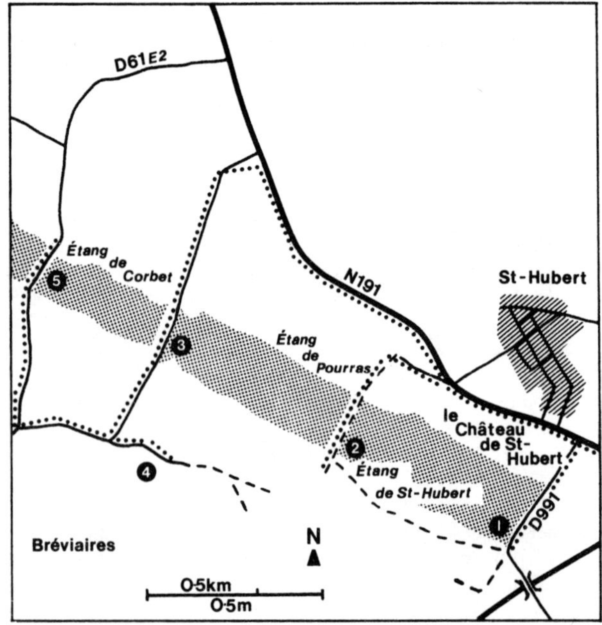

Moulin. If you want to it is possible to get to Bourgneuf Lake embankment ⑤ by taking the D61 for about 500 m (550 yards) and turning right.

Species

- Great Crested Grebe nest in the reed-beds at Saint-Hubert and Pourras Lakes.
- During spring and autumn, Mallard, Pintail, Shoveler, Pochard and Tufted Duck occur, sometimes in large numbers.
- It is mainly in the spring that large numbers of Swift, Swallow and Sand Martin can be seen hunting over the lakes.
- Reed and Great Reed Warblers can be seen in the reed-beds in spring.
- Grey Heron can be seen throughout most of the year.
- Look on the posts in the water for Cormorants during the spring and autumn.
- The best chance of seeing Little Bittern is by standing on the embankment between Corbet and Pourras Lakes, hoping for one to cross the latter.
- Black-headed Gulls nest in places on this same embankment.
- Lapwing and Golden Plover can be seen on Perray Plain in autumn and winter.
- Hen Harrier occur on this plain in winter.

117 L'ÉTANG-VIEUX DE SACLAY NATIONAL NATURE RESERVE

400 m/440 yards
Antony
(IGN 2315 west – 1/25 000)

Habitat and Timing

Saclay lakes, like those of Saint-Quentin and Saint-Hubert, were built in the seventeenth century to supply the châteaux of Versailles. They have been much studied by Parisian ornithologists ever since they became a reserve in the 1950s; but it wasn't until August 1980 that the Étang-Vieux (the west lake) became a full National Nature Reserve (the first in the Île-de-France). The land still belongs to the Ministry of Defence, so that access is very restricted, but it is possible to birdwatch from the road that separates the Étang-Vieux from the Étang-Neuf.

In winter, Saturday and Sunday mornings are often the best times for duck, they come to Étang-Vieux at Saclay having been disturbed at other lakes in the area (hunting, fishing, watersports).

Calendar

Winter: Great Crested Grebe, Grey Heron; Mallard, Shoveler, Wigeon, Pintail, Teal, Pochard, Tufted Duck; Smew and Goosander sometimes occur in February.

Spring: Great Crested Grebe, Greylag Goose (February and March);

Common Sandpiper, Redshank, Little Ringed Plover, Little Gull, Common Tern, Black and Whiskered Terns; Kingfisher, Swift, hirundines.

Autumn: Cormorant, Grey Heron; Shoveler, Gadwall, Teal; Snipe, Lapwing, Golden Plover; migrant passerines.

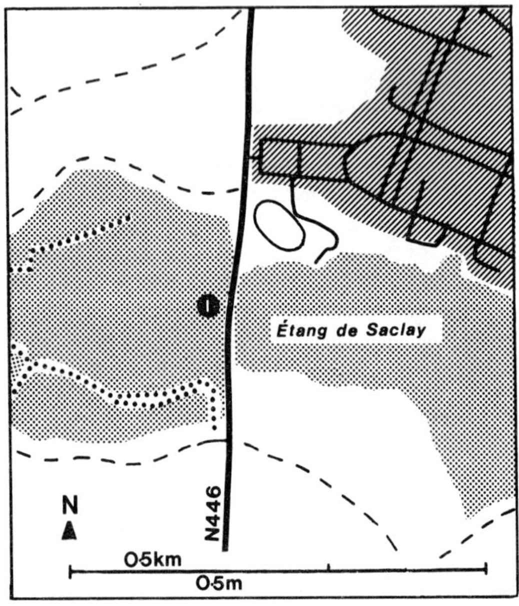

Access

Take the N446 that goes between Christ-de-Saclay and Jouy-en-Josas; take the Saclay exit on the F18 (Paris, Pont de Sèvres–Chartres–Orléans) motorway. It is easy to stop the car on the roadside and birdwatch from a small promontory between the two lakes ①. Access to the rest of the lake is forbidden.

Species

- Great Crested Grebe, visible the whole year, is a common enough nester on both lakes.
- In spring, Swift and hirundines actively hunt insects over the water.
- Duck often flock together in the middle of the Étang-Neuf.
- Black Terns may accompany Swifts in their search for food, Black-headed Gulls are often perched on the vegetation covering the small islands on the right of the lake.
- Cormorants and Grey Herons perch in the dead trees on the lake side.

118 Saulx-les-Chartreux Reserve

Saulx-les-Chartreux Nature Reserve (35 hectares) comprises a reservoir (seven to ten hectares depending on the water-level) primarily used for the regulation of flooding by the Yvette River, and small islands surrounded by arms of the river which form the actual reserve. A tour of the site is made easy by the presence of a raised path (a 'parcours de santé – a health circuit) from which the whole area where birds are likely to be seen can be surveyed. Throughout the year there are Great Crested Grebe, Little Grebe, Grey Heron, Mute Swan, Mallard and Coot; Black-headed Gull and migrant passerines often occur. In winter you can see many species of duck, especially Pochard and Tufted Duck, and in autumn small numbers of waders may pass through ('shanks, Ringed Plovers), depending on the water level. Access is easy from the N20. From Paris, take the Saulx-les-Chartreux exit and turn right towards Saulx-centre and Villebon on the southern side of the CD118. The first road on the right, Route de Champlan, leads to the main car park.

119 Bruyères-le-Châtel Reservoir

Bruyères-le-Châtel Reservoir lies about 35 km (21.75 miles) to the south-west of Paris. To get there, turn left on the D82 after Bruyères church. The reservoir is about 2 km (1.25 miles) from the centre of Bruyères, flanked on both sides by rivers, the Rémarde and the Orge; a footpath goes round the reservoir. Great Crested Grebe, Grey Heron, Mallard, Coot and Black-headed Gull can be seen at all times. In winter there are many species of dabbling duck (Wigeon, Teal) and diving duck (Pochard, Tufted Duck), and in autumn and spring a few waders and many migrant passerines.

120 VILLE-D'AVRAY LAKES AND FAUSSES-REPOSES WOOD

2 km/1.25 miles
Paris-west
(IGN 2314 west – 1/25 000)

Habitat and Timing

Ville-d'Avray occupies the bottom and sides of a wooded valley to the south-west of Paris, between Saint-Cloud and Versailles. Two small lakes surrounded by Fausses-Reposes Wood, well known thanks to the painter Corot and the works of Jean Rostand, lie side by side. The sides are planted with willows, alder, ash, lime and Cypress. At the top end of each lake a small reed-bed is home to a few aquatic species. The close proximity of woodland (oaks, beech, ash, birch and Hornbeam) means that many passerines and woodpeckers can also be seen.

Calendar

Winter: Pochard; Black-headed Gull, Great Spotted, Lesser Spotted and Green Woodpeckers; Crested, Coal, Marsh and Long-tailed Tits; Redpoll, Siskin, Goldfinch.

Spring and summer: Mute Swan, Coot, Swift, Swallow, House Martin, Redstart, Blackcap, Chiffchaff, Willow Warbler, Goldcrest, Spotted Flycatcher and Pied Flycatcher on migration.

Autumn: Grey Heron and passing Greylag Geese.

Access

Coming from Paris via the Pont-de-Sèvres, turn right towards Ville-d'Avray once in Sèvres. At Ville-d'Avray church crossroads turn left on the Rue de Versailles (N185) and take the second or third on the left to get to the lakes. Park at either of two small car parks ① and ②. The tour of the

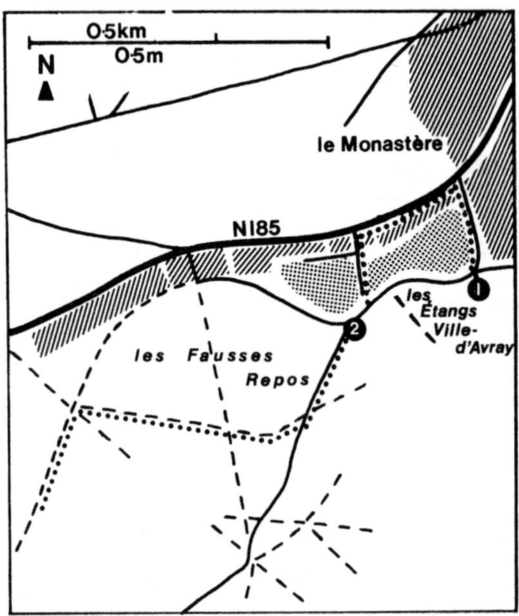

lakes takes about half-an-hour. For a walk in the woods, where many passerines can be seen, take the track that continues on from that of the Vieil-Étang and climb up to the left, along the valley side. It is also possible to take the tarmac track which climbs through the woods behind Vieil-Étang car park towards Chaville and Versailles.

Species

- Mute Swan, Mallard, Coot and Moorhen regularly nest on the lakes. Pochard join them in winter.
- Swift, Swallow and House Martin nesting in the vicinity come to hunt insects over the lakes.
- Many passerines can be seen by walking the paths in Fausses-Reposes wood; Redstart, Blackcap, Wood Warbler, Chiffchaff, Crested, Coal, Marsh and Long-Tailed Tits, Nuthatch, Spotted Flycatcher and Bullfinch all nest.
- In winter other species such as Redpoll and Siskin can be seen.
- Towards the end of winter, at sunset, Tawny Owls start to sing.

121 Sceaux Park

This large and varied park merits a visit. Passerines are numerous, especially in spring and autumn. In winter there are Fieldfare, Redwing, Siskin and sometimes Redpoll. During migration (spring and autumn) many passerines pass through the park and water birds occur on the large lake (duck and grebe).

122 Saint-Cloud Park

Parc Saint-Cloud lies near Ville-d'Avray. It comprises gardens and woodland (English Oak, Hornbeam, lime and many sorts of conifer). Many of the species present at Ville d'Avray can be seen, except the water birds. Among others: Green, Great Spotted and Lesser Spotted Woodpeckers; Short-toed Treecreeper, Song Thrush; Blackcap, Wood Warbler, Crested and Long-tailed Tits, Bullfinch and Jay.

123 La Courneuve County Park

6 km/3.75 miles
Paris-east
(IGN 2314 east – 1/25 000)

Habitat and Timing

A landscaped park built on what was once marshland, part filled with waste material; in other parts lakes have been dug. There are various types of woodland and large meadows (at least for some time to come), and damp and dry scrub. There are heavily-urbanised areas to the south and west, but to the north-east the site opens onto agricultural land and Bourget Airport. It is interesting for birds thanks to its position and its diverse habitats.

Calendar

Winter: Mallard, Pochard, Tufted Duck; Black-headed Gull, Coot, Reed Bunting. Also, more rarely, Long-eared Owl (roost), Brambling, Goldcrest and Firecrest, Coal Tit, Hawfinch.

Spring: Great Crested Grebe, Little Grebe; 'shanks; Stonechat, Wheatear, Willow Warbler. Less frequently, Garganey, Sparrowhawk, Black Kite, Woodcock, Ring Ouzel, Penduline Tit, Redpoll.

Breeding season: Great Crested Grebe, Little Grebe, Moorhen; Little Ringed Plover; Reed and Marsh Warblers. Also, Long-eared Owl, Kestrel, Cirl Bunting, and exceptionally Little Bittern.

Autumn: large flocks of passerines (Redwing, Fieldfare, Linnet, Serin, Greenfinch, Goldfinch, buntings).

Access

From Paris take the Metro (line 7) as far as Aubervilliers Fort, then the 149 bus or the RER (line B) as far as Aubervilliers–La Corneuve station,

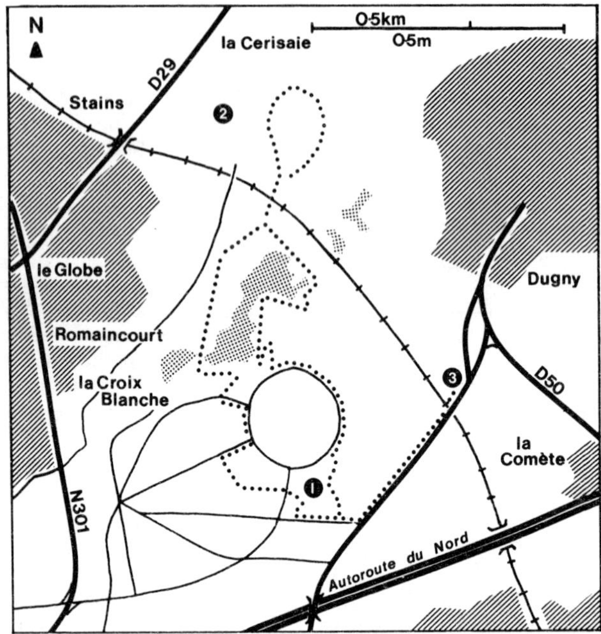

and finally the 150 (or 250) bus, which arrives at the south-west of the park. By car there are various possibilities. The main car park ① is opposite the cemetery on the D114 (beware: the park closes at sunset).

The proposed circuit is about a three-hour walk and passes through most habitats, but not scrub ② to which there is restricted access. It is also possible to look for birds on the settling-beds opposite the station ③.

Species

- The deciduous woodland holds Green, Great Spotted and Lesser Spotted Woodpeckers, and in spring, Golden Oriole can be heard.
- Long-eared Owls occur in the pine wood throughout the year.
- Here also, in winter, it is possible to see flocks of birds containing Goldcrests, Firecrests, Coal and Crested Tits.
- Great Crested Grebe, Little Grebe and Moorhen nest on the main lake. Coot occur in winter.
- The wet scrubland is visited by Redshank and Little Ringed Plover (which nests here), sometimes by other species of wader.
- During periods of migration, Meadow Pipit, Stonechat and Wheatear occur in the scrub.
- Reed and Sedge Warblers nest in the lake's reed-bed.
- In April and May large numbers of hirundines and Swift hunt over the settling-beds.

4 km/2.5 miles
Paris
(IGN 2314 east – 1/25 000)
and Evry
(IGN 2315 east – 1/25 000)

124 CRÉTEIL LAKE

Habitat and Timing

About 10 km (6.2 miles) to the south-east of Paris, between the Marne and Seine Rivers, on an alluvial plain, this old sandpit was not infilled and stayed intact to become Créteil Lake, in the middle of an urban area containing the Hôtel de Ville. This recreation zone was planned for leisure rather than for nature protection, so there is a lot of disturbance from the public; this disturbance only decreases in winter. Nonetheless, the lake is visited by quite a few aquatic birds particularly in autumn during the migration period, or in winter when there can be quite large numbers of duck.

Calendar

Autumn and winter: Great Crested Grebe, Mallard, Pochard, Tufted Duck, sometimes Ferruginous Duck and Scaup, Common and Velvet Scoter.

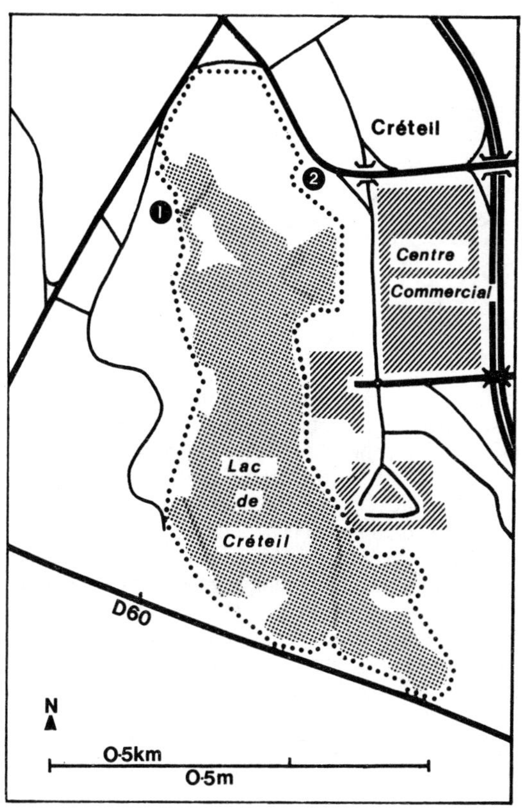

Equally, Goldeneye, Goosander and Smew (in cold winters), Coot, Common Sandpiper, Black-headed Gull.

Spring: Great Crested Grebe, Mallard, Coot, Swift and hirundines, Warblers on migration, Reed Warbler nesting.

Access

From the Pompadour crossroads, access is by the N186 (Route de Choisy) in the direction of the Préfecture, or otherwise by the D60 (Route de la Pompadour). Parking near the lake is possible almost anywhere. A public footpath goes round the lake. You can leave the car at the Rue Jean-Gabin car park ①, and follow the track that passes in front of the Maison de la Nature (nature centre). To do a complete tour, pass by the Préfecture by going up the Boulevard du Général-de-Gaulle ②. You can come by bus (392, stop 'Lac') or on the Metro (station Crétail–Préfecture).

Species

- Mallard are very tame here, taking bread from the hands of passers-by.
- Duck (particularly Pochard) rest in front of the Préfecture in winter.
- A few hundred Coot winter on the lake.
- Migrant passerines (wagtails, warblers) use the bush-covered hillocks and the grass.
- The very small reed-beds hold Reed Warblers in the spring.
- Crested Larks can be seen at the foot of the towers of Offenbach Wharf in winter.

125 L'ISLE-ADAM NATIONAL FOREST

7 km/4.35 miles
Montmorency
(IGN 2313 – 1/25 000)

Habitat and Timing

This site has four principal zones in the form of terraces which spread out progressively from the Oise Valley floor to the Communes Plain above.

Firstly, along the track between the Moulin de Stors to the Porte Noire: to the north of Isle-Adam Forest is an alternating deciduous and coniferous woodland; to the south a steep limestone hillside covered mainly with thick bush. From this high point there is a fine view over the Marais de Stors – a keepered private property, unfenced, of some 50 hectares; access is prohibited and there is no open water – part of the Abbaye du Val. Next, from the Porte Noir to the Communes Plain: the woodland changes from being almost entirely mature hardwoods to abandoned well-grown coppice (private). Then, Communes Plain: a sandy plateau used mainly for cereals, it covers about 50 hectares and still has a few copses. There is a panoramic view over Villiers-Adam, Béthemont-la-Forêt and Isle-Adam and Montmorency National Forests. Lastly, Les

Black Woodpecker

Grez: a ten-hectare hillock bathed in sun where Sessile Oak dominates; the shrub layer is made up of bracken and heather (public and private woodland).

Calendar

Winter: Buzzard, Sparrowhawk, Woodcock, thrushes.

Spring: Honey Buzzard, Water Rail, Stock Dove, Black Woodpecker, Ring Ouzel, Bonelli's and Marsh Warblers, Hawfinch and many other passerines nesting.

Autumn: raptors, geese, Cormorant on migration, Woodlark, chats, Pied Flycatcher, Chaffinch, Brambling, Greenfinch, Siskin.

Access

From Paris-Gare du Nord (railway station), take a train going to Persan-Beaumont via Valmondois, and get off at Mériel (45 minutes by train and a walk of 25 minutes as far as Moulin de Stors). By car from Paris, take the A15 motorway leaving at the Taverny exit, then take the N328 towards Méry-sur-Oise or Auvers-sur-Oise and, on entering Sognolles, get onto the N184 towards L'Isle-Adam, leaving it at Mériel.

From Cergy-Pontoise, take the N184 towards L'Isle-Adam and leave at Mériel. You can leave up to two or three cars parked at Moulin de Stors ①. Follow the Étang Coteau (hillside) and the Marais de Stors on the right to get to Porte Noire ②. From here, take the track that goes

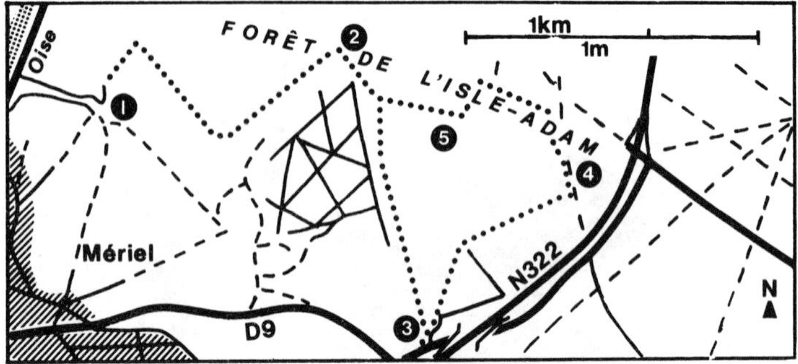

southward towards Carrière Wood ③, then go back north-eastwards in order to get to the point called the 'Petite Commune' ④, and walk along the side of the Communes Plain. Turn left and continue for 700 m (765 yards). Turn left again, then right, passing by the Grez hillock ⑤ for 350 m (380 yards). Turn right and at the Porte Noire take the same track as on arriving.

Species

- Water Rail is present year round on the lake, but it is more easily heard than seen.
- Bonelli's Warbler nests in the pine wood in small numbers (May).
- Reed, Marsh and Grasshopper Warblers can be seen around the edge of the lake.
- A good place to watch Honey Buzzard (May to August), Buzzard (winter) and Sparrowhawk.
- Woodcock are present throughout the year but are more easily seen in November and December.
- Black Woodpeckers are most active in the autumn and in very early spring.
- In the mature woodland Hawfinches are not rare.
- Ring Ouzel is a regular migrant in April, often seen on the ploughed fields.
- Stock Dove are regularly seen in the copses.
- In spring around the Grez hillock, Tree Pipit, Redstart, Wood and Willow Warblers, Chiffchaff, Crested Tit, Spotted Flycatcher and Golden Oriole can be seen. The Pied Flycatcher occurs in August and September.

126 Cergy-Pontoise Leisure Centre

A large sandpit, still in use, progressively being turned into a watersports centre, the present lake covers about 100 hectares. It can be interesting for aquatic birds in winter, especially during cold spells: grebes, diving ducks, sawbills, divers, Common, Herring and Black-headed Gulls. Waders on migration sometimes occur on the banks and Water Pipits are to be found every winter. Crested Larks are common on open areas, such as the car parks. The nearby scrub holds Stonechat, warblers, (including Melodious), buntings, Greenfinch, Goldfinch.

LANGUEDOC-ROUSSILLON

127 GRUISSAN AND CAMPIGNOL LAKE

6 km/3.75 miles
Gruissan
(IGN 2546 east – 1/25 000)

Habitat and Timing

Campignol is a brackish lake receiving fresh water from the north, and sea water from the south (whenever the wind blows from the south-east). To the west and north-east it is edged by large reed-beds and *sansouire* (a low Mediterranean saltmarsh-like vegetation) with a few tamarisks. It is a remarkable area for duck, herons, raptors and marshland passerines. There is restricted access to this reserve but observation of the birds is easy enough.

It is very shallow and adjoins Ayrolle Lake, a vast lagoon whose outlets to the sea are very interesting. On the Île Saint-Martin, lying between Ayrolle and Gruissan Lakes, there is an association of low habitats (vineyards, degraded garrigue), taller habitats (coniferous woods) and some cliffs. It has a typically Mediterranean group of birds. Lastly, the Roc de Conilhac, to the north of Campignol Lake, a small hillock rising from the marsh, is the principal migration watch point.

Calendar

Winter: Greater Flamingo, herons, Mallard, Shoveler, Wigeon, Pintail, Teal, Coot, Marsh Harrier, Bearded and Penduline Tits, buntings.

Spring and autumn: Black and White Storks; Red-crested Pochard, Pochard, Tufted Duck; Honey Buzzard, Short-toed Eagle, Osprey, Hobby, Kestrel, Merlin, Eleonora's Falcon; Black-winged Stilt, Avocet, Ringed Plovers; waders, shrikes, warblers, Chaffinch and Brambling.

Breeding season: Great Spotted Cuckoo, Black-eared Wheatear, Short-toed Lark, Mediterranean warblers.

Access

From Narbonne leave on the A9 and take the Gruissan exit (The Narbonne–Est–les Plages interchange) and get back to Gruissan village on the D32. Cross Grazel Canal (municipal camp site), take the first left then the first right in front of the camp site. Follow the side of the salt-pans for about 1 km (0.6 miles). Turn right and leave the car about 400 m (440 yards) further on, at the fishermens' huts ①. Return on this track, only this time turning left towards the rubbish-tip, going as far as the dirt-track ②. Return to Gruissan; before the canal turn left towards Mandirac, where you can look over Campignol Lake ③ and ④. Lastly, park the car at the Roc de Conilhac ⑤ (for watching during migration).

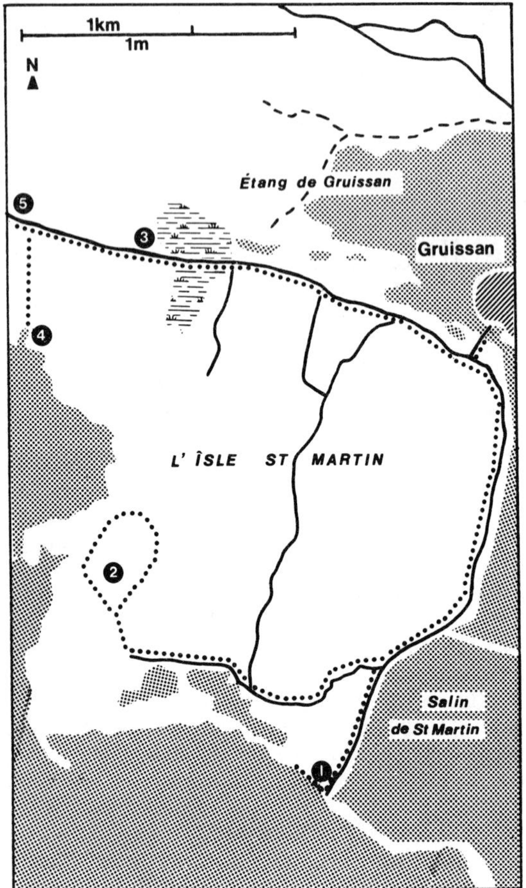

Species

- During migration, many waders stop at Ayrolle (Grey Plover and many of the smaller species), whilst others nest there (Avocet, Kentish Plover).
- Black-headed, Mediterranean and Yellow-legged Gulls and terns can often be seen (from the fishermens' huts) fishing over the sea.
- Great Spotted Cuckoo (in spring) and Hoopoe occur on the garrigue.
- It is also the place for Dartford, Sardinian and Subalpine Warblers and Black-eared Wheatear.
- From Mandirac, when conditions are good, Grey Heron, Purple Heron and Greater Flamingo can be seen.
- The reed-bed conceals many nesting and migrant passerines: Bearded and Penduline Tits. *Acrocephalus* warblers, Moustached Warbler.
- The Roc de Cornilhac is very good for watching raptors between March and May and August and November (also storks, Swift, Bee-eater and hirundines).

128 Leucate

A spring migration study point. The observation site is near the lighthouse (to the left a little after Leucate village) and is situated on the top of a limestone plateau covered in low vegetation. It overlooks the sea and Leucate Lake. A remarkable site in spring and summer. In winter, on the lake or sea, it is possible to see: Black-throated Diver, Red-breasted Merganser, Eider, Teal, Wigeon, Great Crested and Black-necked Grebes, Cormorant, Gannet. In spring, there is visible raptor passage (kites, Honey Buzzard, Short-toed Eagle, harriers, falcons), plus White and Black Storks, herons (Grey, Purple, Night) egrets (Little and Cattle), Woodpigeon, Bee-eater, Hoopoe, swifts, hirundines, wagtails, Serin, Linnet, Chaffinch. On the plateau you can see Great Spotted Cuckoo, Rock and Blue Rock Thrush, Crested Lark, Tawny Pipit, Bonelli's Warbler, Ortolan Bunting and Orphean, Spectacled, Subalpine, Dartford and Sardinian Warblers.

2.5 km/1.55 miles
Lézignan-Corbières
(IGN 2445 east – 1/25 000)
and Peyriac-Minervois
(IGN 2445 west – 1/25 000)

129 JOUARRES LAKE

Habitat and Timing

Once a marsh, the area was flooded in 1980. There is a Réserve de Chasse (no-hunting reserve) on the northern half; an embankment to the south separates the lake from the Canal du Midi. To the west there is a reed-bed, some corn fields and an olive-grove. A few small islands, covered in winter and spring, appear in the summer. The site is interesting for the duck and Coot that stay, as well as the passage of migrants.

Calendar

Spring and autumn: Grey, Purple and Night Herons, Little Bittern; Mallard, Gadwall, Shoveler, Teal, Garganey, Pochard, Coot; 'shanks, Ringed Plovers, other small waders, Lapwing, Snipe; Bee-eater, Great Grey and Woodchat Shrikes; *Phylloscopus* and *Acrocephalus* warblers; Penduline and Bearded Tits, Chaffinch, Brambling, Goldfinch, Buntings.

Breeding season: Great Crested and Little Grebes, Purple Heron, Little Bittern; Mallard, Coot, Kestrel, Little Ringed Plover, Red-legged Partridge, Little Owl, Turtle Dove; Crested Lark, Tawny Pipit, Great Reed and Reed Warblers, Nightingale, Cirl Bunting.

Access

From Narbonne, take the N113 towards Lézignan. At Villedaigne, take the D11 as far as Homps. On leaving Homps on the Carcassonne road, turn right towards Domaine de Jouarres (on the D806) and pass the canal. Take the track that leads to the lake. It is possible to follow the lake on the east for 800 m (875 yards) or on the south-east for 1.5 km (0.9 miles) (access to the pine wood is forbidden).

Penduline Tit

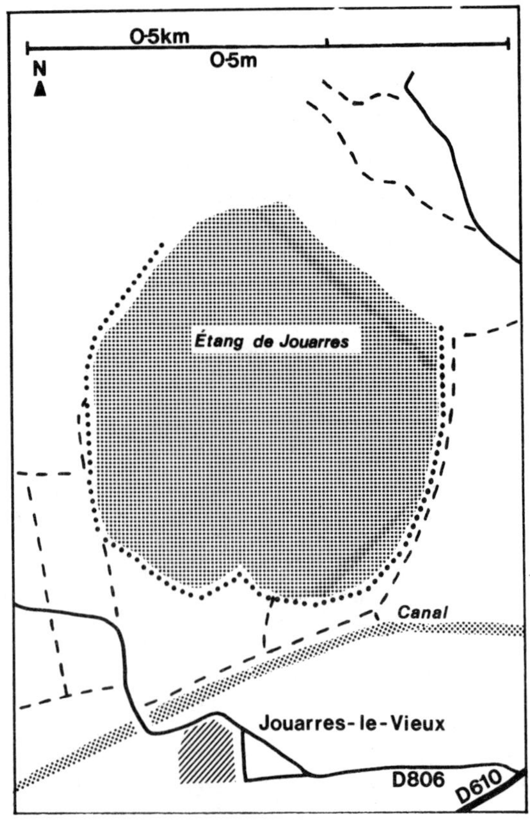

Species

- A good place for watching ducks in winter, also grebes and Coot.
- Near the reed-bed it is sometimes possible to come across Purple Heron or even the rare Little Bittern.
- The surrounding meadows are used by Great Grey and Woodchat Shrikes.
- During migration, small waders including 'shanks, Snipe and Lapwing may stop-over on the lake.
- In the reed-beds, look out for *Acrocephalus* warblers and Bearded and Penduline Tits.

130 THE CAUSSE DE BLANDAS

15.5 km/11.6 miles (of which 6.5 km/4 miles are on foot)
Le Caylar
(IGN 2642 – 1/50 000)

Habitat and Timing

The Causse de Blandas is an outlying 'causse' (limestone plateau of central France) of the Larzac region. The area has a dry limestone soil covered with Box-tree heath and grassy meadows, interspersed with crops and ancient hedgerows. There are also some 'lavognes' (a local word for a watering place for sheep). The Cirque de Navacelles is made up of cliffs and Cedar and pine plantations. It is on a raptor and passerine migration route, both in spring and autumn. The best watching is in the early morning, except during times of migration, when it is best when there are northerly winds.

Calendar

Spring and autumn: Black and Red Kites, harriers, Short-toed Eagle, Honey Buzzard; larks, wagtails, chats; Chaffinch, Brambling, Linnet, Buntings.

Breeding season: Alpine Swift; Tawny Pipit, shrikes (three species), Mediterranean warblers; Blue Rock and Rock Thrushes, buntings (including Ortolan), Chough. Also Little, Scops and Long-eared Owls.

Winter: very variable, thrushes and Blackbird, Chaffinch, Brambling, Wallcreeper, Alpine Accentor.

Access

From Vigan (80 kms/50 miles to the west of Nîmes), go to Avèze and take the D48 as far as Montdardier. Take the second right (D48) after Montdardier towards Blandas and Barral. Stop at the lavogne at Flouirac ①: there is a possible 2 km (1.25 miles) walk here. An excellent place for looking over the Causse for passerines.

Continue along the D48, stopping at the only car park on the left of the road ②. After the village of Rogues, turn right on the D158. Where the road forks, stop at Rogues lavogne ③ and take a 100 m (110 yards) walk.

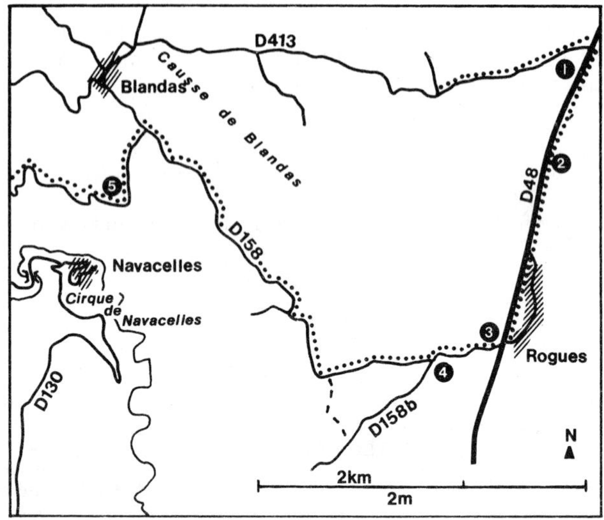

Another 1.5 km (0.9 miles) further on stop at Jurade crossroads ④. Then back onto the road, turn right just before Blandas on the D713 as far as the car park at the Cirque de Navacelles relay ⑤. It is possible to continue along the ridge as far as the Rocher du Loup. Return by the same route.

Species

- Many nesting warblers, including Orphean; and Nightingale. On migration, *Phylloscopus* warblers, Greenfinch, Linnet.
- Great Grey Shrike (the southern European race *meridionalis*) – rare –, Red-backed and Woodchat Shrikes nest on this part of the Causse; Tawny Pipit also.
- Montagu's and Hen Harriers nest here in small numbers.
- Look for Rock Thrush on wires and electricity pylons.
- Corvids, particularly Chough (year round), occur in the fields.
- Rogues village is a very good place for watching raptor migration in the spring: Black and Red Kites, Honey Buzzard, Short-toed Eagle, Marsh Harrier, falcons.
- Near to the lavogne at Rogues, Quail can be heard in spring.
- This part of the Causse is suitable for nesting Scops Owls; Hoopoe also nest.
- From one place or another along the road it is possible to see not only Rock Thrush but also Woodlark, Tawny Pipit, Wheatear and Black-eared Wheatear (rare), Whitethroat and Ortolan Bunting; all nest.
- The typical garrigue vegetation has Sardinian and Subalpine Warblers.
- Around the Cirque de Navacelles, Blue Rock Thrush and Crag Martin nest, Wallcreeper and Alpine Accentor are regular in winter.
- Alpine Swift nest in the cliffs near the Rocher du Loup. Stock Dove also occur.

131 L'Arre/Le Vigan

The footpath running along the Arre River, between Avèze and Le Vigan, is a perfect place for watching Dipper, Kingfisher, Short-toed Tree-creeper, Tree Sparrow, and for hearing Cetti's Warbler, the year through. In winter, the riverside woods have lots of Chaffinch and Greenfinch; some years, Siskin, Citril Finch and Brambling also occur. Woodpeckers and tits are present throughout the year.

132 Fontaret Wood

Fontaret Wood on Blandas Causse is at the crossroads of the D158 and the D813 (a place called the Croix Saint-Jean). It has a footpath on one boundary which leads southwards and from which the birds of this beautiful pine wood can be either seen or heard: Sparrowhawk, Short-toed Eagle, Green, Great Spotted and Lesser Spotted Woodpeckers, Cuckoo, Goldcrest and Firecrest, tits (including Crested), Nightjar and Long-eared Owl.

133 GREC AND PRÉVOST LAKES

Sète
(IGN 2744 – 1/50 000)

Habitat and Timing

Grec Lake is a shallow lagoon, separated from Méjean Lake to the north-west by the Rhône–Sète canal, and from the sea to the south-east by the Carnon–Palavas road. There are two areas of *Salicornia*, one to the north, the other to the south of the lake. Prévost Lake, completely open to the sea not so long ago, now has only a narrow link with it at the fish-farm. It is now separated from the sea by a line of sand-dunes. There is an area of *sansouire* (Mediterranean salt-marsh vegetation) in its south-western part.

Calendar

Winter: divers, Great Crested and Black-necked Grebes, Cormorant, Greater Flamingo, sawbills, Eider, Avocet, Mediterranean Gull.

Spring: Greater Flamingo, Grey and Purple Herons, Little Egret, Shelduck; Grey, Plover, godwits, small waders; Caspian Sandwich, Common and Little Terns; wagtails, Short-toed and Crested Larks.

Autumn: herons; Marsh and Montagu's Harriers, Honey Buzzard, Black Kite, Hobby, Kestrel, Merlin, Osprey; Black-winged Stilt, Avocet, Dunlin; Black-headed and Mediterranean Gulls; terns, wagtails, chats.

Access

From Montpellier, go as far as Carnon on the D21, then turn towards Palavas-les-Flots on the D62E. The road runs alongside Grec Lake; you

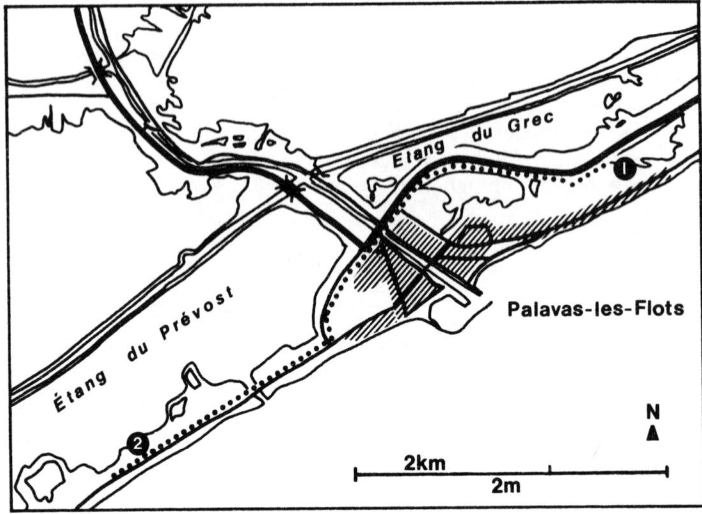

can stop at the roadside ①. At Palavas take the road towards Maguelonne Abbey. To look over Prévost Lake climb onto the sand-dunes ②. Do not forget to look on the sea.

Species

- Greater Flamingos can be seen feeding on Grec Lake throughout the year.
- In winter it is usually easy to see Red-breasted Merganser.
- In spring and autumn, there are concentrations of Yellow-legged Herring, Black-headed and Mediterranean Gulls, as well as terns (including the rare Caspian).
- In winter, there are large concentrations of Great Crested and Black-necked Grebes.
- Avocet and Black-winged Stilt are regular in spring and summer.
- At sea it is possible to see Gannet, Manx Shearwater and skuas during times of migration and in winter.

134 Vic-la-Gardiole Lake

The lake is in Vic-la-Gardiole parish; it is brackish and shallow, separated from the sea by a line of sand-dunes and the Rhône–Sète canal. The most interesting part is near the village; this area is a Reserve de Chasse (a no-hunting reserve). In winter, among others, there are: Greater Flamingo, Grey Heron, Little Egret; Mallard, Shoveler, Pintail, Teal, Shelduck; Marsh Harrier, Water Pipit and Reed Bunting. In spring and autumn many migrants occur: herons, egrets, Cormorant; Redshank, Greenshank and Spotted Redshank, godwits, plovers, small waders; swifts, hirundines, wagtails, pipits. Finally, Avocet, Black-winged Stilt, Kentish Plover, Shelduck and Little Tern all breed. To visit, take the Chemin des Mazets from Vic-la-Gardiole; you need a telescope.

135 BAGNAS LAKE

3.5 km/2.2 miles
Agde
(IGN 2645 east – 1/25 000)

Habitat and Timing

Bagnas is a 375-hectare lake, 100 hectares of which is a dense reed-bed. Probably one of the best birdwatching sites in Languedoc-Roussillon and a very good area for duck and nesting wetland passerines.

Calendar

Winter: Great Crested and Black-necked Grebes, Greater Flamingo, Cormorant, Little Egret; Shoveler, Pintail, Mallard, Wigeon, Teal; Marsh Harrier, Buzzard; Reed Bunting, Bearded and Penduline Tits.
Autumn and spring: Greater Flamingo, Shoveler, Pintail, Garganey, Tufted Duck, Pochard; Coot, swifts, Hoopoe, Bee-eater, Roller; Reed Warblers, Sedge, Aquatic, Savi's and Grasshopper Warblers; Swallow, House and Sand Martins and sometimes Red-rumped Swallow.

Access

Take the N112 from Agde. At the traffic-lights, level with Marseillan beach, turn left and follow the D51E towards Marseillan. After crossing the railway, take the first track on the right in order to look at the Onglous ①, then go back onto the D51E, stop on the left to look at the settling-beds ②. For Bagnas itself, continue as far as the car park on the lake-side ③, the only place for looking at the site as access is prohibited.

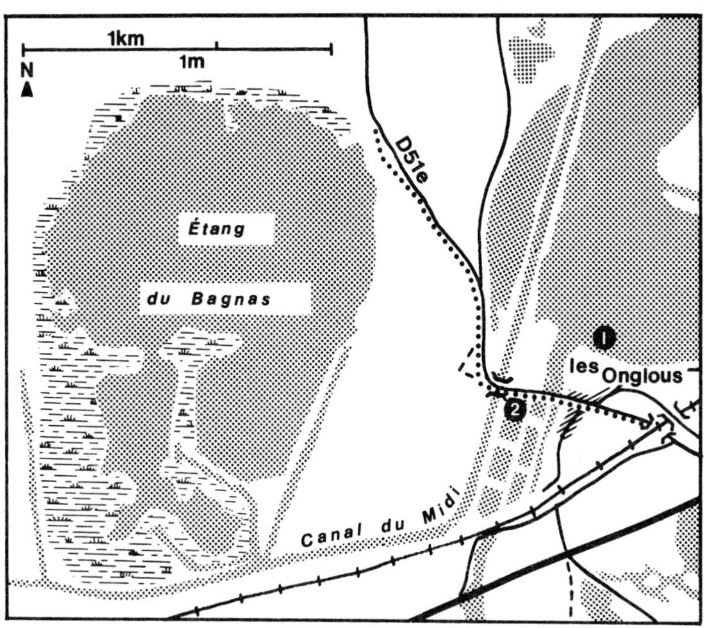

Species

- Grey Heron, Little Egret and Greater Flamingo occur at the southern part of Thau Lake.
- During migration, especially in spring, Avocet, Black-winged Stilt, Redshank and Ringed Plovers also occur here.
- In April and May, Black-headed, Little and Mediterranean Gulls can be seen at the settling-beds.
- Many hirundines (four species) stay here hunting insects.
- In winter large numbers of duck – Mallard, Shoveler, Pintail, Red-crested Pochard and diving duck – can be seen from the bank.
- The reed-beds hold a large number of nesting passerines: Sedge, Reed, Great Reed and Moustached Warblers. Savi's, Grasshopper and Aquatic Warblers occur on migration.

136 Aumelas Causse

Aumelas Causse is covered with a somewhat spoilt open garrigue with rocky outcrops, Holm-oak coppice, old footpaths, burnt areas, and regenerating Holly Oak. To the west of Montpellier, this causse has a typically Mediterranean group of bird species throughout the year

In winter there are sedentary and wintering species: Sardinian Warbler, Great Grey Shrike, Hen Harrier, owls, thrushes, Blackbird and finches. On migration and during the spring it is possible to see: Short-toed Eagle, Montagu's Harrier, Sparrowhawk, Kestrel, Eleonora's Falcon. Sometimes, in summer, you can see: Eagle and Scop's Owls, Little Bustard, Stone Curlew, Bee-eater, Roller, Blue Rock and Rock Thrushes; Sardinian, Subalpine, Dartford, Orphean and Spectacled Warblers; Black-eared Wheatear, Tawny Pipit, Great Grey and Woodchat Shrikes; Cirl and Ortolan Buntings, Rock Sparrow. To get there from Montpellier take the N113 in the direction of Sète, turn right at Fabrègues towards Cournonterral. Watch from any of the many roads that cross the causse.

137 Minerve

Minerve is a fine medieval town surrounded by some splendid garrigue. From Minerve to Boisset (on the D147) the vegetation becomes taller, changing from low garrigue (Holly Oak, Rock Rose, Asphodel) to high garrigue (Holm-Oak). Spring is the best time to see: Red-legged Partridge, Orphean, Sardinian, Dartford and Subalpine Warblers, Whitethroat; Tawny Pipit, Cirl and Ortolan Buntings, Woodlark, Stonechat, Black-eared Wheatear; Great Grey, Woodchat and Red-backed Shrikes; Nightingale. At this time migrating raptors (Honey Buzzard, Black Kite, harriers) mix with local birds (Montagu's Harrier, Sparrowhawk). Raven, Alpine Swift, Crag Martin and Rock Sparrow nest in the cliffs at Minerve; in winter the Wallcreeper is frequently seen.

138 THE CÉVENNES NATIONAL PARK WORLD HERITAGE SITE/SAINT-PIERRE-DES-TRIPIERS AND LE ROZIER

16 km/10 miles
Meyrueis
(IGN 2640 – 1/50 000)
and Saint-Beauzelly
(IGN 2540 – 1/50 000)

Habitat and Timing

The Grands Causses and the Tarn and Jonte Gorges represent a highly original area, with impressive canyons and stretches of high cliffs. Other than its exceptionally rich flora (one quarter of the species in France occur here), the site is also excellent for watching large raptors. It has been particularly good, in recent times, for both Griffon and Egyptian Vultures (there has been a re-introduction scheme and protection organised jointly by the FIR – Fonds d'Intervention pour les Rapaces – and the Cévennes National Park). There is unrestricted access to the area, but it is recommended that visitors stay on the marked paths, as much for the visitors own security as for peace for the local fauna.

Calendar

Year-round: Griffon Vulture, Golden Eagle, Goshawk, Sparrowhawk, Buzzard, Red Kite, Peregrine, Kestrel; Red-legged Partridge; Tawny, Barn and Little Owls; Stock Dove, Raven, Chough and Jackdaw.

Spring: Egyptian Vulture, Short-toed Eagle, Black Kite, Osprey, Honey Buzzard, Montagu's Harrier, Peregrine; Scops Owl; Blue Rock and Rock Thrush, Ring Ouzel; Subalpine Warbler.

Winter: Hen Harrier, Alpine Accentor, Wallcreeper and sometimes Snow Finch.

Access

From the Gorges du Tarn go as far as Rozier to the east of Millau (the department of Aveyron), a parish at the confluence of the Tarn and Jonte Gorges; park the car here ①. From Rozier, walk along the signposted track known as the du Rozier passing via the Rocher de Capluc, the Source du Teil, the Rocher de Cinglegros ②, La Bourgarie, then the plateau Volcegur, Cassagnes, the Vase de Sèvres, the Vase de Chine and back to Le Rozier. This is a hiker's track.

All open viewpoints looking over the gorges are good for watching the antics of raptors. There are many ways of looking for the birds: either by watching from the car at Rozier or on the roads that follow the Tarn and Jonte Gorges; or by using the hiker's track, walks of different lengths being possible, either walk the whole track or take a short cut at Cinglegros ② or at Cassagnes ③.

Species

- Alpine Swift and Crag Martin can be seen the whole length of the Gorge du Tarn.
- The Griffon Vulture – recently re-introduced – can be seen anywhere;

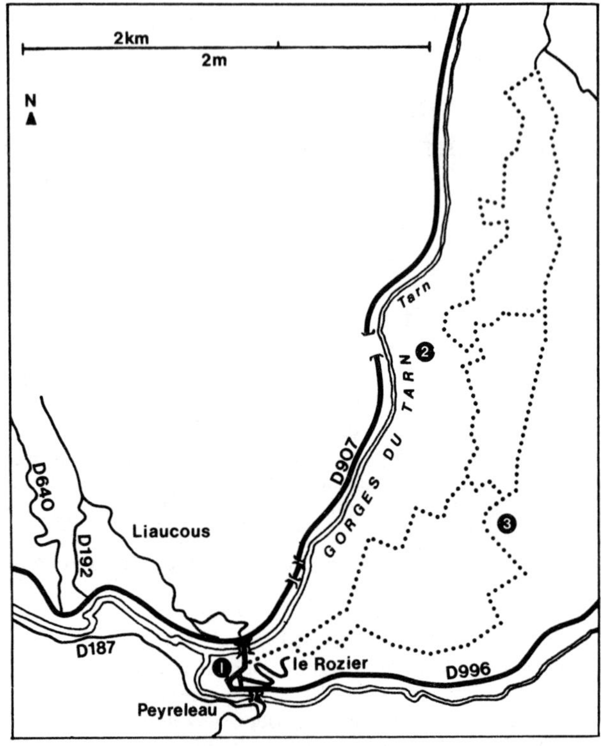

however, open watch-points such as that at Cinglegros may provide better views. Sometimes the rare Egyptian Vulture may be seen.

- In winter the cliffs hold Wallcreeper and Alpine Accentor.
- The whole area is used by Golden Eagle, Red and Black Kites, Honey Buzzard and Montagu's Harrier.
- Mediterranean passerines such as Blue Rock Thrush and Subalpine Warbler occur in the gorges.
- Rock Thrush, Rock Sparrow and Ortolan Bunting are three nesting passerines typical of the causse.
- Hoopoe can regularly be seen around old farm buildings on the causse.
- Noisy Chough can be seen in acrobatic flight along the cliffs. Ravens also occur here.
- Eagle Owls use the scree at the foot of the cliffs, they are most often heard in the spring.

139 Méjean Causse

In Meyrueis, Hures-la-Parade, Mas-Saint-Chély and Vébron parishes, the eastern part of Méjean Causse (the 'Causse nu' or open causse) is in the central part of the Cévennes National Park. Birds typical of open-steppe type vegetation nest here, such as Stone Curlew, Little Bustard, Tawny

Pipit, Short-toed Lark, Skylark, Wheatear, Black-eared Wheatear, Rock Thrush, Rock Sparrow and Ortolan Bunting. Scops Owl and Hoopoe also breed here.

140 The Banks of the Tarn

A footpath runs along the side of the Tarn passing through the parishes of des Vignes La Malène and Saint-Enimie. Other than species normally seen in the Cévennes National Park, which are often less easy to see here, there are some waterside species, notably Dipper, Kingfisher, Grey Heron and Common Sandpiper; the last species breeds here.

141 VILLENEUVE-DE-LA-RAHO

2 km/1.25 miles
Perpignan
(IGN 2449 east – 1/25 000)

Habitat and Timing

This is an artificial lake split into three distinct zones. Part is used as a leisure centre and is visited by the people of Perpignan. The smallest and most interesting zone, in the south-west corner, is a reserve. It is used, particularly in winter, by a large number of duck of all species. There is the largest concentration of Pochard in Languedoc-Roussillon. While the other two zones are very open, the area around the reserve is well planted.

Calendar

Winter: Black-throated Diver (rare), Great Crested and Black-necked Grebes; Mallard, Pintail, Shoveler, Gadwall, Teal, Red-crested Pochard, Pochard, Tufted Duck, Ferruginous Duck (rare).

Spring and autumn: kites, Honey Buzzard, harriers, falcons, herons, duck; Common and Wood Sandpipers, Ringed Plovers; Hoopoe, Bee-eater, swifts, shrikes, leaf warblers, flycatchers.

Access

From Perpignan, take the N9 as far as Pollestres, turn left level with the wine cooperative as far as Monplaisir (1.5 km/0.9 miles). From here take the road to the left and park at the end ①. Use the trail by following the western side of the reserve and turning right at the first junction, going east; follow the southern side of Villeneuve-de-la-Raho Lake as far as the south-east corner ②. Return on the same track. You can go to the village of the same name, from the top of which there is a good view over the lake.

Species

- Small waders – particularly 'shanks – can be seen on the reserve's mudflats at times of migration, in autumn (July–October) and in spring (April and May).

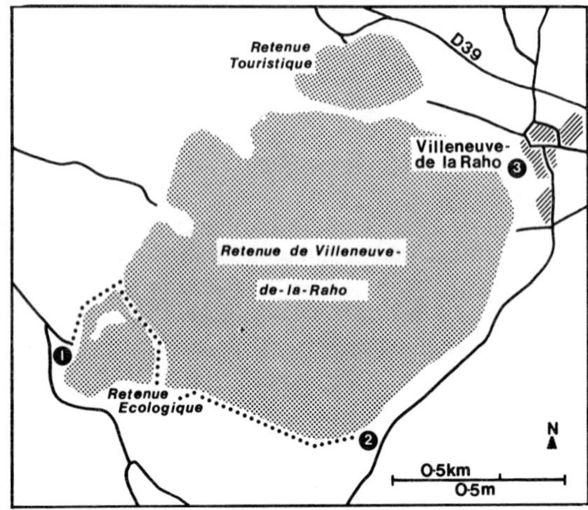

- In spring, hirundines (as early as March) and swifts (from late April) hunt insects over the water.
- Pochard is the most numerous of the diving ducks. There are also Tufted Duck, Red-crested Pochard, Teal, Mallard, Shoveler, Pintail and Gadwall.
- Great-crested and Black-necked Grebes regularly winter. Sometimes a diver may be mixed in with them.
- The top of the village is the best place for watching migrating raptors, in autumn and spring.

142 CANET OR SAINT-NAZAIRE LAKE

6 km/3.75 miles Perpignan (IGN 2545 – 1/50 000)

Habitat and Timing

Canet is a shallow lake of 480 hectares which receives fresh water from three rivers – the Cagarell, the Fosseille and the Réart. Around these three estuaries are large reed-beds. Sea water arrives via the Grau de la Basse (a canal), which is often blocked; the lake's salinity is very variable. Canet Lake is remarkable for the numbers of Greater Flamingo, duck and Coot that occur. The northern part is private, entry is prohibited.

Calendar

Winter: Great Crested and Black-necked Grebes, Greater Flamingo, Grey Heron, Little Egret; Pintail, Mallard, Wigeon, Shoveler, Red-breasted Merganser; Marsh Harrier; Coot; Bearded and Penduline Tits, Moustached Warbler.

Spring and autumn: Greater Flamingo, Grey, Purple and Night Herons; Garganey, Pochard; Little Crake; Black-winged Stilt, sometimes Collared Pratincole; many passerines including Red-throated Pipit (April and May).

Access

From Perpignan, take the D116 to Canet-en-Roussillon, then go towards Saint-Cyprien-Plage. Follow the eastern shore of the lake on the D81 for 2.5 km (1.5 miles) before the first stop ①, near the camp site. The second stop is another 1 km (0.6 miles) further on ②. Further south again, a little less than 1 km (0.6 miles), take a small track on the right ③. Then go back to Canet-en-Roussillon and take the road towards Saint-Nazaire. Once through the village, after the petrol station, take the track on the left ④. Cross the orchards and park the car. Then follow the Réart on foot until its end ⑤.

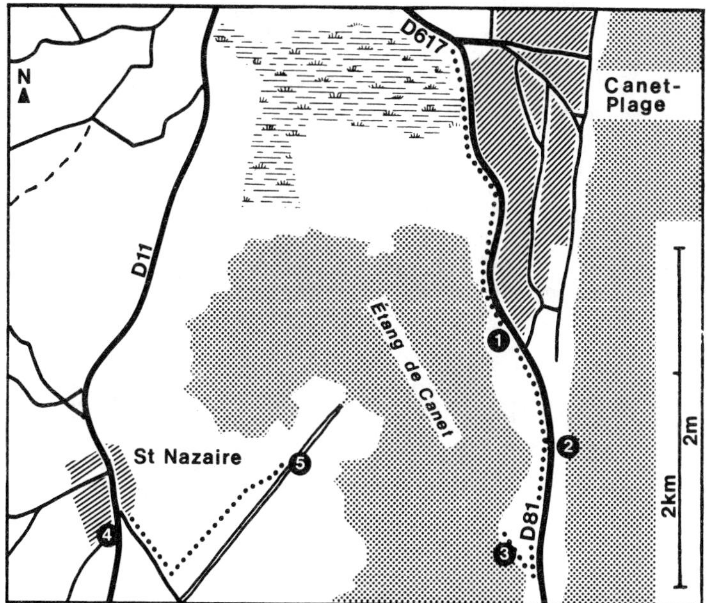

Species

- Greater Flamingos can be seen most of the year.
- In the reed-beds you can see, Reed, Sedge and Savi's Warblers, and Bearded and Penduline Tits.
- Gannet, Manx Shearwater and Razorbill can be seen at sea, particularly in winter.
- Mediterranean and Little Gulls as well as terns can be seen on passage.
- A good place for looking for Red-breasted Merganser in winter, also for Coot and grebes.
- Along the river is a good place for Grey and Purple Herons as well as Little and Cattle Egrets.

- In spring all the European 'shanks can be seen, also the rare Marsh Sandpiper at the point. Collared Pratincole is irregular.
- Larks, pipits (ncluding Red-throated) and Blue-headed Wagtails are often present, particularly between mid-April and mid-May.

143 Eyne

This site is part of a large project studying post-breeding migration across the Pyrenees. The observation station is situated on the pass, overlooking the whole valley. This picturesque site is on a plateau with alternating meadows, cultivated fields, pine woods and poplar- and birch-lined streams.

This site is remarkable in autumn (August and September); 15,000 to 20,000 large soaring birds pass over the site each year, these include: Black and White Storks, Black Kite, Sparrowhawk, falcons, harriers (three species), but especially Honey Buzzard and Short-toed Eagle which pass in big numbers. It is also possible to see good numbers of Bee-eater and Dotterel. To get there leaving from Prades go as far as Montlouis, then on towards Sallagouse. Turn left before Sallagouse towards Eyne, the observation station is on the D29 about 2 km (1.25 miles) after the village.

LIMOUSIN

144 LONGÉROUX PEAT-BOG

5 km/3.1 miles or 16 km/10 miles
Bugeat
(IGN 2232 – 1/50 000)

Habitat and Timing

This site at Longéroux, protected by law, is a vast 255-hectare peat-bog on the southern edge of Millevaches Plateau; it is at an average altitude of 900 m. It is an acid peat-bog evolving towards a peat heath, on a granite bedrock. Surrounded by granitic hills, once covered by a large sheep-grazed heath, today it is largely planted with conifers. Numerous parcels of heather heath still persist, interspersed with a few meadows and crops. It is an interesting area for watching heathland birds and raptors. There is unrestricted access to the area, but camping, lighting fires, the use of vehicles and parking away from official car parks is forbidden.

Calendar

Spring and early summer: Buzzard, Honey Buzzard, Goshawk, Sparrowhawk, Short-toed Eagle, Red Kite, Hen and Montagu's Harrier;

Meadow and Tree Pipits, Whinchat, Linnet, Yellowhammer, Rock Bunting.

Access

From Limoges take the D979 south-eastwards towards Bugeat and Meymac, 10 km (6.2 miles) before Meymac turn left towards Celle on the D109. From Aubusson to the north go towards Felletin, then, on the road to Ussel, turn right 12 km (7.5 miles) after Felletin on the D36 towards Meymac. The peat-bog is about 15 km (9.3 miles) to the north-east of Meymac. There is a car park ① close to the village of Celle.

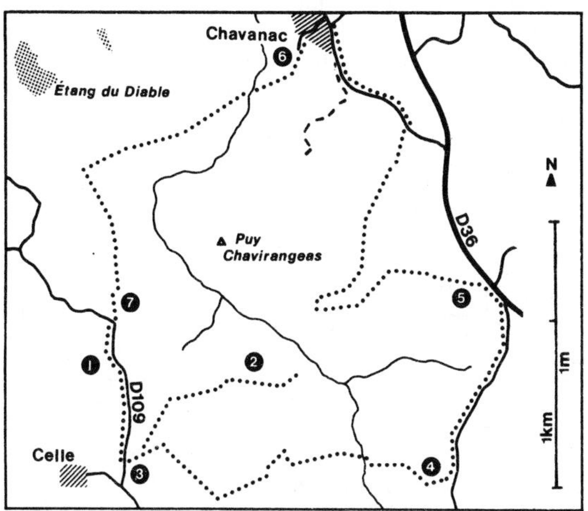

A 5 km (3.1 miles)-round walk is possible, going as far as Cent Pierres ② Otherwise, a long circuit of 16 km (10 miles) can be walked, taking the day. From the car park, take the forest track ③ which rejoins the Chemin du Loup, a forest road ④. Follow this track northwards for a few kilometres, then take the D36 north-westwards for a little less than 1 km (0.6 miles) before taking the track towards Chavanac ⑤. At Chavanac village take the path that crosses the Vézère River ⑥, then rejoin the D109 ⑦ to get back to the car park.

Species

- Whinchat can often be seen in grassy areas around the peat-bog.
- Hen and Montagu's Harriers often occur over the heathland.
- Nightjar can be heard at dusk.
- Passerines such as Coal and Crested Tits, Goldcrest and sometimes Crossbill frequent the conifer plantations.
- On migration, Snipe use the wetter peat heaths.
- Look for Dipper on the Vézère.
- At the foot of Cherfeau hill you can see many raptors using the thermals.
- Quail can be heard to the north of the car park.
- Tree Pipit can be seen, particularly on the drier parts of the heathland.

145 Dordogne-Gorge, between Aigle Dam and the Site de Saint-Nazaire

The Dordogne Gorge is a deep closed valley, the slopes covered with hardwood and coniferous forest. Here and there, there are a few rocky slopes and wooded heaths. The valley is remarkably rich in birds along this whole sector. There is a good selection of raptors: Buzzard, Honey Buzzard, Red and Black Kites, Hen Harrier, Short-toed Eagle, Booted Eagle, Peregrine, Kestrel, Goshawk, Sparrowhawk; all nest in this area or round about. There are also many passerines: Rock Bunting, Dipper, House and Crag Martins, Redstart. Along the circuit three sites stand out: at Saint Nazaire there are raptors and birds of wooded heaths, and there is a very good view over the Dordogne and Diège Valleys; the observation point at Gratte-Bruyère is an excellent site for raptors and has a remarkable view over the valley; finally, Aigle Dam, another good site for watching raptors under good conditions. Red and Black Kites, Peregrine and House and Crag Martins nest on the dam.

146 LANDES LAKE/ LUSSAT

5 km/3.1 miles
Evaux-les-Bains
(IGN 2329 east – 1/25 000)

Habitat and Timing

To the north-east of the department of the Creuse, Landes Lake (of natural origin) lies in a sedimentary depression. There is an important belt of vegetation around the edge, mainly reed, sedge and bulrush. It is a very important site for nesting wetland birds and for the numbers of duck and wader that use the lake on passage, in spring and autumn. It is a private lake, so that anyone wanting to leave the paths should gain permission beforehand. There is some hunting on the lake, which may disturb the birds, particularly in autumn and spring.

Calendar

Spring (February and March): Greylag Goose, Mallard, Shoveler, Pintail, Gadwall, Wigeon, Teal, Garganey, Pochard, Tufted Duck, Scaup, sawbills (three species).
Breeding season: Great Crested Grebe, Little Grebe, Grey and Purple Herons, Bittern, Mallard, Teal, Pochard, Coot, Marsh Harrier, Spotted Crake, Water Rail, Grasshopper, Savi's, Sedge, Reed and Great Reed Warblers, and Reed Bunting all nesting.
Autumn: Cormorant, White and Black Storks, Night Heron, Osprey, Crane, small waders including Snipe, Black, Whiskered, Common and Little Terns, (and almost all these species in the spring).

Access

Leave the N145 level with Gouzon, going towards Chambon-sur-Voueize on the D915. The lake is close to Lussat village, about 10 km (6.2 miles)

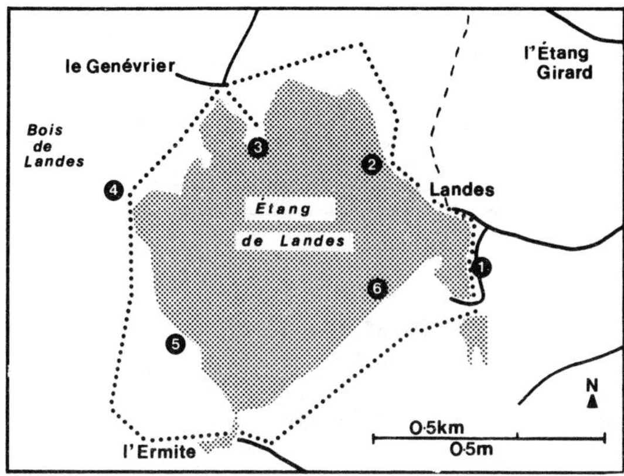

before Chambon-sur-Voueize. Cross the village to arrive at the car park ① on the embankment of the lake. From here, pass in front of the keeper's house and continue on the track along the lake side ②; from here, with a telescope, the whole lake can be watched. Next, skirt around the northern reed-bed to arrive at the western side of the lake ③. The track on the western side goes through thick vegetation, passing close to a large reed-bed mixed with willows ④. Further on, the track passes the side of a large water-meadow ⑤. Next, pass in front of Ermite Farm, and after the bridge over the stream that feeds the lake, pass along the first hedge on the left, in order to see the reed-bed. A little further on, there is a very good view point, from where the whole lake can be seen ⑥.

Species

- During March, most of the duck stopping here during their migration can be seen in the middle of the lake.
- In the spring, the strange call of the Little Grebe is heard in the reed-bed.
- Both Grey and Purple Herons nest on the western side of the lake.
- From May to July, at dusk, the monotonous song of the Spotted Crake can be heard.
- During periods of migration both storks and Cranes may make a stop-over in the large water-meadows.
- The Bittern's strange booming can be heard coming from deep in the reeds during March, April and May.
- Marsh Harriers continually hunt over the lake.
- Where reed and bulrush mingle, large numbers of *Locustella* and *Acrocephalus* warblers nest, particularly the latter.

147 THE PEAT-BOG AT THE SOURCE OF THE DAUGES STREAM/ SAINT-LÉGER-LA-MONTAGNE

4 km/2.5 miles
Ambazac
(IGN 2030 east – 1/25 000)

Habitat and Timing

This is an area of granite in the form of a natural amphitheatre which has a flat bottom surrounded by rounded hills. The slopes around the peat-bog are wooded (especially hardwoods) with some heathland. In the middle is a hillock covered in wooded heath, the Puy-Rond. It is an interesting site for species associated with peat-bog and heathland. There is unrestricted access, but fires, camping and the use of vehicles (except those used locally for agriculture or forestry) is strictly forbidden.

Calendar

Spring and summer: Buzzard, Honey Buzzard, Goshawk, Sparrowhawk; Woodcock; Nightjar, Black Woodpecker; Tree and Meadow Pipits; Nightingale, Stonechat, Whinchat; Willow and Bonelli's Warblers; Linnet, Bullfinch, Rock Bunting, Yellowhammer.

Access

Leave Limoges on the N20 towards Paris, after a few kilometres turn onto the D914 going towards Ambazac. After Ambazac continue on the same road towards Laurière, turning off left on the D28a well before then, going towards Saint-Léger-La-Montagne. Stop at the car park in Sauvagnac village. The peat-bog is found to the west of the village. Cross Sauvagnac ① on a footpath that leads westward; this crosses a wooded

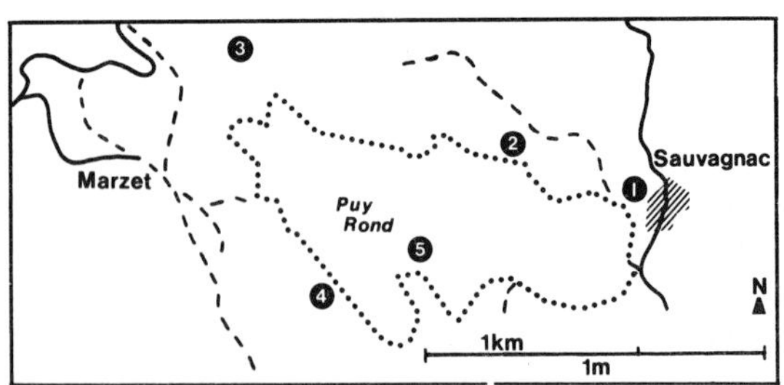

area and arrives at the site, visible from the watch point ②. The footpath continues westward, it crosses a stream ③. In this part the area is a mixture of woodland and heath, there is, therefore, a great variety of bird species. The footpath then loses itself in a wooded zone ④. Steer towards the Puy-Rond where there is a very fine wooded heath ⑤. There are two ways to return, either via the point ② or by using the path to the south of Sauvagnac.

Species

- In the wood near Sauvagnac, Green, Great Spotted and Black Woodpeckers occur.
- The peat-bog has nesting Meadow Pipit and Stonechat.
- On the gently sloping hillsides look out for the brightly coloured but shy Rock Bunting.
- The heath is an ideal habitat for Nightjar.
- Chiffchaff, Willow and Bonelli's Warblers can be heard in spring on the wooded heath near the Puy-Rond.
- Sparrowhawks are not rare here, any sightings are, however, fortuitous.

Rock Bunting

LORRAINE

148 PARROY FOREST AND LAKE

7 km/4.35 miles
Einville-au-Jard
(IGN 3515 west – 1/25 000)

Habitat and Timing

Both lake and forest are found on the Lorraine Plateau, 25 km (15.5 miles) to the east of Nancy just to the north-east of Lunéville, not far from the National Park. The lake is a reservoir for the Marne–Rhin Canal; it is often very low in summer. The northern corners are invaded by aquatic vegetation, while the southern part has steep embankments. The east and west sides are bordered by agricultural land. At its entrance to the lake, the canal is far wider than normal. To the south of the canal, between Sânon and Vezouze, is the vast Parroy National Forest, a mature forest where oak dominates (typical of the forests to be found on the Lorraine Plateau).

Calendar

Breeding season: Bittern, Little Bittern, Purple Heron; Goshawk, Marsh Harrier, Black and Red Kites, Hobby; Water Rail, Woodpeckers (six species); Great Reed and Sedge Warblers, Collared Flycatcher, Treecreeper and Short-toed Treecreeper.

Autumn: Osprey, Merlin; Lapwing, Ringed Plovers, small waders; Black Tern; Skylark, pipits, Blue-headed Wagtail, Whinchat, Wheatear.

Winter: divers, grebes, Mallard, Shoveler, Teal, Tufted Duck and Pochard.

Access

From Lunéville, northwards on the D194 turn right after Einville on the D2. Then, 3 km (1.85 miles) after Bauzemont, turn left towards Bures. On entering the village go right towards the École de Voile (sailing school) and leave the car here ①. From the road the whole of the northern part of the lake can be viewed. In spring, it is possible to walk through the meadows on the edge of the reed-bed ②. At the end of summer, on the other hand, you can pass by the marina and follow the inner edge of the reed-bed, walking on the mud looking for waders. The rest of the lake can be seen from the embankment ③ to the south. This is a good place for diving species outside the breeding season. To visit the forest, continue along the D2 passing through Parroy. After the canal bridge, turn right on the bend. Follow the road for about 2 km (1.25 miles) and park near the crossroads ④. From here you can explore the forest; either follow the two cuttings, the Tranchée de Parroy that leads south-westwards or the Tranchée de Bossupré that goes to the south-east; or go into the forest itself using a compass.

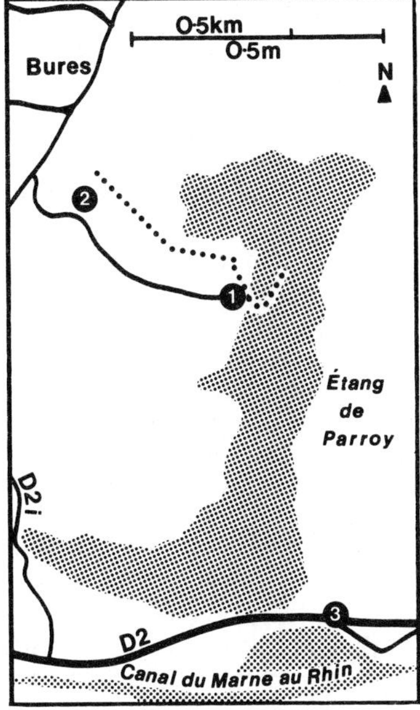

Species

- Great Reed and Sedge Warblers sing from the reed-beds between April and July.
- Lake Parroy's reed-beds hold Purple Heron, Bittern and Little Bittern.
- At the end of summer, many small waders occur on the uncovered mudflats: Ringed Plovers, Lapwing, 'shanks, Dunlin.
- Over the woods, on the other side of the lake, it is often possible to see Black and Red Kites, Hobby and Osprey on migration.
- Small passerines may often stop during migration, particularly in autumn, to the south of the sailing school: pipits, wagtails, Whinchat, Wheatear, Skylark.
- From the embankment, divers, grebes and diving duck (*Aythya* species, Goldeneye, sawbills sometimes) are active in winter on unfrozen parts of the lake or on the canal.
- Six species of woodpecker breed in the forest, including Black and Grey-headed.

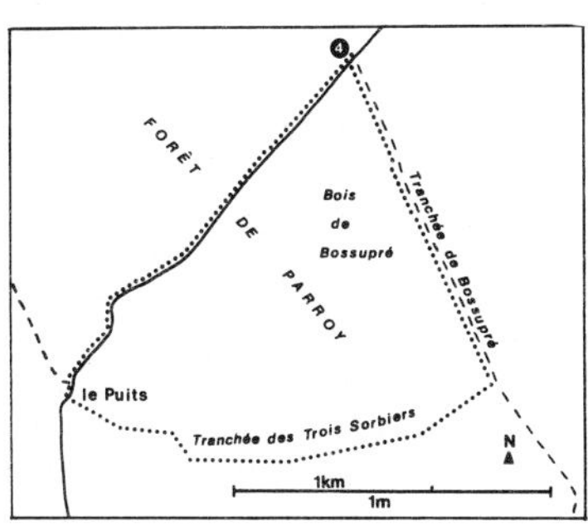

- Collared Flycatcher can be seen in the old oaks in May. Both Treecreeper and Short-toed Treecreeper occur year-round.
- The Goshawk is rather secretive, but is more easily seen when displaying in early spring.

149 The Esche Valley – Petite Suisse in Lorraine

The Esche River has its source in Woëvre in the Reine Forest; it cuts its way through the slopes of the Moselle Plateau before running into the river of the same name, upstream of Pont-à-Mousson. The Martincourt stretch, 10 km (6.2 miles) to the south-west of Pont-à-Mousson, is excellent for walking. The river has Moorhen, Kingfisher, Grey Wagtail and sometimes Dipper. Spotted Flycatchers occur in the riverside woodland. Above Saint-Jean, the path goes through forest where there are Goshawk, Sparrowhawk and many other woodland species.

150 MADINE LAKE

7 km/4.35 miles
Saint-Mihiel
(IGN 3214 – 1/50 000)

Habitat and Timing

Madine Lake is a recently-built reservoir, created by damming the upper Madine flood-plain; the river is a tributary of the Rupt de Mad, and was built in order to provide water for the city of Metz. It is on the Woëvre Plain at the foot of the Meuse Plateau, at an altitude of 227 m. With more than 40 km (25 miles) of shoreline, it is the biggest lake in Lorraine. It was built at the expense of farmland and forests, some of which still border most of the southern shore. Embankments to the north, and large prairies and meadows on the western side, separate it from the Meuse hills. There are two lakes forming the water area; the small Île Verte, opposite Heudicourt, and the large Île du Bois-Gerard in the centre. It is a very important site for water birds. It is also of tourist importance, with two leisure centres, one at Heudicourt to the west and the other at Nonsard to the east (sailing occurs year-round). Regulated fishing attracts many anglers. A present agreement with the ONC (Office National de la Chasse) has made the lake a hunting-free reserve, and disturbance-free areas theoretically control public access.

Calendar

Autumn and winter (October to March): Great Crested Grebe, sometimes Slavonian and Red-necked Grebes, Cormorant, many dabbling and diving duck; Osprey, Hen Harrier, Hobby; Coot, Crane; Lapwing, Golden Plover, many species of small wader, Curlew; Common and Black-headed Gulls.

Spring: Cormorant, dabbling duck, Crane, Penduline Tit.

Breeding season: Grey Heron, Gadwall, Shoveler; Black and Red Kites, Goshawk, Sparrowhawk, Hobby; Middle Spotted Woodpecker, Collared Flycatcher.

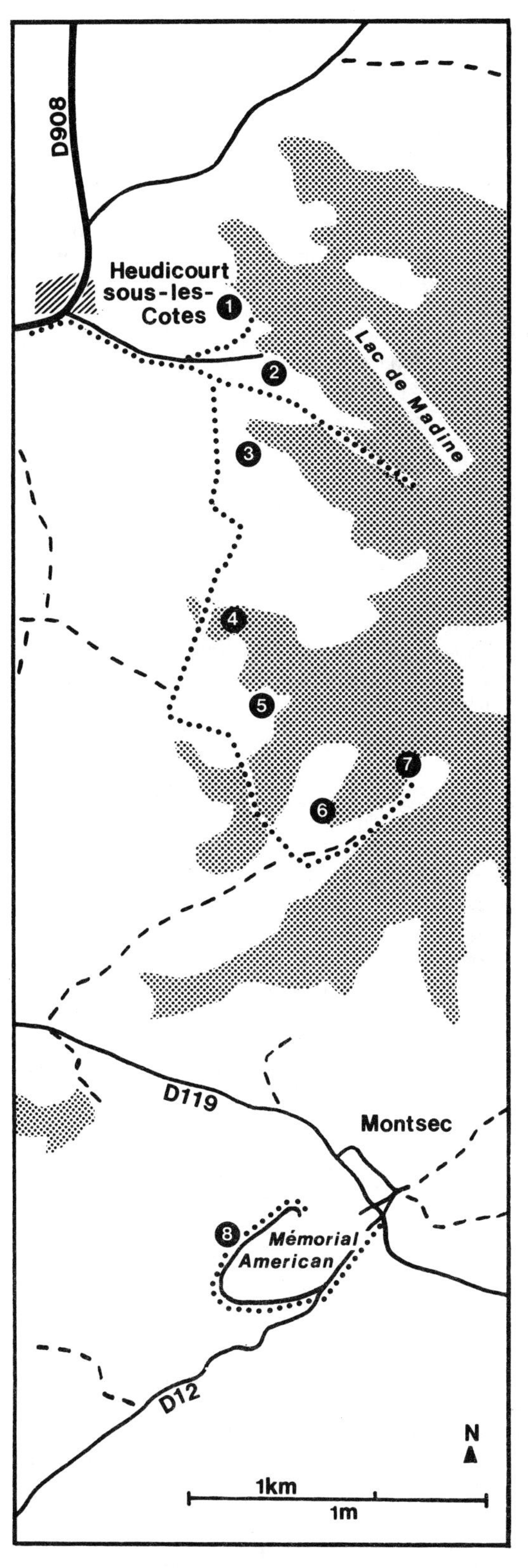
D908
Heudicourt
sous-les-
Cotes
1
2
3
4
5
6
7
8
Lac de Madine
D119
Montsec
Mémorial
American
D12
N
1km
1m

Access

Madine Lake lies some 20 km (12.5 miles) to the west of Pont-à-Mousson. From that town take the D958, then the D3 from which there are several roads to the village of Heudicourt; park here near the church. Take the old road to Nonsard leading eastwards which goes to the lake. The first reservoir on the left ① can be seen from the embankment. Then go to the tip of the G.–Sart Peninsula where there is a hide for watching over the centre of the lake (telescope necessary) ②. Continue southwards on the embankment of the second reservoir which is also worth a glance ③. After skirting the forest, there is a third reservoir ④. Cross the embankment and walk into Sorbière Wood, after crossing the wood the path arrives at the embankment which divides Nouettes inlet ⑤. The more energetic may care to go as far as Madine inlet ⑥ and even as far as the end of the peninsula to look at the southern end of the large island ⑦. Before or after the walk it is worth going by car to Montsec ⑧, a hillock 150 m above the lake offering a fine view over the surrounding area.

Species

- In August and September, when the mudflats are uncovered, many species of small wader are often present.
- There are large numbers of dabbling duck, Tufted Duck and Pochard in winter, Goosander and Smew during hard weather.
- Observing the Grey Heron colony in spring is both easy and instructive.
- In spring you can often come across a family of Gadwall or Shoveler.
- There is a very large Black-headed Gull roost in the centre of the lake in winter, a few Common Gulls are mixed in with them.
- Hen Harriers hunt over the surrounding meadows in winter.
- The mature oak wood near Sorbière holds Collared Flycatcher in May and June.
- Many Cormorant roosts can be seen between October and March.
- This inlet is without doubt the best place for looking for breeding raptors: Black and Red Kites, Goshawk, Sparrowhawk, Hobby, as well as Osprey on migration.
- In April, at the point, Penduline Tits can sometimes be seen.

6.5 km/4 miles
Apremont-la-Forêt
(IGN 3214 east – 1/25 000),
Commercy
(IGN 3215 east – 1/25 000)
and Pont-à-Mousson
(IGN 3314 west – 1/25 000)

151 REINE FOREST

Habitat and Timing

On the Woëvre Plain, to the north-west of Toul, Reine National Forest, with adjoining forests, forms a large area of mainly oak, most of which is regularly cut for timber. Within the area are about 30 lakes used for fish-farming; Romé Lake is the largest.

Meadows and arable land surround the forest; this mixture of arable land/lake/forest is very attractive for birds, particularly raptors.

Calendar

Breeding season: Great Crested Grebe, Bittern; Mallard, Pochard; Marsh Harrier, Red and Black Kites, Honey Buzzard, Sparrowhawk, Hobby; woodpeckers (six species); Wood Warbler, Spotted and Collared Flycatchers.

Spring and autumn: Cormorant, Black Stork, Mallard, Teal, Goldeneye (these last three particularly in March); Osprey, Hobby, marsh terns, Swift, hirundines (three species).

Access

From Toul take the D904 northwards towards Verdun, near Bruley pass onto the D908 at the foot of the Meuse hills going north-westwards. Some 3 km (1.85 miles) after Boucq, turn right on the D147 towards Raulecourt. At the end of a long straight stretch of road there is a crossroads where you can park the car ①. Follow the forestry track going north-eastwards. Stop on Mosée Lake embankment, then continue on to the crossroads and turn right on the Tranchée de la Meuse, which after following the south-east side of the lake, rejoins the D147 ②. Cross this road and take the track directly opposite which passes the Neuf-Château de Rangéval Lake embankment; it is well worth a stop here ③. Continue along the track following a forestry trail which passes round the back of Gérard Lake, then stop on the lake's embankment ④. Turn right a little further on to return to the parking site.

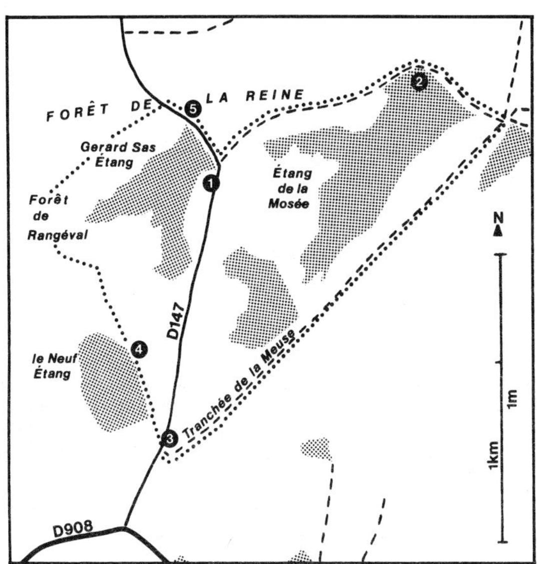

Species

- The call of the Bittern can be heard coming from the reed-bed at Mosée Lake, and equally from the other lakes.

- In winter, Mallard and Pochard are the commonest species.
- Boucq Wood has both Spotted and Collared Flycatchers; May and June are the best months for finding them.
- Six species of woodpecker nest, including Black, Middle Spotted and Grey-headed.
- Honey Buzzard display over the wood in May and June. Sometimes the rare Booted Eagle can be seen.
- The lake's reed-beds are the place to see Marsh Harrier.
- In spring and summer, families of Great Crested Grebe brighten the scene on the lakes.
- Sometimes Black Stork make a short stay on the side of the lakes, especially in August or September.
- Both Reed and Greet Reed Warblers sing from the reed-beds in spring.

152 Mouzay Meadows

These are vast meadows on the right bank of the Meuse some 5 km (3.1 miles) south of Stenay, in Mouzay parish. The most interesting part is the large meadow between the Meuse and the canal near Villefranche. During the breeding season you can find many species typical of valley-bottom hay meadows: Curlew, Quail, Corncrake, Meadow Pipit, Blue-headed Wagtail, Whinchat and Corn Bunting. Also, White Stork recently nested in the area and Black-tailed Godwit has attempted to do so.

On a north-south axis, the valley is important for migrants. Waders pass in large numbers (Lapwing, Golden Plover, 'shanks, Whimbrel) and the sandpits to the east of the canal are used by water birds (duck and waders).

153 LINDRE LAKE

8 km/5 miles
Château-Salins
(IGN 3514 – 1/50 000)

Habitat and Timing

A well-established lake created by barring the upper Seille Valley above Dieuze. It is on the Lorraine Plateau, in the area of the Moselle lakes (210 m), and is an area used mainly for farming and forestry. Lindre Lake belongs to Moselle département and is used for fish-farming. It is enclosed by two national forests – Saint-Jean to the west and Romersberg to the east. There is a peninsula towards the centre of the lake, the Presqu'île de Tarquimpol, which allows for easy watching. At present the lake is empty one year in two; a plan to parcel the lake into several smaller water bodies may lead to a more rational usage, but may be to the detriment of the landscape. The second largest water body in Lorraine, it is probably the best known for birds. This is *the* site in the eastern part of the Lorraine National Park.

Bittern

Calendar

Spring: Great Crested and Black-necked Grebes, Bittern, Grey and Purple Herons, Garganey, Pochard, Tufted Duck, Marsh Harrier, Black and Red Kites, Goshawk, Water Rail, Spotted and Little Crakes, woodpeckers (six species), marshland warblers, Collared Flycatcher, Treecreeper, all nesting.

Summer and autumn: Grebes, Black Stork, Greylag Goose, Osprey, Crane, Lapwing, Snipe, 'shanks.

Winter: divers, grebes, Cormorant, Whooper Swan, Bean Goose, Pochard, Tufted Duck, Black-headed Gull.

Access

The lake is about 45 minutes by road from Nancy, taking first the N74 and then the D38 as far as Dieuze.

For a short visit from the south of Dieuze turn left on the D199E towards Lindre-Basse. Cross the village arriving at the lake's embankment ①. Access is allowed and there is a fine view from here. It is also possible to walk along the track that skirts the fish-farm.

First circuit: leave Dieuze southwards on the D999 towards Gelucourt. The road crosses Saint-Jean Forest. It may be worth stopping at the start of the forestry paths ② to look for Collared Flycatcher. On leaving the forest turn left towards Tarquimpol. Leave the car near the church ③. You can walk around the peninsula from where most of the lake can be seen. A telescope is indispensable. Please respect crops.

Second circuit: leave Dieuze eastwards on the D38, 5 km (3.1 miles) further on turn right towards Guermange. The car must be left in the

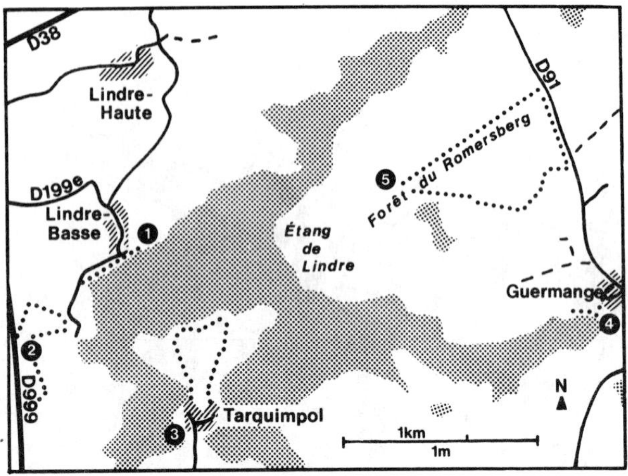

village. A hide ④ allows the most interesting inlet to be watched at ease; Guermange inlet is private but access is possible for scientific and educational activities. The keys have to be asked for: either at the château (from Monsieur Hirtz, responsible for the château, tel: 87.03.93. 48), where useful information on the lake's birds can also be obtained; from the Mairie in Guermange or from FIR (Fonds d'Intervention pour les Rapaces) Lorraine (tel: 87.07.62.13). Then it is on to Romersberg Forest by the D91. Follow the forest edge as far as the forester's house, entering the forest by the Lindre-Basse cutting (Tranchée de Lindre-Basse). You can explore the forest from the tracks which cross at marker 230 ⑤; return via the Tranchée du Milieu and the D91.

Species

- A Grey Heron colony can be seen from the embankment.
- Kingfishers can often be seen on the side of the fish-farm.
- In winter, divers, grebes and diving duck can be seen on the open water in front of the embankment.
- Collared Flycatchers nest in Saint-Jean Wood, and are most easily seen in May and June.
- Middle Spotted Woodpeckers occur here also, they are commoner than the Great Spotted in places.
- In winter, large flocks of duck take refuge in the protected inlets.
- Lapwings occur on arable land.
- The Tarquimpol peninsula is sometimes used by feeding geese.
- There is a large Black-headed Gull roost in the centre of the lake each winter.
- The large reed-beds near Guermange have Bittern and Purple Heron.
- In spring, at night, both Spotted and Little Crakes can be heard calling.
- Romersberg Forest has Black and Red Kites and Goshawk.
- In the large mature woodland both Treecreeper and Collared Flycatcher nest.

154 Maxe Lake

In the Moselle Valley, 3 km (1.85 miles) from Metz, this lake (on the left bank of the river) is below the Metz power-station (the lake supplies the power-station with water). A narrow peninsula separates the lake from the Moselle to the east; to the west there is arable land. There is a track fit for cars along the west bank of the lake. It is most interesting for birds in winter, especially when the Lorraine lakes are frozen. The lake may then have hundreds if not thousands of water birds of at least 15 different species: divers, grebes, Cormorant, Velvet Scoter, Scaup, Goosander, Smew, Goldeneye, and among the more regular, Mallard, Pochard, Tufted Duck and Coot. Bean Geese are present quite often as well as Kingfisher, Grey Heron, Black-headed and Common Gulls.

155 Vaux Valley

This east-facing valley is cut into the side of the slopes of the Moselle about 10 km (6.2 miles) from Metz. The sides of the plateau are wooded (oak and Hornbeam on those parts of the plateau facing south, beech-groves on the northern slopes). The valley bottom is occupied by parks and gardens, with orchards above the village. A stream flows into the Moselle. Some familiar birds are easily seen in the village (Black Redstart, Swallow), and the private parks have Golden Oriole, Serin, Cirl Bunting and Short-toed Treecreeper. In the gardens and orchards are Redstart, Green Woodpecker, Linnet and Greenfinch. Some scrub (once vineyards) has Whitethroat, Grasshopper Warbler and Nightingale. The beech-grove at the back of the valley has Goshawk, Sparrowhawk, Buzzard and Wood Warbler. Coal Tit, Goldcrest and Firecrest can be found in the spruce wood.

156 Falkenstein Château

The impressive site of Falkenstein Château, in Phillippsbourg parish, is on a sandstone peak. From the top of the château there is a magnificent panoramic view over innumerable hills, a typical Vosges du Nord landscape. Liesbach Lake is also of botanical and entomological interest. Some 500m (550 yards) after the car park, the trail skirts an old beech-grove which has Pied Flycatcher, Black and Grey-headed Woodpeckers, and Treecreeper. A Crossbill can sometimes be seen cleaning its bill on the Falkenstein sandstone. You can continue your walk by going into the Rothenbruch, the other side of the car park from the château. This is a large pine wood 1 km (0.6 miles) to 2 km (1.25 miles) from the car park. There are good populations of Pied Flycatcher, Treecreeper, Crossbill and Crested Tit. It is best visited when birds are singing (April to July), preferably in the early morning. Visiting these different habitats offers the chance to see 30 or more species. Other species nesting in the vicinity include: Goshawk, Woodcock, Tengmalm's Owl (very rare), and Peregrine. There is a marked trail to the château, then drop down towards Liesbach Lake and return to Falkenstein car park passing round Landersberg (about a two-hour circuit).

12 km/7.5 miles
Gérardmer
(IGN 3618 – 1/50 000)
and Munster
(IGN 3619 – 1/50 000)

157 THE HOHNECK

Habitat and Timing

The second highest peak in the Vosges, lying on a ridge, the 1,363 m high Hohneck dominates the Gérardmer and Bresse Valleys to the west and Munster to the east. The famous Route des Crêtes (ridge road) runs along its western flank. This track shows a typical vegetation succession, beech–fir–Norway Spruce–high-altitude beech–high meadows. The eastern slopes are more rugged. There are two glacial depressions, the Frankenthal to the north and the Wormspel to the south.

Calendar

Breeding season (May to July): Honey Buzzard, Peregrine; Black Woodpecker; Water, Meadow and Tree Pipits, Grey Wagtail; Alpine Accentor, Wheatear, Rock Thrush, Ring Ouzel; Raven, Nutcracker; Citril Finch, Crossbill, Rock Bunting.

Access

The complete circuit may take the whole day. Reach the Col de la Schlucht (Schlucht Pass) ① via the D417, from Gérardmer on the Lorraine side or from Munster on the Alsace side. Take the Sentier des

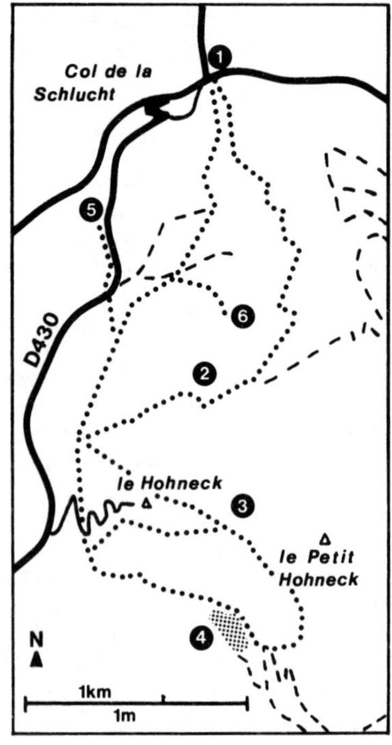

Roches (the rock track) 200 m (220 yards) before the top on the Alsace side (marked with a blue rectangle). For 2 km (1.25 miles) it passes a series of rocky outcrops and many natural spruce woods. Further on, the footpath joins the beech–fir zone and arrives at a wide forestry track which climbs to the right to the Cirque du Frankenthal. Pass by the farm on the moraine ② and skirt the peat-bog, then arrive on the steep footpath that climbs up to the Col de Falimont (Falimont Pass). Skirt around the side of the 'cirque' towards the Col de Shaeferthal ③. Along the path it is possible to look over the high heath on the right, and the southern side of the 'cirque' on the left.

From the 'col' there are two possibilities: – return westwards, skirting the northern side of the Cirque de Wormspel as far as the Col du Fond (Fond Pass), and, along the path, stop from time to time using convenient points to look into the 'cirque'; – or descend towards Schiessrothried Lake ④, skirt around the right side and climb up to the 'col' via the Fond-du-Cirque footpath.

Next, continue directly north on the western side of the Hohneck (on the GR5 (Grandes Randonnées 5 – hiker's route 5) marked by red rectangles). Go back to the Col de Falimont and continue on. A visit to Chitelet high-altitude gardens ⑤ may be worthwhile if the weather allows. Further on a small detour via the Hauteurs de la Martinswand (Martinswand Heights) ⑥ offers a fine view over the Hohneck and the Frankenthal. All that remains now is to follow the line of the ridge northwards (on the GR5) as far as the car park.

Species

- Along the Sentier des Roches (rock track) many forest passerines occur, including Ring Ouzel, Coal and Crested Tits, Goldcrest and Crossbill.
- This is where Black Woodpeckers can be found, they can be most frequently heard in early spring.
- Look for Alpine Accentor on the Frankenthal during the climb, especially on the northern slopes.
- On the high heath, Water and Meadow Pipits breed. Also Wheatear at the Col de Falimont.
- In May and June, when the young are independent, Peregrines are often seen. Other raptors, such as Sparrowhawk, Honey Buzzard and Kestrel, may also be seen.
- Rock Bunting occur on the Wormspel.
- Along the ridge and on the top of the Frankenthal, Rock Thrushes may be found.
- Citril Finch, Dunnock and Ring Ouzel occur on the edges of meadows.

158 Golbey Scrubland

The site is between the Moselle River and the canal, just to the north of Golbey on the outskirts of Épinal. It is on riverside public land so hunting is banned. It is a mixture of bush and scrub. The vegetation is recolonising the area after much of it had been spoilt by various workings. The site should be visited during the spring, during the breeding season. It is possible to familiarise oneself with many scrubland birds, some relatively difficult species can be seen side by side: Reed and Marsh

Warblers, Icterine and Melodious Warblers, Willow Warbler and Chiffchaff, Blackcap, Garden Warbler, Whitethroat and Lesser Whitethroat, and Grasshopper Warbler. The nightingale is common here. On the Moselle River, look for Little Ringed Plover, Kingfisher and Sand Martin. Access is from the south of the Épinal–Drogneville Aerodrome, reached via the D12.

MIDI-PYRÉNÉES

159 THE VICDESSOS UPPER VALLEY

7 km/4.35 miles
Fontargente
(IGN 2149 – 1/50 000)

Habitat and Timing

An area of alpine meadows and rocky outcrops, delimited to the east by the bottom of the Vicdessos Valley and the ridge of the French/Spanish border to the west. The altitude varies between 1,850 and 2,509 metres (at the pass); there is easy access to the alpine zone and the nesting upland birds of the Pyrenees. The area is accessible between June and November without special equipment.

Calendar

Summer: nesting birds include, Ptarmigan, Water Pipit, Black Redstart, Rock Thrush, Wheatear, Alpine Accentor, Chough and Alpine Chough.

Autumn: erratics on migration may include: Lammergeier, Griffon Vulture, Black Kite, Honey Buzzard, Montagu's Harrier, Wryneck, passerines (Ortolan Bunting, Tree Pipit).

Access

Leave the N20 at Tarascon-sur-Ariège (16 km/10 miles) south of Foix, on the D108, which follows the river Vicdessos towards Vicdessos, then go onto Auzat, Marc and Mounicou (24 km/15 miles after Tarascon). Some 2 km (1.25 miles) after Mounicou the road becomes a track, in bad repair in parts. After Soulcem Lake (a reservoir) go on another 2.5 km (1.55 miles) or so and park the car opposite the second stream, which runs into the Vicdessos on its left bank, next to a small house ①. The stream runs down from Soucarrane Lake (at 2,292 m) ②, which can be reached after a 45-minute (1-hour maximum) walk, along a marked trail (spots of red paint on the rocks) climbing up along the right bank of the stream. Pass to the left of the lake climbing south-westwards for 2 km (1.25 miles) as far as the Port de Bouet (2,509 m) ③. Then continue the walk northwards, passing to the west of Soucarrane, at the foot of the Pic de la

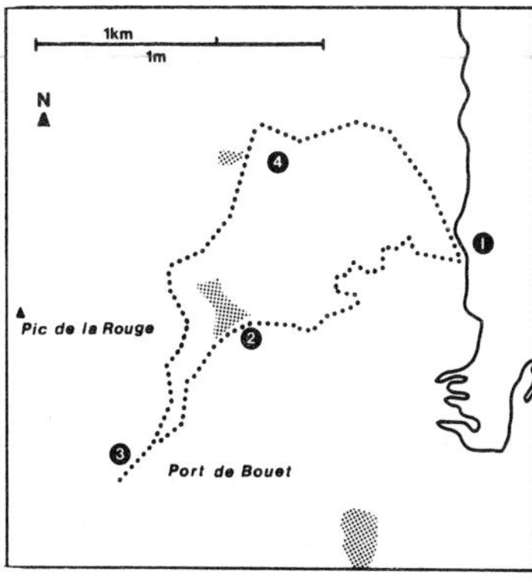

Rouge (2,902 m). It is possible to return down the valley using the same trail as for coming up or via the GR11 (hiker's trail n° 11), which, from Soucarrane, goes northward and drops to Roumazet Lake (2,163 m) ④. Then follow the stream from Roumazet coming out at the bottom of Vicdessos Valley, about 1 km (0.6 miles) to the north of the car.

Species

- Ptarmigan can be seen on the scree, particularly between Soucaranne Lake and the Port de Bouet.
- Rock Thrush can be seen on the slopes of the Pic de la Rouge.
- Alpine Accentor can be seen in the same places as Rock Thrush.
- Water Pipits are common everywhere, even in the valley bottom.
- Migrating raptors (Honey Buzzard, kites, harriers) can be seen anywhere, especially in the afternoon when warm thermals help them to pass over the Pyrenees.

160 Montbel Lake

This lake is 25 km (15.5 miles) to the east of Foix. From Foix, take the D117 as far as Lavelanet, then head towards Laroque d'Olmes from where you take the road to Léran. You can see migrant waders (Ringed Plovers, Black-winged Stilt, 'shanks and other small waders) and marsh terns, in spring and autumn. Cormorant and ducks can be seen during the autumn and winter.

161 DOURBIE GORGES

20 km/12.5 miles
Rodez-Mende
(IGN 58 – 1/100 000)

Habitat and Timing

A deep valley cut by the Dourbie River between the Causse Noir (a limestone plateau) and the Larzac, which dominate the river by more than 400 m. The valley is lined by interesting rocky cliffs, much used by large raptors. Wide open spaces on the plateau are good for birds. This area is one of Aveyron's most picturesque.

Calendar

Winter: Golden Eagle, Griffon Vulture, Peregrine, Merlin, Eagle Owl, Water Pipit, Alpine Accentor, Wallcreeper, Citril Finch.

Spring: Short-toed Eagle, Egyptian Vulture, Hobby, Scops Owl, Alpine Swift, Black Woodpecker, Crag Martin, Dartford Warbler, Raven, Chough. On the plateau, Stone Curlew, Little Bustard, Black-eared Wheatear.

Autumn: Black Stork, Osprey, Ring Ouzel.

Access

From Millau, take the D991 towards Nant. There are small parking sites on the side of the road as far as La Roque-Sainte-Marguerite. Raptors can be seen from the valley. The itinerary on foot: from Millau, take the GR22 (hiker's trail – information from: Sentiers de Pays, BP 600, 12100 Millau), which climbs as far as Cureplats ① on the Causse Noir (a public forest). Follow the GR as far as Caoussou ② and descend into the Dourbie Valley via the Valat Nègre ravine ③. Return to Millau on the D991. This walk takes the whole day with the visits to both the plateau and the valley.

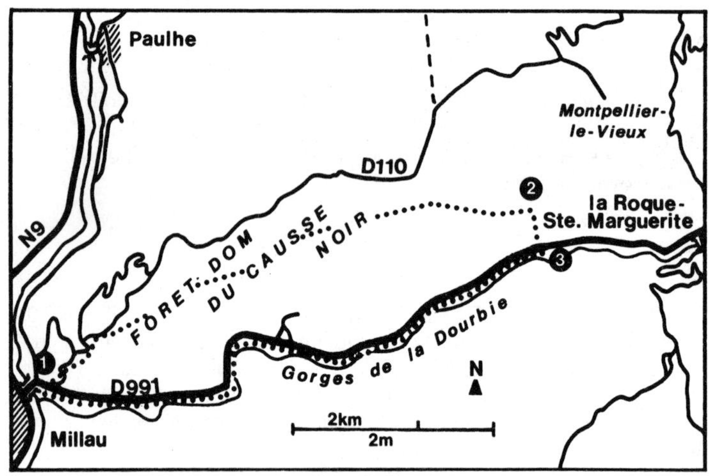

Species

- On the plateau in May, it is possible to come across displaying Little Bustard.
- Black-eared Wheatear nest every year on the Causse Noir.
- On evenings in May or June, the fluty, melancholy call of Stone Curlew can be heard on the plateau.
- Scops Owls sing in the valley from the end of April onwards.
- Each winter there are a few Wallcreepers on the cliffs, look for their butterfly-like flight.

- Griffon Vulture can be seen in winter, visiting from nearby Lozère. Egyptian Vultures are sometimes seen in spring.
- Raven and Chough breed on the cliffs overlooking the Aveyron.

162 The Causse Rouge

To the north of Millau, the southern part (between Millau and Candas) of the Causse Rouge has distinctive (Holm-Oak) vegetation and a Mediterranean fauna: there are Short-toed Eagle, Scops Owl, Short-toed Lark, Dartford, Orphean and Subalpine Warblers; Black-eared Wheatear, Rock Bunting and Rock Sparrow.

163 CARDEILHAC FOREST

17.5 km/10.9 miles
Boulogne-sur-Gesse
(IGN 1845 – 1/50 000)

Habitat and Timing

On the east of the Lannamezan Plateau, Cardeilhac Forest covers a small area of about 1,000 hectares of common land and public forest. In this area local native trees – principally oak and Sweet Chestnut – grow together with introduced species – Maritime and Scots Pine, Red Oak and even larch along the central avenue. There is an arboretum of great interest, with many unusual species of tree, which is well worth a look during the walk.

Calendar

Spring and summer: Buzzard, Honey Buzzard, Sparrowhawk, Hen Harrier, Hobby; Nightjar, Great Spotted, Lesser Spotted and Green

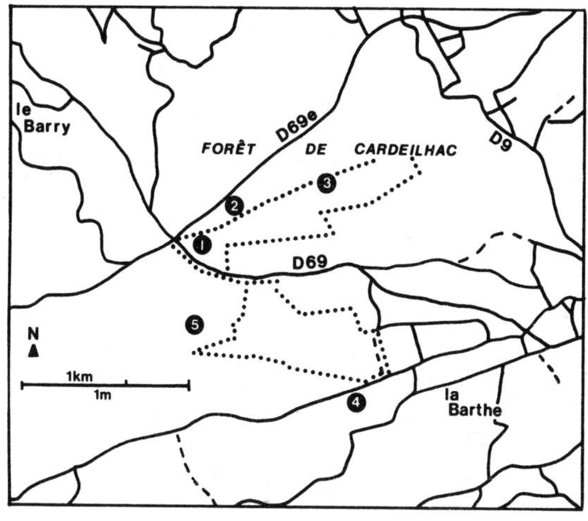

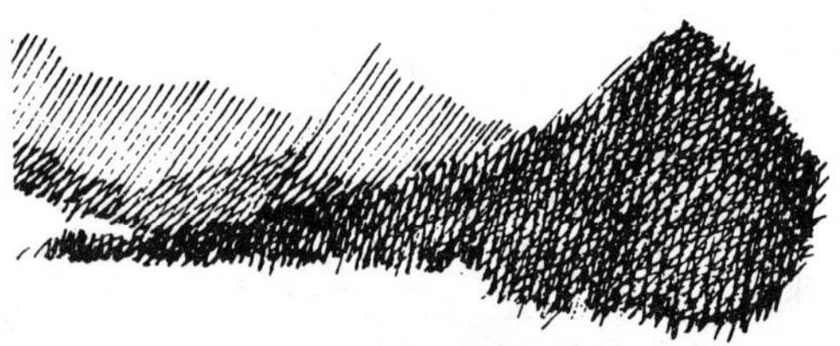

Honey Buzzard

Woodpeckers; Woodlark, Tree Pipit; Mistle Thrush, Melodious Warbler; Marsh, Coal and Crested Tits, Cirl Bunting.

Access

The forest is accessible from the D9 road between Saint-Gaudens and Boulogne-sur-Gesse. Take the D69 north-westwards from Cap-de-la-Vielle and at Lodes turn right towards Cassagne. Park the car 1 km (0.6 miles) further on ① and continue on foot for another 1 km (0.6 miles). Here, turn onto the forest avenue on the right going towards the arboretum ② and continue for a little less than 1.5 km (0.9 miles). Turn right and continue along the main avenue ③ (see map); 100 m (110 yards) before the arboretum, turn left. This leads back onto the D69, (turn left on the road); then take the next path on the right, follow this, referring to the map, as far as the place named Fontaine-des-Champs ④. Turn right and then take the next track on the right and follow this for 3.5 km (2.2 miles). Once again turn right ⑤ and stay on this track as far as the road.

The circuit can be joined at two points: via the forester's house and the arboretum or at Fontaine-des-Champs on the D75. There are very few steep sections on the proposed circuit, so that it can be walked by most people.

Species

- The closed habitat in the arboretum is good for Mistle Thrush.
- Further into the forest, Nuthatch, Treecreeper and Crested Tit can be found.
- This damp part of the forest is good for Hobby (in spring) and Sparrowhawk.
- It is also here that Marsh Tit can be seen.
- Honey Buzzard and Hen Harrier hunt over the more cultivated areas.
- Along the trail, on June evenings, Nightjar can be heard.
- Along the Franqueville Canal at Cardeilhac there are a few Red-backed Shrikes as well as Tree Pipits.

164 Bouconne Forest

Some 15 km (9.3 miles) to the west of Toulouse, this large oak and pine wood (2,300 hectares), in a region almost devoid of forest or hedgerow, is very good for nesting passerines. It needs to be visited in spring to hear Nightjar singing near felled areas where Dartford Warbler also occur; a few pairs of Wood Warbler, alongside the Bonelli's Warbler, breed in the large mature trees to the south. In more open areas many raptors can be seen: Buzzard, Sparrowhawk, Short-toed Eagle, Booted Eagle, and, over newly-felled areas, Hen and sometimes Montagu's Harriers.

165 NÉOUVIELLE NATIONAL NATURE RESERVE

4.5 km/2.8 miles
Vielle-Aure
(IGN 1248 – 1/50 000)

Habitat and Timing

Created in 1935, Néouvielle (which means old, or persistent, snow) National Nature Reserve has a very diversified mountain fauna and flora: rocky scree, alpine meadows, lakes, fast-flowing mountain streams and mountain pine woods offer habitats for many high-altitude species, along with the more common lowland birds.

Calendar

Spring and summer: from June to October, Capercaillie, Black Woodpecker, Grey Wagtail, Water Pipit, Ring Ouzel, Wheatear, Black Redstart, Alpine Accentor, Dipper, Goldcrest, Coal and Crested Tits, Treecreeper, Citril Finch, Snow Finch.

Access

To get to the reserve from Lannamezan, take the N129 southwards towards Arreau and on to Saint-Lary, continue as far as Fabian. From here follow the N129 to the right, pass Orédon Lake and stop at the car park at Aumar Lake ①. The proposed circular hike lasts between four

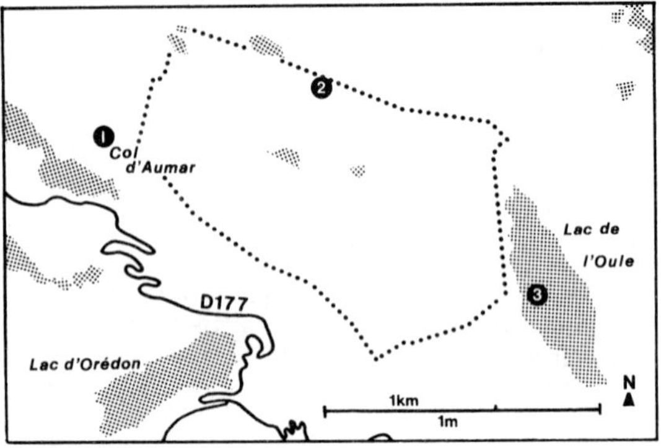

and six hours, depending on the amount of time spent watching; altitude varies between 1,800 m and 2,381 m. From the car park, go towards the Col d'Aumar (Aumar Pass) at 2,381 m crossing the mountain pine wood; after the pass, drop back down into the rocks and alpine meadows of Estibère Valley ②, walking between lakes and streams, before getting to Oule Lake and its forests ③; then go back to the starting point via the GR10 (hiker's trail 10) passing the Col d'Estoudou.

Species

- The mountain pines, just after Aumar Lake, are good for Ring Ouzel, Siskin, Coal and Crested Tits, Goldcrest and Treecreeper.
- Around the Col d'Aumar, you can see Alpine Accentor and sometimes the rarer Snow Finch.
- The meadows and rocky outcrops in Estibère Valley are the domain of Water Pipit, Wheatear and Black Redstart.
- Black Woodpeckers are common in the mountain pine woods.
- Capercaillie is without doubt 'the' bird of the pine woods.

166 The Cirque de Gavarnie

A few kilometres south of Gèdre, the heights around the magnificent Cirque de Gavarnie (a protected natural monument) offer the walker an almost unique panorama of an alpine zone with its many snow-fields. Most members of the high-mountain fauna can be found here: large raptors including Golden Eagle, Griffon Vulture and Lammergeier; and passerines such as Citril Finch, Chough and Alpine Chough, Snow Finch and Wallcreeper. It must be emphasised that this little paradise is only easily accessible in summer.

167 GRÉSIGNE NATIONAL FOREST

18 km/11.2 miles
Nègrepelisse
(IGN 2141 – 1/50 000)

Habitat and Timing

A mature Sessile Oak forest with an undergrowth of Hornbeam, and beech-groves on the north and west slopes. This forest occupies a large natural basin open to the south, from 200 m (220 yards) to 500 m (550 yards) altitude. The forest is remarkable in spring for the diversity and abundance of the woodland birds it contains. There is unrestricted access on foot. The entrance of vehicles is controlled and restricted to those transporting wood; the forest tracks are closed during periods when there is hunting.

Calendar

Spring: Buzzard, Goshawk, Sparrowhawk, Booted Eagle, Short-toed Eagle; Middle Spotted Woodpecker; Wood Warbler, Hawfinch, Woodcock, Marsh Tit.

Access

From Gaillac, take the D964 going through Castelnau-de-Montmiral, and 8 km (5 miles) further on take the D15 towards Vaour. Some 1.5 km (0.9

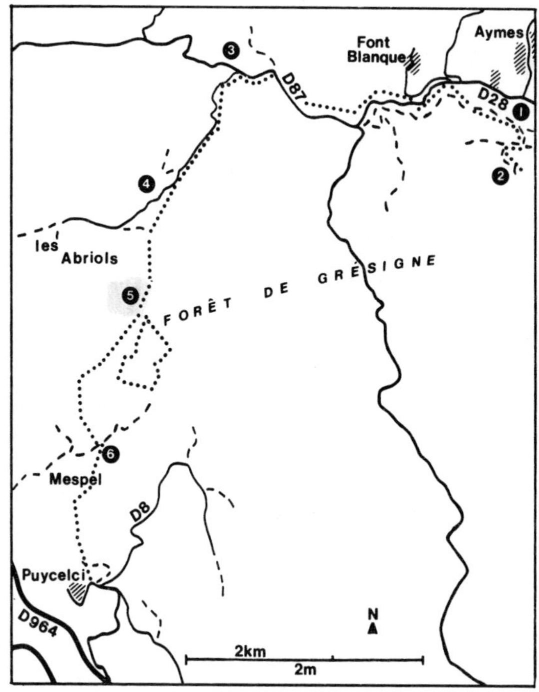

miles) before Vaour turn left on the D28 and left again at the first junction (about 500 m/550 yards on) going as far as Pas-de-Pontraute (where there is a large car park at the entrance to the forest) ①. Take the Baronne Forest Trail, which climbs slightly to a junction under Lafage Château (there is an esplanade with a car park overlooking the national forest) ②. Come back by the same track as far as Pas-de-Pontraute, then take the marked trail that closely follows the Mur de Grésigne (Grésigne wall) as far as Haute-Serre. After Haute-Serre turn right along the road that leads to Fontblanque, at the first bend to the right, continue straight on, still following the Mur de Grésigne, as far as Pech-Aguze (highest point in the forest as 494 m). Continue along the trail as far as Fontbonne holiday camp, then take the D87 to the right for about 600 m (660 yards). Now take the first road to the left ③ as far as Périlhac (forester's house). After the house ④, take the track to the left and at the first junction turn left again. Follow Mespel forest road for about another 1 km (0.6 miles) and park the car in the car park ⑤. Take the barred track to the left walking the 3-km (1.85 miles) circuit around Montoulieu. Back at the car, continue along Mespel forest road as far as the crossroads (car park) ⑥. Walk the GR46 (hiker's trail 46) opposite as far as Puycelci.

Species

- Fage Esplanade is an excellent place for watching displaying raptors such as Buzzard, Short-toed Eagle, Sparrowhawk and Goshawk.
- The southern slope of the ridge has Black Woodpecker.
- Bonelli's Warbler and Red-backed Shrike occur in the limestone scrub on the ridge's northern slope.
- Woodcock occur in the oak wood on the southern slope.
- Tawny Pipits sometimes nest on the limestone slopes.
- Hawfinch, Marsh Tit and Wood Warbler are typical of the oak woods.
- Montoulieu is a good place for finding Honey Buzzard, Hobby and Hen Harrier.
- In the low-coppice areas on Mespel Plateau it is possible to find Dartford and Subalpine Warblers.
- On summer evenings you can hear Scops Owl at Puycelci.

168 The Montagne Noir

A few kilometres to the south-west of Revel, the Montagne Noir is, at all seasons, a place of contrasts. The beech groves on the northern slope touch the Holm-oak woods on the south; this often gives rise to a strange mixture of birds: Crossbill, Bullfinch, Bonelli's Warbler and Goldcrest occur alongside Middle Spotted Woodpecker, Crested, Coal, Marsh, Blue and Great Tits, Red-backed Shrike, Tawny Pipit and Woodlark, whereas some more high-altitude species sometimes occur on passage, for example Alpine Accentor and Snow Finch.

MAP – Page 139

169 THE AVEYRON GORGES

Caussade (IGN 2140 – 1/50 000) and Nègrepelisse (IGN 2141 – 1/50 000)

June 1992 Dull & grey!

Habitat and Timing

This is a 12 km (7.5 miles) long limestone gorge cut into the Limogne Plateau (in lower Quercy); the Aveyron River continues later with a few rapids, riverside woodland with poplar, alder and ash, and limestone cliffs 150 m to 200 m high. These cliffs, as well as the plateau (nearly 350 m at its highest), have a sub-Mediterranean flora. A remarkable area for cliff-dwelling and Mediterranean birds. There is free access using local roads and tracks.

Calendar

Winter: two species in particular pass the winter, Wallcreeper (cliffs, villages and Penne and Bruniquel Châteaux) from December to April, and Grey Heron on the banks of the Aveyron.

Spring: more interesting breeding species include: Dipper, Lesser Spotted Woodpecker, Golden Oriole, Black Kite and Hobby; cliff-dwelling species such as: Crag Martin, Alpine Swift, Stock Dove, x3 Peregrine, Kestrel, Eagle Owl, Raven, Jackdaw. Subalpine and Bonelli's Warblers and Red-backed Shrike occur on the wooded heaths and open coppice within Holm-oak woodland; the Short-toed Eagle hunts here.

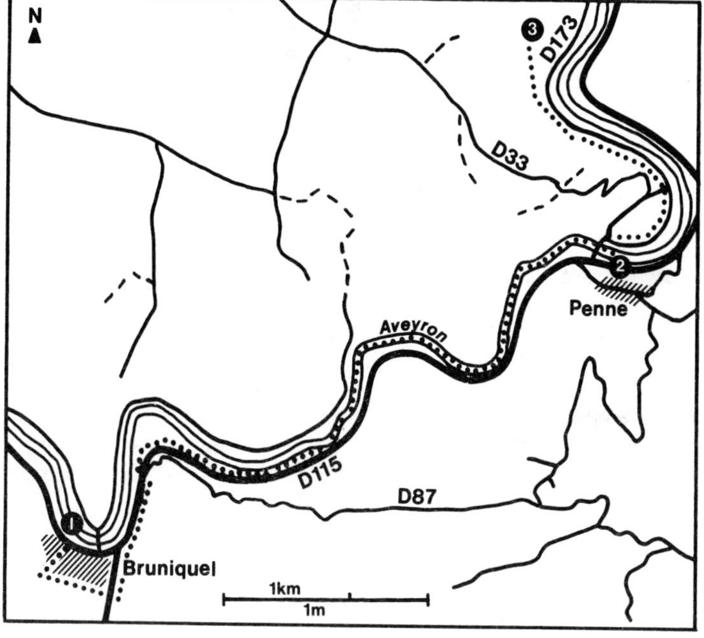

Access

Take the D115 from Montauban as far as Bruniquel (car park) ①, then Penne (car park) ②. From these two villages (from where there are good views) many cliff-dwelling species can be seen. At the bottom of Penne, cross the Aveyron and turn right just after the bridge, on the D173, which follows the right bank (good views over the gorge, particularly at Couyrac ③). From here you can continue along the valley as far as Brousses and Saint-Antonin (D115). You can also explore the gorges by canoe (for information contact; the CPIE de Saint-Antonin, at the Moulin de Rouméqoux).

Wallcreeper

Species

- Alpine Swift can be seen along the cliffs in spring and summer.
- Wallcreeper can be seen on the cliff faces or on Bruniquel Château (December to April). There is also a colony of Jackdaws.
- Red-backed Shrike, Subalpine and Bonelli's Warblers occur in areas of open coppice.
- The Dipper is present year-round on the Aveyron.
- Black Kite and Hobby soar over the gorges in spring and summer.
- Golden Oriole and Lesser Spotted Woodpecker nest in the riverside woodland.
- Grey Herons are present in winter.
- Wallcreepers can often be seen at Penne Château esplanade in winter, there is also a Jackdaw colony.
- Raven can be seen above the cliffs.

170 SAINT-NICOLAS-DE-LA-GRAVE RESERVOIR

5 km/3.1 miles
Saint-Nicholas-de-la-Grave
(IGN 1941 – 1/50 000)

Habitat and Timing

A dam on the Garonne River downstream from where it is joined by the Tarn has given rise to this 400-hectare lake on the flood-plain of the river. There is a marina and leisure centre on the northern part of the lake, where the Tarn flows in, but the southern part upstream of the Garonne is less used by boats and is suitable for duck and waders resting during migration or over-wintering. There is free access to the lakeside, but access is restricted for cars. The track along the bank, when on foot, is excellent for watching over the reservoir, either with binoculars or telescope.

Calendar

Winter: Great Crested Grebe, Cormorant; Mallard, Gadwall, Shoveler, Teal, Tufted Duck, Pochard, sometimes Ferruginous Duck and Red-crested Pochard.

Spring: Pintail; Black-tailed Godwit, Spotted Redshank, Greenshank, Wood Sandpiper; Black-headed Gull, Black Tern.

Breeding season: Mallard, Yellow-legged Gull, Common Tern (rare).

Autumn: Little Grebe, Lapwing, Golden Plover, Kingfisher.

Access

Take the N113 and D15 to get to the lake from Moissac, or the D15 from Saint-Nicholas. Follow the signposts marked Plan d'Eau which lead to the leisure centre. It is best to leave the car at the car park behind the swimming-pool ①, then walk the lakeside via the port as far as La Bernade ② and continue on to the end of the lake ③. This offers a walk of about 5 km (3.1 miles), there and back.

Species

- Sometimes, in winter, a Red or a Black-throated Diver spends a few days here with the Great Crested Grebes.
- In winter, many Cormorants are present along the embankment.
- Shoveler, Teal, Tufted Duck and Pochard roost on the lake in winter, along with the Coot.
- In spring, waders often make a short stay; as early as February for Black-tailed Godwit, not until April for 'shanks.
- In spring, both Black Tern and Little Gull hunt along the embankment.
- Two or three dozen Grey Heron pass the winter, either in the shallows or on the islands in the lake.
- Kingfishers can be found especially in the trees above the flooded embankment.

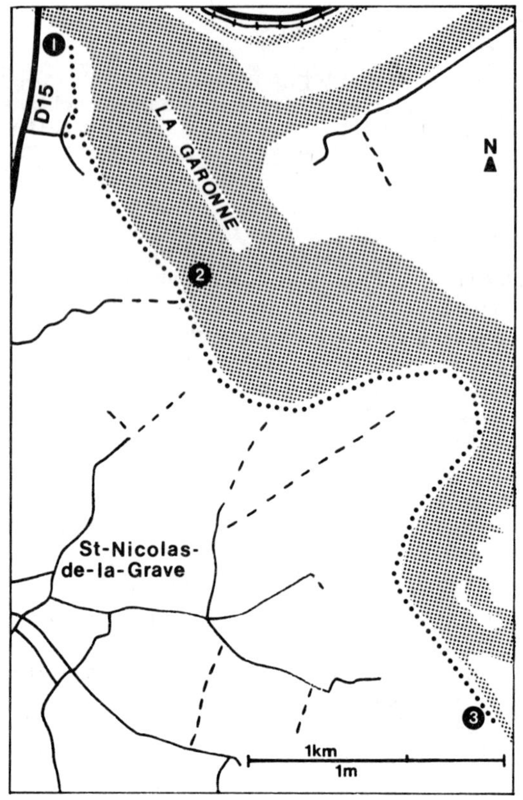

NORD-PAS-DE-CALAIS

171 GORIAUX POND

6 km/3.75 miles
Saint-Amand-les-Eaux
(IGN 2605 west – 1/25 000)
and Denain
(IGN 2606 west – 1/25 000)

Habitat and Timing

Goriaux Pond is a large forest lake formed by mining subsidence (the Wallers–Arenberg pithead can be seen at the south of the site). Settling, which is still occuring, has brought about a decrease in the area of reed-bed, which now only grows in the south-west (where muddy water arrives from the mine). Along the whole of the south side, slag from the mine has been dumped. Around the lake there is degraded humid woodland (birch) or plantations (pines), but the bird life is extraordinary thanks to the amount of food available (insects, particularly mosqitoes, are abundant from May onwards; wear long sleeves and use an insect repellent if going in the forest).

A remarkable area for the diversity of wetland and woodland birds present, and easy to watch from the flat top of the slag heap. Most of the forest roads are freely open to cars (signposts mark otherwise), but access to the western part of the slag heap is controlled. Contact the ONF (Office National des Forêts, 3 Place Jehan-Froissart, BP 422, 59322 Valenciennes Cedex tel: 27.30.35.70). It is important to obtain permission beforehand as a mark of respect to the ONF, especially considering the amount of work they do trying to control public disturbance here; please set an example. In order to watch the birds under good conditions, avoid Sundays and bank holidays. Go first thing in the morning.

Calendar

Winter: ducks (particularly Teal); Bearded Tit.

Spring: Great Crested Grebe; raptors (Buzzard, Honey Buzzard, Hobby, Osprey on passage); Bluethroat; Swift, and hirundines in spectacular numbers on migration.

Autumn: spectacular movements of Lapwing, geese, Chaffinch and Brambling.

Access

Coming from Lille or Valenciennes on the motorway, take the Raisnes-Parc Naturel de Saint-Armand turn-off. From Lille there is direct access to the car park ①; from Valenciennes you have to pass under the motorway. There is a bus from Valenciennes (from the coach station in Valenciennes, Place du Hainaut). From the car park take the maintained path giving access to the top of the flat slag heap. From the summit ②, there is a splendid view over the whole subsidence area and the

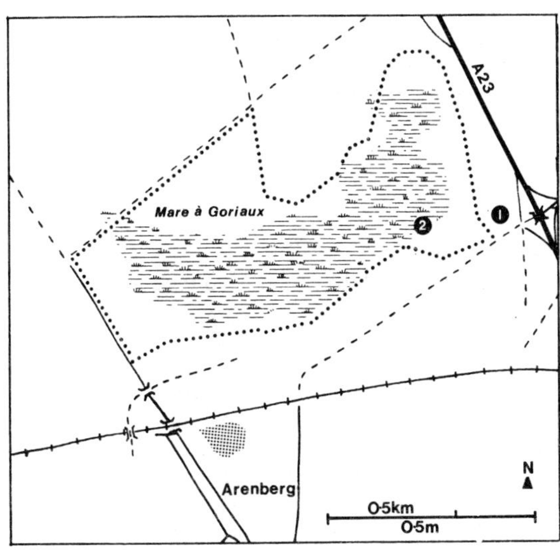

Saint-Amand hills. A magnificent baroque tower 6 km (3.75 miles) away, part of an ancient abbey, marks the north.

In good weather, the Tournai Heights (30 km/19 miles away) can be seen. There are few birds in this sector (much fishing), but there may be some, this is where divers occur. If permission has been obtained, go on to the western part of the slag heap. The grass-covered slopes on its top are being colonised by birch. Put up the telescope where a path descends to the lake. Next take this path. Whilst following the edge of the reed-bed, listen, particularly at dusk in spring. Entry into the reed-bed is prohibited. After walking along the base of the slag heap for 100 m (110 yards) cross a bridge over the stream that feeds into the lake, follow the path that leads to Drève des Boules d'Hérin, a badly-paved sector, (part of the Paris–Roubaix cycle racecourse). Take this to the right for about 400 m (440 yards). At a junction with a red-grit forest track, turn right. After 1 km (0.6 miles) at another junction, turn right on a track that goes towards Mare à Goriaux. At the end, turn left along a winding path that follows the northern bank and leads back to the slag heap and car park.

Species

- Siskin, Redpoll, Twite and Snow Bunting occur together on the near-wooded slopes of the slag heap.
- In winter and on passage, large concentrations of duck occur (saw-bills during cold spells).
- Bluethroat and Savi's Warbler can be heard in the reed-bed in spring; Bearded Tit in winter.
- Grey Heron and Cormorant perch on the dead trees.
- There are many Nightingales, Willow Warblers (and mosquitoes) in the damp forest, from May onwards.
- Woodcock can be found roding in March.
- Large trees in the woods are used by hole-nesting passerines (tits, Short-toed Treecreeper, Nuthatch).
- Raptors display over the forest between February and June (Buzzard, Honey Buzzard, Sparrowhawk, Hobby).
- It is easy to see many woodpeckers (Lesser Spotted, Green and Black).
- In winter, at dusk, Black-headed Gulls fly in to roost.

172 Dunkerque New Outer Harbour

The new outer harbour is situated in the parishes of Loon-Plage and Grande-Synthe. Now abandoned, this enormous construction project was started in the 1960s. Large waste areas created by the construction work are still interesting, particularly during the breeding season (Avocet, sometimes Black-winged Stilt), but to be avoided during the hunting season. On the other hand, hunting is banned in the basin of the harbour. It is an excellent spot for wintering seabirds (divers, Cormorant, Slavonian and Black-necked Grebes, Eider, Long-tailed Duck and rarities often enough). From the eastern jetty, lined by curious cubes of concrete, there are excellent views of seabird migration (August–January and February–May). There are good numbers of Snow Bunting wintering on Braek embankment. The neighbouring basin often has rarities, although there is a plan to build an industrial complex here.

173 Prés-du-Hem/Armentières

Prés-du-Hem Leisure Centre, near Armentières, thanks to some enlightened management, has become the best site in the region for wintering wetland birds. Grey Heron, Cormorant and many species of duck are numerous, except when the water is frozen. The close proximity of Belgian Flanders, a wintering site for geese, means that some occur here, including Pink-footed Goose (otherwise rare in France). Many passerines of open wetlands occur in winter, especially Water and Meadow Pipits. On migration, many waders may occur if conditions are right (low water-level).

174 Heron Lake/Villeneuve-d'Ascq

This lake in semi-urban surroundings, at Villeneuve-d'Ascq, is less protected from disturbance by the public, but local conservationists are active and the local authorities have been sympathetic to their arguments. There are large numbers of duck in winter, Pochard being the most numerous. On migration, birds often do not stay long, but the site is so attractive that almost any wetland species may occur, from White-winged Black Tern to Osprey. A good variety of passerines and owls are found in the surroundings (scrub and woodland).

175 TRÉLON FOREST

7 km/4.35 miles and 9 km/5.6 miles
Trélon
(IGN 2807 – 1/50 000)

Habitat and Timing

This is a vast area of forest at the western end of the Ardennes. At a lower altitude and with more varied (hedgerows) and humid habitats there is a greater diversity of species, albeit that mountain species no longer occur. The best woodland is made up of very old oaks, with a dense undergrowth of Hornbeam. Recent plantations of evergreen have somewhat spoilt a greater part of the forest, although they do provide a more diversified habitat. There are some very fine areas of Foxglove.

The forest and its edges have many raptors (throughout the year), wetland birds (on migration and in winter) and passerines (especially in spring and summer). Movement within private parts of the forest is restricted to the tracks. There is no public access to Folie Lake (a reserve of the Nord Hunters Federation). The Val-Joly area is best given a wide berth in summer (mass tourism).

Calendar

Winter: raptors (Buzzard, Goshawk, Sparrowhawk), Whooper Swan.

Spring: Lesser Spotted, Middle Spotted and Black Woodpeckers; Wood Warbler, Hawfinch; Great Grey and Red-backed Shrikes; Lesser Whitethroat; Fieldfare. Lapwing nests.

Spring and autumn: interesting wetland species (Black Stork) in the wetter parts.

Access

The best areas are to the south and east of the zone, around Trélon. Take the Chimay road; 3 km (1.85 miles) after leaving Trélon, turn left to the village of Wallers-Trélon. There is a parking site for a few cars about 100 m (110 yards) after the last house in the village, on the left on the road to Moustier-en-Fagne at a right-angle bend in the road ①. For the 'hedgerow walk' take the D83 towards Moustier. There are fine views over the south of the Ardennes, and a good little lake 1 km (0.6 miles) further on. Then, for 1 km (0.6 miles), the road offers good views, between woods, of Helpe Majeure Valley; this is a good migration corridor. Turn right at

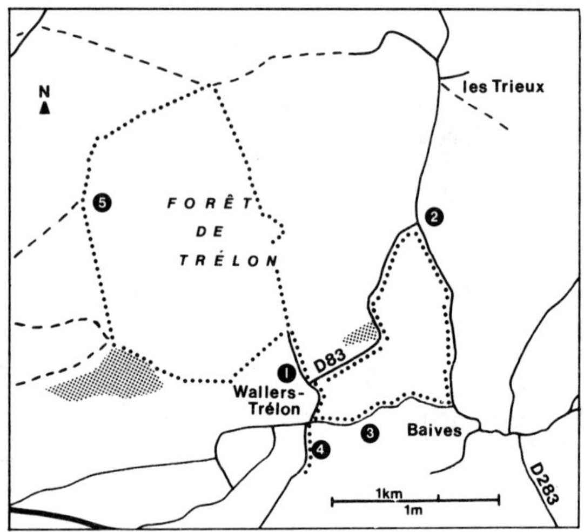

the junction with the D283 ② towards Baives village. There is some nice hedgerow near the cemetery. Turn right directly on entering the village, to climb the 'mont' ③. On its summit are bush, grassland and pines on an old quarry. There is a splendid view over the Trélon Massif and Helpe Majeure Valley. To arrive back at the car, take the first road on the right in Wallers-Trélon village, just before the church (some fine stone-built houses). A small detour can be made in order to follow a pretty river for 500 m (550 yards), by taking the little road just after the church, on the left ④.

For the walk in the forest (9 km/15.6 miles), take the dirt-track that goes towards the forest. Follow the forest track straight on to the Prince-Philippe junction. Turn left taking the winding forest track as far as Blois junction ⑤. Take the third forest track on the left, which after nearly 1.5 km (0.9 miles) without a bend, joins a forest road. Turn left following the fence of Folie Reserve (no access) to get to the forest road that leads back to the starting point.

Species

- On the first fine days in January or February, raptors can be seen displaying over the woods: Buzzard, Sparrowhawk, Goshawk.
- Grey Heron can be seen on the small lake.
- Great Crested Grebe and Coot can be seen in the spring.
- The hedgerows along the road may have Fieldfare, Lesser Whitethroat, Great Grey and Black-backed Shrikes.
- Melodious Warblers are present on the 'mont' at Baives from late April onwards, along with many other warblers.
- Dipper and Grey Wagtail are relatively easy to see along the side of the river.
- Honey Buzzard display along the forest edge in spring.
- Hawfinch can be found in mature woods with little undergrowth.
- Great Grey Shrike and Grasshopper Warbler nest in the larger cleared areas of the forest.
- The mature trees of the forest may have Lesser, Middle Spotted and Black Woodpeckers.
- The shy Woodcock can be seen flying in the woods on spring evenings.
- Coniferous plantations have Goldcrest and Firecrest, Coal and Crested Tits.

176 CAP GRIS-NEZ AND CAP BLANC-NEZ

Marquise
(IGN 2103 east – 1/25 000)

Habitat and Timing

A remarkable peninsula marking the limit of the Channel to the west and the North Sea to the east. Cap Gris-Nez is the closest point to Britain in France; the Straits of Dover are only 28 km (17.5 miles) wide here. The area is in the form of a large bay (Wissant Bay) with a line of sand-dunes, bordered at each end by a rocky headland. To the west, Gris-Nez (Jurassic rock), rises some 50 m above the sea. To the east, the chalk cliffs of Blanc-Nez are more than 100 m high for some kilometres. A large marsh spreads out behind the moving line of dunes. The countryside inland from Cap Blanc-Nez, the Artois, is made up of open fields, whereas that at Gris-Nez, the Boulonnais, is more of a mosaic of habitats with hedgerows.

This is the best place in northern France to observe migration, and one of the best in Europe. Hundreds of thousands of seabirds, waders and passerines pass this stategic point each year. There is unrestricted access onto the cliff tops of both Caps, as well as onto the Courte-Dune. The Dune-d'Aval and Wissant Marsh have restricted public access (contact the Espace Naturel Régional). Mont d'Hubert is now closed to the public, as there is an experiment in place on chalk grassland management using cattle; this has been running since spring 1988. The coast is a no-hunting reserve.

Calendar

Autumn: divers (three species), Great Crested and Red-necked Grebes; Gannet, Sooty, Yelkouan and Manx Shearwaters; Cormorant; Spoonbill, Grey Heron; geese, Shelduck, Goldeneye, sawbills, Long-tailed Duck, Common and Velvet Scoters; skuas, Mediterranean and Sabine's Gulls, terns, Guillemot, Razorbill, numerous passerines.

Winter: divers, grebes, sea duck, Razorbill, Puffin (rare), Guillemot.

Spring: divers, grebes, Gannet, Cormorants, duck, waders, terns, Guillemot and Razorbill.

Access

From Boulogne, to the south, take the D940 which passes through Wimereux, Ambleteuse and Audreselles. From Calais, to the east, take the N1 towards Boulogne and turn onto the D191 at Marquise, going towards Audinghen. The area of the two 'Caps' is some 15 km (9.3 miles) from these two towns. There are railway stations at Calais and Boulogne, with direct links from Lille, Dunkerque and Paris. A bus route between Calais and Boulogne, which stops at villages in the area of the two 'Caps', only runs in summer. There are large car parks at each Cap.

Cap Gris-Nez migration watches are conducted from the cliff top. Stop at the car park at the foot of the lighthouse ① and watch from the cliff a little to the north of the lighthouse ②, looking towards the English coast. It is best to bring a collapsible chair if you are thinking of doing a long watch, as well as warm and waterproof clothes at all seasons (there is often a strong, cool breeze). From Gris-Nez, many interesting walks are possible, either along the coast ③ and ④ or inland ⑤ and ⑥.

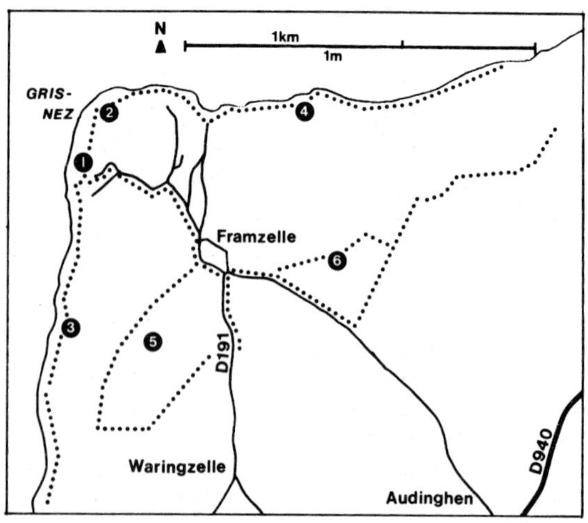

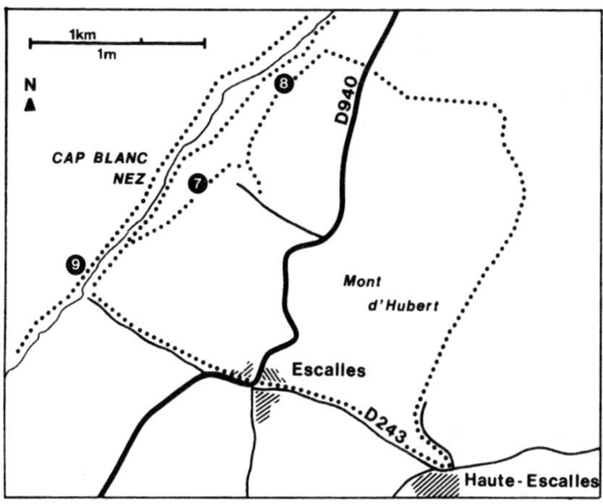

At Cap Blanc-Nez leave the car at the foot of the obelisk ⑦, then traverse the chalkland heath and grass and follow the top of the cliff ⑧ in order to see the seabird colony (Herring Gull and Fulmar). From Cran-d'Escalles ⑨, there is access to the foot of the cliffs. For Wissant/Tardinghen beach, stop at Wissant or at Châtelet (Tardinghen). By following the line of dunes you can watch birds on the foreshore, in the dunes and at sea.

Species

- Eiders are present year-round at the site. Also sometimes Red-breasted Merganser, Common and Velvet Scoters.
- Grebes and divers are on passage from August to May (maximum in December and February). A few stay in the area regularly.
- Razorbill and Guillemot are regularly seen between October and April, more rarely Little Auk or Black Guillemot.
- There is a good passage of Kittiwake and Little Gull at sea (principally in October and November), sometimes Sabine's Gull (in October). Also you can always see the regular species of larger gull (Great Black-backed, Lesser Black-backed, Herring and Common).
- Gannet, Sooty and Manx Shearwaters can be seen out to sea (especially in October), sometimes the rare Leach's Petrel.
- Short-eared Owl is regular over fields and crops from mid-October onwards.
- A few Brent Geese stay on the rocky foreshore between October and April whenever there is a large amount of passage.
- Terns – particularly Common and Arctic – fish in the shallows near the shore, attracting skuas (Arctic, Pomarine and Great).
- Oystercatcher and godwits rest for a while on Tardinghen–Wissant beach during migration.
- Snow Bunting and Twite can be seen from November onwards.
- Pipits (Meadow, Tree and Tawny) occur on the meadows and ploughed fields during autumn.
- The thickets are used as roosts by finches (Greenfinch, Chaffinch, Brambling and Goldfinch) and thrushes between October and December.

- Curlew – and more rarely Dotterel – occur on the stubble, particularly in autumn.
- Lapland Bunting are regularly seen in the stubble.
- The *flavissima* race of the Yellow Wagtail (rare in France) nests commonly in the cultivated areas.
- There are many insectivores (warblers, flycatchers) in April, May, August and September in the coppices and thickets.
- A colony of Fulmars is present from April to October.
- There is a large Herring Gull colony on the chalk cliffs (birds can be seen throughout the year).

177 Boulogne-sur-Mer Port

Boulogne-sur-Mer fishing port is particularly attractive to gulls, thousands are present between August and March. Among them are Great Black-backed, Lesser Black-backed, Herring, Yellow-legged (especially in summer) and Common, as well as Black-headed in large numbers. The Glaucous Gull is rare but regular. Between late August and October, Kittiwakes (nesting at the tip of Carnot Dike), Little Gull, Common Tern, and two or three species of skua occur, sometimes in large numbers. In mid-winter, Eider, Red-necked Grebe and Long-tailed Duck are noted regularly. Finally, Portel beach, to the south of the hovercraft port, is an important roosting site for Mediterranean Gulls.

178 Boulogne-sur-Mer and Hesdin Public Forests

These two forests, Boulogne (2,000 hectares) and Hesdin (1,000 hectares), along the Canche Valley, have very different bird populations. Oak and ash are the dominant trees on the heavy, wet ground at Boulogne, whereas Hesdin is a fine example of a beech wood on alkaline soil. Recently, there has been much felling but there remain some good mature areas. Tawny Owls are common, as well as hole-nesting species (Nuthatch, tits). Raptors have returned to the area in the last few years (Buzzard, Honey Buzzard, Sparrowhawk). Unique in France, the Redpoll (from the north) and the Melodious Warbler (recently arrived from the south) nest side by side at Boulogne. Woodcock is common enough in winter, but rare as a nester.

179 Canche Bay

Canche Bay is the first important estuary on the Picardy coast when arriving from the north. It is not as well known as the Baie de Somme but is probably just as interesting. All of Picardy's estuarine habitats are found here (sea, shore, dunes, buckthorn, etc). Some parts are in a reserve; others are hunted over regularly. For those who like gulls, a close look at the many gulls in the afternoon in late autumn or winter can be well worthwhile (tens of thousand of birds; thousands of Great Black-backed, sometimes rarer species). Leave from the Pointe du

Touquet where there are waders (Curlew) and Shelduck, a telescope is needed. Get to the northern shore to explore the dunes. They are wetter on the left of the road, part of which is a reserve (access 500 m/550 yards after the British cemetery; there are hides), and dry to the right (very calm; a few raptors in winter: including Rough-legged Buzzard and sometimes even a White-tailed Eagle). Among the nesting birds there is an abundance of Lesser Whitethroat in the bushes and Green Woodpeckers in the woods. Redpoll are also present (recent colonists).

180 THE LAKES AND MARSHES OF RUMAUCOURT, ÉCOURT-SAINT-QUENTIN AND OISY-LE-VERGER

6 km/3.75 miles
Douai
(IGN 2506 east – 1/25 000)

Habitat and Timing

The River Hirondelle, a tributary of the Sensée, flows through a valley of peat deposits. Digging peat has lead to the formation of a series of lakes of which the largest considered here is Rumaucourt (20 hectares of open water and 13 hectares of reed-bed). Three-quarters of the banks are in a natural state with a good belt of reeds, areas of mixed willow and alder, and in places some oak woods. Clear water and abundant and varied vegetation mean that there is a diversity of animal life at all seasons. However, hunting from hides and fishing from boats means that the number of duck is not high. These lakes and marshes are leased for hunting and fishing, so that access to the public is limited to the paths, this is sufficient for watching nonetheless.

Calendar

Winter: Great Crested and Little Grebes, Coot, Moorhen and sometimes swans. Around the lake: Buzzard, Sparrowhawk, Kestrel and Merlin (more discreet), Hen Harrier and Kingfisher.

Spring: as soon as the hunting season is closed (end of February), groups of duck (Pochard, Tufted Duck, Shoveler, Wigeon, Pintail, Teal and Garganey). Moorhen, Coot, grebes and Marsh Harrier all nest. Many migrants stop for a while in April and May: Black Tern, hirundines, Swift. In May: Little Bittern (rare breeder); Great Reed and Savi's Warblers, Bluethroat, Nightingale, Golden Oriole. Bittern and Cetti's Warbler have as good as disappeared.

Autumn: late broods of Great Crested Grebe, and passage migrants: Hobby, Osprey, herons. Flocks of geese in flight in October and November.

Access

From Arras (going towards Cambrai) or Cambrai (towards Arras) take the N939 as far as Baralle, turning off to the north on the D19 to get to

Rumaucourt. From Douai take the N43 to Cambrai, leave it after 3 km (1.85 miles) at the Épis crossroads (commercial centre). Turn right towards Rumaucourt, passing through Arleux, Palluel, and Écourt-Saint-Quentin. The entrance is between Écourt-St.-Quentin and Rumaucourt; leave the car near the football pitch, 200 m (220 yards) from the road. From the car park ①, follow the side of the lake straight along to its furthest point ②: which allows you to watch over the whole lake. From here it is possible to turn right, cross a stream and follow a path between a wood and some fields that goes as far as a spring ③, where the lake is visible again. Follow the tarmac track as far as the poplars, just after this take a dirt-track to the right that leads back to the car park.

From point ②, you can continue along the side of some small lakes,

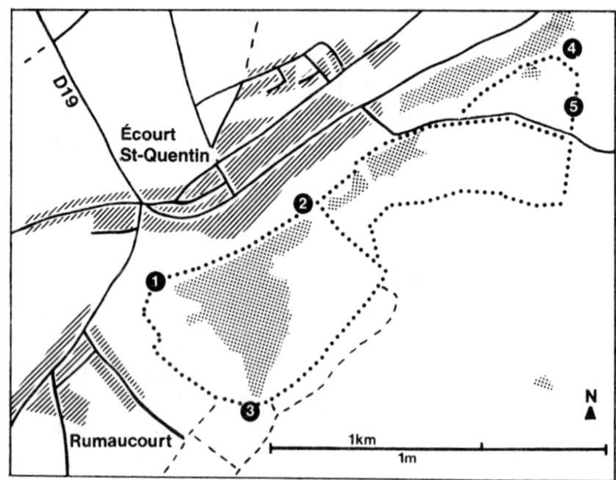

and walk for about 100 m (110 yards) on a tarmac road, turning off to the left just after the camp site, this route passes between Béquerel Lake and a wooded marsh. After a metal bridge ④, the route meets a track which, to the right, following a ditch, leads to a road at an old brick bridge ⑤. Then go back on the same route you used to arrive. Or, cross the road at the bridge and continue along the side of the ditch, turning right at the next bridge to arrive at a path which, following the side of some meadows, arrives at the spring ③. It is also possible to visit the lakes and marshes at Palleul, Écourt-Saint-Quentin and Lécluse (same habitat, same fauna) by taking the GR121 (hiker's trail) from Palleul to Lécluse.

Species

- Snipe can be seen in spring and autumn and Common Sandpiper in May.
- Many Coot and Moorhen can be seen here.
- Great Crested and Little Grebes can be seen throughout the year.
- Reed, Great Reed and Marsh Warblers nest in the reed-beds.
- In spring and early summer many warblers and Nightingale inhabit the waterside bushes.
- Little Bittern may be seen flying over the reed-beds in late May or early June.
- Pochard is an irregular nesting species (July).

- In April and May, hirundines (three species) and Swift can be seen over the lake, as can Black Tern.
- It is easy to see Marsh Harrier, which quarters over the reed-beds from the end of March onwards.
- In the older parts of the marshes both Savi's Warbler and Bluethroat nest.
- Here as well, both Great Crested and Little Grebes occur year-round.
- Willow Tit occur in the wooded parts of the marshes and in the willows.
- A good place for watching Buzzard, Sparrowhawk and Kestrel.
- Hen Harriers hunt over the fields and come into the reed-bed to roost.

181 ROMELAERE NATIONAL NATURE RESERVE

6 km/3.75 miles
Watten
(IGN 2303 west – 1/25 000

Habitat and Timing

Romelaere is part of a 3,600-hectare area devoted to market gardening and tourism. It is formed by a group of large lakes, dug during the nineteenth century for their peat, separated by earthen dikes, edged with reed/beds, water meadows and small woods on peat. For duck it is mainly a stop-over site during the spring which also serves as a roost in winter. It is one of the few remaining wetlands in the Pas-de-Calais that is suitable for *Acrocephalus* warblers and Marsh Harrier. It is best watched in the morning.

Calendar

Winter: dabbling ducks (Mallard, Shoveler, Wigeon, Gadwall and Teal), Hen Harrier, Sparrowhawk, Long-eared Owl; Cormorant, sometimes Bittern.

Spring and summer: many reed-bed and woodland passerines (Reed Warblers, *Locustella* warblers, Cetti's Warbler, Bluethroat, Reed Bunting); hirundines (three species), Swift. A halt for migrating duck in March and April (Teal, Wigeon, Pintail, Shoveler and Pochard).

Migration: Black Tern, Common Sandpiper, Osprey.

Autumn: many passerines (thrushes), waders on passage (Lapwing, Snipe), Cormorant.

All year: Grey Heron, Great Crested Grebe (except in very hard weather).

Access

From Saint-Omer or Arques go as far as Clairmarais. The reserve is signposted from the church onwards. Stop at the Grange-Nature car park ①; this building is an information centre for the national park, it opens at weekends and every day in the summer: there are good videos about the

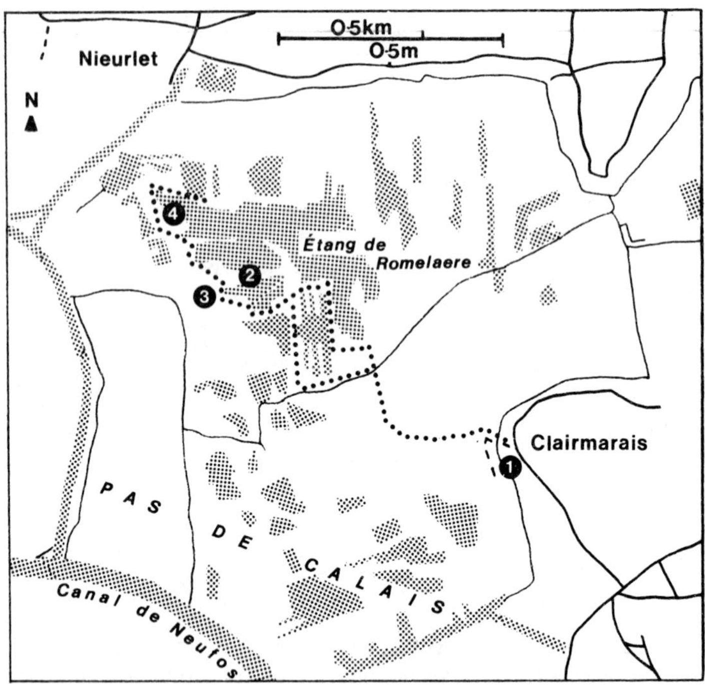

marshes' birds, information on walks in the neighbourhood and a nature exhibition. There are two possible walks:

1) the lakes walk: a circuit of 3 km (1.85 miles); there is a visitors fact sheet for this nature trail.
2) 'the observation trail': A 6-km (3.7 miles) walk, returning by the same patn as on the way out; hides at ②, ③ and ④ are on the sides of lakes.

Species

- Woodland passerines include: Nightingale, Greenfinch, Warblers, tits, Robin and also Sparrowhawk.
- Coot and Moorhen are easily seen.
- Hirundines and Swift hunt over the surface of the lake.
- There are nesting Great Crested Grebe.
- Dabbling duck include: Shoveler, Gadwall, Wigeon and Teal – especially in winter.
- Passerines (especially insectivores) include: Reed Bunting; Savi's, Grasshopper, Reed, Marsh, Great Reed, Cetti's and Sedge Warblers; Bluethroat.
- Cormorant occur mainly in winter.
- Marsh and Hen Harriers can be seen, sometimes Bittern.
- Grey Heron can be found on the side of the lake.

182 SAINT-PIERRE-DU-MONT BIRD RESERVE

1.5 km/0.9 miles
Grandcamp-Maisy
(IGN 1411 south – 1/25 000)

Habitat and Timing

The Bessin cliffs, in lower Normandy, are less well known than the cliffs of the Pays de Caux in upper Normandy. They are better known by tourists for the events of June 1944 than for their birds. Nonetheless, this part of the coast has some good birds which make it one of the most important ornithological sites of the region. The indented limestone lies on top of a clay base, much undermined by the sea; the cliffs are up to 35 m high and run for about 30 km (18.5 miles) along the coast. The coast at Pointe-du-Hoc, at the western end, is heavily eroded. The cliff top is thick with bushes with areas of tarmarisk and gorse heath; unfortunately, work at the Pointe-du-Hoc historic site has considerably reduced the area of heath, a habitat rare in this part of France. The inter-tidal zone is small, difficult to get to and dangerous due not only to the possibility of rock falls from the adjacent cliffs but also because of an often arduous walk on seaweed-covered rocks and flat slabs with many crevices.

The reserve, (created by the Normandy Ornithological Group) to the east of the Pointe-du-Hoc, is one of the most important mainland seabird colonies in France: there is controlled access; climbing onto the cliffs, which can be very dangerous, is not to be recommended. It is possible to see many species at sea, particularly during periods of migration and in winter.

Calendar

Spring and summer: the reserve has a few species of nesting seabirds, such as Fulmar (the largest colony in France), Kittiwake (the first colony to be established in France), Lesser Black-backed and Herring Gulls, cormorants are present year round. Some cliff-dwelling species also bred on the reserve: Starling, Jackdaw, House Sparrow, Black Redstart and Dartford Warbler on the heath.

Autumn: Black Tern, sea terns and skuas.

Winter: on the sea, divers (especially Red-throated), Gannet, Cormorant, Shag, auks (especially Razorbill) and Red-breasted Merganser; also Little Gull; sometimes Mediterranean Gull and more rarely Glaucous Gull. Short-eared and Long-eared Owls, Blackcap (rare) and Chiffchaff.

Access

From the N 13 (Paris–Caen–Cherbourg road), between Bayeux and Isigny, turn either at Formigny, towards Vierville, or at La Cambe or Osmanville, towards Grandcamp, to get onto the D514 coast road. From

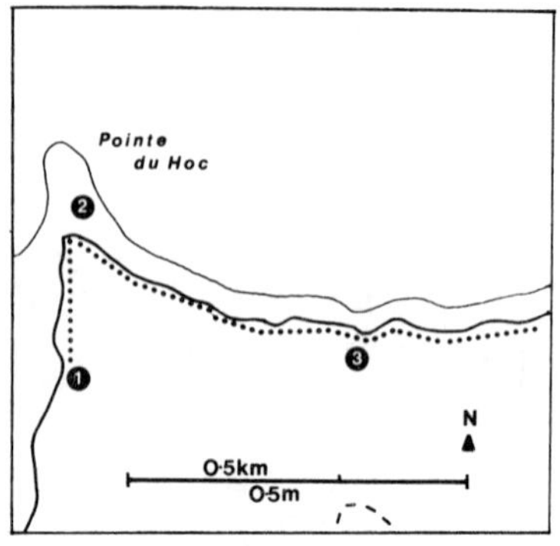

this road, follow the signs to the Pointe-du-Hoc. Park in the car park ①, walk to the monument ② then turn right (east) along the coastal trail, which soon leaves the historic site; the reserve starts less than 1 km (0.6 miles) later ③, and includes a little less than 1 km (0.6 miles) of cliffs. It is easy to watch from the cliff top, but be careful not to get too close to the edge. The edge is unstable and often overhangs. Follow the country code; do not walk through the nearby crops, and close gates after you.

Species

- There are Red-throated Divers and auks on the sea from November to early April.
- Gannet and terns can be seen, mainly between July and October, Cormorant year-round, and Shag between July and January.
- Stonechat, Grasshopper and Dartford Warblers can be found on the heath.
- There is an owl roost in the scrub back from the cliff top, numbers vary from one year to the next (October to March).
- Several pairs of Stock Dove nest on the cliffs. Kestrels occur.

Fulmar

- There are Fulmars between December and August, many gliding along the cliffs; chicks can be seen from late July onwards.
- The Kittiwake colony is easy to watch, it is particularly interesting between May and July.
- There are rock-nesting birds such as Jackdaws, Black Redstart and Starling.
- In winter (October to March) there are sea duck, including Common Scoter and Red-breasted Merganser.

183 The Baie d'Orne

Some 10 km (6.2 miles) to the north of Caen, this bay has a good cross-section of estuarine habitats. There are many birds during the migration seasons. In May, Redshank, Ringed Plover, Turnstone and Avocet are numerous. In August and September, it is an important place of call for terns and skuas, which are easy to watch, particularly at the Pointe de Merville (on the right bank). Shelduck and Ringed Plover both nest here. There is conservation work at present to try to encourage Avocet and terns to nest. The bay also has many Nightingale, Golden Oriole and Long-eared Owl. In winter, Snow Bunting and Shore Lark are present.

184 THE RADE DE SAINT-VAAST-LA-HOUGUE

3.5 km/2.2 miles
Saint-Vaast-la Hougue – Pointe de Barfleur
(IGN 1310 west – 1/25 000)

Habitat and Timing

The Rade (shallows) at Saint-Vaast-la-Hougue, at its northern end, is the limit of the low sandy coast of eastern Cotentin. This area stops abruptly at the level of the Saire Estuary, at its contact with the granitic massif at the Pointe de Barfleur. It is the biogeographical boundary between northern and Atlantic invertebrates. This justified the building of a biological research station of great renown in the nineteenth century. For birds also, the Rade is an area of contact, where those from the North Sea meet those from the Atlantic, Iceland or even North America. The Rade also has many different habitats which increases its attractiveness to birds and thus its interest for the birdwatcher. Of greatest interest are the exceptional numbers of fish-eating birds that occur between September and March, and they are also easy to watch.

Calendar

Breeding season: the Rade has Great Black-backed, Lesser Black-backed and Herring Gulls; Shelduck and Oystercatcher. Eider probably nest as well.

Summer: Gannet, Marsh terns, sea terns, skuas and waders. Sometimes summering Red-necked Grebe, Red-breasted Merganser and Pintail, the latter probably moulting breeders from the nearby Carentan marshes.

Autumn and Winter: divers occur regularly (in order of frequency: Red-throated, Black-throated and Great Northern), grebes, particularly Great Crested, Slavonian and Black-necked (Little and Red-necked are rarer). Also: Shag, Cormorant, Red-breasted Merganser, Gannet, Razorbill, Guillemot, sometimes some late or wintering terns; Eider and Common Scoter, and in smaller numbers, Velvet Scoter, Shelduck, Brent Goose, waders (Curlew, Grey Plover, Ringed Plover, Oystercatcher, Turnstone and Purple Sandpiper. More rarely, Merlin and Peregrine. Lastly, many passerines: Meadow and Rock Pipits, White Wagtail, Black Redstart, Greenfinch, Linnet and Twite, Snow Bunting. In the trees, warblers are abundant during times of migration.

Access

Some 30 km (18.5 miles) to the south-east of Cherbourg, there are two ways of getting to Saint-Vaast-la Hougue; either take the D42 and the D14, which follow Veys Bay, or travel on the D902 if coming from Valognes. Park at the port ① and walk southward towards La Hougue

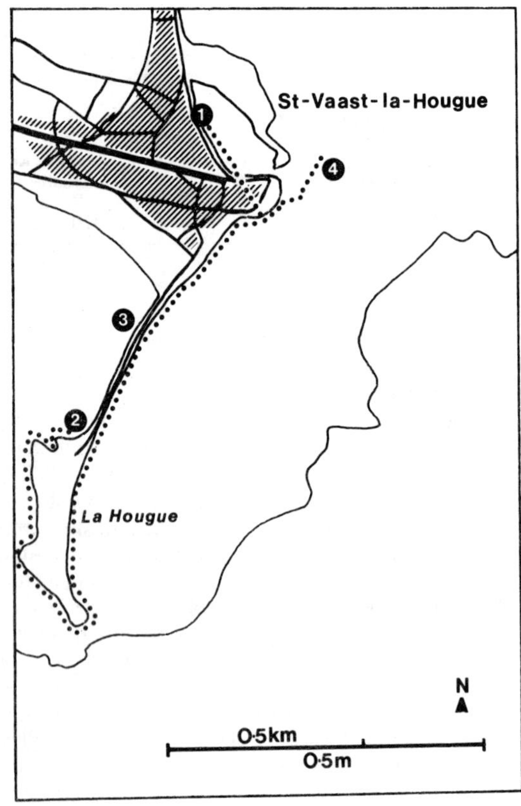

following the signs. At the tennis courts ②, take the path along the side of Cul-de-Loup Cove, marked to the Tour de la Hougue. Along the length of the walk there is easy birdwatching, but the area is only of interest at high tide. Watch what is happening in front, along the foot of the dike, but look also out to sea: there are many divers, and they are not always at the surface. To get back to the port, follow the top of the beach ③ as far as the chapel, then go to the very end of the dike ④; from here, Tatihou Island and surrounds can be watched.

Species

- Shelduck and Brent Geese are present on the mudflats.
- Waders feed on the mudflats (Curlew, Redshank, Grey Plover, Ringed Plover and Dunlin); on the rocks, Oystercatcher, Turnstone and Purple Sandpiper.
- Sea ducks (scoters and Red-breasted Merganser, from September to April) are sometimes present out to sea.
- On the sea, grebes and divers can be seen between October and March/April: Great Crested, Slavonian and Black-necked Grebes, Red-throated Diver; more rarely: Red-necked Grebe, Blackpthroated and Great Northern Divers.
- From July to April, Gannet, terns, Cormorant, Shag, Guillemot and Razorbill feed on the sea in front of La Hougue.
- Eider is present year-round in the waters around Saint-Vaast-la-Hougue.
- On the high-tide line, between September and March, often there are quite a few passerines, such as: White Wagtail, Meadow and Rock Pipits, Black Redstart, Greenfinch, Linnet and Snow Bunting.
- In winter, grebes and divers can be seen close inshore.

185 Veys Bay

In the south-eastern corner of the Cotentin, Veys Bay National Nature Reserve is particularly interesting in autumn and winter: gulls, duck and waders occur by the thousand. It is an important stop-over site for Brent Geese and terns. It is also possible to find some rarer passerines (Snow Bunting, Twite) and many species of raptor, including Merlin and Peregrine. Great Crested Grebe, scoters and Eider occur on the sea. Cormorant is always present. In the polders, Short-eared Owls are very common.

186 The Carentan Marshes

These marshes almost completely separate the Cotentin from the mainland. This is an enormous wetland (25,000 hectares), one of the most important in France. Flood meadows and peat-bogs are omnipresent. Flooding is regular in winter and spring. Various species breed in spring and summer: Teal and Garganey, Shoveler, Pintail; Corncrake (a few hundred pairs); Lapwing, Snipe, Curlew, Black-tailed Godwit, maybe Ruff. Otherwise Montagu's and Marsh Harriers and many passerines (Marsh Warbler and others) also nest.

187 THE HAGUE: THE RESERVE FROM NEZ-DE-JOBOURG TO CAP DE HAGUE

6 km/3.75 miles
Les Pieux
(IGN 1110 – 1/50 000)

Habitat and Timing

The coast, to the north, is low and rocky with many reefs in the sea. The tide-races are some of the strongest in Europe, which explains the lack of seabirds here. Moving southwards, the coast rises and we come to an area of high granite and gneiss cliffs, often an impressive 100 m high with sheer faces of some tens of metres. On the spray-and wind-covered slopes, there are good areas of thrift-covered grassland and gorse heath. Access to the Nez-de-Jobourg reserve is prohibited, but there is easy watching from Nez-de-Voidries. At sea, the other Normandy Ornithological Group reserve, the Hague Isles, is out of bounds to the public during the breeding season. On the other hand, there is easy and unrestricted access to the Cap de Hague.

Calendar

Spring and summer: there are nesting seabirds on the cliffs: Fulmar, Shag (the largest mainland colony in France, outside of Brittany), Great Black-backed and Herring Gulls, Oystercatcher, Kestrel, Stock Dove, Rock Pipit (declining), Jackdaw and Raven. On the heathland: Dartford and Grasshopper Warblers, Stonechat. Some migrant landbirds may be seen: Merlin, Wheatear, Ring Ouzel.

Autumn and spring: depending on the weather there may be good passage of seabirds, petrels, shearwaters (mainly Manx and Yelkouan, sometimes Sooty and even occasionally Cory's), gulls, terns (especially Sandwich), divers (all three species). The commonest species is the Gannet (with some tens of thousands of birds). There are also some migrant passerines; of note are Snow Bunting and sometimes Lapland Bunting. Also Purple Sandpiper, quite a rare wintering species in France. There is a good chance of seeing Mediterranean Gull.

Access

From Cherbourg, take the D901 towards Beaumont-Hague; after Beaumont, go along the side of the Hague nuclear-waste treatment plant and turn left on the D401 to Nez-de-Jobourg. At Dannery, turn right on the D202 which, after 3 km (1.85 miles), runs into a car park ①. Take the track towards the signal-station, then turn left towards the sea; here take the customs trail. At Nez-de-Voidries ②, is, to the left (the south), the Nez-de-Jobourg reserve ③, and beyond the Bréquets Isles ④.

There are two ways of getting to the Cap:

1. Either follow the old customs trail northwards (the GR 223 hiker's trail) as far as Goury; here there is a small harbour with a rescue station (6 km (3.75 miles), one-hour's walk, dangerous in high winds).
2. Or take the car on the D202 as far as Jobourg (village) where it joins

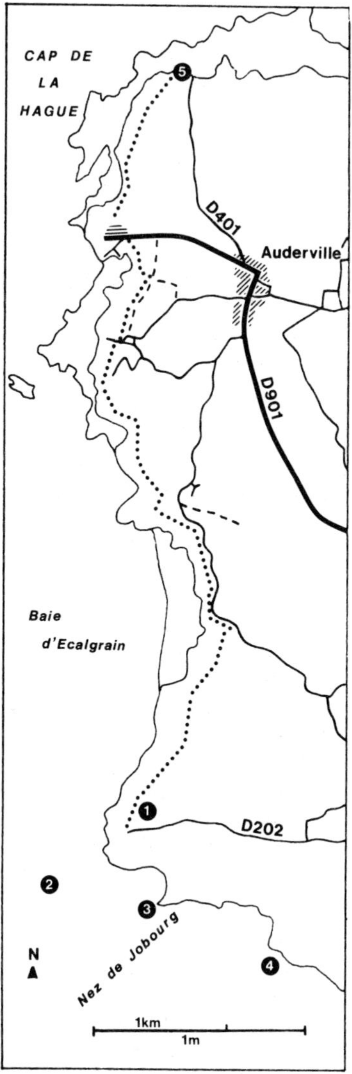

D901, go on to Auderville and then Goury; from here follow the coast to the blockhouse before the signal-station ⑤: this is the best spot for watching migrants.

Species

- Shags are present year-round, those nesting at Jobourg are easy to see; a telescope is needed for those at Voidries.
- Great Black-backed and Herring Gulls nest at Jobourg.
- Typical heathland birds (from April to June/July) are present: Grasshopper and Dartford Warblers, Whitethroat, Stonechat.

- Raven, Jackdaw, Black Redstart, Stock Dove and Rock Pipit all nest on the cliffs.
- Fulmar can be seen between January and July in flight along the whole length of the cliffs, sometimes sitting (Nez-de-Voidries).
- The Lesser Black-backed Gull does not nest but is regularly seen on passage.
- Snow Bunting can be seen at the high-tide mark in autumn and winter.
- Purple Sandpipers are difficult to see (they occur from August to early May), they should be looked for on the tops of rocks at high tide.
- Sea-watching from the Cap (July to December; March to May) can be good particularly for Gannet, terns (especially Sandwich) and divers.

188 Vauville Pond

Vauville Pond National Nature Reserve and the overlooking heath lie to the south of La Hague, some 30 km (19 miles) to the south-west of Cherbourg, and represent fine unspoilt examples of these habitats. In spring a large variety of birds nest here: Kentish Plover, Wheatear and Sand Martin in the dunes; Little Grebe, Shoveler, Pochard, Tufted Duck and wetland warblers on the lakes; Lapwing, Blue-headed Wagtail in the water meadows; Curlew, Grasshopper and Dartford Warblers and Nightjar on the heath; and in the wooded valleys Sparrowhawk and Hobby.

189 CAROLLES CLIFFS AND MONT-SAINT-MICHEL BAY

3 km/1.85 miles
Le Mont-Saint-Michel
(IGN 1215 east – 1/25 000)

Habitat and Timing

At the extreme western end of the Vire granite massif, Carolles Cliffs extend into the sea enclosing the north-eastern part of Mont-Saint-Michel bay. The bay is enclosed by extensive sand and mudflats to the south and a much used tourist beach to the north. The Pointe de Carolles rises to 60 m; of solid appearance, none of the cliffs are more than 15 m in height; the convex slopes are covered with heather, gorse and broom heath, with blackthorn and even trees in the sheltered valleys. Thus, along a few kilometres of cliff top, it is possible to discover a good cross-section of the different plant communities in this area.

The Pointe de Carolles is, therefore, a good place for cliff-dwelling and heathland birds. Its position at the entrance to Mont-Saint-Michel Bay, with a seabed very important for spawning fish, offers excellent chances to watch many seabirds, especially in autumn. And Carolles is an exceptional site for watching passerines on autumn migration; its position at the south-west of the Cotentin Peninsula means that it covers the area where migration routes to the north and east of the Cotentin meet. Hundreds of thousands of daytime migrants pass over Carolles between late August and November; numbers depend on the weather system; conditions are most favourable when there is a wind from the south.

Calendar

Spring: Raven, Kestrel and Black Redstart nest on the cliffs. Shelduck, Dartford and Melodious Warblers and Lesser Whitethroat on the heathland; Sparrowhawk and Hobby in the woods.

Summer: resting on the sea, hundreds of Yelkouan Shearwaters, a few Razorbills and some Guillemots; Common Scoter can be very numerous (around 20,000).

Autumn: an important site for migrating passerines, principally Chaffinch and to a lesser degree Brambling. Also Skylark and Woodlark, Meadow, Tree and sometimes Tawny Pipits, Reed Bunting. Regular in small numbers: Lapland Bunting, tits, Greenfinch, Linnet, Goldfinch, hirundines, sparrows, corvids, pigeons. Sometimes, Ortolan Bunting, Wryneck, and without doubt others!

Access

Carolles is midway between Granville and Avranches, on the D911 coast road. To the south of Carolles (going towards Avranches) turn right after a small bridge, following the signs to Cabane Vauban. After 750 m (820 yards) along a small winding road, park in the car park ①. Take the path on the left that goes to the sea, then right along the old customs trail as

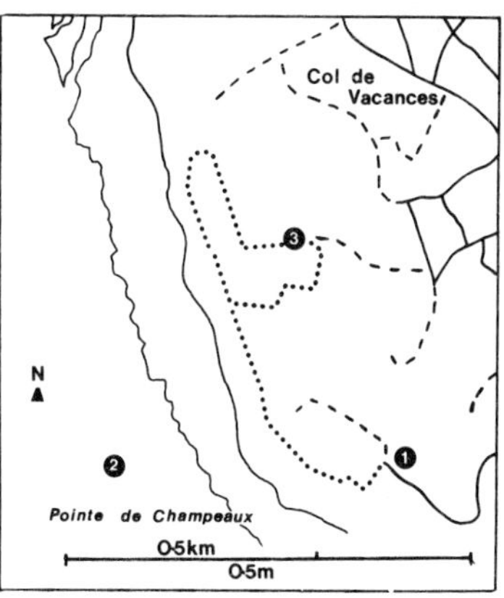

far as Cabane Vauban ② (a customs shelter overlooking the cliff). From here there is an excellent view (especially in the morning at high tide) of the birds at sea; this is the best observation post for the autumn migration. In spring, to find those species occuring on the heath, continue on the path northwards and descend into Lude Valley ③, then go up the stream for 300 m (330 yards) before taking the trail on the right which leads back to the Cabane Vauban.

Species

- As early as the end of June, Common Scoters can be seen at sea, small groups sometimes come close inshore (moult site).
- A superb location for watching daytime migrants (August to November): passing hirundines, wagtails, pipits, finches, larks, buntings, tits, Starling, thrushes and corvids.
- Many seabirds are present in autumn (Yelkouan Shearwater, Guillemot, and in smaller numbers, Razorbill, terns, Gannet, Cormorant and Shag).
- Raven and Black Redstart occur on the cliffs.
- Of the birds that nest on the heath, the most typical of that habitat are Dartford and Melodious Warblers and Lesser Whitethroat.

190 THE EASTERN PART OF MONT-SAINT-MICHEL BAY

5 km/3.1 miles
Le Mont-Saint-Michel
(IGN 1215 – 1/50 000)

Habitat and Timing

At the western limit of Normandy, Mont-Saint-Michel bay is one of Europe's most important natural and cultural sites. Its vast areas of sand and mud stretch north to the Pointe de Cancale and north-east to the Pointe de Carolles. Two islands emerge in the bay, Mont-Saint-Michel itself and Tombelaine (a reserve). The large amount of vegetation (schorre), its great variety, and the large changes in tide here, give rise to a very large diversity of estuarine habitats. Mont-Saint-Michel Bay is of international importance for quite a few bird species, either migrants or wintering species; and especially for duck and waders. But, it is no less interesting in spring and summer; many species nest in the vegetation on the mudflats and there is a seabird colony on Tombelaine (landing is prohibited between March and July). So, the site is worth visiting at any time in the year; but it is worth bearing in mind, due to the size of the bay, that it is often difficult to get close to the birds; on the other hand, large flocks of many species can be seen moving between feeding and roosting grounds. Also, it must be said that the bay can be dangerous: there are some strong tidal races and it is ill-advised to go onto those flats that are uncovered at low tide. In fact, it is better to look for birds from the side of the bay at high tide (best during spring tides, choose those with a coefficient of 80 or more if possible).

Calendar

Spring: many waders on spring migration (Oystercatcher, Grey Plover, Ringed Plover, Turnstone, Curlew, Whimbrel, godwits, 'shanks and many others); Shelduck and dabbling duck; hirundines, Swift and wagtails hunt in numbers over the salt-marsh, as well as raptors, particularly harriers and Hobby. Many species nest on the salt-marsh or on the beaches:

Kentish and Little Ringed Plovers; Mallard; Quail; Skylark, Meadow Pipit, Yellow Wagtail, Reed Bunting. A few Marsh Harriers may nest in the reed-beds, where there are also many nesting warblers. Shelduck are particularly numerous.

Summer and autumn: a stop-over for many species (Black-headed Gull in spectacular numbers, Black-tailed Godwit, Osprey and Spoonbill among others).

Autumn and winter: geese, duck and waders, such as: grey geese in small numbers, Shelduck, Mallard, Wigeon, Teal, Brent Goose (a few of the pale-bellied race). On the mudflats, Oystercatcher, Dunlin, Knot, Bar-tailed and Black-tailed Godwits, Curlew. On the polders to the west of Couesnon: Golden Plover, Lapwing and Ruff. There are wintering raptors (Marsh Harrier, Short-eared Owl, Merlin and Peregrine), numerous gulls, Cormorant, Shag, Grey Heron, Snow and Lapland Buntings. At any time there is a chance of seeing less common species.

Access

Leave Mont-Saint-Michel ①, where there are many birds, at the first junction turn left on the D275 to Bas-Courtils (the cost road to Pontaubault and Avranches); at Bas-Courtils, at a right-angle bend, go straight on towards Rochetorin, follow this road to the sea, turn left along the shore and park about 500 m (550 yards) further on (not on the map): here the grazed salt-marsh can be interesting in winter (Brent Geese, raptors, buntings). Then back on the road as far as Avranches, going towards Granville. At Pont-Gilbert, on leaving Avranches, turn left towards Genêts (D911 coast road). At Pont-de-Vains, turn left towards le Rivage (D591 coast road) and again to the left at Village-du-Rivage. There

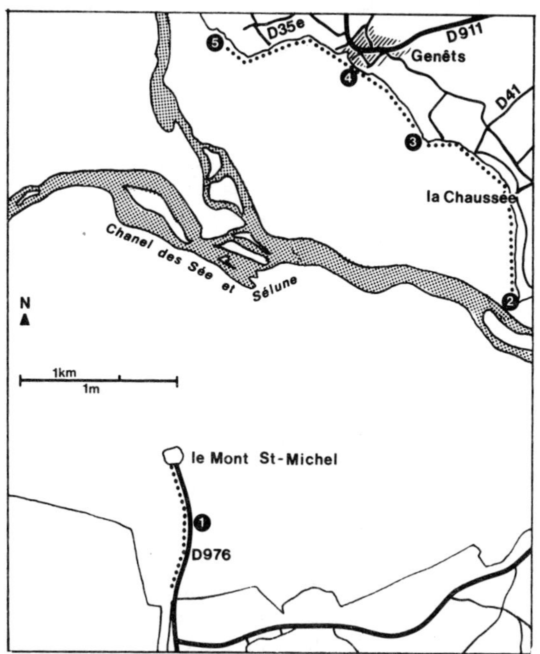

is a good observation spot at Grouin-du-Sud (especially at high tide) ②. Here there are two possibilities:

1. Back on the coast road towards Genêts, on leaving this parish turn left towards Bec-d'Andaine ⑤.
2. It is better to leave on foot following the GR 223 (hiker's trail) northwards as far as Bec-d'Andaine; there is always something to see from the Pointe du Mont-Manet ③, and from Genêts village ④, and Bec-d'Andaine ⑤; the distance between Grouin-du-Sud and Bec-d'Andaine is about 5 km (3.1 miles).

Lapland Bunting (right) and Snow Bunting

Species

- Marsh Harrier year-round, Hen Harrier, Peregrine and Merlin in spring and autumn; in spring and summer, Hobby and sometimes Montagu's Harrier.
- There are Brent Geese from the end of October to late March/April; look for pale-bellied Brent Geese or Barnacle Geese among them.
- Gulls are present throughout the year.
- On the muddy foreshore there are Oystercatcher, Bar-tailed Godwit, Grey Plover.
- On winter evenings, many gulls arrive to roost.
- Salt-marsh nesting passerines include Yellow Wagtail and Reed Bunting.
- Shelduck are present throughout the year (less in August and September); their spectacular displays and crèches are visible between May and July.
- Cormorant and Grey Heron are present throughout the year.
- Skylark and Meadow Pipit nest in spring.
- Peregrine sometimes hunt over the mudflats.
- Curlew are present throughout the year; Black-tailed Godwit can be found from July to March, Bar-tailed Godwit between August and May.

191 Écouves Forest

This is a vast public forest (8,148 hectares), 417 m at its highest point, and 10 km (6.2 miles) to the north of Alençon. A very variable vegetation occurs due to the different variations in exposure and the different types of tree (mature hardwoods mainly of beech, mature conifers and mixed areas). It is worth visiting this forest and its outskirts for: nesting raptors, woodpeckers (Green, maybe Grey-headed in the west, Black, Great, Middle and Lesser Spotted), warblers (particularly Wood, Bonelli's and Dartford), tits (all the species), and Treecreeper and Short-toed Treecreeper side-by-side.

192 GRANDE NOË BIRD RESERVE

1 km/0.6 miles
Les Andelys
(IGN 2012 – 1/25 000)

Habitat and Timing

The reserve is in the meander at Poses, on the left bank of the River Seine. Here the river encircles many islands and, on the right bank, runs against high chalk cliffs; the left bank is low and made up of alluvial material (sand and gravel). Digging of these aggregates has marred the landscape and created many lakes. Some of these are still being worked, others have been infilled and some are used for leisure activities. One of these, despite the surroundings, has become a reserve under the scientific guidance of the GON (Normany Ornithological Group).

There is unrestricted access to the reserve, but signs mark areas that are left aside for the birds and should not be entered; these areas should be respected so that birds can use the reserve to its full potential.

Calendar

Winter: an important wintering site for Cormorant, Grey Heron, Goldeneye, Pochard and Tufted Duck. Also, Smew and Goosander during hard spells; Coot, many dabbling duck, particularly Mallard.

Spring and summer: Gadwall; Grey Heron, Little Bittern (rare); Lapwing, Little Ringed Plover, Stone Curlew; large Sand Martin colonies; Great Crested Grebe, Mallard, Shoveler, Yellow-legged Gull (non-breeders, June to October); Cetti's, Reed and Sedge Warblers; Reed Bunting; Nightingale, Golden Oriole.

Access

The site is between Les Andelys and Rouen, about 12 km (7.5 miles) to the north-east of Louviers, and to the south-east of Val-de-Reuil new town. Coming on the N15 or the Normandy motorway (A13), turn off towards Val-de-Reuil (Le Vaudreuil new town). At the entrance to Val-de-Reuil (crossroads at the commercial centre), go on towards the station, passing the Eure River and the railway bridge. Then, turn right on the Chaussée de l'Andelle ① towards the Saint-Pierre-du-Vauvray indus-

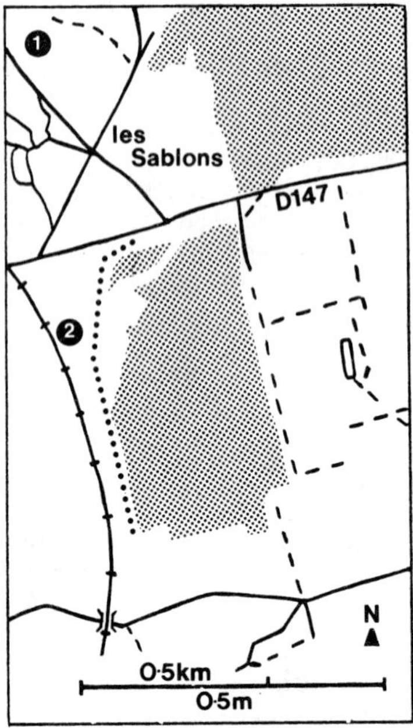

trial estate. About 1 km (0.6 miles) further on, at the junction with the CD147 (the Le Vaudreuil/Tournedos road), is the entrance to the reserve (there is a notice board). Continue for another 400 m (440 yards) and park in the car park on the right ②. Cross the road and walk along the edge of the road southwards. It is worth looking for birds along the whole walk. After about 700 m (770 yards) turn around and go back to the car park. It is well worth visiting the large lake to the west of Poses, which can also be very interesting for birds.

Species

- Cetti's, Reed and Sedge Warblers and Reed Bunting all nest in the reed-bed at the northern end of the lake.
- Thousands of Pochard and Tufted Duck flock together on the lake in winter, among them are Mallard and Teal as well as Goldeneye, Smew and Goosander (the latter two may be numerous during very cold spells).
- Cormorant and Grey Heron can be seen on the islands in the lake.
- During migration, small waders often appear on the freshly-exposed muddy areas. Little Ringed Plover nest.
- Great Crested Grebe can be seen on the open water at most times of the year.
- Sand Martin, a common breeding species along the Poses meander, hunt over the lake in spring.
- In the bushes and scrub, Nightingale is common. The Golden Oriole sings in the surrounding woods from early May.

193 Londe Forest/Les Essarts

Londe public forest is a vast beech wood, interspersed with conifer plantations. It lies to the south of Rouen, and has most species of forest birds to be found in northern France. Buzzard, Honey Buzzard, Sparrowhawk, Hobby and Long-eared Owl all nest; as do Nightjar, Black, Great Spotted, Middle Spotted and Lesser Spotted Woodpeckers. Of the more interesting breeding passerines, Grasshopper and Wood Warblers, Coal Tit and Hawfinch are worthy of note.

194 THE SEINE ESTUARY/ HODE MARSH

16 km/10 miles
Le Havre
(IGN 7 – 1/100 000)

Habitat and Timing

On the northern bank of the estuary, there is a collection of water meadows dotted with numerous ponds and bordered, along the road, by reed-beds. To the south of the road are some immense reed-beds, progressively replaced to the west, by higher sandy ground. On the lower part of the estuary there are large mudflats that are uncovered at low tide. A very interesting area, as much for wintering birds as spring and autumn migrants, but particularly for duck and waders. One part is a maritime reserve, another a local reserve.

Calendar

Spring: Grey Heron, Bittern, Little Egret and Spoonbill (March and April). Greylag Geese (March) and ducks (Garganey, Shoveler). A good variety of waders: large flocks of Lapwing, Black-tailed Godwit and Ruff in March; Bar-tailed Godwit, 'shanks and *Calidris* waders in May. Marsh Harrier, Corncrake and passerines (Bluethroated, Bearded Tit, wetland warblers).

Autumn: Little Egret and Spoonbill, many waders, skuas, large numbers of gulls and terns. Migrant passerines.

Winter: divers, grebes, duck (Shelduck, Pintail, Wigeon, Pochard, Tufted Duck, Goldeneye, Sawbills) and waders (Oystercatcher, Curlew, Dunlin and Avocet). Raptors (Marsh and Hen Harriers, Merlin, Short-eared Owl) and passerines (Snow Bunting and Twite).

Access

To get to the estuary road from Le Havre, go towards Écluse Francois-1er/Terminal de l'Ocean; from the Tancarville bridge, to towards Le Havre; at the intersection, direction ZI Portuaire–Centre Routier, the estuary road is to the left, just after crossing the canal.

All the way along this road, look over the reed-beds and the water meadows. You can get to the Le Havre Grand Canal ① and follow it for about 3 km (1.85 miles) (sometimes impassable in winter). There is access to the embankment opposite the Terminal de l'Ocean ②. There is

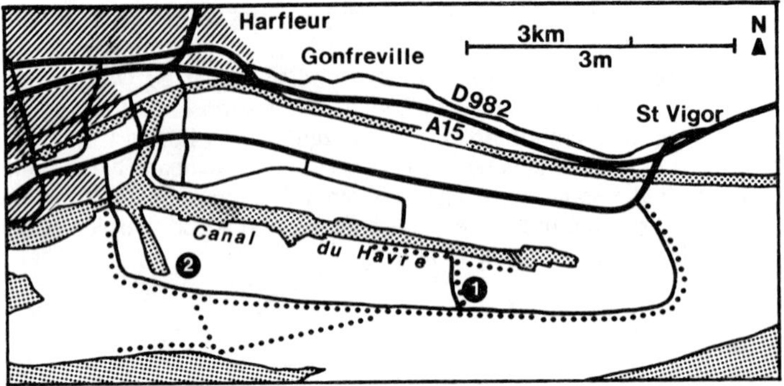

a good view over the mudflats from the embankment, especially from its western end. You can look over the dikes and two reservoirs from the embankment or the road.

Species

- There are Marsh Harriers throughout the year.
- Bearded Tit, Cetti's Warbler and Reed Bunting can also be found year-round.
- In the spring there are Spoonbill, Grey Heron, Greylag Goose, dabbling duck.
- Waders are numerous (Lapwing, Snipe, Black-tailed Godwit, Ruff, 'shanks).
- In winter there are Great Crested and Slavonian Grebes, diving duck, Goldeneye, sawbills and Short-eared Owl.
- In the breeding season there are Bluethroat, Savi's, Grasshopper, Reed and Sedge Warblers.
- Little Grebe, dabbling duck, Pochard, Tufted Duck and Coot can be seen in winter.
- Many waders occur in the autumn.
- There is a roost of Oystercatchers and other waders throughout the year.
- Terns are present in spring and autumn, and there is the chance of seeing skuas in the autumn.
- Little Ringed Plover and Avocet nest on the dikes.
- Snow Bunting and Twite are present in winter.
- It is a roosting and feeding site for coastal waders, gulls, Shelduck and Pintail.

195 Pays de Caux Cliffs

The limestone cliffs of the Caux country occupy 120 km (75 miles) of coast, between Le Havre and Tréport, they reach a height of 80 m. Mainly seabirds are seen here. The commonest nesting species are Fulmar and Herring Gull; Great Black-backed and Lesser Black-backed Gulls are rarer. There is a large Kittiwake colony (Antifer) and some Cormorant colonies. Quite a few other species can be seen during the autumn migration: divers, Gannet, duck, gulls, terns, Guillemot and Razorbill.

PAYS DE LA LOIRE

196 THE GUÉRANDE SALT-MARSHES/CROISIC MUDFLATS

14 km/8.7 miles
Saint-Nazaire
(IGN 1023 – 1/50 000)

Habitat and Timing

This complex of mudflats and salt-marshes is clearly delimited: to the north-west by the La Turballe–Pen-Bron sand-bar, to the east by the Guérande trench, to the south-east by the La Baule sand-bar and to the south-west by the Grande Côte rocky coast of Croisic, Batz-sur-Mer and Le Pouliguen.

This is a remarkable area for duck and grebe in winter, gulls and waders in spring and autumn, and for Common Tern and Bluethroat in the breeding season. Entry into the salt-pans is prohibited, but the many public roads and tracks allow for good viewing. For the gulls, waders and duck it is best to go during an incoming tide or at high tide; this is true for both the mudflats and salt-pans. For passerines, spring mornings are ideal.

Calendar

Winter: Shelduck, Brent Goose, Avocet, Oystercatcher all in large numbers, also Pintail, Wigeon, Teal, Red-breasted Merganser and Goldeneye. The five species of grebe can be seen in the estuary, Great Crested, Black-necked and Little are regular, Red-necked and Slavonian rarer. Also Great Northern Diver and Merlin.

Spring: waders on passage, such as: Grey Plover, Dunlin, Knot, Little Stint, Redshank, Spotted Redshank, Greenshank, Green Sandpiper and sometimes Wood Sandpiper; Black-winged Stilt and Avocet nest. There is a high density of nesting Bluethroat; more than 100 pairs of Common Tern; Kestrel, Marsh Harrier (present year-round).

Summer and autumn: impressive passage of seabirds at the Pointe de Croisic in August and September; Gannet and Yelkouan Shearwaters are numerous, three species of skua. In the salt-pans, Common and Black-headed Gulls, waders (especially *Calidris* species including Curlew Sandpiper, and *Charadrius* species), Spoonbill.

Access

From Guérande take the D99 towards La Turballe. Turn left at Clis as far as the hamlet of Maisons-Brûlées, turn right here to go to Lergat. Take the road to the left here which leads to Pen-Bron Marine Health Centre ①. Back towards Guérande, at Maisons-Brûlées take the road to Batz-sur-Mer and Le Croisic, here you can turn right and go as far as Sissable ②, a good point for looking over the mudflats. Then come back

Bluethroat

the same way and go on to Batz-sur-Mer ③. Whilst driving on the roads in the marsh, go slowly (the route can be difficult and there are always plenty of birds to be seen from the car). You can also leave the car on the side of the road and go by foot on the many paths in the marsh. Take the road to Le Croisic (a shellfish port), parking at the port ④; there is a nice view of the mudflats, the entrance channel, and the breakwater. There is also a good view from the Tréhic jetty ⑤ which goes out into the Pen-Bron shallows. To look at the rocky shore and the Pointe du Croisic ⑥, continue along the D45 which follows the coast.

Species

- Common Scoters (along with Velvet Scoter during hard weather) are common enough on the Pen-Bron shallows; a few summer along the coast. A few Eider are always present.
- Black-necked Grebe are found, especially at the entrance to Croisic port and in the Petit-Traict channel.
- In early autumn, Spoonbill occur on the Petit-Traict mudflats.
- The Point de Sissable is an ideal place for observing waders (particularly 'shanks and calidrids) throughout the year; at high tide, in the salt-pans, they are easily watched from the road.
- Little Egret and Grey Heron are often present at the north bank of the Petit-Traict and are easily seen from Sissable.
- Oystercatcher and Avocet can be seen with an incoming tide.
- In winter, dabbling duck, Red-breasted Merganser and Goldeneye are more numerous on the Petit-Traict.

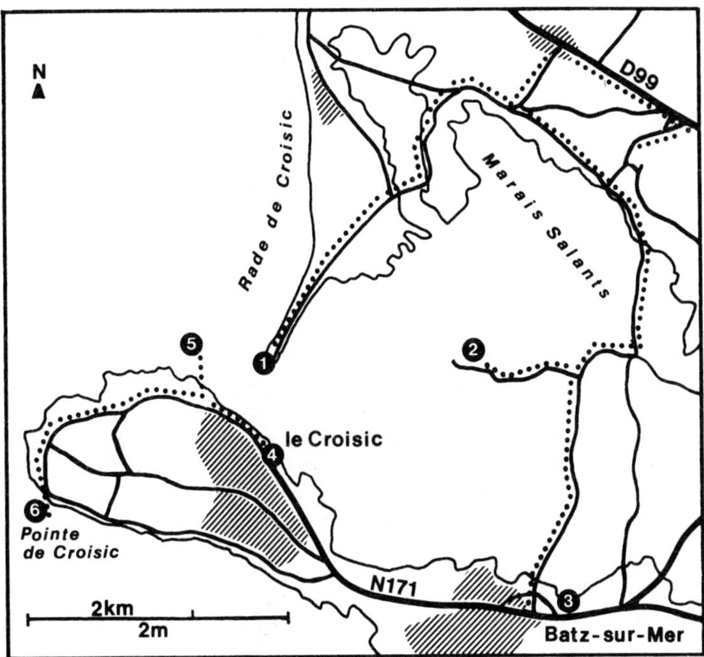

- Shelduck and Brent Geese can be seen on all the mudflats, groups move according to the tide.
- Common Terns nest in small colonies on muddy islands in the salt-pans, they are easily seen from the road, it is best not to get out of the car.
- The Bluethroat (which sings in April and May) is seen everywhere in company with Reed Bunting and Stonechat.
- Black-headed and Common Gull roost in the salt-pans (summer and autumn).
- From Tréhic jetty or the Pointe de Pen-Bron, you can see Slavonian and Red-necked (rarer) Grebes in winter.
- With an incoming tide there are large concentrations of gulls (Black-headed, Great Black-backed, Lesser Black-backed, Herring and Common, more rarely Mediterranean or Yellow-legged) and terns (Common, Sandwich).
- Of the divers, the Great Northern is more common on the Pen-Bron shallows.
- From the Pointe du Croisic it is possible to see skuas (Great, Pomarine and Arctic), shearwaters (mainly Yelkouan with some Manx and Sooty) and many Gannet, mainly in August and September.

197 Grée Marshes

The Grée Marshes, just to the north of Anciens, comprise an area of meadows (periodically flooded in winter) and permanent marshland.

They are most important as a stop-over site for migrants during the spring, for many species of duck (Pintail, Shoveler, Gadwall, Garganey and even Greylag Goose), waders (mainly Black-tailed Godwit and Ruff); passerines such as hirundines, wagtails and pipits also occur. In winter, despite the fact that there is hunting, many thousands of Lapwing occur along with good numbers of Wigeon, Shoveler, Teal and Tufted Duck; after a cold spell, Bewick's and Whooper Swans may join the Mute Swans. In spring, species that are otherwise rare in the area nest – Little Grebe, Garganey, Shoveler, Blue-headed Wagtail and Whinchat.

198 Gâvre Forest

Gâvre Forest, a vast mature beech wood some 45 km (28 miles) to the north-west of Nantes, has an interesting diversity of birds. Spring is the best time to discover the birds: Buzzard, Sparrowhawk and the rare Goshawk display on mild sunny days in February and March; Black Kite arrive in mid-March, Hobby not until mid-April. There are the six species of woodpecker (Great, Middle and Lesser Spotted, while Green and Grey-headed are less common and Black rare). Golden Oriole sing in the foliage, smaller birds are also present: Marsh, Crested and sometimes Coal Tits; Bonelli's and Wood Warblers, Redstart, Spotted Flycatcher; in the evening it is possible to hear Nightjar and Little and Tawny Owls. On the forest edges or in clearings there are Whitethroat, Dartford and Garden Warblers alongside Yellowhammer and Cirl Bunting.

199 BAILLIE MEADOWS

12 km/7.5 miles
Le Lion-d'Angers
(IGN 1521 – 1/50 000)

Habitat and Timing

This is a vast area of alluvial meadows on the right bank of the Sarthe River where it joins the Loir. Periodic flooding almost completely covers them between October and May. The flora is typical of water-meadows (they are still farmed in a traditional manner, cutting hay in July with communal grazing of the regrowth). There is a network of drainage ditches with the occasional willow on their banks. This otherwise open habitat is marred by a few poplar plantations.

There is an increasing amount of hunting which limits its attractiveness in winter for duck (principally Pochard), but in spring the site is a stop-over of major European (even international) importance for many ducks and geese as well as waders. During the breeding period there are many interesting wetland species.

Calendar

Winter: (depending on the water-level) Cormorant; a variety of dabbling duck; Lapwing, Golden Plover, Snipe; Skylark, Meadow and Water Pipits, Reed Bunting.

Spring: principally between mid-February and April when the meadows are still partially flooded, large numbers of migrants, such as dabbling duck (mainly Pintail), Greylag Goose (February and March); Lapwing, Golden Plover, Ringed Plover, Dunlin, Ruff, Black-tailed Godwit by the thousand (late February to mid-March), Curlew, Snipe, different 'shanks; Black-headed, Common and Lesser Black-backed Gulls; marsh terns; passerines include hirundines, pipits and Blue-headed Wagtail. These concentrations attract birds of prey such as Peregrine.

Breeding season: from May to July, Grey Heron, Garganey; Quail, Corncrake, sometimes Spotted Crake; Lapwing; Kingfisher, Blue-headed Wagtail; Whinchat, Savi's, Grasshopper, Sedge and Reed Warblers, Reed and Corn Buntings.

Access

On leaving Angers northwards, about 5 km (3.1 miles) to the south of the area, take the D107 towards Cantenay-Épinard. At the entrance to the village, turn right in the direction of Châtillon and Vieux-Cantenay ①,

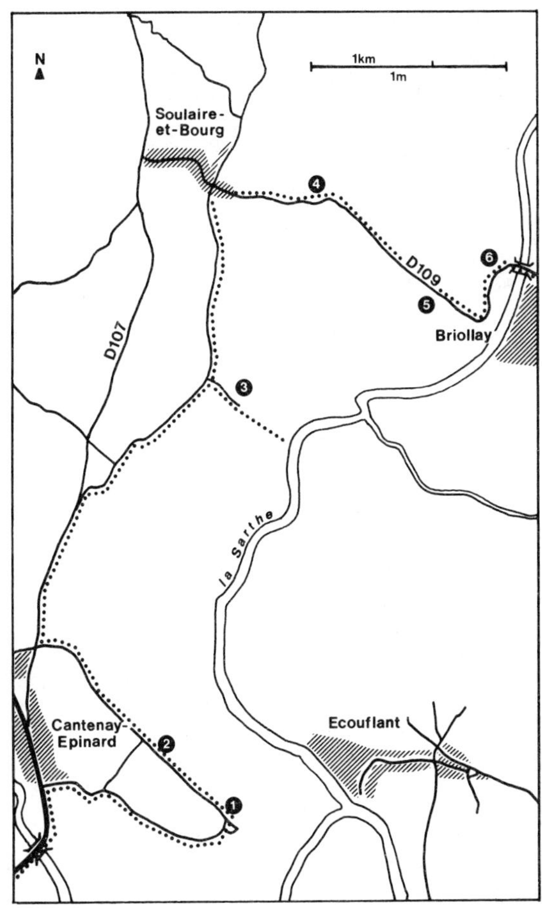

where the road comes into the Sarthe Valley. Between Chantenay and Vaux, there are many possible sites for watching birds ②. From Vaux, go onto the D107 towards the hamlet of Noyant, and here, take the tarmac track which runs along the flood bed of the Sarthe, crossing the meadows on the right bank. There is an excellent view over the whole Baillie area ③. If groups of birds are close, it is better to stay in the car in order not to frighten them. In summer, there is a network of tracks that can be used on foot to discover the whole area.

Returning from Noyant, turn north towards Soulaire-et-Bourg as far as the hamlet of Les Chapelles, then turn right on the D109 towards Briollay. Drive 2.5 km (1.6 miles), this allows observation, once again, of the meadows of the right bank, and it is easy to stop along the road at the access points to the fields ④, ⑤, ⑥.

Beware: when there is a lot of flooding (when the level of the Maine at Angers is 3.5 m or more), most of the access roads indicated here are under water.

Black-tailed Godwit

Species

- From mid-February to April, it is a migration stop-over for waders, particularly Black-tailed Godwit, but also Ruff and Golden Plover.
- A resting site in spring (February and March) for dabbling duck and Greylag Goose.
- In spring, Sedge and Savi's Warblers can be found on the lowest-lying ground, where a few reeds grow.
- In April, the *flavissima* race of the Yellow Wagtail is frequently observed. Also Water and Meadow Pipits can be seen.
- In April there are many hirundines on migration.
- Corncrakes can be heard in the late afternoon, evening and at night (May and June) singing in the meadows.

200 The Loire, between La Daguenière and Saint-Mathurin

The river-bed of the 'wild Loire' with its numerous islands and sandbanks, can easily be watched from the roads on the protection embankments. Above Angers, the most interesting circuit is on the left bank on the D952 between La Daguenière and Saint-Martin. In winter you can see Cormorant, Goosander (in hard weather), Lesser Black-backed and Yellow-legged Gulls. During times of migration and when the river is low (April, May, and July to November) you can see Spoonbill, waders and marsh terns. In the nesting season, on the sandbanks, there are colonies of Little Ringed Plover, Common and Little Terns, and on the steep banks, Kingfisher and Sand Martin.

201 The Loire at Parnay

Above Saumur, the river is of interest for watching migrants and overwintering birds. Its big attraction is the Isle de Parnay, near to the left bank, level with Parnay (located on the D947 between Saumur and Montsoreau). From Parnay, there is a network of footpaths which gives access to the river-bank, from where there are good views over the island. This treeless island is protected by law; it has the largest Black-headed Gull colony in the region and good numbers of Little Ringed Plover, Common and Little Terns.

202 MONT DES AVALOIRS/ PRÉ-EN-PAIL

3 km/1.85 miles
Carrouges
(IGN 1616 east – 1/25 000)

Habitat and Timing

Very undulating countryside, with the highest point in the west of France (417 m), the Mont des Avaloirs has large areas of heather moor, conifer and deciduous woods with an undergrowth of Bilberry and bracken. It is a nesting area for many species otherwise rare in the region. It is also a good place for seeing migrants. Many footpaths wind their way through the area, allowing good views of the birds.

Calendar

Spring (the best time): many nesting species, Hen Harrier, Honey Buzzard, Dartford Warbler, Nightjar, Grasshopper Warbler, Hawfinch, Crossbill, Treecreeper. Also many species on spring migration: raptors, passerines, Ring Ouzel.

Winter: Woodcock, Coal Tit, Redpoll and Crossbill.

Access

Leaving Pré-en-Pail (70 km/44 miles to the north of Laval and 30 km/ 19 miles) to the west of Alençon, on the N12), take the D144 towards Saint-Pierre-de-Nids. After 3 km (1.85 miles), turn left towards Mont-des-Avaloirs; 2.5 km (1.9 miles) later, leave the car at the car park

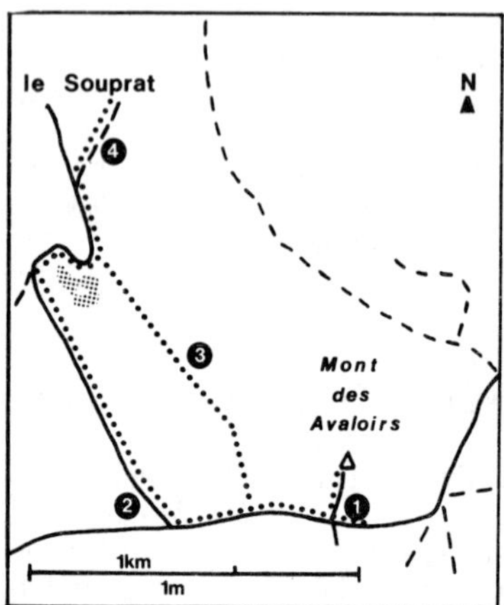

near the information board. In this type of habitat, you have to walk a good distance to find the birds. From the car park ①, return via the entrance and turn right at the end of the track; 300 m (330 yards) further on take the tarmac track towards Souprat. On each side of this little road is some magnificent moorland/heath ②. Turn around before arriving at Souprat Farm, and take the marked trail going in the direction of Pierre-au-Loup; this little track crosses some sparse deciduous woodland, with an undergrowth of Bilberries ③. Continue on to Pierre-au-Loup ④. Return along the same track. Other interesting walks can be taken.

Species

- In spring it is easy to see some typical heathland birds: Whitethroat, Grasshopper and Dartford Warblers, Stonechat, Linnet.
- There are ground-dwelling passerines (Wheatear, pipits, larks).
- There are good numbers of some forest passerines (all the tits, treecreepers).
- Woodpeckers are also seen in the wood.
- A good point for looking for raptors (Buzzard, Hen Harrier, Honey Buzzard), especially in spring.

203 La Chapelle-Erbrée Lake

Recently created (in 1984), La Chapelle-Erbrée Lake is on the border of two departments, Mayenne (the parish of Bourgon) and Ille-et-Vilaine (La Chapelle-Erbrée and Saint-M'Hervé). From July to October, with a low water-level, mudflats appear, attracting waders on autumn migration. More than 20 species have been observed, including Marsh

Sandpiper, Knot and Curlew Sandpiper. During hard weather the lake freezes less quickly than others in the neighbourhood and this attracts hundreds of duck. At present there are few nesting species (Great Crested Grebe, Coot, Mallard), due to the number of tourists and the lack of vegetation.

204 Gué-de-Selle Lake

In Mésangers parish (in north-east Mayenne), Gué-de-Selle Lake has been part of a protected area since 1963. In the middle of an area with many lakes, it plays an important role as a reserve. A path has been made round the lake which provides good birdwatching. The birds tend to be less shy here. Its main interest is for the many duck in winter (especially when neighbouring lakes are hunted). There is also a large Black-headed Gull roost and its reed-beds have nesting warblers (Reed, Marsh and Sedge).

205 PARCÉ-SUR-SARTHE PLAIN

8 km/5 miles
Sablé-sur-Sarthe
(IGN 1620 west – 1/25 000)

Habitat and Timing

This is a plain of regrouped farmland now used for cereal growing (Maize, Wheat, Barley, Rape and Sunflowers) with a very stony, chalky soil. Nearby, there is the sinuous, wooded valley of the River Sarthe. In winter and spring, it is an important wintering and stop-over site for some species. Watching in the early morning or the evening is recommended.

Calendar

Winter: Merlin, Marsh Harrier, sometimes Short-eared Owl. Large numbers of Lapwing and Golden Plover. Large flocks of passerines, including Lapland Bunting.

Spring: Hen and Montagu's Harrier; Lapwing, Quail, Stone Curlew, Grey and Red-legged Partridges, sometimes Little Bustard.

On migration: waders on ploughed fields, Lapwing, Golden Plover, Dotterel, Ruff, Curlew, Snipe. Many passerines (Wheatear, Whinchat, Blue-headed Wagtail), also Greylag Goose and Black Kite.

Access

From Sablé-sur-Sarthe (to the west) take the D306 towards La Flèche. Just before Louailles village, turn left taking the D53 to Vion (3.5 km/2.2 miles). Park at Vion church car park ①. Take the road opposite the church going towards La Lucerie Farm (poultry breeding), drop down to the water-tower and turn left (D53). Just after La Richardière Farm, take the track to the left which cuts across a corner of the plain, then come

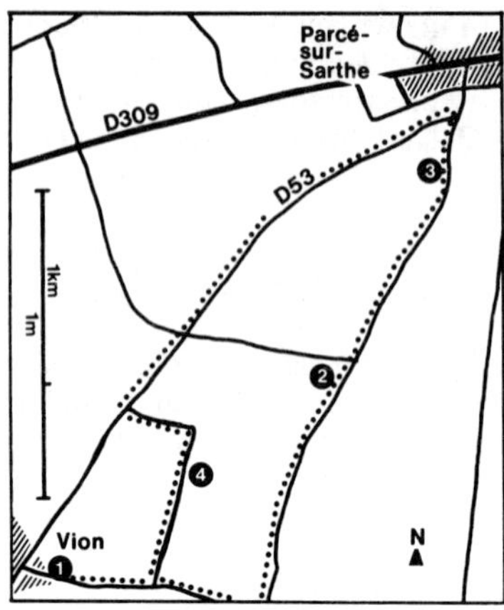

back to Vion. You are advised to stop at points ②, ③ and ④, in order to see raptors and waders under good conditions.

Species

- During times of migration and in winter, Lapwing, Golden Plover, Dunlin, Ruff and sometimes the rare Dotterel occur.
- An ideal place for searching for raptors: Merlin, Marsh Harrier, sometimes Short-eared Owl, Hen Harrier, Sparrowhawk, Kestrel, Buzzard. In the summer Montagu's Harrier and Hobby. On migration, Black Kite and Honey Buzzard can be seen. Long-eared and Barn Owls come to hunt.
- There are many passerines including Reed and Lapland Buntings in winter. Corn Bunting is present as a breeder and in winter.
- Stone Curlew and Lapwing nest on the plain.
- Red-legged and Grey Partridges and Quail nest here; sometmes Little Bustards are also seen on the plain.
- You can see Blue-headed Wagtail, Whinchat and Wheatear on migration.
- In winter, buntings (Reed, Lapland and Corn) can be seen in the stubble.

206 Bercé Forest

This public forest lies to the south-east of Mans, on a 150 m-high plateau. This is a splendid wood of mature Sessile Oaks nearly 300 years old, mixed with areas of slender beech and Sweet Chestnut, covering 5,415 hectares.

The site holds a remarkable number of species and is best visited in the spring (April or May) in order to see raptors displaying (Hobby, Kestrel, Goshawk, Sparrowhawk, Buzzard, Honey Buzzard and Hen Harrier). It is possible to see woodpeckers (Middle, Great and Lesser Spotted, Green, Grey-headed and Black) in the same sectors. Also present are: Stock Dove, Redstart, the four species of *Phylloscopus* warblers, Goldcrest and Firecrest as well as the two treecreepers, Woodcock and Nightjar.

207 Perseigne Forest

About 50 km (31 miles) to the north of Mans and some 10 km (6.2 miles) to the south-east of Alençon, Perseigne Forest sits on one of the Normandy hills. English and Sessile Oaks dominate the site. The six species of woodpecker (Great, Middle and Lesser Spotted, Black, Green and Grey-headed) give away their presence by their calls and drumming as early as February. Goshawk, Honey Buzzard and Hobby all nest here. In the more open areas you can see: Blackcap, Garden and Grasshopper Warblers, Tree Pipit, Woodcock and Nightjar. Crossbill can sometimes be seen in winter.

208 The Bourgneuf-Passage du Gois Bay Maritime Reserve

4 km/2.5 miles
Beauvoir-sur-Mer
(IGN 1125 west – 1/25 000)

Habitat and Timing

This is a vast bay about 20 km (12.5 miles) to the south of the Loire estuary; it is shallow, and is situated between the mainland and Noirmoutier Island; this has favoured, over the centuries, the deposit of marine mud. At low tide the area provides food and sanctuary for thousands of waders and duck. Protected by an embankment, the polders (used for agriculture and oyster-farming) lie alongside the tidal area. The time and state of the tides influence the movements and observation of the birds. A high tide coefficient of 55 to 70 is ideal.

Calendar

Autumn and winter: on the mudflats with an incoming tide, many Dunlin, Grey Plover, Oystercatcher, Curlew, Avocet (from September onwards). At high tide on the sea (from November to March) Cormorant, Shelduck, Brent Goose, dabbling duck (Pintail, Shoveler, Wigeon, Teal). On the polders, passerines (pipits, larks, buntings), raptors hunting (Hen and Marsh Harriers, Merlin), Lapwing, Golden Plover.

Spring: on the mudflats, passage of hundreds of Knot, Bar-tailed Godwit, Redshank, Whimbrel, Ringed Plover, Turnstone. On the salt-marshes and in bushes on the embankments, Bluethroat and different races of Yellow Wagtail on migration. On the polders, Montagu's Harrier, Kestrel. Common on the ploughed fields, Wheatear. Whatever the season, start the visit about three hours before high tide.

Access

Take the D948 out of La-Roche-sur-Yon via Challans, staying on this road going towards Beauvoir-sur-Mer. Go in the direction of Île de Noirmoutier on leaving Beauvoir-sur-Mer to pass on the 'Gois' (a mudflat road, covered at high tide) ①. The Gois road was built on a sand-bar, the

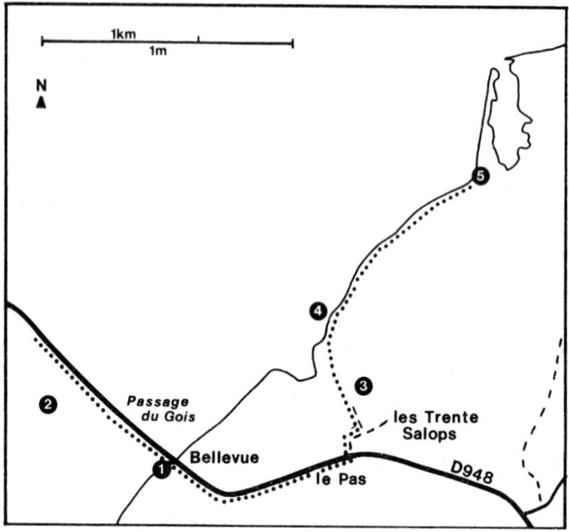

result of two sea currents from opposite directions meeting. Park the car at the entrance to the Gois, on the left. Look at the information board about tide times, on the right of the road. Walk along the Gois for about 1 km (0.6 miles). There is a superb view over the mudflats and of the oyster-farming ②. Return with the rising tide. Take the same road back in the car for about 1 km (0.6 miles) and turn left towards the place called Trente-Salops. Park the car on the roadside, about 100 m (110 yards) after coming onto the track. Take the dust road which goes towards the sea (forbidden to cars). On the right there are polders and meadows ③. On reaching the sea-wall, climb discreetly on top ④. Continue northwards either on the sea-wall or along the track. Once at point ⑤, stop and return by the same route, watching birds coming into feed as the tide recedes.

Species

- There are old salt-pans next to the road. It is possible to see nesting Lapwing and Redshank in the spring.
- There are groups of Brent Geese in front of the incoming tide.
- Waders move in front of the incoming tide (Oystercatcher, Bar-tailed Godwit, Curlew, Dunlin, Knot – in summer plumage in the first half of May –, Grey Plover, Avocet).
- There are good numbers of Blue-headed Wagtail nesting in the summer.
- Dabbling duck (Pintail, Shoveler, Wigeon, Mallard, Teal) and Shelduck (November to March) roost. Waders pass in flight going to their high-tide roosts.
- Marsh and Montagu's Harriers hunt over the polders, Kestrel too. Merlin hunt passerines (pipits, larks, buntings) in winter.
- In spring, the bushes on the salt-marsh and along the embankments hide passerines: Bluethroat, Willow Warbler, Chiffchaff, Whitethroat, Chaffinch, Brambling, Linnet, Twite.
- There is a big roost of waders and other birds at high tide: Oyster-

catcher and Cormorant on posts of an old embankment; Avocet, Curlew and godwits preen at the edge of the tide. In late April and early May, there is a large passage of Dunlin, Knot and Grey Plover in summer plumage. There is also a night roost of Whimbrel.

209 Jacobsen Jetty/Noirmoutier

To the east of the Island of Noirmoutier, the jetty separates the entrance channel to the port from an area of ancient salt-pans, a few of which are still used. A remarkable number of nesting birds use this area in the spring (Avocet, Black-winged Stilt, Shelduck, Black-headed Gull, Common Tern, Redshank, Bluethroat). It is also a wader roost, including Spotted Redshank and Greenshank, and Little Tern on spring migration. In winter there are concentrations of Shelduck and Brent Goose.

210 Olonne Marsh

This is one of the best birdwatching spots in the Vendée. A little less than 8 km (5 miles) to the north of Les Sables-d'Olonne, these marshes have many nesting species in spring: Avocet (the biggest colony in France), Black-winged Stilt, Redshank, Lapwing, Common Tern, Lesser Black-headed, Yellow-legged, Herring and Black-headed Gulls. In autumn, there are many waders on migration, and in winter dabbling duck. To the south of Île d'Olonne there is a bird observatory with guides from the ADEV (Association de Défense de L'Environment en Vendée) in the summer only. Chaume Lighthouse, at Les Sables-d'Olonne, is an excellent spot for watching seabird passage (August and September). The coast between Saint-Gilles-Croix-de-Vie and Les Sables-d'Olonne has a spectacular concentration of Yelkouan Shearwaters (5,000–10,000) in summer, visible from the coast, particularly from the beach at Sauveterre.

211 Belle-Henriette Lagoon

This lagoon, on the side of the D46 between La Tranche-sur-Mer and La Faute-sur-Mer, has many small waders in late summer (Black-winged Stilt, Ringed and Little Ringed Plovers, *Calidris* and *Tringa* waders, Black-tailed Godwit) as well as gulls (Black-headed and Little) and terns (Common, Little, Sandwich and Black). Shelduck are regular in small numbers. It is a breeding site for the Tawny Pipit, and passerines migrate through in autumn (hirundines, wagtails, Blackcap, Chiffchaff, Willow Warbler, Redstarts and Spotted and Pied Flycatchers). There are, however, a lot of holiday-makers in summer, to the detriment of the birds.

212 Beauvoir-sur-Mer Ancient Salt-pans

These old salt-pans just to the south-east of Beauvoir lie near some freshwater marshes and limestone hillsides. This is one of the most interesting sites in the Brittany-Vendée marshes (between April and July), notably for waders and duck in the breeding season. At this time the meadows and ponds have nesting Lapwing, Redshank, Black-tailed Godwit, Avocet and Black-winged Stilt; there are also Mallard, Garganey and Shoveler. Ruff, Whimbrel and various 'shanks stop here during the spring migration. In the spring the hedges of tamarisk, Blackthorn and bramble attract many passerines: Nightingale, Bluethroat, Cetti's, Sedge and many other Warblers.

213 AIGUILLON BAY

7.5 km/4.7 miles
L'Aiguillon-sur-Mer
(IGN 1328 – 1/50 000)

Habitat and Timing

This 6,500-hectare bay lies on the borders of two departments, Charente-Maritime and Vendée. The larger part, in the Vendée, has been a maritime no-hunting reserve since 1972. At low tide, the bay is a series of mudflats which provide the necessary food for coastal waders; it is the most important site in France for these birds (from July to May inclusive). In winter large flocks of duck can be seen (October to March). The bay is surrounded by polders used for agriculture, they have many diurnal and nocturnal birds of prey. Altogether, this is one of the richest sites on the coast of France. The best watching is from the sea-walls and the 'mizottes' during a rising tide, if possible with a coefficient of 75–80. A telescope is vital for looking at birds in the bay.

Calendar

Winter: Cormorant, Grey Heron; Greylag Goose, sometimes White-fronted Goose, Brent Goose (in small numbers); tens of thousands of dabbling duck (Wigeon, Mallard, Pintail, Shoveler, Teal); sometimes Crane; Marsh and Hen Harriers, Kestrel, Merlin, Peregrine; Oystercatcher, Avocet, Grey Plover, Dunlin, Knot, Curlew; thousands of Black-tailed Godwit, Bar-tailed Godwit, Redshank, Spotted Redshank, Ringed Plover, Great Black-backed, Lesser Black-backed, Herring, Common and Black-headed Gulls; Barn Owl (year-round), Short-eared Owl; Skylark, Meadow and Water Pipits, Reed and sometimes Lapland Buntings.

Breeding Season: Mallard, Montagu's Harrier, Hobby, Red-legged Partridge, Quail, Lapwing, Turtle Dove, Blue-headed Wagtail, Bluethroat, Stonechat, Melodious Warbler, Whitethroat, Linnet. Many over-summering waders.

Spring and autumn: as well as many of the wintering birds already mentioned, Little Egret, Spoonbill, Black Stork; Black Kite, Sparrowhawk; Dotterel (rare), Sanderling, Little Stint, Curlew Sandpiper, Ruff, Snipe, Whimbrel (late April and early May), Greenshank, Wood, Green and Common Sandpipers, Turnstone; Caspian, Common, Sandwich and Little Terns; hirundines, Tawny Pipit, Whinchat, Wheatear; Aquatic Warbler (rare), flycatchers.

Access

From Saint-Michel-en-l'Herm or Triaize, take the D746 and at Vignaud turn directly south on the road called Route des Prises. After Serinière ①

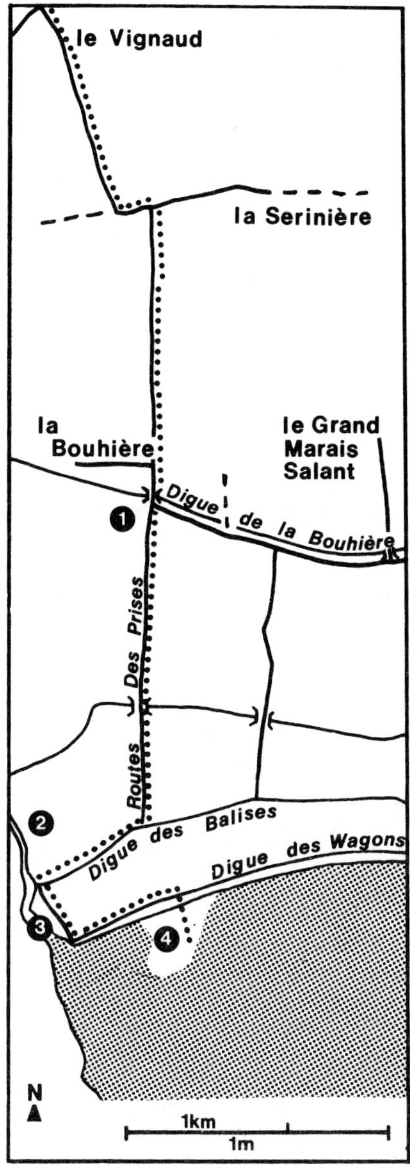

continue on the same road for another 1.5 km (0.9 miles). It is worth looking over the cultivated polders, especially in late summer. On arriving at the end of the road, turn left and after another 200 m (220 yards) park the car ②. Walk the embankment going directly southwards, leaving the Chenal-Vieux lock-gate ③ on your right. At the end of this embankment, you can see other birds by continuing east along the Digue des Wagons. It is also possible to advance some few hundred metres out onto the mizottes (best avoided at high tide so as not to disturb the roosting waders) and look over the salt-marshes ④. Return the same way as you came. It is also worth driving around the polder roads, to the north of the bay.

Species

- Marsh and Hen Harriers are present, especially in autumn and winter. As early as the end of April Montagu's Harriers are back nesting.
- Yellow Wagtail is a common nesting bird in the cereals. From August onwards many Whinchat and Wheatear use the polders.
- Black-headed, Lesser Black-backed, Yellow-legged, Herring and Common Gulls come onto the ploughed fields to roost at high tide, especially in summer.
- Bluethroat nest in the ditches at the bottom of the embankments.
- It is quite easy to see Barn Owl at dusk, hunting around the groups of Cypress trees. Also, Short-eared Owl occur in winter.
- In the ponds on the salt-marshes in August and September you can see Dotterel (rare), Ruff, Greenshank, Wood Sandpiper and Redshank, feeding there. At the end of April you can see Whimbrel.
- Greylag Goose can be found on the salt-marshes in winter and in March.
- As the tide rises, innumerable groups of waders group together at the top of the salt-marsh.
- Grey Heron, Little Egret and even Spoonbill, plus Cormorant on the posts, wait for the tide to go out.
- It is worth looking through the flocks of gulls roosting at high tide, there may well be some terns – perhaps the imposing Caspian Tern.
- Out in the bay, large groups of Shelduck and Avocet as well as dabbling duck are present from October to March.

214 Saint-Denis-du-Payré

This National Nature Reserve lies between the villages of Saint-Denis-du-Payré and Triaize; it is managed by the Association de Défense de L'Environnement en Vendée (ADEV); there are organised visits in July and August. It has thousands of dabbling duck in winter (Pintail, Wigeon, Shoveler, Mallard, Gadwall, Teal), and Garganey are seen in spring, as are Black Tern (which sometimes nest here) and Little Gull. A good number of raptors visit the reserve and the surrounding countryside: Marsh and Montagu's Harriers, Short-toed Eagle, Black Kite, Buzzard, Hobby and Kestrel; Peregrine in autumn and winter. In summer and autumn, many species of wader occur on the mud, also White and Black Storks and Spoonbill. Access is from Luçon via the D746 as far as Triaize, then on the D25. When there are no organised visits, watch from the road.

215 Poiré/Velluire Common

About 20 km (12.5 miles) to the south-west of Luçon, this 250 hectares of common land is mainly grazing meadows and is a no-hunting reserve. Spectacular numbers of Lapwing occur as well as many Golden Plover (from September to March). Black-tailed Godwit and Greylag Goose occur in early spring, sometimes in large numbers. Mute Swan are resident. In the autumn (September and October) it is a traditional gathering ground for Little Bustard, a few tens occur. The Parc Naturel Régional du Marais Poitevin has erected a hide in the eastern part of the common at the crossroads of the L'Anglée and La Taillée roads. Access is via the D949 as far as Mouzeuil-Saint-Martin, then on the D68.

216 Boucheries Lake

Boucheries Lake is 45 km (28 miles) to the south-east of Nantes, in Landes-Genusson parish. It welcomes, principally in winter and spring, many diving and dabbling duck, and Smew and Goosander during hard weather. Grebes and waders are mainly seen on migration. Shoveler, Gadwall, Garganey, Pochard and Great Crested Grebe all nest here. Bought by Vendée County Council, the area has been a no-hunting reserve since 1986. To get there from Nantes, take the N137 as far as Tiffauges, then the D37. There is a car park and a visitor centre.

PICARDIE

217 AILETTE LAKE

8 km/5 miles
Beaurieux
(IGN 2711 west – 1/25 000)

Habitat and Timing

This is an enormous artificial lake, built in 1983 in the Ailette Valley as part of a leisure centre of 450 hectares; it is some 12 km (7.5 miles) to the south of Laon (about 40 minutes from Reims and 90 minutes from Paris). The various habitats (open water, reed-bed, willow and alder beds, water-meadows, mudflats) have many birds, particularly at the back of the lake (north-east of Chamouille and south-east of Neuville-sur-Ailette). Hunting is forbidden, so that birds find calm here throughout the year. A remarkable site, particularly for waders and duck from October to March/April.

Calendar

Summer: Great Crested and Little Grebes, Coot; Mallard; Black-headed Gull, Reed Warbler and Reed Bunting. Mute Swan and a few pairs of Tufted Duck also nest.

Winter: thousands of duck (Mallard; Tufted Duck, Pochard, Pintail, Shoveler, Gadwall, Teal). Also, Black-headed Gull, Grebes, Cormorant, sawbills, Grey Heron. On the sides of the lake, Meadow Pipit, Lapwing, 'shanks and sandpipers.

Autumn and spring: wagtails (three species), marsh terns, hirundines and Swift.

Access

From Paris, Laon or Reims, go first to Chamouille village. Then take the D967 towards Cerny-en-Laonnais. One kilometre (0.6 miles) on, there is a good view over the embankment ①. Then go back to Chamouille and take the D19 towards Neuville-sur-Ailette. Stop again at the top end of the lake ②. Next, go 600 m (660 yards) further on and turn right towards the camp site, turn right again towards the watersports centre ③: from here it is possible to look over the lake. Go back towards Neuville-sur-Ailette.

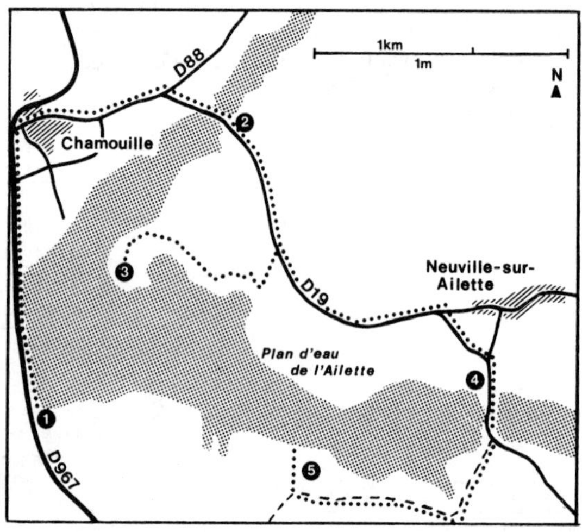

Some 200 m (220 yards) before the village, turn right and park the car near the eastern arm of the lake ④. Watch from here and walk along the southern bank ⑤.

Species

- There are concentrations of Tufted Duck, Pochard and Mallard in winter, also Mute Swan.
- Great Crested Grebe, Mallard, Tufted Duck and Coot nest at the top end of the lake.
- Sawbills may be present near the watersports centre in winter, Black-headed Gull also.
- Coot are present throughout the year.
- Lapwing nest on the side of the lake.
- Reed Bunting nest in the reed-bed on the eastern arm.
- Swift and hirundines (three species) are seen during migration in spring and autumn.
- Waders and Black Tern occur during migration.

218 The Isle de Saint-Quentin Marsh National Nature Reserve

This 50-hectare reserve (no hunting since 1973) is in the Somme Valley, in the heart of the town of Saint-Quentin (department of Aisne). This area contains a variety of habitats (ponds, reed-beds, wooded islands) and some rare plants (Cowbane, Great Fen Sedge) and many species of bird. Nesting species include Great Crested Grebe, Mallard, Coot and Reed Warbler; some migrants also occur in addition to swans, geese, duck and herons. The natural history centre welcomes groups; there is a peripheral path and information boards.

219 COMPIÈGNE PUBLIC FOREST

5 km/3.1 miles
Compiègne
(IGN 2411 east – 1/25 000)
and Attigny
(2511 west – 1/25 000)

Habitat and Timing

This forest is the largest and most varied in the department. The management techniques used by the ONF (Forestry Commission) mean that there are always mature trees. The majority of the forest comprises hardwoods: oaks, beech, Hornbeam, often mixed. However, the centre of the forest is planted with Scots Pine; and the southern and south-eastern edges are pure beech. Many parts have been replanted with conifers. A good area for woodpeckers, Woodcock and forest-dwelling passerines. A good number of tracks are closed to vehicles. The area is best visited in the spring.

Calendar

Spring: Buzzard, Honey Buzzard, Sparrowhawk; Woodcock; Stock Dove; Black and Middle Spotted Woodpeckers, Wryneck; Redstart; Grasshopper, Melodious, Wood and Bonelli's (uncommon) Warblers, Lesser Whitethroat; Willow Tit, Spotted and Pied Flycatchers; Hawfinch, Crossbill.

Winter: Redwing, Brambling, Siskin.

Access

Leave Compiègne on the D973 going towards Pierrefonds. At the Faisanderie crossroads (at the traffic-lights in the middle of the forest, 2 km (1.25 miles) after leaving the town), go straight on towards Pierrefonds turning right after 1 km (0.6 miles). Take a tarmac forest road which soon arrives at the Nymphes crossroads ①, starting point for the walk. There is a car park. From here the route crosses an arm of mature and regenerating oaks, excellent for hole-nesting species. Three hundred metres (330 yards) further on, a track goes off to the right into an area of thorn bushes and birch ②. Come back to the original track by skirting the side of some mature oak forest. Before arriving at Puits-de-Berne junction ③, the trail

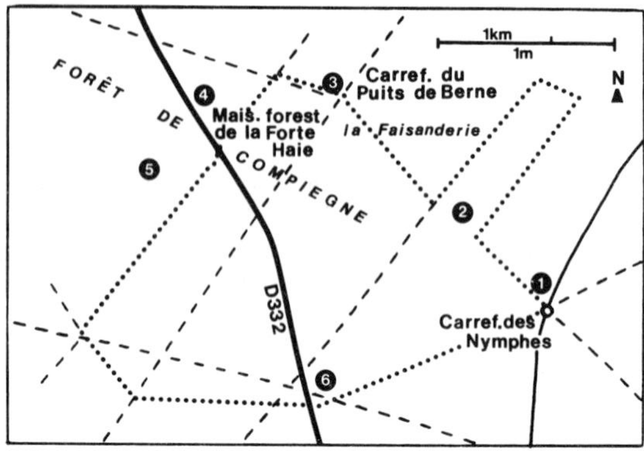

crosses an area of conifers. Soon after it passes before a recently-planted hardwood stand. Now go towards the Forte-Haie forester's house ④ and, after crossing a main road, go into a stand of mature beech ⑤. The return track passes through some quite thick stands of mature hardwood ⑥.

Crested Tit

Species

- As early as the end of February, both Black and Middle Spotted (very common) Woodpeckers can be heard in the mature oaks.
- In spring there is every chance of seeing Lesser Whitethroat or Melodious Warbler in the area of thorns and birch.
- In the conifers near the Puits-de-Berne junction, typical species include Coal and Crested Tits and Goldcrest.
- Where the forest has been cleared, you can see nesting raptors such as Buzzard and Honey Buzzard.

- It is also in the cleared areas that Stonechat, Grasshopper Warbler and Whitethroat nest.
- The beech grove is the best place for Wood Warbler, its metallic song is easily heard.
- In the nearby, denser woodland there are Spotted and Pied Flycatchers.

220 The Oise Valley Gravel-pits between Creil and Compiègne

This is a group of large water-bodies and sugar-beet factory settling-beds which attract many birds in winter or on migration. Verneuil, Moru-Pontpoint and Verberie gravel-pits are the most interesting of those open to the public (but not always still working and sometimes hunted over); Beaurepaire fish pond is also worth visiting (especially in winter). Visiting these lakes can easily fill a day. A telescope is useful. Many waders may be seen, especially in autumn (Dunlin, Little Stint, Lapwing, Redshank, Spotted Redshank, Greenshank, Green, Wood and Common Sandpipers, Black-tailed Godwit, Snipe); and also Black-headed Gull, Black Tern, the three common hirundines, Blue-headed and White Wagtails, warblers.

221 Wallus Lake

This is a private lake in Retz Forest of importance in winter for the number of Teal that occur. They nest in small numbers and are visible throughout the year. Other species can be seen or heard, including duck, Water Rail, Bittern (exceptional) and Grey Heron. The lake is in very beautiful countryside, but watching is only possible from the embankment (other areas are prohibited), and you need a telescope.

222 THE SOMME BAY MARITIME RESERVE (NO-HUNTING)

5 km/3.1 miles
Rue
(IGN 2106 – 1/50 000)

Habitat and Timing

A mud and sand estuary with all the typical habitats of such an area. To the north is a line of man-made sand-dunes which protect Marquenterre Bird Park (private); this gives place to a system of natural sand-dunes, stabilised with marram grass, Sea Buckthorn and plantations of pine, stretching as far as the Baie d'Authie. To the east there are water-meadows and marsh. The bird park is a mosaic of all the habitats found above the shore. The mudflats and sand are suitable for duck and waders either on migration or in winter. Marquenterre acts as a reserve for birds, some use it to roost at high tide throughout the year and certain species nest there (duck, herons, waders, passerines). The no-hunting reserve (Réserve de Chasse) is forbidden to motorised vehicles; dogs should be on a lead. The bird park is open to the public (pay to enter). It is best to visit the bay with a rising tide (followed by Marquenterre Bird Park), as the birds move up with the water.

Calendar

Winter: many dabbling duck (Pintail, Wigeon, Mallard, Shoveler, Teal), some diving duck in the bird park (Pochard and Tufted Duck). During periods of hard weather, sawbills, Whooper and Bewick's Swans. Many thousands of waders roost (Oystercatcher, Curlew, Dunlin, Bar-tailed Godwit) in addition to gulls and Shelduck. The Hooded Crow regularly over-winters. Some raptors are present during the winter (Rough-legged Buzzard, Peregrine, Merlin, Sparrowhawk). In the Mollières de la Maye, you find Snipe and passerines (Twite, pipits, larks, sometimes Shore Lark).

Spring: many migrants, duck, Greylag Goose, Brent Goose, waders, Spoonbill and raptors.

Breeding season: many species in Marquenterre Bird Park: Grey Heron, Avocet, Oystercatcher, Ringed Plover; some duck (Mallard, Gadwall, Shoveler, Teal, Shelduck), passerines (wetland warblers, Stonechat).

Autumn: many West European migrants. In the reserve, roosts of waders, Terns (Arctic, Common, Sandwich, Little and Roseate), accompanied by Arctic Skuas. Important numbers of passerines (pipits, finches, larks, thrushes and Blackbird) and raptors (Buzzard, Sparrowhawk, Merlin, Osprey); each year, North American waders are seen in the bird park between July and September (among others, Buff-breasted Sandpiper). Although the Baie de Somme is interesting at all times, autumn is the best season, for both quantity and quality.

Access

Marquenterre Bird Park is sign-posted from Abbeville (open April to November). For the Baie de Somme reserve, go to Crotoy on the D260 (if coming from Abbeville) or on the D938 (if coming from Rue). From here turn left towards La Maye, follow the winding road for 2 km (1.25 miles) as far as the car park overlooking the sea (Parking de Maye) ①. Park the car here, there are two possibilities:

1. Walk north-westwards on the estuary on the Voie de Rue to get to Saint-Quentin Point ⑤; you can do this at low tide but La Maye must be crossed ②. It can be done barefoot in summer, boots are needed in winter.
2. At high tide La Maye is impossible to cross; walk north-eastwards crossing the 'mollières' (beware of the water-filled creeks) and follow the embankment as far as Férolles Lock ③, where you can cross the small river. The second option offers a view over the channels in the Marquenterre Bird Park from over the embankment, a hide has been built here ④. Then follow the exterior of the park to get to Saint-Quentin Point ⑤. From here, there is a sandbank in the form of an arc called Banc de L'Illette which serves as a wader roost during

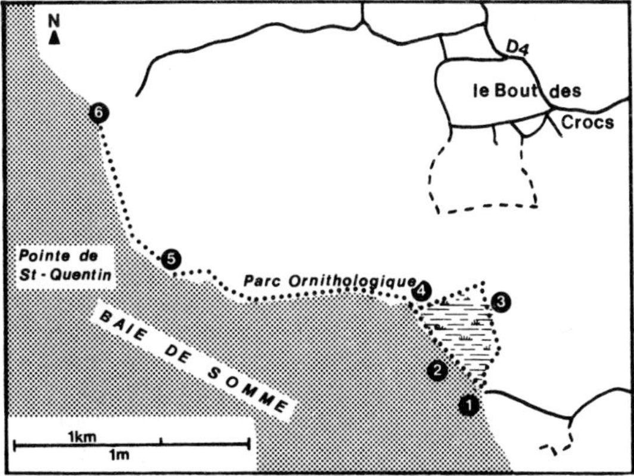

spring tides. It is here that the largest flocks of birds occur. To observe them, all that you need to do is to stay along the line of dunes. Continuing northwards, a blockhouse is a useful hide ⑥. Return by the same route. *Beware:* it is very dangerous to venture out into the estuary without knowing the times and heights of the tides.

Species

- Jack Snipe can be seen in winter.
- Waders use the old hunting marshes during migration.
- As early as March, Lapwings display over the water-meadows.
- Avocet, on migration, stop in the wetter depressions.
- Warblers nest in the reed-beds in summer (Reed, Sedge and Savi's).
- In winter there are many passerines in the 'mollières' (Twite among others).
- From the hide it is possible to see dabbling and diving duck, and Coot throughout the year.
- Avocet are present in the breeding season.
- This is an important high-tide roost of Oystercatcher and other waders during times of migration.
- An area used by Hooded Crow in winter.
- Smew, Goosander and even Whooper and Bewick's swans may be seen during hard weather.
- Osprey hunt over the canal in August and September.
- There is a large passerine and raptor migration in the autumn (October/November).
- Thousands of waders come in to roost at high tide (Oystercatcher, Curlew, Dunlin, Bar-tailed Godwit, plovers).
- In winter, the inter-tidal zone is used by Pintail, Wigeon, Mallard and Shelduck.
- It is a gull roost during rising tides in winter. In autumn it is also a tern roost (July to September) with the chance of seeing an Arctic Skua.
- Avocet and Kentish Plover nest here (April and May).
- Rough-legged Buzzard hunt in the dunes in winter.

223 HABLE D'AULT (NO-HUNTING RESERVE)

9.5 km/5.9 miles
Saint-Valery-sur-Somme
(IGN 2107 – 1/50 000)

Habitat and Timing

This reserve is an ancient coastal lagoon, now separated from the sea; there are some good reed-beds around its edges, and ponds to the north and south. To the east lie meadows and cultivated fields. To the west there are some dry flats with wet hollows, of interest for duck, waders and gulls. Access to the reserve is strictly controlled, but the gravel paths on the edge allow for easy watching in the early morning and the evening.

Calendar

Winter: plenty of diving duck (Pochard, Tufted Duck, Scaup, Goldeneye, Red-breasted Merganser, Smew); Coot, Cormorant, Great Crested and Red-necked Grebes, Red-throated and Black-throated Divers, gulls (including Glaucous). Also, Short-eared Owl, Rough-legged Buzzard, Shore Lark, Bearded Tit, Lapland and Snow Buntings. Scoters and Eider at sea.

Spring: large numbers of migrants in March and April, such as Pintail, Shoveler, Teal and Garganey, Greylag Goose; waders ('shanks, Ringed Plovers, godwits, Curlew, Avocet); terns and marsh terns (Black and Whiskered); Little and Mediterranean Gulls. Many passerines, notably hirundines, wagtails and pipits; harriers (three species), Hobby, Merlin, Kestrel and Peregrine (rare), sometimes Red-footed Falcon.

Breeding season: Shelduck, Shoveler, Garganey, Pochard, Tufted Duck; Ringed Plovers, Lapwing; Bearded Tit, Wheatear.

Autumn: Greylag Goose (October), dabbling duck; Curlew, godwits, snipes. Many migrants: raptors (Sparrowhawk, Buzzard, Falcons); seed-eating passerines and pipits. Good sea-watching from the sea-wall (duck, waders, gulls and terns).

Access

On leaving Abbeville, take the D204 as far as Saint-Valery-sur-Somme. From here go towards Cayeux, still on the D204. At Cayeux, take the Chemin Sud towards the reserve which skirts the beach. From Ault take the N40. At Hautebut, take a track on the right towards the reserve's marsh (there are signposts). From Hautebut, visit the meadows ① and the first extraction lakes ② by car, stop to look over the sea ③; then follow the coast going northwards (Hable d'Ault); it is worth stopping at ④. Park at the level of Hable d'Ault, where there is a good view over the reserve ⑤. Continue northwards, with a possible stop at the ballast pits ⑥, and continue on towards Cayeux ⑦. You can do the route the other way round.

Species

- Lapwing nest on the meadows and crops.
- In winter the ballast pits have diving ducks including sawbills.

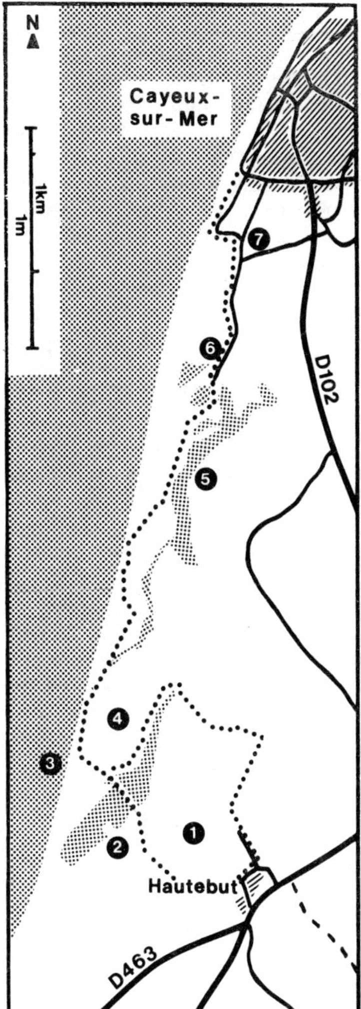

- Ringed Plover nest on the top of the sea shore.
- Scoters and Eider may be seen on the sea.
- Snow and Lapland Buntings and Shore Lark can be seen here in winter.
- Wheatear nest on the dunes.
- Raptors on migration are seen in the autumn.
- Many Swift and hirundines hunt over Hable d'Ault in April and May.
- Large numbers of dabbling duck occur in spring, diving duck in winter.
- Bearded Tit and *Acrocephalus* warblers nest in the vast reed-beds.
- The ballast pits attract migrant godwits, Ringed Plovers and 'shanks.
- Migrant terns and gulls can be seen at sea.

224 Ault-Onival Cliffs

To the south of the Hable d'Ault, these chalk cliffs continue for about 7 km (4.35 miles) between Ault-Onival and Mers-les-Bains. They vary in height between 60 m and 80m. You can birdwatch from the cliff top (take care) or from below (do not get caught out by the tide). For the latter, access is via Ault beach, walk southwards; or via Mers, from there walk northwards; or again via the Bois de Cise, between these first two places. Spring is the best time to visit this special area; Fulmar, Herring Gull (prospering), Jackdaw, Stock Dove, House Martin, Starling and Kestrel all nest. During the migration period, there is excellent birdwatching over the sea.

225 Crécy-en-Ponthieu Forest

This public forest, some 15 km (9.3 miles) to the north-west of Abbeville, is a beech wood of 4,314 hectares, rich in birds and mammals (Roe Deer, Wild Boar). In spring there are nesting raptors (Buzzard, Honey Buzzard, Sparrowhawk), and many passerines: Nuthatch, Great Spotted, Lesser Spotted and Green Woodpeckers; Wood Warbler, Redstart, Hawfinch, Stock Dove (in the mature trees). In the clearings and areas of regrowth there are: Melodious and Grasshopper Warblers, Tree Pipit, Hen Harrier and sometimes Short-eared Owl. In winter, there are large flocks of Chaffinch and Brambling; Woodpigeons are particularly plentiful and roost here. There are regular Long-eared Owl roosts in conifer plantations.

POITOU-CHARENTES

226 TOUVRE VALLEY

10 km/6.2 miles
Angoulême
(IGN 1732 east – 1/25 000)

Habitat and Timing

The Touvre is really the reappearance of an underground river (the second most important in France, after the Fontaine de Vaucluse). Three natural ducts bring water from two other rivers (the Bandiat and the Tardoire) to the surface. So the waters of the Touvre are very clear, well oxygenated and of an almost constant temperature, winter and summer alike. This explains why, despite heavy urbanisation, the valley is still important for birds in winter; they find abundant and varied food. Although easy, access to the valley is more or less restricted to the areas mentioned here.

Calendar

Winter: Little Grebe, Moorhen, passerines, notably Water Pipit, wagtails, *Phylloscopus* warblers; Black Redstart, Stonechat, Blackcap, Siskin, Hawfinch; Great Grey Shrike; Teal, Pochard, Tufted Duck; Grey Heron, Snipe, Water Rail, Lapwing; Black-headed Gull; Kingfisher, Cetti's Warbler, Reed Bunting, Redpoll.

Spring: many nesting Little Grebe. The only nesting site of Common Sandpiper in west-central France; Golden Oriole, Lesser Spotted Woodpecker, Reed and Sedge Warblers, Water Rail. Also migrant Black-necked Grebe, Garganey and waders.

Access

Take the N141 from Angoulême towards Limoges. On leaving Ruelle take the D57 as far as the village of Touvre. Park at Touvre source ①. Then leave on the D408 towards Magnac. After the level-crossing, you can park at ②. Descend to the wash-house and skirt the river bank and the reed-bed. Return by the same path. Go onto the bridge on the D699 ③. Other than watching from the bridge, it is possible to take a path ④ which follows the river (the right bank) for about 1 km (0.6 miles). Return on the same path. Now take the road in the direction of Ruelle running along the right of the railway. You can park at the sports ground ⑤ and walk on the left bank. Finally, once you reach the foot-bridge ⑥, there is a good view over the valley. Visiting is rewarding at any time of the day.

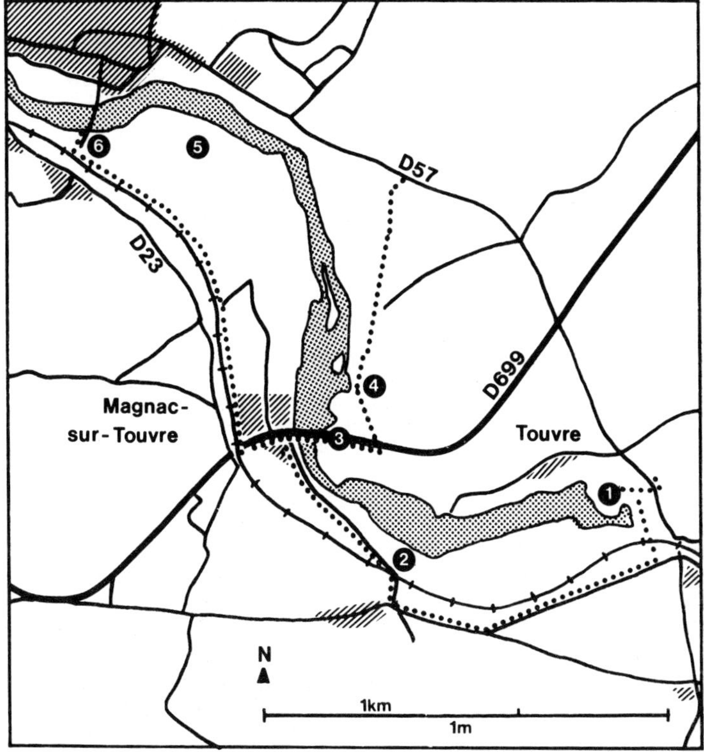

Species

- Little Grebe are present throughout the year.
- Water Pipit, Grey and White Wagtails are present in winter.
- Reed and Sedge Warblers and Reed Bunting can be found on migration and in the breeding season.
- Water Rail can be heard throughout the year.
- Mallard, Teal, Pochard and Tufted Duck occur in winter.
- Waders occur in the wetter areas, especially during migration, sometimes in winter.
- Chiffchaff are found in the bushes and shrubs in winter.

227 Braconne Forest

This is a state forest of 4,000 hectares situated 15 km (9.3 miles) to the north-east of Angoulême, on the N141 in the direction of Limoges. Beech, oak and Hornbeam of various ages are mixed together, their structural differences are accentuated by the forestry practice of natural regeneration from mature trees. There are many nesting raptors (Short-toed Eagle, Honey Buzzard, Goshawk, Sparrowhawk, Buzzard, Hobby, Black Kite, Montagu's and Hen Harriers), equalled only by the woodpeckers (Lesser, Middle and Great Spotted, Green, and also Grey-headed and a recent coloniser, the Black). Tawny and Long-eared Owls and Nightjar fly here at night, and the forest resounds to the song of passerines during spring dawns. There are four 'leaf' warblers (Wood, Bonelli's, Willow and Chiffchaff); Redstart, Song Thrush, Nightingale and Golden Oriole. Hawfinch also occur.

228 FIER-D'ARS AND LILEAU-DES-NIGES NATIONAL NATURE RESERVE/ÎLE DE RÉ

12 km/7.5 miles (by car) and 3.5 km/2.2 miles (on foot)
Île de Ré
(IGN 1229 – 1/50 000)

Habitat and Timing

The north of the Île de Ré is a mosaic of habitats which is responsible for the great diversity of birds to be found there. A large area of salt-marsh and salt-pans, some used, others not, encircles a nearly closed-off bay, the Fier-d'Ars; a line of dunes and a flat rocky foreshore protect the Fier from the ocean. There are two reserves, so the birds are not disturbed: Lileau-des-Niges National Nature Reserve to the south of Portes-en-Ré (no entry) managed by the LPO (Ligue Français pour la Protection des Oiseaux), and a maritime no-hunting reserve lying between Pointe du Lizay and Pointe du Grouin.

In order not to disturb the birds, it is very important that visitors stay on the paths. The best times for watching are two or three hours either side of high tide; for the marshes, try to go when there is a high tide in the morning.

Calendar

Winter: divers (three species), grebes (all species), Grey Heron, Little Egret, Spoonbill; Brent Goose, Shelduck, Mallard, Wigeon, Teal, Red-breasted Merganser, Goldeneye, Long-tailed Duck, Common Scoter; Oystercatcher, Dunlin, Sanderling, Grey and Ringed Plover, Curlew, Bar-tailed Godwit, Turnstone; Mediterranean Gull, Redwing, Blackcap.

Spring: waders on passage (March to late May). Equally: Shelduck, Marsh Harrier; Avocet, Black-winged Stilt, Kentish Plover, Little Ringed Plover, Redshank; Lesser Black-backed, Herring and Yellow-legged Gulls; Common Tern; Hoopoe, Blue-headed Wagtail, nesting Bluethroat.

Autumn: Spoonbill, Common Scoter, Waders (more than 30 species), migrant passerines.

Access

The itinerary varies according to the tide. By car: drive to the village of Portes-en-Ré, at the north of the island. Follow the signs Centre-Ville and take the third road to the right, then the second left and the first right 800 m (880 yards) later: here there is a car park close to the camp site ①. Go

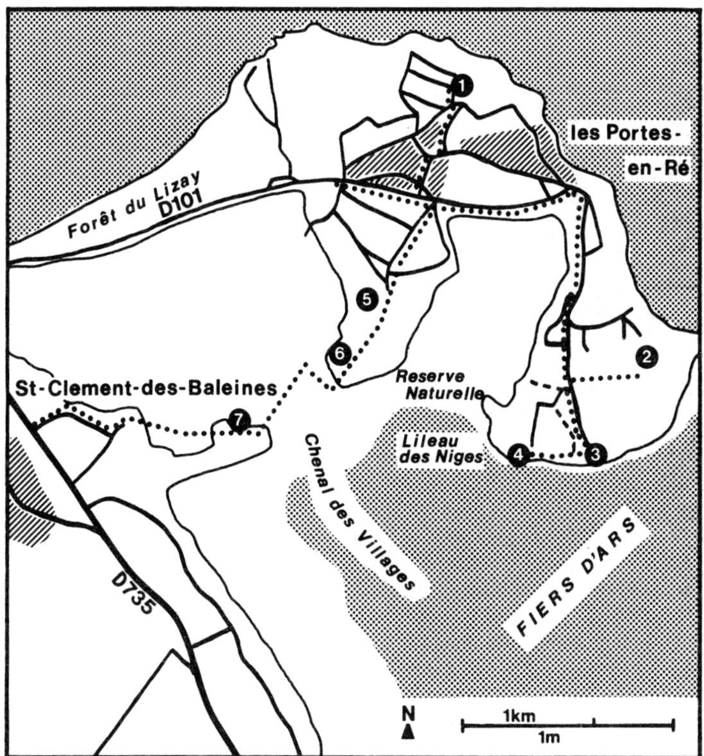

to the Marchais beach. Then go back to the car and continue along the D101 towards the Bois de Trousse-Chemise. 800 m (880 yards) before the Patache car park, turn left (opposite an electricity transformer), then take the second right. After 400 m (440 yards), the road comes to Trousse-Chemise car park ②. Leave the car and continue on foot to the sea, passing the wood and dunes. Then go back to the car and on to Patache car park ③. Walk the wrong way down the one-way road to the left for 100 m (110 yards) as far as the sea. At the back of the car park, turn left and again take the second turning on the left, where there is another car park ④. Look out over the Fier-d'Ars.

Return to Les Portes-en Ré, without entering the village. Turn left, opposite a supermarket, along a small road, following the signs Piste Cyclable as far as a large black building on the left (an old salt warehouse) ⑤. Leave the car and continue on foot (or bicycle) along the cycle track as far as Saint-Clément-des-Baleines. There is a possible stop in front of the reserve's information board ⑥; then take the Passerelle du Grand Vasais ⑦. Return via the same route, or via the D101 if you have a bicycle (or on to Ars-en-Ré).

Species

- An ideal spot in winter for watching Great Northern and Black-throated Divers, Great Crested, Slavonian and Black-necked Grebes.
- Sanderling, Ringed Plover and Turnstone feed on the beach and the high-tide wrack.
- Gulls and Common and Sandwich Terns roost on the sandbanks during the rising tide.
- A good point for watching migrant passerines in autumn.
- In the Fier narrows, it is possible to see Red-breasted Merganser, Goldeneye, Eider and sometimes Long-tailed Duck under excellent conditions (November to March). This is also a good place for seeing divers and grebes.
- At high tide for most of the year, Brent Geese, Shelduck and dabbling duck flock in front of Lileau-des-Niges.
- Many waders gather at high tide including Oystercatcher, Grey Plover, Bar-tailed Godwit and Curlew.
- In spring, Black-winged Stilt nest in the old salt-pans. Redshank and Avocet can be seen here too.
- Blue-headed Wagtail and Bluethroat are two typical breeding passerines to be found in this habitat.
- Brent Geese occur around the Grand Vasais in winter.

229 Baleines Lighthouse/Île de Ré

At the extreme north-west tip of Ré, the lighthouse is a good place for seawatching: Yelkouan Shearwater, Gannet, sometimes Storm Petrel, skuas (three species), gulls and terns all pass here, principally between August and November, but also in spring (April and May), Kittiwakes nest on the lighthouse; winter can be good for seeing divers, grebes and Red-breasted Merganser. It is also a good place for migrant passerines in the autumn, many insectivorous species may be noted.

230 La Lasse/Loix-en-Ré

Still on the Île de Ré, La Pointe de Lasse, opposite La Patache, is another good bird spot. Large movements can be observed when the tide is coming in or going out (Brent Goose, waders, gulls). At high tide, Oystercatcher, Curlew and Turnstone congregate here; there is a tern roost, especially in autumn; duck (especially Red-breasted Merganser), divers and grebes are present. It is a good spot for watching daytime passerine migrants in October. Bluethroat nest here.

231 YVES MARSHES NATIONAL NATURE RESERVE

5 km/3.1 miles
Rochefort
(IGN 1430 west – 1/25 000)

Habitat and Timing

This is a shallow ancient coastal lagoon (it only receives salt water during the highest tides). Fringed to the west by dunes, the main lagoon is in four parts. To the north there is a sandy area, overgrown with willows, with ponds from old sand workings which have been invaded by bulrush and reed. It is an interesting area for the number of duck and waders that occur, especially in winter and spring. Access to the reserve, which is managed by the LPO, is strictly controlled, but it is easy enough to see things well from the edge, particularly during high tide and in the morning, if possible.

Calendar

Winter: many Pintail, Shoveler, Pochard, Brent Goose, Dunlin, Grey Plover and Curlew. Also Penduline and Bearded Tits.

Spring: dabbling duck (including Garganey) and Greylag Goose (late February-March). Hirundines and Swift.

Autumn: Little Egret, freshwater waders (all *Tringa* species), Black-winged Stilt, Avocet, Snipe, Golden Plover, Lapwing. Many migrant passerines (both insectivores and granivores).

Access

From La Rochelle (to the north) or Rochefort (to the south), use the N137. The reserve is about 15 km (9.3 miles) from each of these towns. Park at Le Marouillet, or to the east of Les Boucholeurs. There are buses between La Rochelle and Rochefort. Starting from the car park at Le Marouillet there are two possibilities:

1. Simply park the car in the car park at Marouillet ①, level with Belle-Espérance and look over the marshes from here.
2. The walk: from the car park ①, go to the beach and walk northwards for about 2 km (1.28 miles). From ② it is possible to look over the dunes (no entry) as well as the sea (high or incoming tide). Arriving at

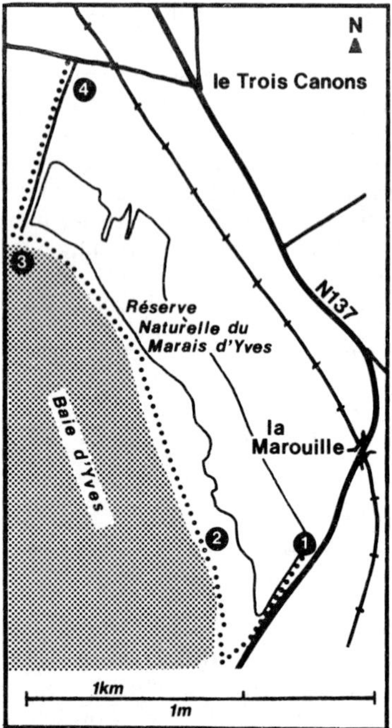

a sea-wall ③ (good view over the bay), take the tarmac road that goes northwards along the side of the oyster-farm. After about 500 m (550 yards), there are some interesting sandpits on the right ④. Those on the left may also be interesting, but between March and September only, as they are used for hunting. Return by the same route.

Species

- There are many hirundines and Swift in May.
- Dabbling duck and Greylag Geese occur in early spring.
- Little Egret and Grey Heron can be seen (autumn).
- Whinchat and Wheatear occur during migration. Sometimes Tawny Pipit and Short-eared Owl can be found on the 'Dune Grise'.
- On the sea side as the tide rises it is possible to see Brent Goose, duck and coastal waders.
- There is an important Black-headed and Common Gull roost in winter. Little Ringed Plover nest on the dunes.
- Bearded and Penduline Tits occur in winter, also migrant passerines (especially in autumn). Savi's, Great Reed, Reed and Sedge Warblers can be seen in the breeding season.
- There are Snipe, Ringed Plovers, Common Sandpiper and other *Tringa* waders (July to September).
- Little Grebe, Pochard and Tufted Duck are easily seen.
- Marsh Harriers occur year-round. Sometimes you can find Little Bittern and Spotted Crake (August and September).

232 The Île d'Oleron

This island, the second largest in France, is in many ways similar to the Île de Ré. Three places, at least, are worth visiting.

The Pointe de Chassiron in Saint-Denis parish, is excellent in autumn (September and October) for watching seabirds such as: Gannet, Yelkouan Shearwater, Storm and Leach's Petrels; Common Scoter, skuas Kittiwake, terns, Guillemot and Razorbill. In May there are often large movements of waders (Knot, Sanderling, Bar-tailed Godwit, Turnstone). Mediterranean Gulls are common enough near the cliffs in winter. The fields around the point are excellent for passerines in autumn as are the hedges between then (beware of hunters). La Cotinière port attracts many gulls in autumn and winter (Glaucous Gull often occur in winter). Autumn gales can produce some interesting species such as: Grey Phalarope, Kittiwake and Little Gulls, and Arctic Tern. Lastly, Douhet Marsh, near Saint-Georges, harbours many nesting species in the spring: Shelduck, Black-winged Stilt, Redshank, Herring and Yellow-legged Gulls, Bluethroat, and during times of migration it is an important site for small waders.

233 CÉBRON-PUY-TERRIER LAKE/SAINT-LOUP-SUR-THOUET

10 km/6.2 miles (of which 7.5 km/ 4.7 miles are on foot)
Parthenay
(IGN 1626 – 1/50 000)

Habitat and Timing

First filled with water in 1982, Cébron Reservoir was built in order to provide drinking water for all the parishes in the north of the Deux-Sèvres, and secondly to help irrigate 1,500 hectares of agricultural land. The countryside round about is mainly open permanent meadows, with many small valleys. As soon as it was flooded, the lake attracted many birds, despite the presence of incompatible activities (fishing, sailing). There is some protection with leisure and sports activities being controlled.

Calendar

Winter: Mallard, Gadwall, Wigeon, Teal, Pochard, Tufted Duck; Black-headed Gull; Lapwing, Golden Plover, Curlew, Snipe.

Spring: grebes, Greylag Goose (late February), all the species of dabbling duck, diving duck, waders, gulls. Great Crested Grebe, Mallard, Lapwing, Little Ringed Plover and Stone Curlew all nest.

Autumn: dabbling duck, waders and sometimes Black Stork.

Access

Take the D938 from Parthenay towards Thouars-Saumur for 15 km (9.3 miles). Take the D46 (to the right going to Saint-Loup-sur-Thouet), from

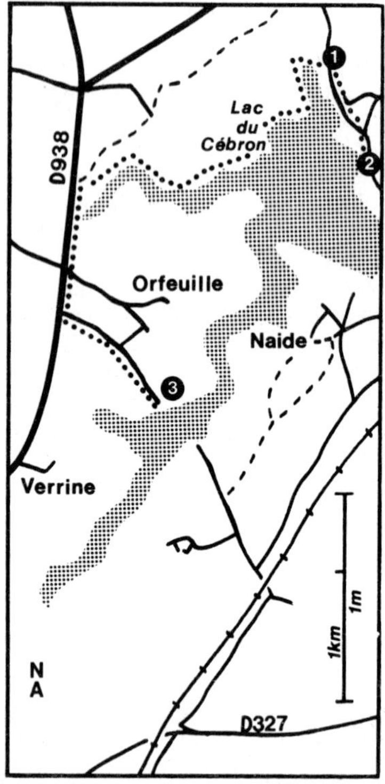

where the Barrage de la Retenue (dam) is clearly indicated. Park in the north car park ①; walk along the dam for about 900 m (985 yards) ②. It is then advisable to take the car back along the D938 (towards Lageon). One kilometre (0.6 miles) further on turn left onto the D137 and a further one kilometre (0.6 miles) one arrives at ③. You can look over the lake from here.

Species

- A good place at the end of winter and in spring for seeing: Mallard, Gadwall, Wigeon, Teal, Pochard and Tufted Duck.
- When the water-level is lower, in late summer and autumn, you can see various species of wader.
- From the hide there are good views of Greylag Geese, on their way north at the end of February.
- In the neighbourhood in winter you can see various species, such as Dunnock, Stonechat, Black Redstart and several species of bunting.
- Little Owl and Hoopoe nest not far from the lake.
- Nightingale, Melodious Warbler and Whitethroat all nest in the hedgerows.
- In autumn many migrant passerines can be seen in the area: Blue-headed Wagtail, Wheatear, Whinchat, Redstart, Chiffchaff, Spotted and Pied Flycatchers.
- Many raptors nesting in the area hunt over the back of the lake.

234 Niort and its Surrounding Plains

The plains around Niort are home, in spring, to Little Bustard, Stone Curlew and Hen and Montagu's Harriers, and it is worth spending a little time here. In winter there are a few Merlin which, coupled with the birds on Niort-Noron Lake, allow the birdwatcher to pass an agreeable few hours.

235 Chevais Heath

On the D45, which goes between Lezay and Clussais-la-Pommeraie, Chevais (the nearby village) Heath, along with its lake, is a good place for birds in spring. A breeding area for Curlew, it also has many breeding Red-backed Shrike and many pipits, chats and buntings. The lake has Great Crested and Little Grebes, Mallard, Garganey and Coot. Finally, a few Little Bustard and Stone Curlew, nesting on the nearby plain, can also be seen, as well as Black Kite, Buzzard and Honey Buzzard.

236 PINAIL NATIONAL NATURE RESERVE AND MOULIÈRE PUBLIC FOREST

Vouneuil-sur-Vienne
(IGN 1826 – 1/50 000)

Habitat and Timing

Some 20 km (12.5 miles) to the north-east of Poitiers, Le Pinail is a natural prolongation of Moulière Forest and covers 800 hectares of a clay plateau. This heather heath, a habitat once common in this area ('Terres de Brandes'), became the first mainland reserve in the Poitou-Charentes region in 1980. The quarrying of millstones has left thousands of ponds. These ponds gradually invaded with vegetation, have compressed to form peat-bogs of great botanical interest. The Moulière has a large Sessile Oak wood with much beech and now many conifers.

Access to the reserve is controlled; please abide by the regulations shown at the entrance. The paths in the forest are open to the public (except where indicated). Pinail is of interest for the raptors that nest and for passerines (in the spring and on migration, particularly); Moulière Forest has many woodland species, raptors, Nightjar and passerines. Pinail has a remarkable flora, especially in and around its many acid ponds, with some insectivorous plants. It is best to birdwatch in the morning (winter and spring) or in the evening (spring and summer). Between October and February, there is hunting on Tuesdays and Saturdays. There is sometimes hunting with beaters (for Wild Boar or hinds), usually on a Thursday morning.

Calendar

Winter: tits, Short-toed Treecreeper, Nuthatch, Song and Mistle Thrushes, Great Spotted and Middle Spotted Woodpeckers; Merlin, Dartford Warbler, Reed Bunting, Buzzard, Goshawk, Woodcock.

Spring: Sparrowhawk, Kestrel, Hobby, Hen and Montagu's Harriers, Short-toed Eagle, Honey Buzzard. Many passerines: Grasshopper Warbler; Meadow, Tree and Tawny Pipits; Woodlark, Redstart, Wood Warbler, Hawfinch, Woodpeckers; Nightjar. Also, many migrant passerines and Osprey and Crane.

Access

Coming from Poitiers, take the N10 towards Châtellerault; leave it 3 km (1.85 miles) after Jaunay-Clan, at Maison-Neuve, turning right on the D4 towards Dissay. In front of the château, go left, then right, following the D15 as far as Bondilly. Here, there are two possible routes:

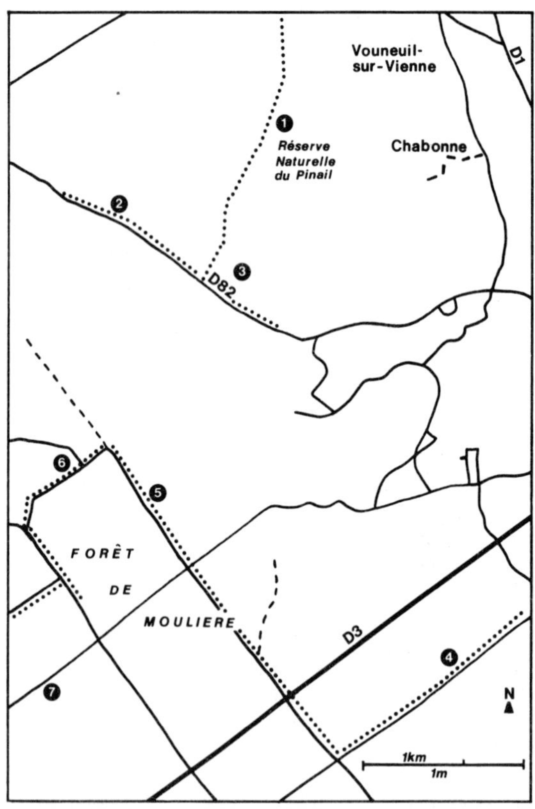

1. Towards Vouneuil-sur-Vienne. Arriving at a crossroads, about 1 km (0.6 miles) after the Château du Fou, take the track to the right for about 1 km (0.6 miles) as far as the car park (1), at the entrance to Pinail Reserve. Walk the forest paths that border the reserve.
2. Take the D82 to the right towards Bonneuil-Matours. Stop on the side

of the road ②, at the crossroads with the Allée de la Fontaine Salée. Continue as far as the Rivau Bridge ③; 500 m (550 yards) after the power-lines, a gravel track to the left leads to the car park at the reserve's entrance ①, 3 km (1.85 miles) further on.

From the reserve, take the D15 towards Bondilly then the D82 on towards Bonneuil-Matours. Turn right on the D3 towards Poitiers. Turn left at the forester's house and after about 1 km (0.6 miles) turn right onto the Sommière des Chirons Noirs. Stop on the side of the road ④ and take one of the forest tracks through the mature woodland (towards the D3) or the south-east forest edge (towards the Fontaine de Bourre). Next take the road as far as the next crossroads and turn right on the Défens forest road. At the crossroads continue straight on, taking the forest road opposite for about 3 km (1.85 miles) as far as the Fosse-au-Loup roundabout ⑤. Walk along the Allée du Plan-des-Aises on the right; 600 m (660 yards) further on, take the second track on the right in a managed woodland, as far as the forest road. Then back on the Défens forest road; at the next crossroads turn left going as far as point ⑥, 100 m (110 yards) before a forester's house: you can walk along the track to the right of the road. Then, turn left at the Closures roundabout and go as far as the Saint-Georges roundabout, then right as far as the bottom of the slope; park on the side ⑦. Take a forest track, a 'sommière', towards the Plan-des-Aises through a recently-cut area; cross the road following the sommière as far as the Allée du Grand-Soubis to the left, then left again to get back to the forest road at the starting point ⑦.

Grasshopper Warbler

Species

- On the heath, passerines include: Stonechat, Dartford and Grasshopper Warblers and Linnet.

- There are Hobby, Sparrowhawk, Short-toed Eagle, Honey Buzzard and Montagu's and Hen Harriers between April and December, Merlin in winter.
- There are Meadow, Tree and Tawny Pipits on the heath in spring.
- Osprey and Red Kite occur on migration.
- Passerines during the time of migration include: Willow Warbler, Whinchat, Wheatear and Ring Ouzel.
- Nightjar occur at the forest edge and on the heath and in newly-cleared areas, during spring and summer evenings.
- There are Snipe all year, Lapwing around the ponds and on the recently-planted heaths, and Woodcock in winter.
- Crane on migration can be seen during the first days of November or early March.
- Wood Warbler can be seen in undergrowth-free forest, and Bonelli's Warbler in the pine plantations.
- Buzzard occur throughout the year.
- Hawfinch can be seen in areas of mature trees in spring.
- Woodcock occur in the thickets in winter.
- Honey Buzzard display between May and July.
- Nuthatch, Short-toed Treecreeper, Long-tailed Tit can be seen.
- Black, Great, Middle and Lesser Spotted Woodpeckers can be found in the mature trees in winter and spring.
- Hobby hunt near the forest edge in the evening.
- It is easy to find Coal and Crested Tits and Goldcrest in the pine plantations.

237 Neuville Plain

Neuville-de-Poitou Plain is some 15 km (9.3 miles) to the north-west of Poitiers. It is an area of large expanses of cereal, divided by many Lucerne fields and small vineyards. The area is characterised by its shallow soils, locally called Terres de Groies. The area is delimited by a rectangle formed by the villages of Cherves, Mirebeau, Neuville-de-Poitou and Vouillé. It holds a high number of breeding Little Bustard and Stone Curlew. In the orchards and vineyards around the villages, Ortolan Bunting and Scops Owl breed; Quail, Montagu's Harrier and Kestrel breed on the plain. In winter there are large flocks of Rook, Lapwing and Golden Plover. Merlin occur regularly. Pre-migratory groups of Bustard and Stone Curlew (August and September) are frequent.

238 Combourg Lake

Some 80 km (50 miles) to the south-east of Poitiers, Combourg Lake is not far from Gençay. In the heart of a natural area formed of a mosaic of woods, heaths, hedgerows and some scattered lakes, it is one of the most important wetlands of inland Poitou-Charentes. Grebes, duck and Coot breed. The nearby woods hold a Grey Heron colony. In the reed-beds and marshland vegetation, Purple Heron, Reed, Sedge, Cetti's and Savi's Warblers as well as Marsh Harrier, all breed. Many raptors occur over the lake and woods. The area is particularly interesting during migration, with many waders as well as gulls and terns, especially Black and Whiskered, most of the duck and also Cormorant and Crane. Greylag Geese stop-over regularly. Passerines are numerous at all times; there are many species of warbler.

PROVENCE-ALPES-CÔTE D'AZUR

239 BACHELARD VALLEY/ PETITE-CAYOLLE PASS

25 km/15.5 miles
Nice-Barcelonnette
(IGN 61 Green Series – 1/100 000)

Habitat and Timing

The Ubaye Valley stretches west to east in the north-east of the department. Just to the south, forming two right-angle bends, is the Bachelard mountain stream, in the valley of the same name. The stream rises in the Petite-Cayolle Valley and flows into the Ubaye River some 20 km (12.5 miles) further on, passing through different vegetation zones. A good part of the valley is in the central part of the Mercantour National Park. The rules of the park and their application mean that the fauna is relatively well protected; not long ago there was quite a lot of hunting. Choose a nice day and leave in the car early in the morning.

Calendar

Spring: Golden Eagle, Short-toed Eagle, Goshawk; Ptarmigan, Rock Partridge; Alpine Swift, Black Woodpecker; Woodlark; Crag Martin, Tree and Water Pipits, Alpine Accentor; Wheatear, Rock Thrush, Ring Ouzel, Black Redstart; Lesser Whitethroat, Treecreeper, Citril Finch, Crossbill, Wallcreeper, Snow Finch, Chough, Alpine Chough, Raven.

Access

Take the D902 from Barcelonnette (Nice via the Col de Cayolle – the Cayolle Pass). Some 2.5 km (1.6 miles) after Uvernet village, the road enters the Gorges de la Corbière. Watch from the bridge ①. Then on another 1.5 km (0.9 miles) and stop at a large bridge next to a cabin ②. Walk along the footpath in the spruce wood for twenty minutes or so. Go back to the car and continue out of the gorge. The valley widens after the little village of Villard-d'Abat ③; the contrast between the north- (spruce

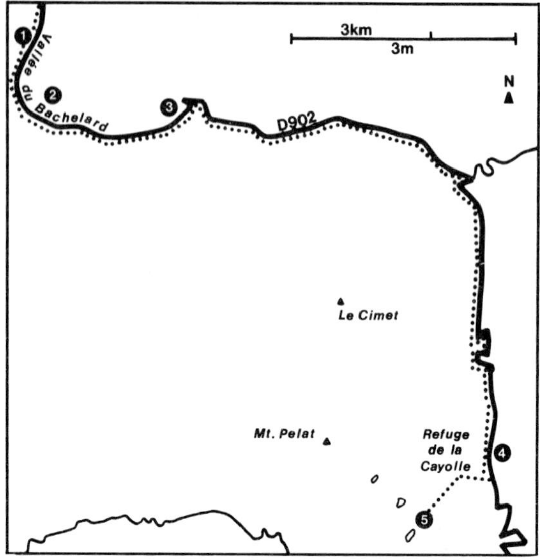

and larch) and south-facing slopes (rocky) is striking. After crossing the bridge on the outskirts of the village of Bayasse, the road enters the Mercantour National Park (read the rules on the large green notice board, just after the bridge).

The narrow road then climbs into an increasingly alpine environment: larch, scree, alpine meadows and rocks. About 1 km (0.6 miles) before the pass you can park at the Cayolle Refuge car park ④ (at an altitude of 2,296 m). Either stop here and look for birds around the refuge, or, continue on foot as far as Petite-Cayolle Lake (altitude 2,610 m). From the refuge, take the departmental trail n°1 (SD 1) marked in red and yellow, which climbs to Petite-Cayolle Pass (altitude 2,642 m and visible from the refuge) to the south-west between the Trou de l'Aigle and the Garrets summit ⑤. An easy walk of 40 minutes climbing 350 m. However, please stay on the marked trail so as not to disturb the birds. Use the same trail back to the refuge.

Species

- From the bridge you can see Wallcreeper on the steeper cliffs and Dipper on the stream.
- Firecrest, Treecreeper, Willow Tit and Crossbill can be seen in the spruce forest.
- Black Woodpecker also occur here, but they are easier to hear than see.
- Chough, Alpine Chough and Raven occur along the cliffs.
- Rock Bunting and Lesser Whitethroat are two typical species of the south-facing slopes.
- Raptors can be seen, particularly Golden Eagle, Short-toed Eagle and Kestrel.
- Tree Pipit, Whinchat, Ring Ouzel and Citril Finch can be seen where there is mixed larch and scree.

- On the alpine meadows are Woodlark, Skylark, Water Pipit and Wheatear.
- In rocky areas are black Redstart and Rock Thrush, Alpine Accentor; and Snow Finch may also be seen.
- Ptarmigan also occur here.

240 Sisteron

On the right bank of the Durance Valley to the north of Sisteron is a very interesting plateau of mixed cereal fields and heath. To cross the area, from Siseron take the N85 road towards Gap, and 1.5 km (0.9 miles) after the large junction with the Grenoble–Gap road, take the D4 to the right as far as Thèze, passing by Vaumeilh Aerodrome. Spring is the best time, when it is possible to see: Montagu's Harrier, Stone Curlew, Nightjar, Short-toed Eagle, Tawny Pipit, Quail, Rock Sparrow, Stonechat, and, with a little luck, Egyptian Vulture. In winter you can see: Merlin, Hen Harrier, Red Kite, Peregrine, Great Grey Shrike and Chough.

241 QUEYRAS NATIONAL PARK: NORTH-WEST ZONE (THE CLAPEYTO CHALLETS SECTOR/ARVIEUX PARISH)

12 km/3.75 miles
Guillestre
(IGN 3537 – 1/50 000)

Habitat and Timing

The park is in an old glacial valley, drained by the mountain stream – the Rivière. The stream's source (1,800 m) is in a deep-sided valley, cut into the limestone. A dense mountain pine wood with a few larch trees grows on the scree and on the moraines. Higher up, (2,000 m) there are three glacial bars flanked by cliffs which form successive shelves, once lakes, now filled with alluvium, which have been transformed into hay meadows and are surrounded by old chalets. Above this (2,300–2,500 m), the valley opens up and gives rise to a landscape reminiscent of Scotland, where each hollow in the grass has become a small peat-bog. However, the north and south of the valley are bordered by large limestone blocks. The pine wood should be visited early in the morning (6 am–8 am). The biggest cliff-face (south-east part), which overlooks the Pra-Premier, is best watched between 8 am and 11 am.

Calendar

Spring and summer (May to mid-August): Ptarmigan (June and July); Common and Green Sandpipers; Alpine Swift, Crag and House Martins; Water Pipit, Alpine Accentor; Whinchat, Wheatear, Ring Ouzel, Mistle

Thrush; Coal, Crested and Willow Tits; Siskin, Citril Finch, Serin; Wallcreeper, Snow Finch.

Access

Whether coming from Briançon via the Izoard Pass, or from Guillestre going towards the same pass, use the D902 as far as the small village of Brunissard (at the foot of the pass, southern side). Take the public track which goes to the amenities area at the Planet camp site; park near here ①. The medium-length walk of 12 km (7.5 miles) climbs some 700 m.

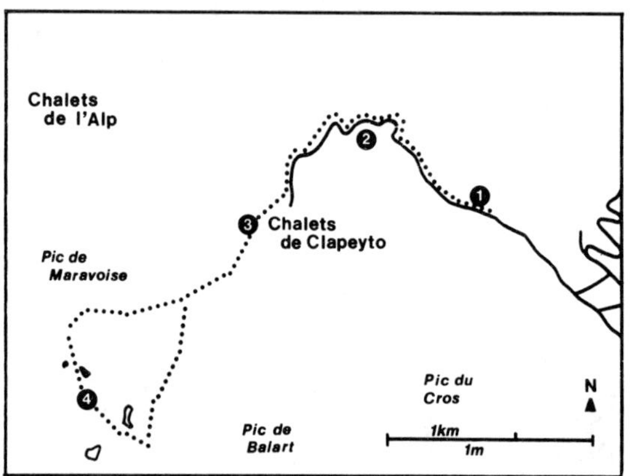

This will take the whole day. On the way up, the track is marked in red and white (the GR 5), then in yellow (to see the birds better, do not hesitate to leave the trail). The start of the trail is on a track forbidden to tourist vehicles which climbs in a wood – the Pré des Vaches. Then you move onto the larger rocky areas and onto the Pra-Premier flat shelf ② (at 2,000 m and a good observation point). Take the winding track under the cliffs, staying on it until it ends ③. Cross the stream by taking the yellow trail. This leads by steps through varied and scented meadows as far as the peat-bogs ④ at Cogour and Marion Lakes and later to Néal Pass (avoid trampling the fragile bog edges).

To go back, use either the same route or follow the yellow markings; this route, on a low ridge, passes via Favière Lake then drops down to the left (to the north-east) through an area of boulders to get back to Clapeyto.

Species

- Crossbill start to breed in the mountain pines as early as February. Here there are also: Coal, Crested and Willow Tits, Bullfinch, Serin, Siskin and Citril Finch.
- In the undergrowth you may be able to find the spectacular Great Spotted Woodpecker anvil.
- Mistle Thrush and Ring Ouzel are often seen side-by-side in this habitat.
- House Martins nest on the lower overhangs, Crag Martin is scarce on the cliffs and Alpine Swift occupy the higher parts.

- With the first rays of the sun the Wallcreeper comes out onto the rock-face, the boulders or even the chalet walls.
- Chough and Alpine Chough occur wherever there are cracks in the rock-face.
- This is the place for Black Redstart, Whinchat and Wheatear.
- In the austere surroundings of glaciers and rocky outcrops the mimetic Ptarmigan can be found, principally on north-facing slopes where there are creeping willow and saxifrages growing. Often all one sees of the bird are its droppings.
- In the meadows with boulders and rocks, Alpine Accentor and Snow Finch can be found.

242 Queyras National Park: East and South Zones (Upper Guil Valley – the Mont Viso Area)

The remarkable country above Ristolas has a markedly variable appearance. On the gentle eastern slopes, which were once cultivated, it is possible to see Rock Partridge and Rock Thrush (Marmots are numerous). The western slopes, very broken, are covered in dense ancient forests of larch and Arolla Pine and contain Nutcracker, Black Grouse, Goshawk, Sparrowhawk, Ring Ouzel and Crossbill. In winter the calls of Tengmalm's and Eagle Owls can be heard from the cross-country ski trails along the Guil River. Above here are Roe Deer, Chamois, Moufflon and Alpine Ibex; breeding Golden Eagle visit the area. Beware! The area is very susceptible to damage by tourists. Queyras National Park has opened a number of nature-trails (with explicatory leaflets) allowing an in depth look at the local habitats.

243 Lautaret Pass

It is worth stopping, even for a short while, at Les Sestrières, below the Marionnaise avalanche-protection tunnel. It is some 1.5 km (0.9 miles) from Lautaret Pass (in the parish of Monêtier-les-Bains), on the N91 at an altitude of about 1,970 m. A few yards along the old Galibier Pass, a path leads to where the road parts and on to an area of alpine meadows, traversed by many streams and lined with stands of green alder; this is a good area for seeing Alpine Chough, Chough, Alpine Accentor, Snow Finch, Water Pipit and Whinchat. The northern slopes near to Combeynot National Nature Reserve (managed by the Écrins National Park – an information centre at the Col du Lautaret and at Casset) and the southern slopes of the Grand Galibier are a hunting area for a pair of Golden Eagle. The larger limestone rock-faces and the scree lower down are good for seeing Rock Thrush and Wallcreeper, and also Chamois and Alpine Ibex. From Lautaret, the Crevasses trail leads into some green alders that have Marsh Warbler.

244 ÉCRINS NATIONAL PARK

6 km/3.75 miles
Orcières
(IGN 3437 west – 1/25 000)

Habitat and Timing

From the Séveraisse Valley, at La Chapelle-en-Valgaudemar (1,100 m), as far as the granite ridge at Pétarel peak (2,618 m), three vegetation layers succeed each other: northern-facing mountain forest, of mainly beech, birch and fir; subalpine heath and scree, a mosaic of Juniper and rhododendrons; and the very rocky landscape of the Cirque des lacs de Pétarel, where there is little space for the few alpine meadows. This succession of habitats and their surrounds support all those mountain birds typical of the western Alps.

While respecting the present rules of the central area of the Écrins National Park (92,000 hectares), it is still quite possible to see everything: do not disturb the animals, photography can upset nesting birds; do not take your dog, it may disturb wildlife or domestic animals. Some hunted species (such as Rock Partridge and Black Grouse), whose populations are low despite total protection within the central area of the park, are easily disturbed. In order to protect them, please be quiet and do not try to get too close as the birds are easily scared.

Calendar

Spring and summer (mid-April to August): Golden Eagle; Black Grouse, Ptarmigan, Rock Partridge; Black and Great Spotted Woodpeckers; Water Pipit, Alpine Accentor; Wheatear, Black Redstart, Rock Thrush, Ring Ouzel, Mistle Thrush; Lesser Whitethroat, Blackcap, Garden and Bonelli's Warblers, Chiffchaff; Goldcrest, Coal and Willow Tits; Treecreeper, Nutcracker; Redpoll, Crossbill, Citril Finch, all of these nest.

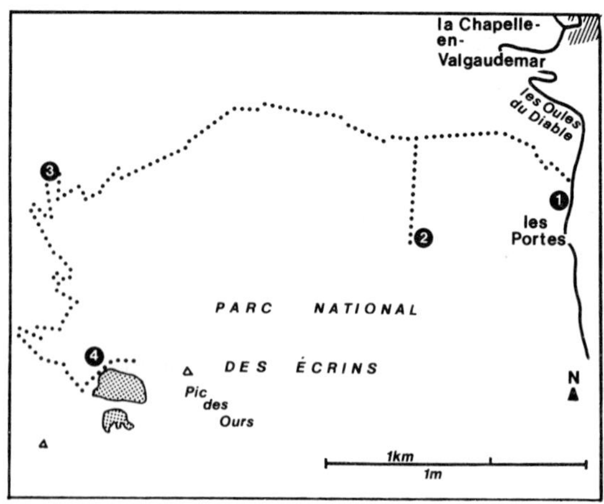

Access

By rail and bus: take the train to Gap station then go by bus as far as La Chapelle-en-Valgaudemar, changing at Sant-Firmin. By road: take the N85 between Gap and Grenoble, then the D985a from Saint-Firmin to La Chapelle-en-Valgaudemar, where there is the Écrins National Park Visitor Centre (information, exhibitions). For the walk, take the small road which goes up to the car park ① before arriving at the small village of Les Portes (1,280 m). The path, the Sentier de Pétarel, is signposted from the middle of the village. The melting of the snow from mid-April, normally allows you to walk the first part of the track and with a deviation to get to the Châtelard Belvedere ② at 1,572 m. The trail climbs above the pine forest and crosses the Pétarel stream via a ford, fed from lakes higher up. It climbs onto a public area planted with larch and arrives at a view point ③ off the trail. Higher up, it leaves the forest and passes the Casinière rocky area and scree before arriving at the glacial bar which blocks the lakes ④.

Species

- It is easy to see Bonelli's Warbler below the small village of Portes, in the mountain forest where conifers predominate.
- On slabs of snow, hardened by the night frosts, during April and May, Black Grouse cocks display fervently with their broken hoots and coos, giving the place a strange atmosphere.
- More difficult to see than hear, Rock Partridges incessantly reply to one another's short calls, creeping in and out of the ground-hugging shrubs on the Clos des Portes.
- Willow and Coal Tits and Goldcrest occur in the mixed beech and fir woods.
- Spring migrants – such as the Rock Thrush – follow the receding line of the melting snow.
- Nutcrackers will hide seeds from August onwards at the Banc du Marchand.
- The Ring Ouzel's loud song carries far, when heard in the spring.
- The Golden Eagle's silhouette can be seen in uplifting thermals.
- Fir woods hold Crossbill and Treecreeper, also Black Woodpecker.
- Areas of alder may have Lesser Whitethroat and even Redpoll and Citril Finch.
- Stuck onto the shear rock face, looking like a large pink-and-grey butterfly, you can often surprise a Wallcreeper.
- On the higher alpine meadows and scree, you can find Alpine Accentor, Wheatear and Water Pipit.
- Ptarmigan may be seen above Pétarel Lake, not far from the Pic de l'Ours.

245 THE MOUTH OF THE VAR, SAINT-LAURENT-DU-VAR

1.5 km/0.9 miles
Nice
(IGN 3743 west – 1/25 000)

Habitat and Timing

The mouth of the Var is delimited by an embankment on each side. It separates an airport, to the east, from a commercial centre, to the west. The form of the mouth is very much influenced by the amount of floodwater: at the time of writing, there are shingle banks above where the waters meet; these form islands, the less exposed are covered in vegetation. A reed-bed on the western bank is being invaded by willows and alders, with brambles on the edges and on the side of the embankment. It is a no-hunting reserve and remarkable for the variety of species that occur within such a small area, especially in the spring. There is strictly no access to the islands up-river of the Napoleon III bridge, but there are no restrictions further south; it is better watching from the embankment (in the afternoon, except in autumn).

Calendar

Winter: duck, Coot and waders, sometimes numerous. Black-headed and Mediterranean Gulls, Yellow-legged Gulls in number. Blackcap, Chiffchaff and Penduline Tit.

Spring: a large variety of species – herons, duck (especially Garganey and Shoveler), Spotted Crake, many waders; Mediterranean (abundant in March) and Little Gulls, terns including all three marsh terns (April and May). And many migrant passerines, especially insectivorous species.

Access

From Nice (to the east) or Cannes (to the west), take either the N98 (the coast road) or the N7, towards Saint-Laurent-du-Var. Go to Cap 3000 and use the Parking Supérieur Sud (upper-south car park). Buses and trains run from Menton, Nice or Cannes, buses only from Grasse. According to the service, get off at either Cap 3000 or Saint-Laurent-du-Var station and go to the bank of the Var, either via the commercial centre, or via the north car park and the Napoleon III bridge. Stop outside the car park, alongside the eucalyptus trees, near the shingle banks opposite the runways ①. There is an uninterrupted view over the river mouth, the islands, the airport and its bay. Go onto the sewage farm causeway ②; watch over the sea and some man-made islands. Return to the starting point ①, and go up-river along the embankment. Stop after 150 m (165 yards) on a projecting causeway ③. There is another view over the river mouth, over a bare island opposite and directly over a reed-bed somewhat choked with thickets. Continue up-river. Before arriving at the Napoleon III bridge, you can go down into the undergrowth and to the side of the Var. Then continue along the embankment passing under the bridge where there is an unobstructed view over some islands ④.

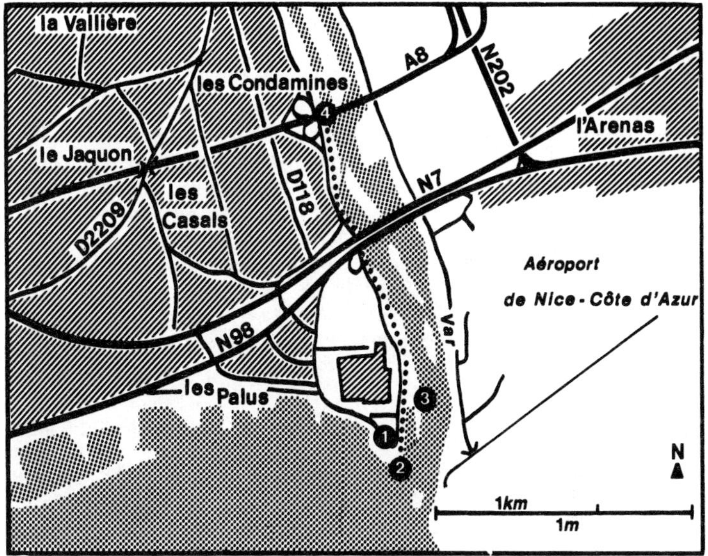

Species

- Yelkouan Shearwater (spring), and gulls and terns (April and May) can be seen at sea.
- There is a gull roost (Black-headed, Mediterranean, Yellow-legged). Sometimes Cormorant and Sandwich Tern occur (winter and spring).
- This is a feeding area for gulls, especially in the afternoon. Sometimes Great Crested and Black-necked Grebes (in winter) and Razorbill (January–February) are present.
- Spotted Crake and sometimes other species of Rallidae and Bluethroat (from mid-March to mid-April) occur. There are also waders on open areas.
- Cetti's, Reed and Great Reed Warblers, and Red-backed Shrike nest.
- There is a roost of smaller herons: Night (April and May), sometimes Squacco (May).
- Melodious Warbler and Nightingale nest. Blackcap, Willow Warbler, flycatchers and shrikes can be seen on migration.
- There is a common Tern colony, with Little Ringed Plover and Common Sandpiper (all nesting).

246 Le Boréon

There are many different habitats around the small village of Boréon, some 70 km (44 miles) to the north of Nice, of both mountain and conifer forest (at the Cimes du Mercantour – Mercantour summits). From mid-May to mid-October walk along the forest tracks: Black Woodpecker, Song Thrush, Coal and Willow Tits, Firecrest, Nutcracker, Goshawk, Little Owl are all found here. On the river, Grey Wagtail and Dipper can be seen. Above the tree-line there are Chough and Alpine Chough; sometimes Ptarmigan and Golden Eagle can be seen on the slopes of Mont Pélago.

247 Carros

Hydro-electric dams on the Var River near Carros, to the north of Nice, form lakes which are attractive to aquatic birds. In winter (from December to March), this area has a good variety of species: Cormorant, duck (Mallard, Teal, Tufted Duck), Coot, Moorhen and Dipper. In spring there are Garganey, Shoveler and waders. During rainy periods hundreds of hirundines and Swift collect over the lakes. Gulls are numerous throughout the year. In the neighbourhood there are Turtle Dove (embankment), Subalpine Warbler (bushy steppe) and Cirl Bunting (crops).

248 CAMARGUE NATIONAL NATURE RESERVE

20 km/12.5 miles
Arles
(IGN 2943 – 1/50 000)
and
Saintes-Maries-de-la-Mer
(IGN 2944 – 1/50 000)

Habitat and Timing

The Camargue is in the heart of the vast Rhône delta (85,000 hectares make up the national park). The 13,117 hectares of the reserve are successively transformed into an immense wetland each year with the autumn and winter rains; where any real or fossil dunes break the surface, then it becomes a dry, salty desert between March and September due to evaporation. Only a few permanent lakes still have water – Vaccarès, Le Lion and La Dame being the most important.

An annual water deficit, due in a large part to violent north-west winds (the famous Mistral), is compensated for by water coming from agricultural land (rice fields), some of which flows into Vaccarès Lake.

The appearance of the reserve changes from south to north.

1. Coastal beaches and dunes: protected, access on bike or foot.
2. The Digue-à-la-Mer embankment: built in 1867, it protects the Camargue from gales. It provides one of the best walks for looking at the reserve, 12 km (7.5 miles) are within its limits. There is access on bike or foot from two car parks.
3. The Sansouires: one of the most typical of Camargue landscapes, a salty steppe with much Glasswort, a favourite area of waders and duck when flooded (October to March). The same birds also flock together on the shallow lakes.
4. The Bois des Rièges: this is a group of bush-covered islands, on an east-west aligned area of fossil dunes, in the heart of the reserve.
5. Vaccarès Lake: this is a 6,500 hectare refuge for Coot, duck and grebes. Its reed-beds, along the edges, are good for passerines.

Calendar

Autumn and winter: grebes, Grey Heron, Bittern; Great White, Little and Cattle Egrets, Glossy Ibis (rare); dabbling duck, Red-crested Pochard,

Pochard, Tufted Duck, Goldeneye; Marsh Harrier, Spotted Eagle (rare), Kestrel; waders; Black-headed, Little and Yellow-legged Gulls, Marsh terns; Bearded and Penduline Tits, many migrant passerines.

Spring and summer: some spectacular breeding colonies, such as Greater Flamingo, many heron species, Black-headed, Mediterranean and Slender-billed Gulls, Sandwich, Common, Little and Gull-billed Terns; raptors, waders (Black-winged Stilt, Avocet, Kentish Plover); Collared Pratincole, Bee-eater, Roller, Hoopoe, hirundines (sometimes Red-rumped Swallow); Blue-headed Wagtail, *Acrocephalus* warblers, Moustached and Spectacled warblers, many migrant passerines (March–May).

Access

From Arles take the D570 towards Saintes-Maries-de-la-Mer, then the D36 towards Salin-de-Giraud and later the D36d towards Vaccarès Lake (passing the two small villages of Gageron and Villeneuve). At Villeneuve take the D37 towards Saintes-Maries-de-la-Mer. After 3 km (1.85 miles), turn right towards the Mas d'Agon ①. Watch from various points along the road for 2 km (1.25 miles). Then go back onto the D37, continue 2 km (1.25 miles) as far as Basse-Méjanes Marsh ②. Look over the marsh to the right of the road. To get to the eastern part of Vaccarès Lake, go back to Villeneuve, turn right in the village towards Salin-de-Badon. Some 4 km (2.5 miles) further on is the information centre at La Capelière, which also has the reserve's offices ③. There is a 1.7 km (1.1 mile) nature trail with several hides. Next continue southwards, it may be worth stopping

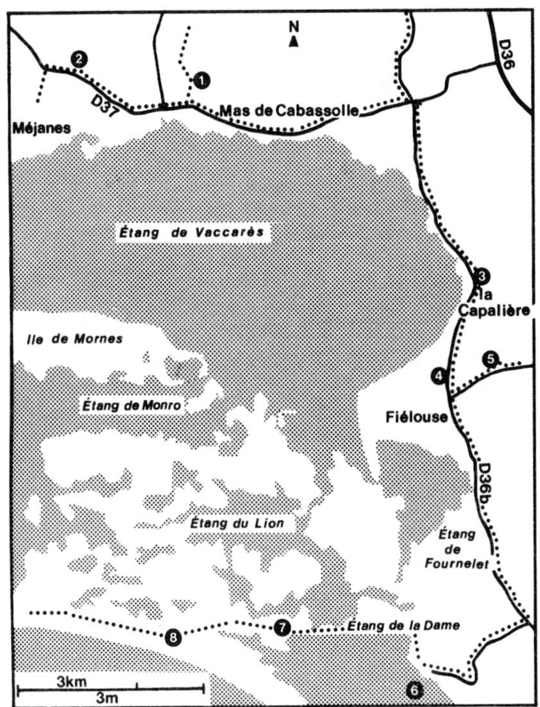

on the side of Vaccarès Lake at ④. At the junction at the Mas de Fièlouse turn left and continue for 1 km (0.6 miles), stop to look over Grenouillet Marsh ⑤, as far as Fiélouse. Return to the main road and continue southwards for about 3 km (1.85 miles), where the road turns sharply right. After the corner keep going straight on for 4 km (2.5 miles), following the northern edge of the Fangassier salt-pan ⑥, going as far as the Comtesse car park. Leave the car here and walk along the Digue-à-la-Mer.

Species

- In spring, Grey, Purple and Squacco Herons, Cattle and Little Egrets can be seen. There are Bittern calling in the reed-beds.
- Black-winged Stilt nest. Sometimes, in spring, it is possible to see Collared Pratincole.
- There are dabbling duck in winter (Wigeon, Gadwall, Mallard and Teal). Bewick's Swans also occur.
- You will find Great White Egret in winter, sometimes Glossy Ibis.
- On Vaccarès Lake in winter you can see grebes, dabbling duck, Red-crested Pochard, Pochard, Tufted Duck, also Goldeneye and Eider.
- You can see Penduline Tit on migration and in winter, sometimes they nest.
- Wetland passerines: *Acrocephalus* warblers, Sedge Warbler (in spring), Moustached Warbler (most easily located singing before migrant warblers occur – even as early as January, on warm, calm days) abound.
- Marsh Harrier occur year-round.
- Bee-eaters hunt around here, and perch on overhead wires.
- Black and Whiskered Terns occur, sometimes White-winged Black (in May).

Greater Flamingos

- This salt-pan is the only nesting place of the Greater Flamingo in France.
- In spring and summer, terns (Sandwich, Common, Little) and gulls (Black-headed, Mediterranean, Slender-billed) can be watched easily.
- There are nesting Avocet.
- Shelduck occur throughout the year and dabbling duck in winter.
- Spectacled Warbler nest in the Grasswort.
- Groups of Greater Flamingo are often seen from the Digue-à-la-Mer.
- This is a superb site for waders (Curlew, Avocet, 'shanks and many others).

249 Camargue/Vieux Rhône

You can continue along the track along the side of the Fangassier by passing below the Vieux Rhône, reaching the sea (the Mediterranean) at the Crau-de-la-Dent. Return via Salin-de-Giraud, passing Faraman Marshes (tracks are open to cars during dry weather): Greater Flamingo, Black-winged Stilt, both Avocet and Kentish Plover nest; you can also see Little Gull (on migration – sometimes hundreds), terns and insectivorous passerines in the tamarisk (warblers, flycatchers, redstarts and others). At Crau-de-la-Dent you can see Slender-billed Gull and waders. On the sea, grebes, sea duck, Razorbill (winter and spring) occur.

250 Saintes-Maries-de-la-Mer

Still in Camargue, this area is well worth a visit. From the town of Saintes-Maries-de-la-Mer, either take the Digue-à-la-mer to the east (Cormorant, herons, terns, waders), or go towards the mouth of the Petit Rhône to the west. In winter, out at sea you can watch Gannet, Eider, Razorbill and scoters. At times of migration, you can watch skuas, terns and grebes (Slavonian and Black-necked in breeding plumage, late March and early April, are all easily seen).

5.5 km/3.4 miles
Eyguières
(IGN 3043 – 1/50 000)

251 CRAU PLAIN

Habitat and Timing

This is the old delta of the Durance; it has been dry for the last twelve thousand years. It is uniformly flat and covered throughout with large pebbles, although a few scattered bushes find a hold; the whole area looks like steppe. There is uniform vegetation, even though there is a marked north–south climatic gradient. Herbs dominate, especially Thyme and different spurges. There are large areas of Lavender in the north, whereas Asphodel occurs mainly in the south. A very remarkable area for its steppe animals and its endemic insects and plants. The area of steppe (locally called Coussous) is grazed by 35,000 sheep in about 40 flocks, between mid-February and mid-June. The Crau is still not protected and about 80 per cent of the land is in private hands. It is advisable not to leave the tracks, nor to go to close to the sheep flocks, and to keep out of the signposted military areas.

Calendar

Winter: Little Bustard and Pin-tailed Sandgrouse flock together, their erratic movements make them hard to find. Also at this time: Lapwing, Golden Plover, large flocks of Corn Bunting, Hen Harrier and maybe Peregrine.

Spring: Little Bustard and Pin-tailed Sandgrouse displaying (easy to see). Also: Stone Curlew, Little Owl, Egyptian Vulture, Short-toed Eagle and Black Kite. Larks are abundant, Skylark and Short-toed.

Summer: best time for seeing Roller, which flock, with as many as 15 together.

Autumn: large flocks of Stone Curlew.

Access

From Arles, take the N113 which goes to Salon and Aix. There is useful information to be had at the Crau Ecomuseum (at Saint-Martin-de-Crau, near the church, entry free), which organises guided visits of the coussous (ask for times). Turn right some 7 km (4.35 miles) after Saint-Martin-de-Brau, on the D5 towards Istres. 8 km (5 miles) after the junction, just after Entressen, the road crosses a large area of coussous. Park the car near the electricity transformer, to the south of this zone ①. There is no set route. A possible circuit starts by taking the track towards Mas Guilhem ②, then turns northwards crossing an ancient Almond plantation, then turns eastwards passing in front of a sheep-pen and returns to the starting point by skirting the area. The middle of this area is a military zone. This walk will take about two hours.

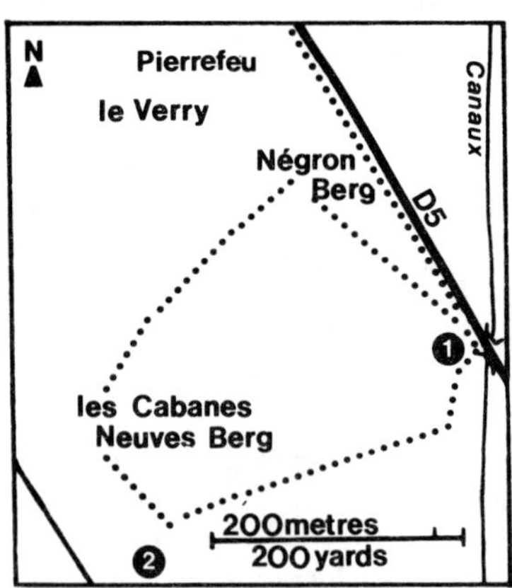

Species

- Skylark and Short-toed Lark are omnipresent.
- Here you can see Great Grey, Lesser Grey and Woodchat Shrikes in the Rockrose bushes.

Pin-tailed Sandgrouse

- Rollers can be seen in the wood around Mas Guilhem.
- Red-legged Partridge can be seen on the edge of the coussous.
- There may be a Great Spotted Cuckoo in the old Almond trees.
- Hoopoe and Little Owl can be seen near the sheep-pen.
- Little Bustard, Pin-tailed Sandgrouse and Stone Curlew are all difficult to observe, but are present on the coussous.
- Black Kite is common, look for Egyptian Vulture and Short-toed Eagle.

252 Entressen

On the D5, before arriving at Entressen, turn right on the road leading to the Étang d'Entressen (signposted). After 1 km (0.6 miles), park the car near Mas de la Tour (which belongs to the town of Istres). The poplar elm and Holm-oak wood has many Black Kite, Roller and Green Woodpecker. Coot nest on the lake. Egyptian Vulture are seen regularly.

253 Berre Lake

Berre Lake is the second biggest lake in France, after the Franco-Swiss Lac Léman. In winter there are two to three thousand Black-necked Grebe, plus many other wintering birds. The length of its banks means that its better visited by car than on foot; each side is of interest, except the western bank which is too steep. In front of Jaï sandy beach, between Châteauneuf and Marignane, there are often many species otherwise rare in Provence: Common and Velvet Scoters, Eider, Long-tailed Duck and divers are regular. In the bay at Saint-Chamas, and visible from the top of the village, there are always plenty of diving duck (mainly Tufted Duck) in winter. With the neighbouring Réaltor Lake, the many thousands of diving duck outnumber those in the whole of the Camargue. Entry into the Salins de Berre (Berre salt-pans) is strictly forbidden. However, a walk from Berre to the port of La Pointe allows you to look over some of the area. In winter Greater Flamingo and Shelduck are numerous. In summer the salt-pans have a large tern colony and many Black-headed and Yellow-legged Gulls, Avocet, Kentish Plover and Oystercatcher.

254 La Caume

In Saint-Rémy-de-Provence parish, the Caume relay station is on a spot which dominates the whole of the Alpilles range of hills and surrounding plains. As soon as the Egyptian Vulture arrives in the vicinity in March, this is one of the best places to see it and other Mediterranean species such as: Short-toed Eagle, Bonelli's Eagle, Alpine Swift, Crag Martin, Blue Rock Thrush and other cliff-dwelling species, plus warblers in the surrounding garrigue. Up until April it is also possible to see Wallcreeper, Alpine Accentor, and Snow Finch, the latter only on migration. The garrigue information centre – run by the Centre d'Étude sur les Écosystèmes de Provence (CEEP) and the Fonds d'Intervention pour les Rapaces (FIR) – is open from April to August. In recent summers the road up to the Caume has been shut to cars, to try to prevent fires.

255 Durance and the Puy-Sainte-Réparade Gravel-pits

This zone continues for 5 km (3.1 miles) along the left bank of the Durance downstream from Pertuis bridge. In spring and summer there are quite a few aquatic birds, in particular Little Bittern and Moustached Warbler, and also Great Crested Grebe, Reed and Great Reed Warblers. On the bed of the Durance you can see Common Tern and Little Ringed Plover; on the embankments there are Short-toed and Crested Larks and Sardinian Warbler. On migration it is possible to see Osprey and Squacco Heron, both occur regularly. Also, there is a chance of seeing Egyptian Vulture.

256 GIENS PENINSULA AND HYÈRES SALT-PANS

4.5 km/2.8 miles
Hyères
(IGN 3446 – 1/50 000)

Habitat and Timing

Two areas of salt-pans are still being worked, some 6 km (3.15 miles) apart. The freshwater marshes have all been filled in except for the Marais des Estagnets (about four hectares). The salt-pans have areas of high human activity, where the salt is harvested, but there are also large reservoir pans and ancient salt-pans that are more or less overrun with vegetation (Grasswort): these are the best areas for birds (principally herons, Greater Flamingo and waders). Access to the interior of the salt-pans is strictly controlled, but is is easy to obtain good views from the road that runs around the edge.

Calendar

Winter: Dunlin, Little Stint, Kentish and Grey Plovers, Curlew. Also Cormorant, Cattle and Little Egret, Sandwich Tern.

Spring: Shelduck, Black-winged Stilt, Avocet, Kentish Plover all nest; many waders including Marsh Sandpiper, Whiskered, Black and White-winged Black Terns, Little Tern nest.

Autumn: Greater Flamingo abundant.

Access

From Hyères, go southwards towards Giens. The best areas are seen from the salt road, that is to say the west side of the peninsula: you can park along the whole length of the road, but it is better to walk its length. At the southern end is Estagnets Lake ①, with unrestricted access and it is well worth a visit especially in spring. To the north of Hyères-Plage it may be worth visiting Ceinturon Lake ②.

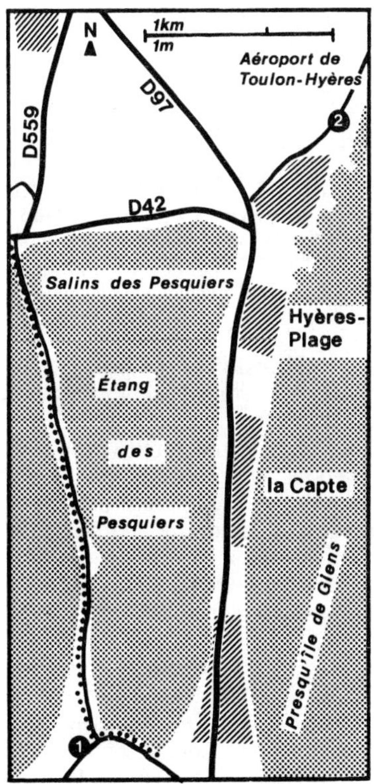

Species

- Little Egrets are common along the canals that surround the salt-pans.
- During times of migration, Pesquiers salt-pans have Dunlin, Little Stint, Kentish Plover and other waders.
- There are always some Greater Flamingos on the salt-pans, it is impossible not to see them.
- Shelduck can also be seen on the salt-pans.
- Black-winged Stilt and Avocet regularly nest in the Hyères salt-pans. During May, at sunset, you can see Little Bittern.

- Little Tern also nest on the salt-pans.
- Little Grebe regularly pass the winter on Ceinturon Lake.

257 Villepey Lakes

Villepey Lakes in Fréjus parish are at the mouth of the Argens. There is a large salinity gradient between the deeper lakes (gravel-pits) and the sea which gives rise to a diversity of vegetation and birds. April to June is the time for migrants (waders, Greater Flamingo, duck, passerines). There is a good chance of seeing Little Bittern and Bee-eater, both nest. The best place for watching is from the side of the N98, between the lakes and the sea; the area is being bought by the Conservatoire du Littoral (the Coastal Conservancy), and a nature trail along the lakes is planned.

258 THE DENTELLES DE MONTMIRAIL

11.5 km/7.2 miles
Orange
(IGN 3040 – 1/50 000)
and Vaison-la-Romaine
(IGN 3140 – 1/50 000)

Habitat and Timing

The Dentelles de Montmirail is a typical provençal range of hills, limited to the north and west by Ouvèze Valley, to the east by the Malaucène basin, and ending abruptly to the south where it drops to Carpentras Plain. The cliffs overlooking wooded slopes give the Dentelles their name. The southern slopes are overgrown with a Kermes Oak and Rosemary maquis, areas of Holm-oak and Aleppo Pine woods; on the north it is Downy Oak that dominates.

The cliffs have many uncommon birds, and the garrigue on the southern slopes has Mediterranean warblers.

Calendar

Spring: Egyptian Vulture, Short-toed Eagle; Alpine Swift, Hoopoe, Bee-eater, Nightjar; Tawny and Tree Pipits; Crag Martin; Great Grey (Mediterranean race) and Woodchat Shrikes, Blue Rock Thrush; Subalpine, Dartford, Sardinian, Orphean and Bonelli's Warblers; Raven, Scops and Eagle Owls.

Winter: Eagle Owl, Kestrel; Alpine Accentor, Sardinian and Dartford Warblers, Wallcreeper, Snow Finch, Raven.

Access

Three areas can be reached by car. There are also many forestry tracks which should not be used by a car so as not to harm this fragile habitat.

Le Grand-Montmirail ①: from Carpentras to the south, go through Aubignan and Beaumes-de-Venise then take the D90 towards Lafare. After 2.5 km (1.6 miles) there is a small tarmac road to the left (often in a bad state of repair). After crossing the Salette it climbs up towards the

Grand-Montmirail cliffs. Leave the car in the car park and explore the surroundings.

Gigondas ②: from the village go as far as the hamlet of Florets, leave the car here, and walk up as far as the Col du Cayron–Cayron Pass. There are good views over the Dentelles Sarrasines. The forest road skirts the cliffs to the west.

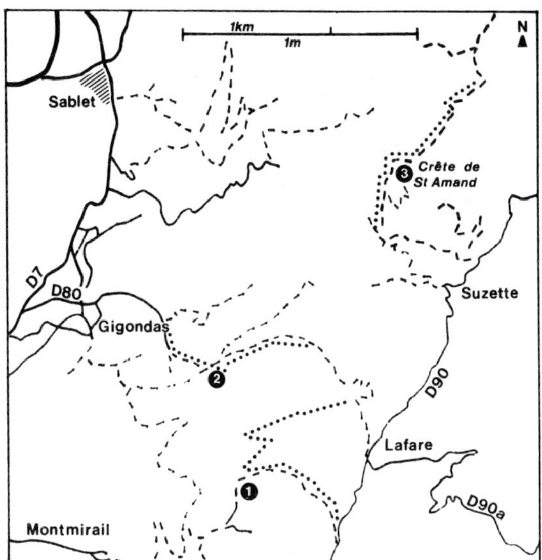

Le Mont Saint-Amand ③: from Suzette (to the east of the hills) take the Château–Neuf–Redortier road (the road is narrow and it is not always easy to park). Continue a little past the farm before leaving the car, then it is on foot to get to the northern slope of the Saint-Amand ridge. Marked trails allow for a circuit around the hills or access to the summit.

Species

- Hoopoe and Scops Owl can be seen from April to August.
- Subalpine and Orphean Warblers occur from April to August; Sardinian and Dartford Warblers as well as Great Grey Shrike (*meridionalis*) throughout the year.
- Blue Rock Thrush are sedentary, but are more easily observed in April and May.
- Kestrel can be seen throughout the year, Egyptian Vulture and Short-toed Eagle between April and August.
- Alpine Swift and Crag Martin can be seen from April to September, Wallcreeper in winter.
- Eagle Owl can be heard especially between December and March.
- Bonelli's Warbler are present from April to July and Nuthatch year-round.
- Raven nests, Wallcreeper and Alpine Accentor can be found in winter, Black Redstart throughout the year.

Sardinian Warbler

- Short-toed Eagle may be seen from April to September.
- Firecrest, Mistle Thrush, Bonelli's Warbler and Woodpigeon occur during the breeding season.
- Snow Finch are irregular, Alpine Accentor may be seen in winter.
- Tree and Tawny Pipits and Woodlark nest.

259 The Little Luberon

From the village of Mérindol, some 16 km (10 miles) south-east of Cavaillon, take the road up to the Font-de-l'Orme forester's house, through the forest. Walk up the GR6 hiker's trail; it takes three or four hours. It crosses all of the principal habitats of the Petit Luberon and a large area that was burnt a few years ago. It is best to visit during fine weather (late March to late June). It is possible to see quite a few species of raptor: Bonelli's Eagle, Egyptian Vulture, Short-toed Eagle, and also Red-legged Partridge, Nightjar, Alpine Swift, Tawny Pipit, Black-eared Wheatear, Orphean, Dartford and Sardinian Warblers, Ortolan Bunting and Raven.

260 Île-Vieille Marsh

This marsh is in Mondragon parish, it lies between the Rhône River and the deviation canal belonging to the Compagnie Nationale du Rhône. It was once an ox-bow lake, but has been separated from the river for a long time. Most birds are present in spring (April to June) and autumn (August to October). It has some good breeding species: Purple Heron, Little Bustard, Marsh Harrier, Black Kite, Hobby, Lesser Spotted Woodpecker. There are many migrants: Little Egret, Night Heron, Osprey, Bee-eater, Chiffchaff, Willow Warbler, other warblers and Penduline Tit. Reed Bunting occur in winter.

RHÔNE-ALPES

261 ÉTOURNEL RIVERSIDE MARSH

2.5 km/1.55 miles
Bellegarde-sur-Valserine
(IGN 3229 west – 1/25 000)

Habitat and Timing

In the parishes of Collonges, Pougny (Ain), Vulbens and Chevrier (Haute-Savoie), this Reserve de Chasse (no-hunting reserve) is at the south-west extremity of the Geneva Basin, above Fort-l'Ecluse Gorge. It marks the start of the Rhône River in France corresponding to the top of Génissiat Dam lake. The habitat at the bottom of the natural funnel of the Alpes–Jura mountains attracts migrant and wintering birds. Twenty-six plant communities have been described, one of the most important is the well developed reed-bed and that part of the marsh occupied by sedges fringed by willows and alders. There are many species of orchid and cotton-grass. Three rare plants justify the interest botanists show in this site. The site has been evolving for the last forty years (slowing of the river's current, increasing afforestation, gravel extraction) and is not without threat despite its national ecological importance.

Calendar

Autumn: Ruff, Black-tailed Godwit, Greenshank, Marsh, Green, Wood and Common Sandpipers; Common and White-winged Black Terns. Rarer: Bluethroat, Moustached Warbler, Penduline Tit.

Winter: divers, Shelduck, Teal, Gadwall, Pochard, Goldeneye, Black-headed, Common and Yellow-legged Gulls.

Spring: Grasshopper, Reed, Marsh and Sedge Warblers, tits (eight species and Reed Bunting, all nest). Aquatic Warbler on migration.

Access

Leave Collonges (Ain) on the D906, taking the N206 off to the right. Cross over the railway and after crossing the Rhône, park the car at the Carnot bridge car park ①. From the bridge there is a view over the Étournel upstream and Fort-l'Ecluse downstream; take the path on the side of the Rhône (left bank) as far as the Ravoire promontory ②, some 2 km (1.25 miles) distant. A visit to Fort-l'Ecluse Gorge ③ can be well worthwhile between September and November, particularly for the passage of raptors.

Species

- In spring, Reed and Sedge Warblers and Reed Bunting nest in the reed-beds. In April and May the rare Aquatic Warbler occurs. Bluethroat and Moustached Warbler occur in autumn.
- Many waders stop at Étournel in the autumn; *Tringa* and *Calidris* species, Lapwing and Black-tailed Godwit are the commonest.

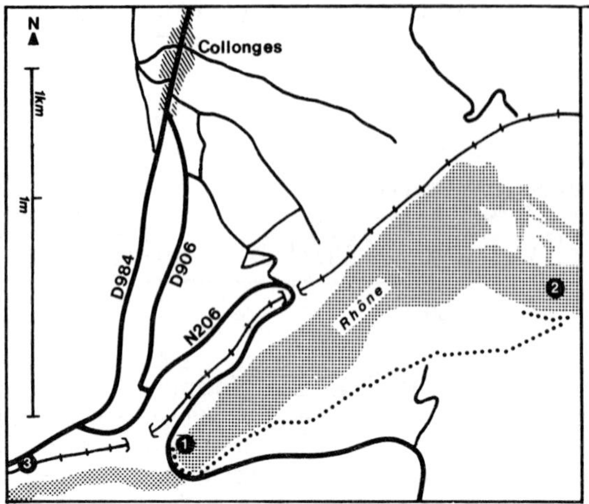

- Marsh and Grasshopper Warblers can be found in the willows in the reed-beds in spring.
- Étournel is the most important site for Teal between Switzerland and the Camargue. Gadwall, diving duck, including Goldeneye, are also present.
- The Black-headed gull roost in winter attracts Common and Yellow-legged gulls.
- Many raptors pass down Fort-l'Ecluse Gorge in autumn, they include: Buzzard, Sparrowhawk, Red Kite, Osprey and Merlin.

262 Fort-l'Écluse Gorge

This gorge, in Collonges parish, is a traditional autumn migration watch point. Between the end of August and end of October flights of Woodpigeon and passerines (Chaffinch, Brambling, Hawfinch, White Wagtail, Greenfinch) are forced to take this funnel to get to the Rhône Valley. Gliding birds (Osprey, Storks, Crane) occur in good numbers. Honey Buzzard, Buzzard, Kestrel and Sparrowhawk are abundant here; Short-toed Eagle, harriers and Golden Eagle rarer. Wallcreepers occur on the walls of the fort. Leave the car at Collonges post office car park; take the road behind the post office for 300 m (330 yards), at the junction on the left, take the track, the Sentier du Fortin, marked with black circles surrounded with white; this is a 2-km (1.25 miles) walk.

263 The Dombes

To the south of Bourg-en-Bresse, the Dombes is an area of lakes used for fish-farming. It has a complex system of pools, constantly filling or emptying according to their use. Many aquatic birds breed here, the include: Little, Great Crested and Black-necked Grebes; Purple, Grey, Night and Squacco (rare) Herons; Mallard, Gadwall, Shoveler, Teal, Garganey, Red-crested Pochard, Pochard, Tufted Duck. Marsh Harrier,

Black-headed Gull and Whiskered Tern are common. Lapwing and a few pairs of Black-tailed Godwit and Black-winged Stilt nest. Many waders occur on migration, particularly *Tringa* and *Calidris* species and Snipe. Rarer species from eastern Europe often occur in April or May: Red-footed Falcon, White-winged Black Tern, Red-throated Pipit. White Storks from introduced stock breed near Villars-les-Dombes Ornithological Park. Hoopoe is common and there are many reed-bed passerines. The N83 (Bourg-en-Bresse to Lyon road) crosses the Dombes. Be careful, most of the lakes are private and it is advisable to watch from the roadside only. A visit to the ornithological park may well be worthwhile.

264 Cormaranche-Hauteville Marsh

This is a natural curiousity near Bugey, in the limestone southern Jura; it is a quiet area with little water. The marsh is next to a water-meadow, and is bordered with rushes and a small reed-bed. It offers refuge to some relatively rare species such as Corncrake. The nearby beech and spruce wood allows for easy viewing of Black Woodpecker and Hazelhen. Peregrine, Raven and Nutcracker are not exceptional here. Access is from the D21 (Tenay–Hauteville road); at Nantuy take the road that leads to Lésines. A little further on there is a path that goes around the marsh. Spring is the best time, as much for the flowers as the birds.

265 ESCRINET PASS/ SAINT-ÉTIENNE-DE-BOULOGNE

Privas
(IGN 2937 – 1/50 000)

Habitat and Timing

This pass, overlooking Aubenas Valley, is at the limits of different regions: the Cévenne to the south, the high Vivarais to the north, the high plateau of the Ardèche to the east, and Coiron basalt plateau to the east. The pass is at 787 m and is a very good place for watching migration. More than 160 species have been seen migrating over Escrinet. Passerines are observed in the early morning; raptors and other gliding species at almost any hour.

Calendar

Spring: Black Stork; Buzzard, Black and Red Kites, Marsh Harrier, Booted Eagle, Osprey, Honey Buzzard, Merlin; Swift, Cuckoo, hirundines; White and Blue-headed Wagtail, Chaffinch and Brambling.

Access

Take the N104 out of the Rhône valley, going towards Privas. The pass is on this road, between Privas some 11 km (6.85 miles) to the north and

Aubenas, 20 km (12 miles) to the south. There is a car park and information point at the pass. You can get there by bus: use the Valence–Aubenas service. There are lodgings near the pass. There is no circuit; the migrants are watched from the hillock at the top of the pass. (**No map**).

As early as the end of February, Buzzard, Woodpigeon, Stock Dove, grebes and finches start passing. In early March it is the turn of Cormorant, Red and Black Kites, Crane and White Wagtail. Next come Marsh Harrier, Osprey and a few Black and White Storks. April sees the migration of many harriers, Turtle Dove, Cuckoo, Swift and thousands of passerines including: hirundines, Chaffinch, Brambling, Greenfinch, Siskin, Serin, Goldfinch, Golden Oriole. Also Short-toed Eagle and Booted Eagle. Lastly, May is the best month for seeing Honey Buzzard.

266 THE DOUX VALLEY

7.5 km/4.7 miles
Tournon
(IGN 3035 west – 1/25 000)

Habitat and Timing

The Doux flows into the Rhône; it is a fast-flowing river which passes through wide, open gorges in its lower stretches; these gorges are very sunny and offer an ideal home for the Beavers that occur here. The oak wood, mixed with Scots Pine, ancient Sweet Chestnuts (memories of former times when this was an important crop in the Ardèche), and a few Holm-oak, shows a marked Mediterranean influence. The mixed agriculture on the plateau, quite environmentally friendly, encourages many species of passerine.

Calendar

Spring: Goshawk, Sparrowhawk, Buzzard, Honey Buzzard, Short-toed Eagle, Black Kite, Kestrel; Great Spotted Woodpecker, Wryneck; Bonelli's Warbler, Short-toed Treecreeper, Rock and Corn Buntings.

Winter: Eagle Owl.

Access

Tournon is on the N86 where the Doux enters the Rhône. A little before the northern edge of the town, take the N532 towards Lamastre. Leave the car at the entrance to the Duzon bridge ① (look below at the Beavers' work). Walk along the side of the N534 for a while (the only way into the gorges), but the road is little used. At the level of the hydro-electric station, after the hairpin bend ②, take the track to the right which climbs onto the plateau and joins the D238 leading back to Duzon bridge.

Species

- Honey Buzzard and Buzzard are easy to see in spring, as is Black Kite which comes from the nearby Rhône.

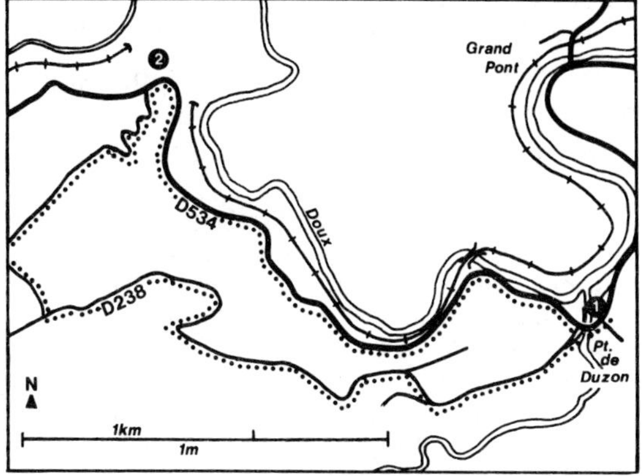

- The Wryneck's plaintive song can be heard in the oak wood from April onwards.
- The best time to hear the Eagle Owl's impressive call resounding in the gorges is December.
- Sparrowhawk hunt over the crops and on the edge of the gorges. Goshawk display noisily in the valley.
- On the hillside you can see Bonelli's Warbler and Rock Bunting.
- Short-toed Eagle nest in the scattered Scots Pine woods.

267 Vogüé

Vogüé is a small village on the side of the Ardèche; it is situated near dead trees and meanders created by the river in flood. Chauzon cirque nearby is a limestone cliff with a Mediterranean climate and vegetation. The village is 8 km (5 miles) to the south of Aubenas. Walk in the vicinity of the village, especially on the water's edge and in the garrigue. During spring, the best time, it is possible to see Grey Heron, Black Kite and migrating waders along the ox-bow lakes; Tawny Pipit, Black-eared Wheatear and all the Mediterranean warblers in the garrigue, while the cliff-face has Eagle Owl, Alpine Swift, Blue Rock Thrush and Raven.

268 The Tanargue Massif

In June and July the Tanargue range of hills holds a rich variety of birds. On the heaths are Montagu's Harrier, Short-toed Eagle, Woodlark and Skylark. In the forests are Black Woodpecker and Crossbill, to mention only two of the most interesting species. From Aubenas, take the N102 towards Thueyts. On reaching Lalevade-d'Ardèche, take the D19 as far as Croix-de-Bauzon. Park, and follow the marked trails which go into the Massif du Tanargue.

269 THE SAOU FOREST MASSIF

3.5 km/2.2 miles (IGN 3137 west – 1/25 000 and IGN 3138 west – 1/25 000)

Habitat and Timing

This is a densely-wooded mountain valley (except at its summit), to the south of the Drôme Valley, and it is surrounded by high cliffs. The range of altitude (between 400 m and 600 m), and the effect of its orientation, give the massif a large diversity of plants. The oak and beech/spruce woods are among the finest in the Drôme. The cliffs (a total length of 25 km, 15.5 miles) are much used by rock-dwelling birds. There is free access to the private forest. Cars are not allowed on the forest roads.

Calendar

Spring and summer: Golden Eagle, Short-toed Eagle, Peregrine, Eagle and Tengmalm's Owls; Tawny Pipit, Alpine Accentor, Subalpine Warbler, Alpine Chough.

Access

Some 50 km (31 miles) to the south-east of Valence. It is reached by going via Crest-Aouste, entering the forest via the Pas de Lauzun. From Montélimar, 40 km (25 miles) to the south-west, via Pont-de-Barret-Saou, you enter the forest via the Défilé du Pertuis. For more direct access to the summit of the Saou Massif, go to Les Trois-Becs, via Chaudière Pass on the main road between Bourdeau and Saillans. There is a biological research station in the heart of Saou Forest, welcoming both professional and amateur naturalists.

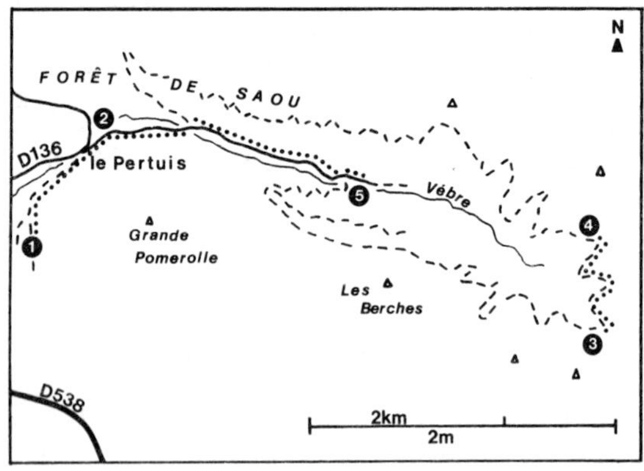

There is a short circuit: park the car near Lestang Farm, walk on the track towards Pertius, passing via the Pas de Lestang ① and the Long de la Vèbre ②. Hiker's circuit: the Trois-Becs ③, via Chaudière Pass, where there is a car park. Go up on the Pas de la Sierra which takes 30 minutes. There is a refuge (without frills) one hour's walk away towards the north

(Girards Refuge) ④, or three hours away if passing via the Trois-Becs ridge. It is possible to climb to the Trois-Becs by passing via a forest circuit which leaves from the Château de la Forêt (the biological research station) ⑤; arriving at Girards in two and a half hours.

Species

- Mediterranean passerines include: Tawny Pipit, Subalpine Warbler. Also Raven and Crag Martin.
- Eagle Owl can be seen, particularly at dusk.
- Short-toed Eagle is frequent enough.
- Kingfisher and Dipper are easy to see along the river.
- Black Woodpecker can be found in the forest.
- Honey Buzzard and Goshawk are seen in the spring.
- Tengmalm's Owl is found in the spring (calling).
- In the forest and on its edges you can see Ring Ouzel, Citril Finch and Willow Tit.
- Alpine Swift and Alpine Chough are often seen in flight.
- Alpine Accentor, Wallcreeper and Water Pipit can be seen (scree and cliff-faces).
- Golden Eagle and Peregrine fly over the area.

270 Printegarde (No-Hunting Reserve)

This is the best site for birds in the Rhône Valley between Lyon and Avignon. Wintering ducks (upto 2,000 birds) start arriving in October. There are many Cormorants in winter. Their roost is next to a heronry (Grey Heron) partially visible from the N86, some 3 km (1.85 miles) to the south of La Voulte (Ardèche). The area is interesting for migrants in March and April: Osprey, Penduline Tit, gulls and herons. There is easy access to the two banks of the Rhône: it is worth walking the embankments which are closed to cars.

271 Malsanne Gorge

The gorge is in the Valbonnais region, between La Mure and Le Bourg-d'Oisans; here it is easy to see cliff-dwelling and torrent-loving species, during a stop on the D526 at a spot called La Barrière, 1.2 km (0.75 miles) from Entraigues (where there is an information centre and museum for the Écrins National Park). A lay-by provides parking near the central zone of the park; the zone is marked by tricolours. Cliff-dwelling birds nest in the impressive rock-faces: Kestrel, Crag Martin and Raven. Others occur in winter: Alpine Chough, Chough and Wallcreeper. The rocky hillsides are favoured by Rock Bunting and Short-toed Eagle which arrive in April, while the river is home to Dipper and Grey Wagtail.

272 THE HILLSIDES OF THE RHÔNE VALLEY, BETWEEN SAINT-PIERRE-DE-BOEUF AND BESSEY

11.5 km/7.2 miles
Vienne
(IGN 3033 west – 1/25 000)

Habitat and Timing

The Malleval Gorges are some of the more typical of the many small valleys that occur between the Piedmont Massif Central and the Rhône Valley. Protected from chilly winds, facing directly south on one slope (the adret) or directly north (the ubac), there were cultivated terrasses in the past, with gardens and vineyards; they are now abandoned. The north-facing slope (often shaded and damp) is still occupied by a forest of Downy and Sessile Oaks, the south-facing slope has a Mediterranean flora, where the presence of Prickly Pear, coupled with its sunny character, give this valley the appearance and atmosphere of the countryside of southern France. The best time to visit the area is in the spring, early in the morning.

Calendar

Spring: Short-toed Eagle; Woodlark, Skylark, Grey Wagtail; Nightingale, Stonechat, Whinchat; Blackcap, Chiffchaff, Bonelli's and Garden Warblers; Red-backed and Woodchat Shrikes, Dipper, Cirl and Ortolan Buntings.

Access

Leave the car near the cemetery ① at Saint-Pierre-de-Boeuf, a small village between Vienne (Isère) and Valence (Drôme), on the N86. Some 500 m (550 yards) after the hairpin bend take the track off to the right, which should soon be a marked trail. The circuit then crosses the N503 and joins a small road that you follow for 1.7 km (1.05 miles). Take a small track off to the left then a road that leads to Goëly ②. Then it is onto the Toucheboeuf road and on straight to Bessey. Return by the same route until it joins the main road, from here drive to Malleval. Then follow the marked trail which leads to Saint-Pierre-de-Boeuf, this time on the road from the north.

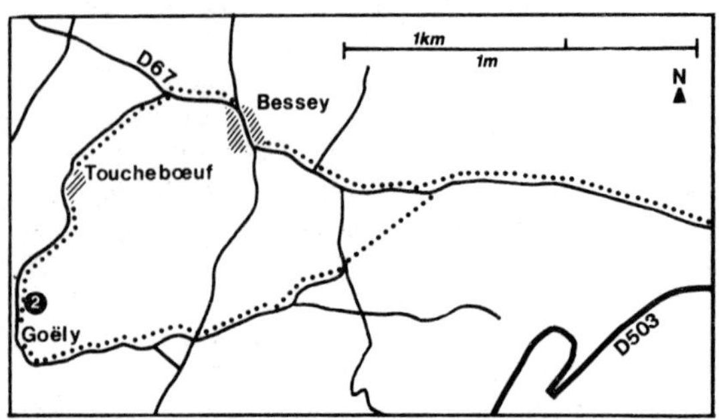

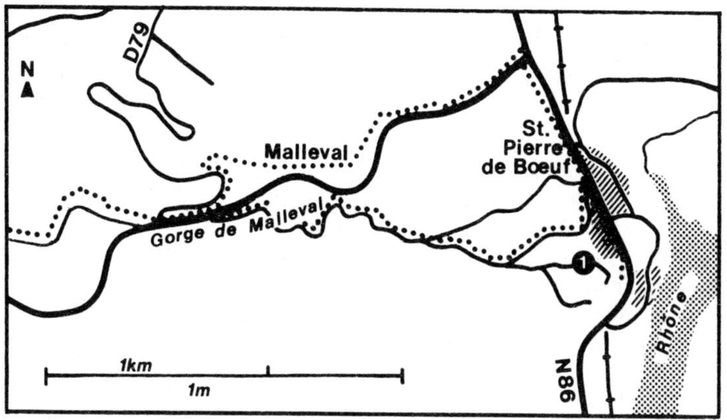

Species

- On leaving Saint-Pierre-de-Boeuf, the abandoned orchards are good for seeing the shy Nightingale.
- Crossing the oak wood, listen for the melodious songs of Blackcap and Garden Warbler.
- Look for Red-backed and Woodchat shrikes, passerines with the habits of raptors.
- In an area of sunny hedgerows and orchards look for Skylark and Woodlark.
- Further on, on the cultivated plateau, near the vineyards, it is possible to see Stonechat, Whinchat, Greenfinch, Serin and Goldfinch.
- On the stream in the valley bottom there are Grey Wagtail and Dipper.
- Cirl Bunting can be seen to the south of Toucheboeuf.
- On the way back look in the abandoned gardens on the Chemin des Cigales for Ortolan Bunting.

273 The Southern Gorges of the Loire

These gorges have the reputation of being the best areas in the region for raptors; it is easy to see many birds of prey including some of the rarer species. A three-hour walk is sufficient. The track, near Saint-Victor-sur-Loire, follows in places the old railway track and follows the side of the reservoir of Grangent Dam on the Loire River; you can go back by the same route. The gorges normally have: Black and Red Kites, Eagle Owl, Short-toed Eagle, Honey Buzzard, and Hen and Montagu's (rarer) Harriers. For more than ten years now, the Red Kite has occurred in winter and there is a roost of 20 to 50 birds, to the south of Roche-la-Molière (within a 3-km/1.85 mile radius of the small village of Bécizieux).

274 HAUTES-CHAUMES/ FOREZ HILLS

9 km/5.6 miles or 18 km/11.2 miles Ambert (IGN 2732 – 1/50 000)

Habitat and Timing

The chain of the Forez Hills is some 60 km (37 miles) long, from north to south, and is at the boundary of two departments, the Loire and the Puy-de-Dôme. It is a crystalline massif with some granitic incursions, the highest point being the 1,634 m Pierre-sur-Haute. These Hautes-Chaumes are covered with heather heathland, with Bilberry and Hairy Greenweed, dotted with peat-bogs containing some interesting plants. The area has a mountain climate, with much snow between December and April; a subalpine vegetation and forest allow for varied birdwatching – sometimes unexpected, different from season to season, and even from day to day in autumn. One of the passes in this massif, (Barracuchet) is an observation centre (between mid-September and early November); it has been open for several years. Be very careful during times of mist, tracks are not marked (except the GR3) and some of the open, barren areas have no distinctive features, especially when there is snow.

Calendar

Spring and summer: Buzzard, Honey Buzzard, Short-toed Eagle, Goshawk, Sparrowhawk, Montagu's and Marsh Harriers, Red Kite; Woodcock, Swift, Black Woodpecker, Wryneck; Skylark, Water, Meadow and Tree Pipits; Wheatear, Black Redstart, Rock Thrush, Ring Ouzel; Willow Warbler, tits, Nuthatch.

Autumn: Crane, many raptors, Woodpigeon, Woodlark, thrushes, Hawfinch, Siskin, Citril Finch. Sometimes, Black Stork, Osprey, Peregrine, Dotterel.

Winter: many thrushes, including Fieldfare.

Access

The car can be left at the Col de Béal ① (access via Chalmazel or Saint-Pierre-de-Bourlhonne); take the GR3 hiker's trail as far as the Rocher rocky ridge ②; descend to the Col de Chamboite, then, using the Rocher Ravé, a rocky crest, reach the Dôme de Pierre-sur-Haute ③. Beware, this area can be very dangerous, there are water-filled holes more than 7 m deep. From here you can continue further going to the Gros-Fumé ④ by skirting Jasseries-du-Colleigne Nature Reserve, and coming back by the same route; or, a little before Pierre-sur-Haute, take the summit ski-lift track as far as Traverse ⑤. Here, turn left towards Chalet Gauchon, and arrive back at the Col du Béal via the ruins of Font-Noire. It is also possible to walk up from the east, starting from Sauvain.

Species

- On the nearby alpine meadows you can find Tree, Meadow and Water Pipits.
- On the Rocher rocky ridge look for Rock Thrush as well as the commoner Wheatear and Black Redstart.

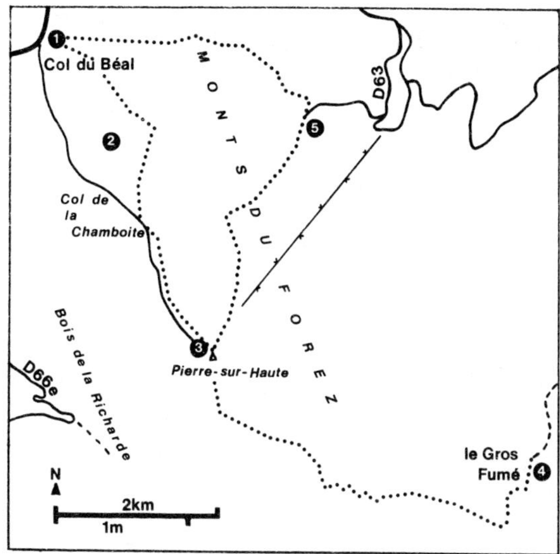

- From Pierre-sur-Haute, in autumn, you can see many migrating raptors.
- Chaffinch, Brambling, thrushes, Siskin, Goldfinch and larks pass in large numbers in the autumn.
- Red Kite and Buzzard hunt over the heathland, and in spring and summer there are Short-toed Eagle and Honey Buzzard.
- Ring Ouzel sing at the wood edges. There are many tits in the forest, including Coal, Crested and Marsh; also Crossbill.
- There is a good place for Black, Green, Great Spotted and Lesser Spotted Woodpeckers.

275 The Pilat

Between the charming little village of Verrane and Saint-Sabin chapel, the birdwatcher crosses the mountain zone of the Pilat Massif, where conifers, beech/spruce woods, open heathland and small fields of crops form a rich and diverse mosaic of habitats. It is possible to find Wryneck, and Bonelli's and Melodious Warblers near the village. Further up there are Mistle and Song Thrushes, and Coal and Crested Tits. Tree Pipit sing at the forest edge and three species of bunting can be seen in the broom heath (Rock, Cirl and Yellowhammer). There are Citril Finch and Crossbill in the pine wood near Saint-Sabin and, lastly, on arriving at the chapel, there is a good chance of finding Rock Bunting again.

276 FOREZ PLAIN, MAGNEUX-HAUTE-RIVE

Veauche (IGN 2832 east – 1/25 000)

Habitat and Timing

The area has a large number of lakes and reservoirs; the plain also collects water from the surrounding mountains (Monts du Forez and Monts du Lyonnais). This circuit of about 12 kilometres (7.5 miles) (with many possible deviations), winds between the Loire, the lakes, a few English Oak woods, some coppice and some agricultural land (chambons) on the flood-plain. A part of the gravel-pits, on the side of the Loire, belongs to the Fédération Rhône-Alpes de Protection de la Nature which is undertaking conservation work here. For the moment there is no official protection, and there is free access.

Calendar

Spring: Great Crested Grebe; Grey and Night Herons, Little Egret; Marsh and Hen Harriers; Stone Curlew, Curlew, Lapwing, Little Ringed Plover, Redshank; Black-headed Gull; Kingfisher, Sand Martin, Grey and White Wagtails, Reed Warbler.

Autumn: White and Black Storks, Cormorant, geese, swans, Osprey, Crane, small waders, Penduline Tit.

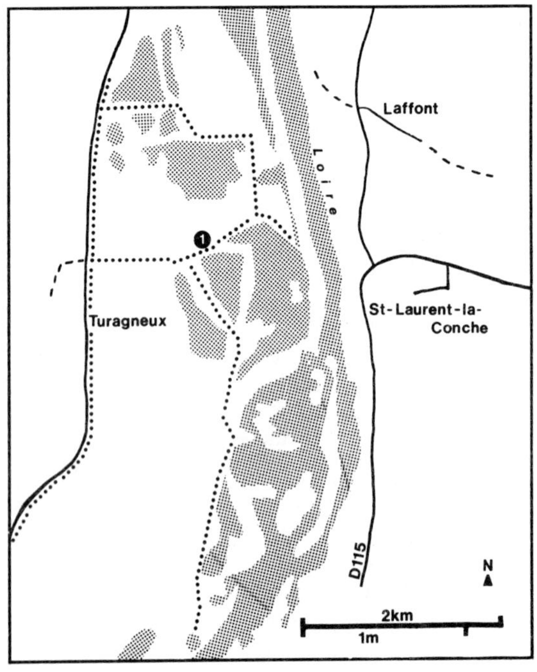

Access

From Saint-Etienne, take the N82 as far as Montrond-les-Bains; turn left here on the D496 towards Montbrison, then right on the D6 as far as Magneux-Haute-Rive. Turn right here to get to the gravel-pits on the side of the Loire. There is easy parking anywhere ①. Walk southwards following the paths that wind between the various pits.

Little Egrets

Species

- Stone Curlew, Lapwing and Curlew all nest on the cultivated plain.
- In the coppices on the side of the gravel-pits there are Whitethroat and Melodious Warbler.
- Grey and Night Herons nest here in spring, there are Little Egrets mixed in with them.
- This is also a good area for Sand Martin.
- In autumn, a few of the smaller waders occur on the gravel-pits.
- Marsh and Hen Harriers from the nearby plain often hunt over the area.
- Kingfishers are seen on the Loire as much as on the lakes.
- On the banks of the Loire, Little Ringed Plover and Common Sandpiper (rare) nest.

277 Forez Lakes

Forez Plain, between the Loire to the east and the Forez Hills to the west, contains many lakes. Spring is the best time to birdwatch in this little-known area where many wetland birds nest: Great Crested and Little Grebes, Mallard, Gadwall, Shoveler, Garganey, Red-crested Pochard, Pochard and Tufted Duck. Marsh Harrier, Hobby and Black Kite all nest in small numbers. Osprey regularly pass in spring and autumn. There are large colonies of Black-headed Gull. Stone Curlew occur on the drier parts of the plain, but are rare. Access to this area of lakes is via Feurs, Montbrison or Montrond-les-Bains. The lakes are private and entry is prohibited. Nevertheless, it is quite easy to obtain good views of the birds from the local roads.

278 Montagny Heathland

Despite its rather unexciting countryside, the Monts du Lyonnais, which is a favourite area for walks for the people of Lyon, is of interest to the naturalist. On a sunny piedmont (glacial plain), along the road between Mornant and Montagny, these heaths have a surprisingly rich and diverse fauna; Curlew and Lapwing nest on the ground in the wet meadows. Stone Curlew occur in the drier, more stony fields. Curlew can be seen as early as the end of February, whereas Stone Curlew, which come from further afield, arrive later, around 20 March.

279 Bellevaux Forest

The little-managed Bellevaux Forest, some one hundred years old, grows on a small part of the Bauges Massif which overlooks Annecy Lake. This heterogeneous beech/spruce forest, cultivated in small parts, has a typical fauna of the mountain zone (Black Woodpecker, Hazelhen, Treecreeper, Ring Ouzel, etc); the upper limit in contact with alpine meadow is very rich: Black Grouse, Raven, Alpine Chough, Alpine Accentor, Peregrine and Golden Eagle can be seen. The closeness of Bauges no-hunting reserve means that Chamois and Mouflon may be seen. There is free access from École-en-Bauges (on the D911 coming from Saint-Pierre-d'Albigny).

INDEX TO SPECIES BY SITE